Course	Introduction to Business Information Systems
Course Number	**MIS 301**
	George Mason University
	ISOM

http://create.mheducation.com

ISBN-10: 1308148674   ISBN-13: 9781308148670

Contents

Credits

CHAPTER 1

Business Driven Technology

Competing in the Information Age

LO 1.1 Describe the information age and the differences among data, information, business intelligence, and knowledge.

Did you know that . . .

- The movie *Avatar* took more than four years to create and cost $450 million.
- Lady Gaga's real name is Stefani Joanne Angelina Germanotta.
- Customers pay $2.6 million for a 30-second advertising time slot during the Super Bowl.[2]

A *fact* is the confirmation or validation of an event or object. In the past, people primarily learned facts from books. Today, by simply pushing a button people can find out anything, from anywhere, at any time. We live in the *information age,* when infinite quantities of facts are widely available to anyone who can use a computer. The impact of information technology on the global business environment is equivalent to the printing press's impact on publishing and electricity's impact on productivity. College student startups were mostly unheard of before the information age. Now, it's not at all unusual to read about a business student starting a multimillion-dollar company from his or her dorm room. Think of Mark Zuckerberg, who started Facebook from his dorm, or Michael Dell (Dell Computers) and Bill Gates (Microsoft), who both founded their legendary companies as college students.

You may think only students well versed in advanced technology can compete in the information age. This is simply not true. Many business leaders have created exceptional opportunities by coupling the power of the information age with traditional business methods. Here are just a few examples:

- Amazon is not a technology company; its original business focus was to sell books, and it now sells nearly everything.
- Netflix is not a technology company; its primary business focus is to rent videos.
- Zappos is not a technology company; its primary business focus is to sell shoes, bags, clothing, and accessories.

Amazon's founder, Jeff Bezos, at first saw an opportunity to change the way people purchase books. Using the power of the information age to tailor offerings to each customer and speed the payment process, he in effect opened millions of tiny virtual bookstores, each with a vastly larger selection and far cheaper product than traditional bookstores. The success of his original business model led him to expand Amazon to carry many other types of products. The founders of Netflix and Zappos have done the same thing for videos and shoes. All these entrepreneurs were business professionals, not technology experts. However, they understood enough about the information age to apply it to a particular business, creating innovative companies that now lead entire industries.

Students who understand business along with the power associated with the information age will create their own opportunities and perhaps even new industries, as co-founders Chris DeWolfe and Tom Anderson did with Myspace and Mark Zuckerberg did with Facebook. Our primary goal in this course is to arm you with the knowledge you need to compete in the information age. The core drivers of the information age are:

- Data
- Information
- Business intelligence
- Knowledge (see Figure 1.1)

DATA

Data are raw facts that describe the characteristics of an event or object. Before the information age, managers manually collected and analyzed data, a time-consuming and complicated task without which they would have little insight into how to run their business. Lacking data, managers often found themselves making business decisions about how many products to make, how much material to order, or how many employees to hire based on intuition or gut feelings. In the information age, successful managers compile, analyze, and comprehend massive amounts of data daily, which helps them make more successful business decisions.

FIGURE 1.1

The Differences among Data, Information, Business Intelligence, and Knowledge

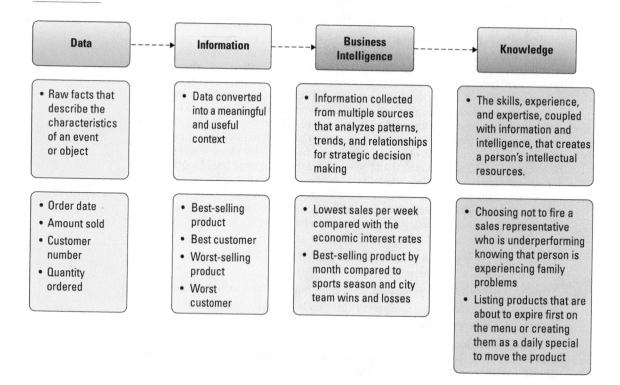

Data	Information	Business Intelligence	Knowledge
• Raw facts that describe the characteristics of an event or object	• Data converted into a meaningful and useful context	• Information collected from multiple sources that analyzes patterns, trends, and relationships for strategic decision making	• The skills, experience, and expertise, coupled with information and intelligence, that creates a person's intellectual resources.
• Order date • Amount sold • Customer number • Quantity ordered	• Best-selling product • Best customer • Worst-selling product • Worst customer	• Lowest sales per week compared with the economic interest rates • Best-selling product by month compared to sports season and city team wins and losses	• Choosing not to fire a sales representative who is underperforming knowing that person is experiencing family problems • Listing products that are about to expire first on the menu or creating them as a daily special to move the product

Figure 1.2 shows sales data for Tony's Wholesale Company, a fictitious business that supplies snacks to stores. The data highlight characteristics such as order date, customer, sales representative, product, quantity, and profit. The second line in Figure 1.2, for instance, shows that Roberta Cross sold 90 boxes of Ruffles to Walmart for $1,350, resulting in a profit of $450 (note that Profit = Sales − Costs). These data are useful for understanding individual sales; however, they do not provide us much insight into how Tony's business is performing as a whole. Tony needs to answer questions that will help him manage his day-to-day operations such as:

■ Who are my best customers?
■ Who are my least-profitable customers?
■ What is my best-selling product?
■ What is my slowest-selling product?
■ Who is my strongest sales representative?
■ Who is my weakest sales representative?

What Tony needs, in other words, is not data but *information*.

INFORMATION

Information is data converted into a meaningful and useful context. Having the right information at the right moment in time can be worth a fortune. Having the wrong information at the right moment; or the right information at the wrong moment can be disastrous. The truth about information is that its value is only as good as the people who use it. People using the same information can make different decisions depending on how they interpret or analyze the information. Thus information has value only insofar as the people using it do as well.

Tony can analyze his sales data and turn them into information to answer all the above questions and understand how his business is operating. Figures 1.3 and 1.4, for instance, show us that Walmart is Roberta Cross's best customer, and that Ruffles is Tony's best product measured in terms of total sales. Armed with this information, Tony can identify and then address such issues as weak products and underperforming sales representatives.

A *variable* is a data characteristic that stands for a value that changes or varies over time. For example, in Tony's data, price and quantity ordered can vary. Changing variables allows managers to create hypothetical scenarios to study future possibilities.

FIGURE 1.2

Tony's Snack Company Data

Order Date	Customer	Sales Representative	Product	Qty	Unit Price	Total Sales	Unit Cost	Total Cost	Profit
4-Jan	Walmart	PJ Helgoth	Doritos	41	$24	$ 984	$18	$738	$246
4-Jan	Walmart	Roberta Cross	Ruffles	90	$15	$1,350	$10	$900	$450
5-Jan	Safeway	Craig Schultz	Ruffles	27	$15	$ 405	$10	$270	$135
6-Jan	Walmart	Roberta Cross	Ruffles	67	$15	$1,005	$10	$670	$335
7-Jan	7-Eleven	Craig Schultz	Pringles	79	$12	$ 948	$ 6	$474	$474
7-Jan	Walmart	Roberta Cross	Ruffles	52	$15	$ 780	$10	$520	$260
8-Jan	Kroger	Craig Schultz	Ruffles	39	$15	$ 585	$10	$390	$195
9-Jan	Walmart	Craig Schultz	Ruffles	66	$15	$ 990	$10	$660	$330
10-Jan	Target	Craig Schultz	Ruffles	40	$15	$ 600	$10	$400	$200
11-Jan	Walmart	Craig Schultz	Ruffles	71	$15	$1,065	$10	$710	$355

Order Date	Customer	Sales Representative	Product	Quantity	Unit Price	Total Sales	Unit Cost	Total Cost	Profit
26-Apr	Walmart	Roberta Cross	Fritos	86	$ 19	$ 1,634	$ 17	$ 1,462	$ 172
29-Aug	Walmart	Roberta Cross	Fritos	76	$ 19	$ 1,444	$ 17	$ 1,292	$ 152
7-Sep	Walmart	Roberta Cross	Fritos	20	$ 19	$ 380	$ 17	$ 340	$ 40
22-Nov	Walmart	Roberta Cross	Fritos	39	$ 19	$ 741	$ 17	$ 663	$ 78
30-Dec	Walmart	Roberta Cross	Fritos	68	$ 19	$ 1,292	$ 17	$ 1,156	$ 136
7-Jul	Walmart	Roberta Cross	Pringles	79	$ 18	$ 1,422	$ 8	$ 632	$ 790
6-Aug	Walmart	Roberta Cross	Pringles	21	$ 12	$ 252	$ 6	$ 126	$ 126
2-Oct	Walmart	Roberta Cross	Pringles	60	$ 18	$ 1,080	$ 8	$ 480	$ 600
15-Nov	Walmart	Roberta Cross	Pringles	32	$ 12	$ 384	$ 6	$ 192	$ 192
21-Dec	Walmart	Roberta Cross	Pringles	92	$ 12	$ 1,104	$ 6	$ 552	$ 552
28-Feb	Walmart	Roberta Cross	Ruffles	67	$ 15	$ 1,005	$ 10	$ 670	$ 335
6-Mar	Walmart	Roberta Cross	Ruffles	8	$ 15	$ 120	$ 10	$ 80	$ 40
16-Mar	Walmart	Roberta Cross	Ruffles	68	$ 15	$ 1,020	$ 10	$ 680	$ 340
23-Apr	Walmart	Roberta Cross	Ruffles	34	$ 15	$ 510	$ 10	$ 340	$ 170
4-Aug	Walmart	Roberta Cross	Ruffles	40	$ 15	$ 600	$ 10	$ 400	$ 200
18-Aug	Walmart	Roberta Cross	Ruffles	93	$ 15	$ 1,395	$ 10	$ 930	$ 465
5-Sep	Walmart	Roberta Cross	Ruffles	41	$ 15	$ 615	$ 10	$ 410	$ 205
12-Sep	Walmart	Roberta Cross	Ruffles	8	$ 15	$ 120	$ 10	$ 80	$ 40
28-Oct	Walmart	Roberta Cross	Ruffles	50	$ 15	$ 750	$ 10	$ 500	$ 250
21-Nov	Walmart	Roberta Cross	Ruffles	79	$ 15	$ 1,185	$ 10	$ 790	$ 395
29-Jan	Walmart	Roberta Cross	Sun Chips	5	$ 22	$ 110	$ 18	$ 90	$ 20
12-Apr	Walmart	Roberta Cross	Sun Chips	85	$ 22	$ 1,870	$ 18	$ 1,530	$ 340
16-Jun	Walmart	Roberta Cross	Sun Chips	55	$ 22	$ 1,210	$ 18	$ 990	$ 220
				1,206	$383	$20,243	$273	$14,385	$5,858

Sorting the data reveals the information that Roberta Cross's total sales to Walmart were $20,243 resulting in a profit of $5,858. (Profit $5,858 = Sales $20,243 − Costs $14,385)

FIGURE 1.3

Tony's Data Sorted by Customer "Walmart" and Sales Representative "Roberta Cross"

Tony may find it valuable to anticipate how sales or cost increases affect profitability. To estimate how a 20 percent increase in prices might improve profits, Tony simply changes the price variable for all orders, which automatically calculates the amount of new profits. To estimate how a 10 percent increase in costs hurts profits, Tony changes the cost variable for all orders, which automatically calculates the amount of lost profits. Manipulating variables is an important tool for any business.

BUSINESS INTELLIGENCE

Business intelligence (BI) is information collected from multiple sources such as suppliers, customers, competitors, partners, and industries that analyzes patterns, trends, and relationships for strategic decision making. BI manipulates multiple variables and in some cases even hundreds of variables including such items as interest rates, weather conditions, and even gas prices. Tony could use BI to analyze internal data such as company sales, along with external data about the environment such as competitors, finances, weather, holidays, and

Tony's Business Information	Name	Total Profit
Who is Tony's best customer by total sales?	Walmart	$ 560,789
Who is Tony's least-valuable customer by total sales?	Walgreens	$ 45,673
Who is Tony's best customer by profit?	7-Eleven	$ 324,550
Who is Tony's least-valuable customer by profit?	King Soopers	$ 23,908
What is Tony's best-selling product by total sales?	Ruffles	$ 232,500
What is Tony's weakest-selling product by total sales?	Pringles	$ 54,890
What is Tony's best-selling product by profit?	Tostitos	$ 13,050
What is Tony's weakest-selling product by profit?	Pringles	$ 23,000
Who is Tony's best sales representative by profit?	R. Cross	$1,230,980
Who is Tony's weakest sales representative by profit?	Craig Schultz	$ 98,980
What is the best sales representative's best-selling product by total profit?	Ruffles	$ 98,780
Who is the best sales representative's best customer by total profit?	Walmart	$ 345,900
What is the best sales representative's weakest-selling product by total profit?	Sun Chips	$ 45,600
Who is the best sales representative's weakest customer by total profit?	Krogers	$ 56,050

FIGURE 1.4

Information Gained after Analyzing Tony's Data

even sporting events. Both internal and external variables affect snack sales, and analyzing these variables will help Tony determine ordering levels and sales forecasts. For instance, BI can predict inventory requirements for Tony's business for the week before the Super Bowl if, say, the home team is playing, average temperature is above 80 degrees, and the stock market is performing well. This is BI at its finest, incorporating all types of internal and external variables to anticipate business performance.

Top managers use BI to define the future of the business, analyzing markets, industries, and economies to determine the strategic direction the company must follow to remain profitable. Tony will set the strategic direction for his firm, which might include introducing new flavors of potato chips or sport drinks as new product lines or schools and hospitals as new market segments.

KNOWLEDGE

Knowledge includes the skills, experience, and expertise, coupled with information and intelligence, that creates a person's intellectual resources. *Knowledge workers* are individuals valued for their ability to interpret and analyze information. Today's workers are commonly referred to as knowledge workers and they use BI along with personal experience to make decisions based on both information and intuition, a valuable resource for any company.

Imagine that Tony analyzes his data and finds his weakest sales representative for this period is Craig Schultz. If Tony considered only this information, he might conclude that firing Craig was a good business decision. However, because Tony has knowledge about how the company operates, he knows Craig has been out on medical leave for several weeks; hence, his sales numbers are low. Without this additional knowledge, Tony might have executed a bad business decision, delivered a negative message to the other employees, and sent his best sales representatives out to look for other jobs.

The key point in this scenario is that it is simply impossible to collect all the information about every situation, and yet without that, it can be easy to misunderstand the problem. Using data, information, business intelligence, and knowledge to make decisions and solve problems is the key to finding success in business. These core drivers of the information age are the building blocks of business systems.

The Challenge: Departmental Companies

LO 1.2 Identify the different departments in a company and why they must work together to achieve success.

Companies are typically organized by department or functional area such as:

- **Accounting:** Records, measures, and reports monetary transactions.
- **Finance:** Deals with strategic financial issues including money, banking, credit, investments, and assets.
- **Human resources:** Maintains policies, plans, and procedures for the effective management of employees.
- **Marketing:** Supports sales by planning, pricing, and promoting goods or services.
- **Operations management:** Manages the process of converting or transforming or resources into goods or services.
- **Sales:** Performs the function of selling goods or services (see Figure 1.5).

Each department performs its own activities. Sales and marketing focus on moving goods or services into the hands of consumers; they maintain transactional data. Finance and accounting focus on managing the company's resources and maintain monetary data. Operations management focuses on manufacturing and maintains production data, while human resources focuses on hiring and training people and

FIGURE 1.5

Departments Working Independently

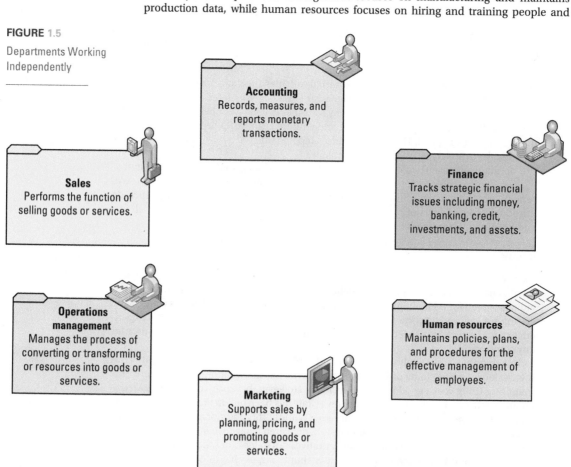

Accounting
Records, measures, and reports monetary transactions.

Sales
Performs the function of selling goods or services.

Finance
Tracks strategic financial issues including money, banking, credit, investments, and assets.

Operations management
Manages the process of converting or transforming or resources into goods or services.

Human resources
Maintains policies, plans, and procedures for the effective management of employees.

Marketing
Supports sales by planning, pricing, and promoting goods or services.

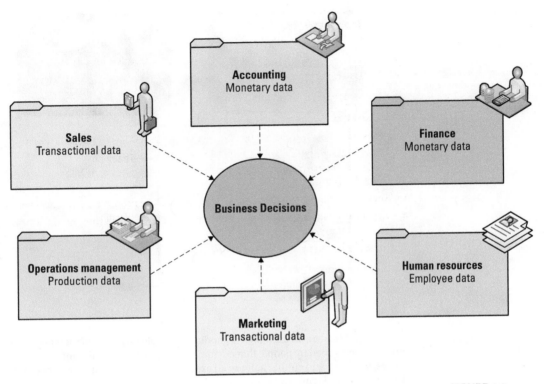

FIGURE 1.6

Departments Working
Together

maintains employee data. Although each department has its own focus and data, none can work independently if the company is to operate as a whole. It is easy to see how a business decision made by one department can affect other departments. Marketing needs to analyze production and sales data to come up with product promotions and advertising strategies. Production needs to understand sales forecasts to determine the company's manufacturing needs. Sales needs to rely on information from operations to understand inventory, place orders, and forecast consumer demand. All departments need to understand the accounting and finance departments' information for budgeting. For the firm to be successful, all departments must work together as a single unit sharing common information and not operate independently or in a silo (see Figure 1.6).

The Solution: Management Information Systems

LO 1.3 Explain systems thinking and how management information systems enable business communications.

You probably recall the old story of three blind men attempting to describe an elephant. The first man, feeling the elephant's girth, said the elephant seemed very much like a wall. The second, feeling the elephant's trunk, declared the elephant was like a snake. The third man felt the elephant's tusks and said the elephant was like a tree or a cane. Companies that operate departmentally are seeing only one part of the elephant, a critical mistake that hinders successful operation.

Successful companies operate cross-functionally, integrating the operations of all departments. Systems are the primary enabler of cross-functional operations. A *system* is a collection of parts that link to achieve a common purpose. A car is a good example of a system, since removing a part, such as the steering wheel or accelerator, causes the entire system to stop working.

Before jumping into how systems work, it is important to have a solid understanding of the basic production process for goods and services. *Goods* are material items or products that customers will buy to satisfy a want or need. Clothing, groceries, cell

FIGURE 1.7

Different Types of Goods
and Services

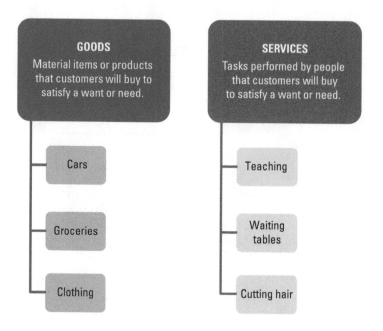

phones, and cars are all examples of goods that people buy to fulfill their needs. ***Services*** are tasks performed by people that customers will buy to satisfy a want or need. Waiting tables, teaching, and cutting hair are all examples of services that people pay for to fulfill their needs (see Figure 1.7).

Production is the process where a business takes raw materials and processes them or converts them into a finished product for its goods or services. Just think about making a hamburger (see Figure 1.8). First, you must gather all of the *inputs* or raw materials such as the bun, patty, lettuce, tomato, and ketchup. Second, you *process* the raw materials, so in this example you would need to cook the patty, wash and chop the lettuce and tomato, and place all of the items in the bun. Finally, you would have your *output* or finished product—your hamburger! ***Productivity*** is the rate at which goods and services are produced based upon total output given total inputs. Given our previous example, if a business could produce the same hamburger with less expensive inputs or more hamburgers with the same inputs it would see a rise in productivity and possibly an increase in profits. Ensuring the input, process, and output of goods and services work across all of the departments of a company is where systems add tremendous value to overall business productivity.

FIGURE 1.8

Input, Process, Output
Example

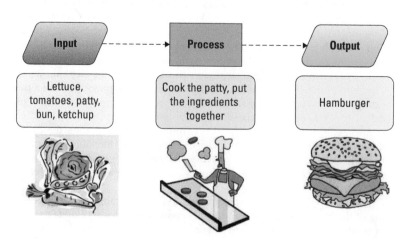

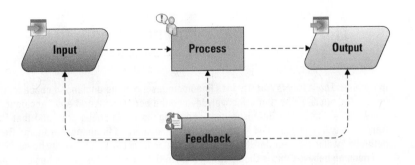

FIGURE 1.9

Overview of Systems
Thinking

Systems thinking is a way of monitoring the entire system by viewing multiple inputs being processed or transformed to produce outputs while continuously gathering feedback on each part (see Figure 1.9). *Feedback* is information that returns to its original transmitter (input, transform, or output) and modifies the transmitter's actions. Feedback helps the system maintain stability. For example, a car's system continuously monitors the fuel level and turns on a warning light if the gas level is too low. Systems thinking provides an end-to-end view of how operations work together to create a product or service. Business students who understand systems thinking are valuable resources because they can implement solutions that consider the entire process, not just a single component.

Management information systems (MIS) is a business function, like accounting and human resources, which moves information about people, products, and processes across the company to facilitate decision making and problem solving. MIS incorporates systems thinking to help companies operate cross-functionally. For example, to fulfill product orders, an MIS for sales moves a single customer order across all functional areas including sales, order fulfillment, shipping, billing, and finally customer service. Although different functional areas handle different parts of the sale, thanks to MIS, to the customer the sale is one continuous process. If one part of the company is experiencing problems, however, then, like the car without a steering wheel, the entire system fails. If order fulfillment packages the wrong product, it will not matter that shipping, billing, and customer service did their jobs right, since the customer will not be satisfied when he or she opens the package.

MIS can be an important enabler of business success and innovation. This is not to say that MIS *equals* business success and innovation, or that MIS *represents* business success and innovation. MIS is a tool that is most valuable when it leverages the talents of people who know how to use and manage it effectively. To perform the MIS function effectively, almost all companies, particularly large and medium-sized ones, have an internal MIS department, often called information technology (IT), information systems (IS), or management information systems (MIS). For the purpose of this text, we will refer to it as MIS.

OPENING CASE STUDY QUESTIONS

1. Explain how Apple achieved business success through the use of information, information technology, and people.

2. Describe the types of information employees at an Apple store require and compare it to the types of information the executives at Apple's corporate headquarters require. Are there any links between these two types of information?

Chapter One Case: The World Is Flat—Thomas Friedman

In his book *The World Is Flat,* Thomas Friedman describes the unplanned cascade of techno-logical and social shifts that effectively leveled the economic world and "accidentally made Beijing, Bangalore, and Bethesda next-door neighbors." Chances are good that Bhavya in Bangalore will read your next X-ray, or as Friedman learned firsthand, "Grandma Betty in her bathrobe" will make your JetBlue plane reservation from her Salt Lake City home.

Friedman believes this is Globalization 3.0. "In Globalization 1.0, which began around 1492, the world went from size large to size medium. In Globalization 2.0, the era that introduced us to multinational companies, it went from size medium to size small. And then around 2000 came Globalization 3.0, in which the world went from being small to tiny. There is a difference between being able to make long-distance phone calls cheaper on the Internet and walking around Riyadh with a PDA where you can have all of Google in your pocket. It is a difference in degree that's so enormous it becomes a difference in kind," Friedman states. Figure 1.10 displays Friedman's list of "flatteners."

FIGURE 1.10

Thomas Friedman's 10 Forces That Flattened the World

1. Fall of the Berlin Wall	The events of November 9, 1989, tilted the worldwide balance of power toward democracies and free markets.
2. Netscape IPO	The August 9, 1995, offering sparked massive investment in fiber-optic cables.
3. Work flow software	The rise of applications from PayPal to VPNs enabled faster, closer coordination among far-flung employees.
4. Open-sourcing	Self-organizing communities, such as Linux, launched a collaborative revolution.
5. Outsourcing	Migrating business functions to India saved money *and* a Third World economy.
6. Offshoring	Contract manufacturing elevated China to economic prominence.
7. Supply-chaining	Robust networks of suppliers, retailers, and customers increased business efficiency.
8. Insourcing	Logistics giants took control of customer supply chains, helping mom-and-pop shops go global.
9. Informing	Power searching allowed everyone to use the Internet as a "personal supply chain of knowledge."
10. Wireless	Wireless technologies pumped up collaboration, making it mobile and personal.

Friedman says these flatteners converged around the year 2000 and "created a flat world: a global, Web-enabled platform for multiple forms of sharing knowledge and work, irrespective of time, distance, geography, and increasingly, language." At the very moment this platform emerged, three huge economies materialized—those of India, China, and the former Soviet Union—"and 3 billion people who were out of the game, walked onto the play-ing field." A final convergence may determine the fate of the United States in this chapter of globalization. A "political perfect storm," as Friedman describes it—the dot-com bust, the attacks of 9/11, and the Enron scandal—"distract us completely as a country." Just when we need to face the fact of globalization and the need to compete in a new world, "we're looking totally elsewhere."

Friedman believes that the next great breakthrough in bioscience could come from a 5-year-old who downloads the human genome in Egypt. Bill Gates's view is similar: "Twenty years ago, would you rather have been a B-student in Poughkeepsie or a genius in Shanghai? Twenty years ago you'd rather be a B-student in Poughkeepsie. Today, it is not even close. You'd much prefer to be the genius in Shanghai because you can now export your talents anywhere in the world."[3]

Questions

1. Do you agree or disagree with Friedman's assessment that the world is flat? Be sure to justify your answer.

2. What are the potential impacts of a flat world for a student performing a job search?

3. What can students do to prepare themselves for competing in a flat world?

4. Identify a current flattener not mentioned on Friedman's list.

CHAPTER 2

Identifying Competitive Advantages

LEARNING OUTCOMES

2.1. Explain why competitive advantages are temporary.

2.2. Describe Porter's Five Forces Model and explain each of the five forces.

2.3. Compare Porter's three generic strategies.

2.4. Demonstrate how a company can add value by using Porter's value chain analysis.

LO 2.1 Explain why competitive advantages are temporary.

Identifying Competitive Advantages

Running a company today is similar to leading an army; the top manager or leader ensures all participants are heading in the right direction and completing their goals and objectives. Companies lacking leadership quickly implode as employees head in different directions attempting to achieve conflicting goals. To combat these challenges, leaders communicate and execute business strategies (from the Greek word *stratus* for army and *ago* for leading). A **business strategy** is a leadership plan that achieves a specific set of goals or objectives as displayed in Figure 2.1.

FIGURE 2.1

Examples of Business Strategies

Business strategies
Leadership plans that achieve a specific set of goals or objectives

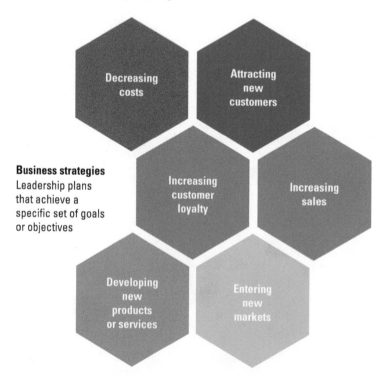

Good leaders also anticipate unexpected misfortunes, from strikes and economic recessions to natural disasters. Their business strategies build in buffers or slack, allowing the company the ability to ride out any storm and defend against competitive or environmental threats. Of course, updating business strategies is a continuous undertaking as internal and external environments rapidly change. Business strategies that match core company competencies to opportunities result in competitive advantages, a key to success!

A *competitive advantage* is a feature of a product or service on which customers place a greater value than they do on similar offerings from competitors. Competitive advantages provide the same product or service either at a lower price or with additional value that can fetch premium prices. Unfortunately, competitive advantages are typically temporary, because competitors often quickly seek ways to duplicate them. In turn, organizations must develop a strategy based on a new competitive advantage. Ways that companies duplicate competitive advantages include acquiring the new technology, copying the business operations, and hiring away key employees. The introduction of Apple's iPod and iTunes, a brilliant merger of technology, business, and entertainment, offers an excellent example.

In early 2000, Steve Jobs was fixated on developing video editing software when he suddenly realized that millions of people were using computers to listen to music, a new trend in the industry catapulted by illegal online services such as Napster. Jobs was worried that he was looking in the wrong direction and had missed the opportunity to jump on the online music bandwagon. He moved fast, however, and within four months he had developed the first version of iTunes for the Mac. Jobs' next challenge was to make a portable iTunes player that could hold thousands of songs and be completely transportable. Within nine months the iPod was born. With the combination of iTunes and iPod, Apple created a significant competitive advantage in the marketplace. Many firms began following Apple's lead by creating portable music players to compete with the iPod. In addition, Apple continues to create new and exciting products to gain competitive advantages, such as its iPad, a larger version of the iPod that functions more as a computer than a music player.[1]

When a company is the first to market with a competitive advantage, it gains a particular benefit, such as Apple did with its iPod. This *first-mover advantage* occurs when a company can significantly increase its market share by being first with a new competitive advantage. FedEx created a first-mover advantage by developing its customer self-service software, which allows people to request parcel pickups, print mailing slips, and track parcels online. Other parcel delivery companies quickly began creating their own online services. Today, customer self-service on the Internet is a standard feature of the parcel delivery business.

Competitive intelligence is the process of gathering information about the competitive environment, including competitors' plans, activities, and products, to improve a company's ability to succeed. It means understanding and learning as much as possible as soon as possible about what is occurring outside the company to remain competitive. Frito-Lay, a premier provider of snack foods such as Cracker Jacks and Cheetos, does not send its sales representatives into grocery stores just to stock shelves; they carry handheld computers and record the product offerings, inventory, and even product locations of competitors. Frito-Lay uses this information to gain competitive intelligence on everything from how well competing products are selling to the strategic placement of its own products.[2]

Managers use three common tools to analyze competitive intelligence and develop competitive advantages including:

1. The Five Forces Model (for evaluating industry attractiveness).

2. The three generic strategies (for choosing a business focus).

3. Value chain analysis (for executing business strategies).

LO 2.2 Describe Porter's Five Forces Model and explain each of the five forces.

The Five Forces Model— Evaluating Industry Attractiveness

Michael Porter, a university professor at Harvard Business School, identified the following pressures that can hurt potential sales:

- Knowledgeable customers can force down prices by pitting rivals against each other.
- Influential suppliers can drive down profits by charging higher prices for supplies.
- Competition can steal customers.
- New market entrants can steal potential investment capital.
- Substitute products can steal customers.

Formally defined, ***Porter's Five Forces Model*** analyzes the competitive forces within the environment in which a company operates to assess the potential for profitability in an industry. Its purpose is to combat these competitive forces by identifying opportunities, competitive advantages, and competitive intelligence. If the forces are strong, they increase competition; if the forces are weak, they decrease competition. This section details each of the forces and its associated MIS business strategy (see Figure 2.2).[3]

BUYER POWER

Buyer power is the ability of buyers to affect the price they must pay for an item. Factors used to assess buyer power include number of customers, their sensitivity to price, size of orders, differences between competitors, and availability of substitute products. If buyer power is high, customers can force a company and its competitors to compete on price, which typically drives prices down.

One way to reduce buyer power is by manipulating ***switching costs,*** costs that make customers reluctant to switch to another product or service. Switching costs include financial as well as intangible values. The cost of switching doctors, for instance, includes the powerful intangible components of having to build relationships with the new doctor and nurses, as well as transferring all your medical history. With MIS, however, patients can store their medical records on DVDs or thumb drives, allowing easy transferability. The Internet also lets patients review websites for physician referrals, which takes some of the fear out of trying someone new.[4]

FIGURE 2.2

Porter's Five Forces Model

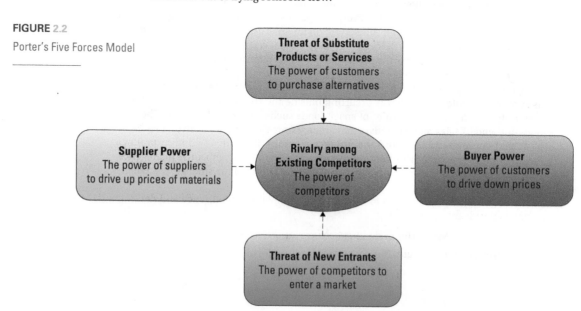

Companies can also reduce buyer power with **loyalty programs,** which reward customers based on their spending. The airline industry is famous for its frequent-flyer programs, for instance. Because of the rewards travelers receive (free airline tickets, upgrades, or hotel stays), they are more likely to be loyal to or give most of their business to a single company. Keeping track of the activities and accounts of many thousands or millions of customers covered by loyalty programs is not practical without large-scale business systems, however. Loyalty programs are thus a good example of using MIS to reduce buyer power.[5]

SUPPLIER POWER

A **supply chain** consists of all parties involved, directly or indirectly, in obtaining raw materials or a product. In a typical supply chain, a company will be both a supplier (to customers) and a customer (of other suppliers), as illustrated in Figure 2.3. **Supplier power** is the suppliers' ability to influence the prices they charge for supplies (including materials, labor, and services). Factors used to appraise supplier power include number of suppliers, size of suppliers, uniqueness of services, and availability of substitute products. If supplier power is high, the supplier can influence the industry by:

- Charging higher prices.
- Limiting quality or services.
- Shifting costs to industry participants.[6]

Typically, when a supplier raises prices, the buyers will pass on the increase to their customers by raising prices on the end product. When supplier power is high, buyers lose revenue because they cannot pass on the raw material price increase to their customers. Some powerful suppliers, such as pharmaceutical companies, can exert a threat over an entire industry when substitutes are limited and the product is critical to the buyers. Patient who need to purchase cancer-fighting drugs have no power over price and must pay whatever the drug company asks because there are few available alternatives.

Using MIS to find alternative products is one way of decreasing supplier power. Cancer patients can now use the Internet to research alternative medications and practices, something that was next to impossible just a few decades ago. Buyers can also use MIS to form groups or collaborate with other buyers, increasing the size of the buyer group and reducing supplier power. For a hypothetical example, the collective group of 30,000 students from a university has far more power over price when purchasing laptops than a single student.[7]

THREAT OF SUBSTITUTE PRODUCTS OR SERVICES

The **threat of substitute products or services** is high when there are many alternatives to a product or service and low when there are few alternatives from which to choose. For example, travelers have numerous substitutes for airline transportation including automobiles, trains, and boats. Technology even makes videoconferencing and virtual meetings possible, eliminating the need for some business travel. Ideally, a company would like to be in a market in which there are few substitutes for the products or services it offers.

Polaroid had this unique competitive advantage for many years until it forgot to observe competitive intelligence. Then the firm went bankrupt when people began taking digital pictures with everything from video cameras to cell phones.

A company can reduce the threat of substitutes by offering additional value through wider product distribution. Soft-drink manufacturers distribute their products through vending machines, gas stations, and convenience stores, increasing the availability of

FIGURE 2.3

Traditional Supply Chain

soft drinks relative to other beverages. Companies can also offer various add-on services, making the substitute product less of a threat. For example, iPhones include capabilities for games, videos, and music, making a traditional cell phone less of a substitute.[8]

THREAT OF NEW ENTRANTS

The *threat of new entrants* is high when it is easy for new competitors to enter a market and low when there are significant entry barriers to joining a market. An *entry barrier* is a feature of a product or service that customers have come to expect and entering competitors must offer the same for survival. For example, a new bank must offer its customers an array of MIS-enabled services, including ATMs, online bill paying, and online account monitoring. These are significant barriers to new firms entering the banking market. At one time, the first bank to offer such services gained a valuable first-mover advantage, but only temporarily, as other banking competitors developed their own MIS services.[9]

RIVALRY AMONG EXISTING COMPETITORS

Rivalry among existing competitors is high when competition is fierce in a market and low when competitors are more complacent. Although competition is always more intense in some industries than in others, the overall trend is toward increased competition in almost every industry. The retail grocery industry is intensively competitive. Kroger, Safeway, and Albertsons in the United States compete in many different ways, essentially trying to beat or match each other on price. Most supermarket chains have implemented loyalty programs to provide customers special discounts while gathering valuable information about their purchasing habits. In the future, expect to see grocery stores using wireless technologies that track customer movements throughout the store to determine purchasing sequences.

   Product differentiation occurs when a company develops unique differences in its products or services with the intent to influence demand. Companies can use differentiation to reduce rivalry. For example, while many companies sell books and videos on the Internet, Amazon differentiates itself by using customer profiling. When a customer visits Amazon.com repeatedly, Amazon begins to offer products tailored to that particular customer based on his or her profile. In this way, Amazon has reduced its rivals' power by offering its customers a differentiated service.

   To review, the Five Forces Model helps managers set business strategy by identifying the competitive structure and economic environment of an industry. If the forces are strong, they increase competition; if the forces are weak, they decrease it (see Figure 2.4).[10]

ANALYZING THE AIRLINE INDUSTRY

Let us bring Porter's five forces together to look at the competitive forces shaping an industry and highlight business strategies to help it remain competitive. Assume a shipping

FIGURE 2.4

Strong and Weak Examples of Porter's Five Forces

	Weak Force: Decreases Competition or Few Competitors	Strong Force: Increases Competition or Lots of Competitors
Buyer Power	An international hotel chain purchasing milk	A single consumer purchasing milk
Supplier Power	A company that makes airline engines	A company that makes pencils
Threat of Substitute Products or Services	Cancer drugs from a pharmaceutical company	Coffee from McDonald's
Threat of New Entrants	A professional hockey team	A dog walking business
Rivalry among Existing Competitors	Department of Motor Vehicles	A coffee shop

	Strong (High) Force: Increases Competition or Lots of Competitors
Buyer Power	Many airlines for buyers to choose from forcing competition based on price
Supplier Power	Limited number of plane and engine manufacturers to choose from along with unionized workers
Threat of Substitute Products or Services	Many substitutes including cars, trains, and busses. Even substitutes to travel such as video conferencing and virtual meetings.
Threat of New Entrants	Many new airlines entering the market all the time including the latest sky taxis.
Rivalry among Existing Competitors	Intense competition—many rivals.

FIGURE 2.5

Five Forces Model in the Airline Industry

company is deciding whether to enter the commercial airline industry. If performed correctly, an analysis of the five forces should determine that this is a highly risky business strategy because all five forces are strong. It will thus be difficult to generate a profit.

- **Buyer power:** Buyer power is high because customers have many airlines to choose from and typically make purchases based on price, not carrier.

- **Supplier power:** Supplier power is high since there are limited plane and engine manufacturers to choose from, and unionized workforces (suppliers of labor) restrict airline profits.

- **Threat of substitute products or services:** The threat of substitute products is high from many transportation alternatives including automobiles, trains, and boats, and from transportation substitutes such as videoconferencing and virtual meetings.

- **Threat of new entrants:** The threat of new entrants is high because new airlines are continuously entering the market, including sky taxies offering low-cost on-demand air taxi service.

- **Rivalry among existing competitors:** Rivalry in the airline industry is high, and websites such as Travelocity.com force them to compete on price (see Figure 2.5).[11]

The Three Generic Strategies— Choosing a Business Focus

LO 2.3 Compare Porter's three generic strategies.

Once top management has determined the relative attractiveness of an industry and decided to enter it, the firm must formulate a strategy for doing so. If our sample company decided to join the airline industry, it could compete as a low-cost, no-frills airline or as a luxury airline providing outstanding service and first-class comfort. Both options offer different ways of achieving competitive advantages in a crowded marketplace. The low-cost operator saves on expenses and passes the savings along to customers in the form of low prices. The luxury airline spends on high-end service and first-class comforts and passes the costs on to the customer in the form of high prices.

Porter has identified three generic business strategies for entering a new market: (1) broad cost leadership, (2) broad differentiation, and (3) focused strategy. Broad strategies reach a large market segment, while focused strategies target a niche or unique market with either cost leadership or differentiation. Trying to be all things to all people is a recipe for disaster, since doing so makes it difficult to project a consistent image to the entire marketplace. For this reason, Porter suggests adopting only one of the three generic strategies illustrated in Figure 2.6.[12]

FIGURE 2.6

Porter's Three Generic
Strategies

FIGURE 2.6

Porter's Three Generic
Strategies

Cost Strategy

	Low Cost	High Cost
Broad Market	Cost Leadership	Differentiation
Narrow Market	Focused Strategy	

Competitive Scope

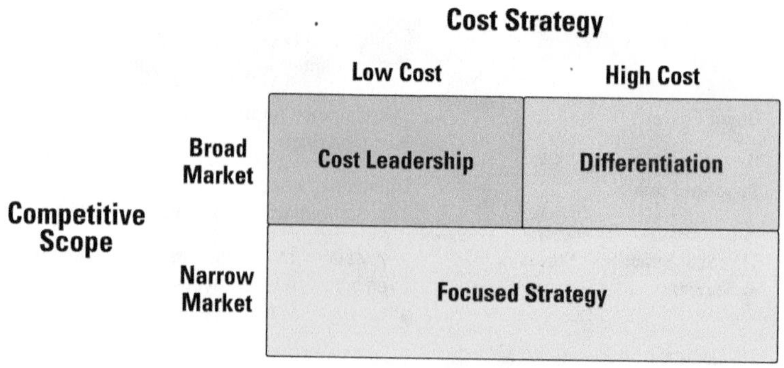

FIGURE 2.7

Examples of Porter's Three
Generic Strategies

Cost Strategy

	Low Cost	High Cost
Broad Market	Walmart	Neiman Marcus
Narrow Market	Payless Shoes	Tiffany & Co.

Competitive Scope

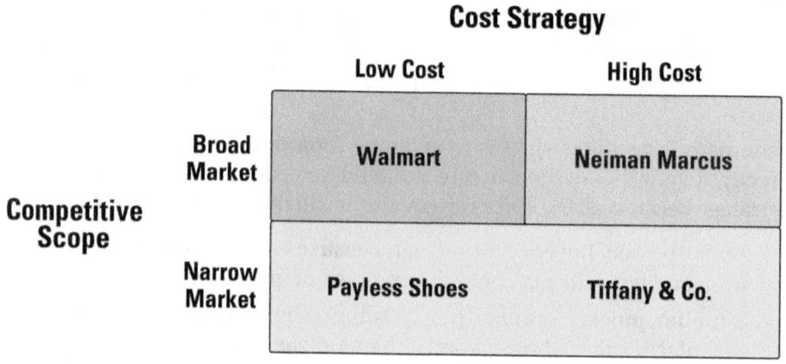

Figure 2.7 applies the three strategies to real companies, demonstrating the relationships among strategies (cost leadership versus differentiation) and market segmentation (broad versus focused).

■ **Broad market and low cost:** Walmart competes by offering a broad range of products at low prices. Its business strategy is to be the low-cost provider of goods for the cost-conscious consumer.

■ **Broad market and high cost:** Neiman Marcus competes by offering a broad range of differentiated products at high prices. Its business strategy offers a variety of specialty and upscale products to affluent consumers.

■ **Narrow market and low cost:** Payless competes by offering a specific product, shoes, at low prices. Its business strategy is to be the low-cost provider of shoes. Payless competes with Walmart, which also sells low-cost shoes, by offering a far bigger selection of sizes and styles.

■ **Narrow market and high cost:** Tiffany & Co. competes by offering a differentiated product, jewelry, at high prices. Its business strategy allows it to be a high-cost provider of premier designer jewelry to affluent consumers.

LO 2.4 Demonstrate how a
company can add value by using
Porter's value chain analysis.

Value Chain Analysis—
Executing Business Strategies

Firms make profits by taking raw inputs and applying a business process to turn them into a product or service that customers find valuable. A ***business process*** is a standardized set of activities that accomplish a specific task, such as processing a customer's order. Once a firm identifies the industry it wants to enter and the generic strategy it will focus on, it must then choose the business processes required to create its products or services. Of course, the firm will want to ensure the processes add value and create competitive advantages. To identify these competitive advantages, Michael Porter created *value chain analysis*, which views a firm as a series of business processes that each add value to the product or service.

Value chain analysis is a useful tool for determining how to create the greatest possible value for customers (see Figure 2.8). The goal of value chain analysis is to identify processes in which the firm can add value for the customer and create a competitive advantage for itself, with a cost advantage or product differentiation.

The *value chain* groups a firm's activities into two categories, primary value activities, and support value activities. *Primary value activities*, shown at the bottom of the value chain in Figure 2.8, acquire raw materials and manufacture, deliver, market, sell, and provide after-sales services.

1. **Inbound logistics:** acquires raw materials and resources and distributes to manufacturing as required.
2. **Operations:** transforms raw materials or inputs into goods and services.
3. **Outbound logistics:** distributes goods and services to customers.
4. **Marketing and sales:** promotes, prices, and sells products to customers.
5. **Service:** Provides customer support after the sale of goods and services.[13]

Support value activities, along the top of the value chain in Figure 2.8, include firm infrastructure, human resource management, technology development, and procurement. Not surprisingly, these support the primary value activities.

- **Firm infrastructure:** includes the company format or departmental structures, environment, and systems.
- **Human resource management:** provides employee training, hiring, and compensation.
- **Technology development:** applies MIS to processes to add value.
- **Procurement:** purchases inputs such as raw materials, resources, equipment, and supplies.

It is easy to understand how a typical manufacturing firm takes raw materials such as wood pulp and transforms it into paper. Adding value in this example might include using high-quality raw materials or offering next-day free shipping on any order. How, though, might a typical service firm take raw inputs such as time, knowledge, and MIS and transform them into valuable customer service knowledge? A hotel might use MIS to track customer reservations and then inform front-desk employees when a loyal customer is checking in so the employee can call the guest by name and offer additional

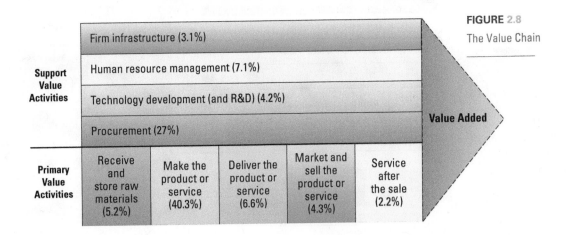

FIGURE 2.8

The Value Chain

services, gift baskets, or upgraded rooms. Examining the firm as a value chain allows managers to identify the important business processes that add value for customers and then find MIS solutions that support them.

When performing a value chain analysis, a firm could survey customers about the extent to which they believe each activity adds value to the product or service. This step generates responses the firm can measure, shown as percentages in Figure 2.9, to describe how each activity adds (or reduces) value. Then the competitive advantage decision for the firm is whether to (1) target high value-adding activities to further enhance their value, (2) target low value-adding activities to increase their value, or (3) perform some combination of the two.

MIS adds value to both primary and support value activities. One example of a primary value activity facilitated by MIS is the development of a marketing campaign management system that could target marketing campaigns more efficiently, thereby reducing marketing costs. The system would also help the firm better pinpoint target market needs, thereby increasing sales. One example of a support value activity facilitated by MIS is the development of a human resources system that could more efficiently reward employees based on performance. The system could also identify employees who are at risk of quitting, allowing manager's time to find additional challenges or opportunities that would help retain these employees and thus reduce turnover costs.

Value chain analysis is a highly useful tool that provides hard and fast numbers for evaluating the activities that add value to products and services. Managers can find additional value by analyzing and constructing the value chain in terms of Porter's Five Forces Model (see Figure 2.9). For example, if the goal is to decrease buyer power, a company can construct its value chain activity of "service after the sale" by offering high levels of customer service. This will increase customers' switching costs and reduce their power. Analyzing and constructing support value activities can help decrease the threat of new entrants. Analyzing and constructing primary value activities can help decrease the threat of substitute products or services. Revising Porter's three business strategies is critical. Firms must continually adapt to their competitive environments, which can cause business strategy to shift.[14]

FIGURE 2.9

The Value Chain and Porter's Five Forces Model

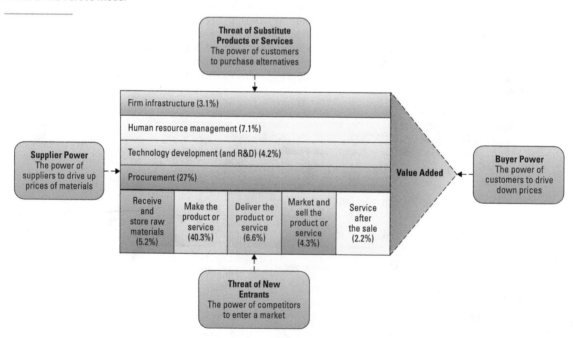

1. How can Apple use competitive intelligence to gain business intelligence?

2. Using Porter's Five Forces Model, analyze Apple's buyer power and supplier power.

3. Which of the three generic strategies is Apple following?

4. Which of Porter's Five Forces did Apple address through the introduction of the iPhone and customer-developed iPhone applications?

Chapter Two Case: *BusinessWeek* Interview with Michael Porter

The Harvard professor and popular author explains the "location paradox" and talks about the competitive challenges facing the United States. Ever since his 1990 book *The Competitive Advantage of Nations,* Harvard Business School professor Michael Porter has been regarded as a leading authority on the economic development of nations, regions, and cities. Both as an academic and consultant, Porter is best known for his work on the importance of developing a specialty in industrial clusters—high concentrations of companies in a sector such as semiconductors, cars, or textiles. In an interview with Senior Writer Pete Engardio, Porter explains why he believes globalization has actually made industry clusters and local advantages even more important, rather than weakened them.

If globalization means that work, technology, and money can now move anywhere over the Internet, does the physical location of an industry still really matter?
"I call it the location paradox. If you think of globalization, your first reaction is to think that location doesn't matter anymore. There are no barriers to investment. But the paradox is that location still matters. The U.S. is still the most important space in the world, for example, and regions have tremendous specialization. Anything that can be easily accessed from a distance no longer is a competitive advantage. But the more there are no barriers, the more things are mobile, the more decisive location becomes. This point has tripped up a lot of really smart people.

"As a result, the bottom half of U.S. locations are facing more stress. Many cities used to have a natural advantage just because they were in the U.S. But that is not such an advantage anymore. We are finding a tendency for the rich regions to get richer."

How has globalization affected the idea of regional clusters?
"Now that globalization continues to power forward, what has happened is that clusters must become more specialized in individual locations. The global economy is speeding up the process by which clusters get more focused. There is a footwear cluster in Italy, for example, where they still produce very advanced products. The design, marketing, and technology still are in Italy. But much of the production has shifted to Romania, where the Italians have developed another cluster. All of the production companies actually are Italian-owned. Taiwan has done the same by shifting production to China. The innovation is in Taiwan, but its companies are moving aspects of their cluster that don't need to be in Taiwan."

What are the big differences in the way communities approach development today compared to 1990, when you wrote *The Competitive Advantage of Nations*?
"There has been tremendous change in the last 15 or 20 years. Before *Competitive Advantage* was published, the dominant view was that you need to get costs down, offer incentives, and have a development department that hunts for investment. I think the level of sophistication has risen at the state and local level. They now understand that competitiveness does not just mean low costs.

"Another big change from 20 years ago is that the notion of industry clusters is now pretty much ubiquitous. Many regions now look at development in these terms, and have identified hundreds and hundreds of different clusters. I think that the fact that productivity growth has risen dramatically shows that economic development has been a big success over the past few years."

If every community is developing the same industry clusters, how do they stand out?

"I think it's very important to understand that the bar has risen substantially. Everything matters now. The schools matter. The roads matter. You have to understand this is a marathon. Also, you can't try to build clusters across the board and be into everything. You have to build on your strengths."

Many local officials in the U.S. talk a lot about collaboration among universities, companies, and governments across an entire region. Is this new?

"There is a growing recognition that the interaction between one region or metropolitan area and its neighbors is important. The overlap between clusters is very important in stimulating growth. Isolated clusters are less powerful than integrated clusters. That's because new clusters often grow out of old clusters. I also think there is more recognition that you need a lot of cross-company collaboration in a region. Companies realize they have a lot of shared issues. Meanwhile, universities used to be seen as standalone institutions. Now, more regional economies see universities as players and are integrating them into industrial clusters."

Does the U.S. have a competitiveness problem?

"I think the U.S. is facing some very serious challenges. But the most important drivers of competitiveness are not national. They are regional and local. National policies and circumstances explain about 20 percent to 25 percent of why a regional economy is doing well. What really matters is where the skills and highly competitive institutions are based. Some of these assets take a very long time to build. But competitiveness essentially is in the hands of regions."[15]

Questions

1. In today's global business environment, does the physical location of a business matter?
2. Why is collaboration among universities important?
3. Is there a competitiveness problem in the United States?
4. What are the big differences in the way communities approach development today compared to 1990, when Porter wrote *The Competitive Advantage of Nations?*

13

Creating Innovative Organizations

13.1. Compare disruptive and sustaining technologies, and explain how the Internet and WWW caused business disruption.

13.2. Describe Web 1.0 along with ebusiness and its associated advantages.

LO 13.1 **Compare disruptive and sustaining technologies, and explain how the Internet and WWW caused business disruption.**

Disruptive Technologies and Web 1.0

Polaroid, founded in 1937, produced the first instant camera in the late 1940s. The Polaroid camera, whose pictures developed themselves, was one of the most exciting technological advances the photography industry had ever seen. The company eventually went public, becoming one of Wall Street's most prominent enterprises, with its stock trading above $60 per share in 1997. In 2002, the stock dropped to 8 cents and the company declared bankruptcy.[2]

How could a company such as Polaroid, which had innovative technology and a captive customer base, go bankrupt? Perhaps company executives failed to use Porter's Five Forces Model to analyze the threat of substitute products or services. If they had, would they have noticed the two threats—one-hour film processing and digital cameras—which eventually stole Polaroid's market share? Would they have understood that their customers, people who want instant access to their pictures, would be the first to try these alternatives? Could the company have found a way to compete with one-hour film processing and the digital camera to save Polaroid?

Many organizations face the same dilemma as Polaroid—what's best for the current business might not be what's best for it in the long term. Some observers of our business environment have an ominous vision of the future—digital Darwinism. ***Digital Darwinism*** implies that organizations that cannot adapt to the new demands placed on them for surviving in the information age are doomed to extinction.

DISRUPTIVE VERSUS SUSTAINING TECHNOLOGY

A ***disruptive technology*** is a new way of doing things that initially does not meet the needs of existing customers. Disruptive technologies tend to open new markets and destroy old ones. A ***sustaining technology,*** on the other hand, produces an improved product customers are eager to buy, such as a faster car or larger hard drive. Sustaining technologies tend to provide us with better, faster, and cheaper products in established markets. Incumbent companies most often lead sustaining technology to market, but they virtually never lead in markets opened by disruptive technologies. Figure 13.1 positions companies expecting future growth from new investments (disruptive technology) and companies expecting future growth from existing investments (sustaining technology).[3]

Disruptive technologies typically enter the low end of the marketplace and eventually evolve to displace high-end competitors and their reigning technologies. Sony is a

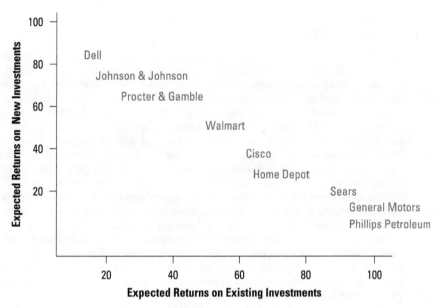

FIGURE 13.1

Disruptive and Sustaining
Technologies

perfect example. Sony started as a tiny company that built portable, battery-powered transistor radios. The sound quality was poor, but customers were willing to overlook that for the convenience of portability. With the experience and revenue stream from the portables, Sony improved its technology to produce cheap, low-end transistor amplifiers that were suitable for home use and invested those revenues in improving the technology further, which produced still-better radios.[4]

The Innovator's Dilemma, a book by Clayton M. Christensen, discusses how established companies can take advantage of disruptive technologies without hindering existing relationships with customers, partners, and stakeholders. Xerox, IBM, Sears, and DEC all listened to existing customers, invested aggressively in technology, had their competitive antennae up, and still lost their market-dominant positions. They may have placed too much emphasis on satisfying customers' current needs, while neglecting new disruptive technology to meet customers' future needs and thus losing market share. Figure 13.2 highlights several companies that launched new businesses by capitalizing on disruptive technologies.[5]

Company	Disruptive Technology
Apple	iPod, iPhone, iPad
Charles Schwab	Online brokerage
Hewlett-Packard	Microprocessor-based computers, ink-jet printers
IBM	Minicomputers; personal computers
Intel	Low-end microprocessors
Intuit	QuickBooks software; TurboTax software; Quicken software
Microsoft	Internet-based computing; operating system software; SQL and Access database software
Oracle	Database software
Quantum	3.5-inch disks
Sony	Transistor-based consumer electronics

FIGURE 13.2

Companies That Capitalized
on Disruptive Technologies

THE INTERNET AND WORLD WIDE WEB—THE ULTIMATE BUSINESS DISRUPTORS

The **Internet** is a massive network that connects computers all over the world and allows them to communicate with one another. Computers connected via the Internet can send and receive information including text, graphics, voice, video, and software. Originally the Internet was essentially an emergency military communications system operated by the U.S. Department of Defense Advanced Research Project Agency (DARPA), which called the network ARPANET. No one foresaw the dramatic impact it would have on both business and personal communications. In time, all U.S. universities that had defense-related funding installed ARPANET computers, forming the first official Internet network. As users began to notice the value of electronic communications, the purpose of the network started shifting from a military pipeline to a communications tool for scientists.

Millions of corporate, educational, and research networks now connect billions of computer systems and users in more than 200 countries. Internet users are expected to top the 2 billion mark, about one-third of the world's population.[6]

Although the Internet was an excellent communication tool for scientists and government officials, it was technically challenging for everyday people to operate. This changed with the inventions of the World Wide Web and web browsers. The **World Wide Web (WWW)** provides access to Internet information through documents including text, graphics, audio, and video files that use a special formatting language called HTML. **Hypertext markup language (HTML)** links documents, allowing users to move from one to another simply by clicking on a hot spot or link. **Web browsers,** such as Internet Explorer or Mozilla's Firefox, allow users to access the WWW. **Hypertext transport protocol (HTTP)** is the Internet protocol web browsers use to request and display web pages using universal resource locators. A **universal resource locator (URL)** is the address of a file or resource on the web such as www.apple.com. A domain name identifies a URL address and in the previous example apple.com is the domain name.

Notice that the Internet and the World Wide Web are not synonymous. The WWW is just one part of the Internet, and its primary use is to correlate and disseminate information. The Internet includes the WWW and also other forms of communication systems such as email. Figure 13.3 lists the reasons for the massive growth of the WWW.[7]

WEB 1.0: THE CATALYST FOR EBUSINESS

As people began learning about the WWW and the Internet, they understood that it enabled a company to communicate with anyone, anywhere, at anytime, creating a new way to participate in business. The competitive advantages for first movers would be enormous, thus spurring the beginning of the Web 1.0 Internet boom. **Web 1.0** is a term to refer to the World Wide Web during its first few years of operation between 1991 and 2003. **Ecommerce** is the buying and selling of goods and services over the Internet. Ecommerce refers only to online transactions. **Ebusiness** includes ecommerce along with all activities related to internal and external business operations such as servicing customer accounts, collaborating with partners, and exchanging real-time information. During Web 1.0, entrepreneurs began creating the first forms of ebusiness.

FIGURE 13.3

Reasons for Growth
of the World Wide Web

The microcomputer revolution made it possible for an average person to own a computer.
Advancements in networking hardware, software, and media made it possible for business computers to be connected to larger networks at a minimal cost.
Browser software such as Microsoft's Internet Explorer and Netscape Navigator gave computer users an easy-to-use graphical interface to find, download, and display web pages.
The speed, convenience, and low cost of email have made it an incredibly popular tool for business and personal communications.
Basic web pages are easy to create and extremely flexible.

Industry	Business Changes Due to Technology
Auto	AutoTrader.com is the world's largest used-car marketplace, listing millions of cars from both private owners and dealers. AutoTrader.com actually helps to increase used-car dealers' business as it drives millions of qualified leads (potential used-car buyers) to participating automotive dealers and private sellers.
Publishing	With the Internet, anyone can publish online content. Traditionally, publishers screened many authors and manuscripts and selected those that had the best chances of succeeding. Lulu.com turned this model around by providing self-publishing along with print-on-demand capabilities.
Education and Training	Continuing medical education is costly, and just keeping up-to-date with advances often requires taking training courses and traveling to conferences. Now continuing education in many fields is moving online, and by 2016 more than 50 percent of doctors will be building their skills through online learning. Companies such as Cisco save millions by moving training to the Internet.
Entertainment	The music industry was hit hard by ebusiness, and online music traders such as iTunes average billions of annual downloads. Unable to compete with online music, the majority of record stores closed. The next big entertainment industry to feel the effects of ebusiness will be the multibillion-dollar movie business. Video rental stores are closing their doors as they fail to compete with online streaming and home rental delivery companies such as Netflix.
Financial Services	Nearly every public efinance company makes money, with online mortgage service Lending Tree leading the pack. Processing online mortgage applications is more than 50 percent cheaper for customers.
Retail	Forrester Research predicts ebusiness retail sales will grow at a 10 percent annual growth rate through 2014. It forecasts U.S. online retail sales will be nearly $250 billion, up from $155 billion in 2009. Online retail sales were recently up 11 percent, compared to 2.5 percent for all retail sales.
Travel	Travel site Expedia.com is now the biggest leisure-travel agency, with higher profit margins than even American Express. The majority of travel agencies closed as a direct result of ebusiness.

Ebusiness opened up a new marketplace for any company willing to move its business operations online. A *paradigm shift* occurs when a new radical form of business enters the market that reshapes the way companies and organizations behave. Ebusiness created a paradigm shift, transforming entire industries and changing enterprise-wide business processes that fundamentally rewrote traditional business rules. Deciding not to make the shift to ebusiness proved fatal for many companies (see Figure 13.4 for an overview of industries revamped by the disruption of ebusiness).[8]

FIGURE 13.4

Ebusiness Disruption of Traditional Industries

Advantages of Ebusiness

LO 13.2 **Describe Web 1.0 along with ebusiness and its associated advantages.**

Both individuals and organizations have embraced ebusiness to enhance productivity, maximize convenience, and improve communications. Companies today need to deploy a comprehensive ebusiness strategy, and business students need to understand its advantages, outlined in Figure 13.5. Let's look at each.

EXPANDING GLOBAL REACH

Easy access to real-time information is a primary benefit of ebusiness. *Information richness* refers to the depth and breadth of details contained in a piece of textual, graphic, audio, or video information. *Information reach* measures the number of people a firm can communicate with all over the world. Buyers need information richness to make informed purchases, and sellers need information reach to properly market and differentiate themselves from the competition.

Ebusinesses operate 24 hours a day, 7 days a week. This availability directly reduces transaction costs, since consumers no longer have to spend a lot of time researching

FIGURE 13.5

Ebusiness Advantages

purchases or traveling great distances to make them. The faster delivery cycle for online sales helps strengthen customer relationships, improving customer satisfaction and ultimately sales.

A firm's website can be the focal point of a cost-effective communications and marketing strategy. Promoting products online allows the company to precisely target its customers whether they are local or around the globe. A physical location is restricted by size and limited to those customers who can get there, while an online store has a global marketplace with customers and information seekers already waiting in line.

OPENING NEW MARKETS

Ebusiness is perfect for increasing niche-product sales. ***Mass customization*** is the ability of an organization to tailor its products or services to the customers' specifications. For example, customers can order M&M's in special colors or with customized sayings such as "Marry Me." ***Personalization*** occurs when a company knows enough about a customer's likes and dislikes that it can fashion offers more likely to appeal to that person, say by tailoring its website to individuals or groups based on profile information, demographics, or prior transactions. Amazon uses personalization to create a unique portal for each of its customers.

Chris Anderson, editor-in-chief of *Wired* magazine, describes niche-market ebusiness strategies as capturing the ***long tail,*** referring to the tail of a typical sales curve. This strategy demonstrates how niche products can have viable and profitable business models when selling via ebusiness. In traditional sales models, a store is limited by shelf space when selecting products to sell. For this reason, store owners typically purchase products that will be wanted or needed by masses, and the store is stocked with broad products as there is not room on the shelf for niche products that only a few customers might purchase. Ebusinesses such as Amazon and eBay eliminated the shelf-space dilemma and were able to offer infinite products.

Netflix offers an excellent example of the long tail. Let's assume that an average Blockbuster store maintains 3,000 movies in its inventory, whereas Netflix, without physical shelf limitations, can maintain 100,000 movies in its inventory. Looking at sales data, the majority of Blockbuster's revenue comes from new releases that are rented daily, whereas older selections are rented only a few times a month and don't repay the cost of keeping them in stock. Thus Blockbuster's sales tail ends at title 3,000 (see Figure 13.6) However, Netflix, with no physical limitations, can extend its tail beyond 100,000 (and with streaming video perhaps 200,000). By extending its tail, Netflix increases sales, even if a title is rented only a few times.[9]

Intermediaries are agents, software, or businesses that provide a trading infrastructure to bring buyers and sellers together. The introduction of ebusiness brought about ***disintermediation,*** which occurs when a business sells directly to the customer online and cuts out the intermediary (see Figure 13.7). This business strategy lets the company shorten the order process and add value with reduced costs or a more responsive and efficient service. The disintermediation of the travel agent occurred as people began to book their own vacations online, often at a cheaper rate. At Lulu.com anyone can publish and sell print-on-demand books, online music, and custom calendars, making the publisher obsolete.[10]

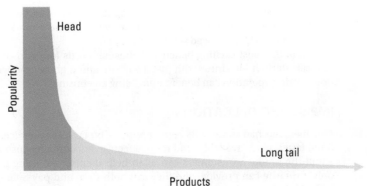

FIGURE 13.6

The Long Tail

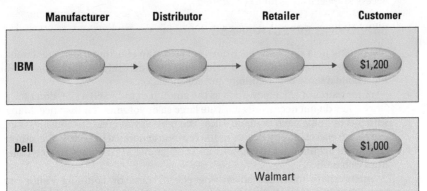

FIGURE 13.7

Business Value of Disintermediation

The more intermediaries that are cut from the distribution chain, the lower the product price. When Dell decided to sell its PCs through Walmart many were surprised, because Dell's direct-to-customer sales model was the competitive advantage that had kept Dell the market leader for years.

In *reintermediation,* steps are *added* to the value chain as new players find ways to add value to the business process. Levi Strauss originally thought it was a good business strategy to limit all online sales to its own website. A few years later, the company realized it could gain a far larger market share by allowing all retailers to sell its products directly to customers. As ebusiness matures it has become evident that to serve certain markets in volume, some reintermediation may be desirable. *Cybermediation* refers to the creation of new kinds of intermediaries that simply could not have existed before the advent of ebusiness, including comparison-shopping sites such as Kelkoo and bank account aggregation services such as Citibank.[11]

REDUCING COSTS

Operational benefits of ebusiness include business processes that require less time and human effort or can be eliminated. Compare the cost of sending out 100 direct mailings (paper, postage, labor) to the cost of a bulk email campaign. Think about the cost of renting a physical location and operating phone lines versus the cost of maintaining an online site. Switching to an ebusiness model can eliminate many traditional costs associated with communicating by substituting systems, such as Live Help, that let customers chat live with support or sales staff.

Online air travel reservations cost less than those booked over the telephone. Online ordering also offers the possibility of merging a sales order system with order fulfillment and delivery so customers can check the progress of their orders at all times. Ebusinesses can also inexpensively attract new customers with innovative marketing and retain present customers with improved service and support.[12]

One of the most exciting benefits of ebusiness is its low start-up costs. Today, anyone can start an ebusiness with just a website and a great product or service. Even a dog-walking operation can benefit from being an ebusiness.

IMPROVING OPERATIONS

Ebusiness has had some of its biggest impacts on customer service. Communication is often faster, more available, and more effective, encouraging customers to learn more about the product. Customers can often help themselves, using the content richness only a website can provide, and they can both shop and pay online without having to leave the house. Companies can also use email, special messages, and private password access to special areas for top customers.

IMPROVING EFFECTIVENESS

Just putting up a simple website does not create an ebusiness. Ebusiness websites must create buzz, be innovative, add value, and provide useful information. In short, they must build a sense of community and collaboration.

IT measures of efficiency, such as the amount of traffic on a site, don't tell the whole story. They do not necessarily indicate large sales volumes, for instance. Many websites with lots of traffic have minimal sales. The best way to measure ebusiness success is to use *effectiveness* IT metrics, such as the revenue generated by web traffic, number of new customers acquired by web traffic, and reductions in customer service calls resulting from web traffic.

Interactivity measures advertising effectiveness by counting visitor interactions with the target ad, including time spent viewing the ad, number of pages viewed, and number of repeat visits to the advertisement. Interactivity measures are a giant step forward for advertisers, since traditional advertising methods—newspapers, magazines, radio, and television—provide few ways to track effectiveness. Figure 13.8 displays the

FIGURE 13.8

Marketing Received Tremendous Benefits from Ebusiness

Marketing via Ebusiness
An **associate (affiliate) program** allows a business to generate commissions or referral fees when a customer visiting its website clicks on a link to another merchant's website. For example, if a customer to a company website clicks on a banner ad to another vendor's website, the company will receive a referral fee or commission when the customer performs the desired action, typically making a purchase or completing a form.
A **banner ad** is a box running across a website that advertises the products and services of another business, usually another ebusiness. The banner generally contains a link to the advertiser's website. Advertisers can track how often customers click on a banner ad resulting in a click-through to their website. Often the cost of the banner ad depends on the number of customers who click on the banner ad. Web-based advertising services can track the number of times users click the banner, generating statistics that enable advertisers to judge whether the advertising fees are worth paying. Banner ads are like living, breathing classified ads. Tracking the number of banner ad clicks is an excellent way to understand the effectiveness of the ad on the website.
A **click-through** is a count of the number of people who visit one site and click on an advertisement that takes them to the site of the advertiser. Tracking effectiveness based on click-throughs guarantees exposure to target ads; however, it does not guarantee that the visitor liked the ad, spent any substantial time viewing the ad, or was satisfied with the information contained in the ad.
A **cookie** is a small file deposited on a hard drive by a website containing information about customers and their browsing activities. Cookies allow websites to record the comings and goings of customers, usually without their knowledge or consent.
A **pop-up ad** is a small web page containing an advertisement that appears outside of the current website loaded in the browser. A pop-under ad is a form of a pop-up ad that users do not see until they close the current web browser screen.
Viral marketing is a technique that induces websites or users to pass on a marketing message to other websites or users, creating exponential growth in the message's visibility and effect. One example of successful viral marketing is Hotmail, which promotes its service and its own advertisers' messages in every user's email notes. Viral marketing encourages users of a product or service supplied by an ebusiness to encourage friends to join. Viral marketing is a word-of-mouth type advertising program.

ebusiness marketing initiatives allowing companies to expand their reach while measuring effectiveness.[13]

The ultimate outcome of any advertisement is a purchase. Organizations use metrics to tie revenue amounts and number of new customers created directly back to the websites or banner ads. Through *clickstream data* they can observe the exact pattern of a consumer's navigation through a site. Figure 13.9 displays different types of clickstream metrics, and Figure 3.10 provides definitions of common metrics based on clickstream data. To interpret such data properly, managers try to benchmark against other companies. For instance, consumers seem to visit their preferred websites regularly, even checking back multiple times during a given session.[14]

Types of Clickstream Data Metrics
The number of page views (i.e., the number of times a particular page has been presented to a visitor).
The pattern of websites visited, including most frequent exit page and most frequent prior website.
Length of stay on the website.
Dates and times of visits.
Number of registrations filled out per 100 visitors.
Number of abandoned registrations.
Demographics of registered visitors.
Number of customers with shopping carts.
Number of abandoned shopping carts.

FIGURE 13.9

Clickstream Data Metrics

METRICS MEASURING WEBSITE SUCCESS	
Website Visit Metrics	
Stickiness (visit duration time)	The length of time a visitor spends on a website.
Raw visit depth (total web pages exposure per session)	The total number of pages a visitor is exposed to during a single visit to a website.
Visit depth (total unique web pages exposure per session)	The total number of unique pages a visitor is exposed to during a single visit to a website.
Website Visitor Metrics	
Unidentified visitor	A visitor is an individual who visits a website. An "unidentified visitor" means that no information about that visitor is available.
Unique visitor	A unique visitor is one who can be recognized and counted only once within a given period of time.
Identified visitor	An ID is available that allows a user to be tracked across multiple visits to a website.
Website Hit Metrics	
Hits	When visitors reach a website, their computer sends a request to the site's computer server to begin displaying pages. Each element of a requested page is recorded by the website's server log file as a "hit."

FIGURE 13.10

Website Metrics

1. Do you consider Pinterest a form of disruptive or sustaining technology? Why or why not?
2. What types of security and ethical dilemmas are facing Pinterest?

Chapter Thirteen Case: Failing to Innovate

It is a sad but common tale—a dynamic company comes up with an innovative new product that utilizes cutting-edge technology in an exciting way that generates lots of hype and attention. But for some reason this new product fails to click with the masses and falls into oblivion, only to see other products gain massive success by following in its footsteps.

It's not always a case of right technology at the wrong time. Sometimes these first movers failed to build on their innovation, instead sitting on their initial achievements and letting more nimble competitors refine their idea into something more attractive and functional. And some just made too many mistakes to succeed.

Obtaining the first-mover advantage is critical to any business that wants to compete in the Internet economy. However, gaining a first-mover advantage is typically temporary, and without remaining innovative the company can soon fail. Here is a list of the top 10 first movers that flopped, according to Jim Rapoza of *eWeek*.

1. **Apple Newton PDA**—When it was launched in the early 90s, the Apple Newton was first lauded but later mocked because of its failings (it even had the honor of being spoofed on *The Simpsons)*. But one can draw a straight line from the Newton to current products such as tablet PCs, smartphones, and the Apple iPhone.

2. **PointCast**—In 1997, one of the hottest products found on the desktop of nearly every IT worker was PointCast, which delivered selected news items directly to the desktop. It quickly launched the "push" craze, which just as quickly imploded spectacularly. But today's RSS and news feeds all owe a debt to PointCast.

3. **Gopher Protocol**—It was so close. Launched just before the web itself, Gopher quickly became popular in universities and business. Using search technology, it worked very much like a website, but it could not compete with the web itself.

4. **VisiCalc**—Often lauded as the first killer application for the PC, the VisiCalc spreadsheet was a must-have for early PC-enabled businesses but quickly fell behind more polished spreadsheets from Lotus and Microsoft.

5. **Atari**—For those of a certain age, the word *Atari* is synonymous with video games. The pioneer in home gaming consoles failed to innovate in the face of more nimble competitors.

6. **Diamond Rio**—For $200 and with 32MB of RAM (with a SmartMedia slot for memory expansion), the Rio helped launch the MP3 revolution. That is, until white earbuds and a thing called the iPod took over.

7. **Netscape Navigator**—Netscape Navigator was essentially the web for users in the early to mid-1990s. But Netscape could not withstand the Microsoft onslaught, along with plenty of mistakes the company made itself, and now only lives on as the original basis of the Mozilla browsers.

8. **AltaVista**—Not the first search engine, but the first to use many of the natural language technologies common today and the first to gain real web popularity, AltaVista failed to keep up with technological changes.

9. **Ricochet Networks**—Nothing created geek lust like sitting next to someone who had a Ricochet card plugged into the laptop. Look, she is in a cab and accessing the Internet at ISDN speeds! But Ricochet never expanded to enough cities to be a serious player.

10. **IBM Simon Phone**—The iPhone's $499 price is nothing compared with the $900 price tag the IBM Simon had when it finally became available in 1994. But it pioneered most of the features found in today's smartphones and even beat the iPhone when it came to a buttonless touch-screen interface.[15]

Questions

1. If these companies all had a first-mover advantage, then why did the products fail?
2. For each of the listed products, determine if the technology used was disruptive or sustaining.
3. Choose one of the products listed and determine what the company could have done to prevent the product from failing.
4. Can you name another technology product that failed? Why did it fail? What could the company have done differently for it to succeed?

Business Process

1. Describe business processes and their importance to an organization.
2. Compare the continuous process improvement model and business process reengineering.
3. Describe the importance of business process modeling (or mapping) and business process models.
4. Explain business process management along with the reason for its importance to an organization.

LO 1. Describe business processes and their importance to an organization.

Introduction

The benefits of business process improvement vary, but a rough rule of thumb is that it will, at a minimum, double the gains of a project by streamlining outdated practices, enhancing efficiency, promoting compliance and standardization, and making an organization more agile. Business process improvement involves three key steps:

1. Measure what matters to most customers.
2. Monitor the performance of key business processes.
3. Assign accountability for process improvement.

Comprehensive business process management systems help organizations model and define complete business processes, implement those processes integrated with existing systems, and provide business leaders with the ability to analyze, manage, and improve the execution of processes in real time.

Examining Business Processes

Waiting in line at a grocery store is a great example of the need for process improvement. In this case, the "process" is called checkout, and the purpose is to pay for and bag groceries. The process begins when a customer steps into line and ends when the customer receives the receipt and leaves the store. The *process* steps are the activities the customer and store personnel do to complete the transaction. A ***business process*** is a standardized set of activities that accomplish a specific task, such as processing a customer's order. Business processes transform a set of inputs into a set of outputs (goods or services) for another person or process by using people and tools. This simple example describes a customer checkout process. Imagine other business processes: developing new products, building a new home, ordering clothes from mail-order companies, requesting new telephone service from a telephone company, administering Social Security payments, and so on.

Examining business processes helps an organization determine bottlenecks and identify outdated, duplicate, and smooth running processes. To stay competitive, organizations must optimize and automate their business processes. To identify which business processes need to be optimized, the organization must clearly understand its business processes, which typically have the following important characteristics:

- The processes have internal and external users.
- A process is cross-departmental. Departments are functional towers of expertise, but processes cut across departments.
- The processes occur across organizations.
- The processes are based on how work is done in the organization.
- Every process should be documented and fully understood by everyone participating in the process.
- Processes should be modeled to promote complete understanding.

A business process can be viewed as a "value chain." By contributing to the creation or delivery of a product or service, each step in a process should add value to the preceding step. For example, one step in the product development process consists of conducting market acceptance tests. This step adds value by ensuring that the product meets the needs of the market before the product or service is finalized. A tremendous amount of learning and improvement can result from the documentation and examination of the input-output linkages. However, between every input and every output is a process. Knowledge and improvement can only be completed by peeling the layers of the onion and examining the processes through which inputs are converted into outputs. Figure B2.1 displays several sample business processes.

UNDERSTANDING THE IMPORTANCE OF BUSINESS PROCESSES

Organizations are only as effective as their business processes. Developing logical business processes can help an organization achieve its goals. For example, an automobile manufacturer might have a goal to reduce the time it takes to deliver a car to a customer. The automobile manufacturer cannot hope to meet this goal with an inefficient ordering process or a convoluted distribution process. Sales representatives might be making mistakes when completing order forms, data-entry clerks might not accurately code order information, and dock crews might be inefficiently loading cars onto trucks. All of these errors increase the time it will take to get the car to the customer. Improving any one of these business processes can have a significant effect on the total distribution process, made up of the order entry, production scheduling, and transportation processes.

IBM Business Consulting Services helped Bank of America's card services division identify $40 million of simplification and cost savings projects over two years by improving business processes to identify opportunities, eliminate redundancies, consolidate systems/applications, and remove duplicate processes. Within the card services and ecommerce division were several fragmented strategies and IT architectures. These were consolidated and simplified to streamline the business area and provide better and faster response to customer demand.

The scope of the IT strategy and architecture business process realignment project included all consumer card segments (including military, school, airlines, etc.), ATM cards and services, and ecommerce.

Sample Business Processes
ACCOUNTING BUSINESS PROCESSES
■ Accounts payable
■ Accounts receivable
■ Bad/NSF checks
■ Bank account reconciliation
■ Cash receipts
■ Check requests
■ Check signing authority
■ Depreciation
■ Invoice billings
■ Petty cash
■ Month-end closing procedures
CUSTOMER SERVICE BUSINESS PROCESSES
■ Customer satisfaction survey
■ Customer service contact/complaint handling
■ Guarantee customer service satisfaction
■ Postsale customer follow-up
■ Warranty and service policies
ENVIRONMENTAL BUSINESS PROCESSES
■ Environmental protection
■ Hazardous waste management
■ Air/water/soil resource management
FINANCE BUSINESS PROCESSES
■ Account collection
■ Bank loan applications
■ Banking policy and relations
■ Business plans and forecasts
■ Customer credit approval and credit terms
■ Exercise of incentive stock options
■ Property tax assessments
■ Release of financial or confidential information
■ Stock transactions
■ Weekly financial and six-week cash flow reports
HUMAN RESOURCES BUSINESS PROCESSES
■ Board of directors and shareholders meetings, minutes, and protocol
■ Disabilities employment policies
■ Drug-free workplace employment policies
■ Employee hiring policies
■ Employee orientation
■ Family and medical leave act
■ Files and records management
■ Health care benefits
■ Paid and unpaid time off
■ Pay and payroll matters
■ Performance appraisals and salary adjustments
■ Resignations and terminations
■ Sexual harassment policies
■ Training/tuition reimbursement
■ Travel and entertainment
■ Workplace rules and guidelines
■ Workplace safety

Sample Business Processes
MANAGEMENT INFORMATION SYSTEMS BUSINESS PROCESSES
■ Disaster recovery procedures
■ Backup/recovery procedures
■ Service agreements, emergency services, and community resources
■ Emergency notification procedures
■ Office and department recovery
■ User workstation standards
■ Use of personal software
■ Computer security incident reporting
■ Control of computer virus programs
■ Computer user/staff training plan
■ Internet use policy
■ Email policy
■ Computer support center
MANUFACTURING BUSINESS PROCESSES
■ Assembly manuals
■ Bill of materials
■ Calibration for testing and measuring equipment
■ FDA inspections
■ Manufacturing change orders
■ Master parts list and files
■ Serial number designation
■ Quality control for finished goods
■ Quality assurance audit procedure
SALES AND MARKETING BUSINESS PROCESSES
■ Collection of sales tax
■ Copyrights and trademarks
■ Marketing plans model number
■ Designation public relations
■ Return of goods from customers
■ Sales leads
■ Sales order entry
■ Sales training
■ Trade shows
SHIPPING, PURCHASING, AND INVENTORY CONTROL BUSINESS PROCESSES
■ Packing, storage, and distribution
■ Physical inventory procedures
■ Purchasing procedures
■ Receiving, inspection, and stocking of parts and materials
■ Shipping and freight claims
■ Vendor selection, files, and inspections

FIGURE B2.1

(Continued)

Business Process Improvement

Improving business processes is paramount for businesses to stay competitive in today's marketplace. Over the past 10 to 15 years, companies have been forced to improve their business processes because customers are demanding better products and services; if they do not receive what they want from one supplier, they have many others to choose from (hence the competitive issue for businesses). Figure B2.2 displays several opportunities for business process improvement.

Many organizations began business process improvement with a continuous improvement model. A *continuous process improvement model* attempts to understand and measure the current process, and make performance improvements accordingly. Figure B2.3

LO 2. Compare the continuous process improvement model and business process reengineering.

Business Process Improvement Examples
Eliminate duplicate activities
Combine related activities
Eliminate multiple reviews and approvals
Eliminate inspections
Simplify processes
Reduce batch sizes
Process in parallel
Implement demand pull
Outsource inefficient activities
Eliminate movement of work
Organize multifunctional teams
Design cellular workplaces
Centralize/decentralize

FIGURE B2.2

Opportunities for Business
Process Improvement

illustrates the basic steps for continuous process improvement. Organizations begin by documenting what they do today, establish some way to measure the process based on what customers want, perform the process, measure the results, and then identify improvement opportunities based on the collected information. The next step is to implement process improvements, and then measure the performance of the new process. This loop repeats over and over again and is called continuous process improvement. It might also be called business process improvement or functional process improvement.

This method for improving business processes is effective to obtain gradual, incremental improvement. However, several factors have accelerated the need to improve business processes. The most obvious is technology. New technologies (like the Internet and wireless) rapidly bring new capabilities to businesses, thereby raising the competitive bar and the need to improve business processes dramatically.

Another apparent trend is the opening of world markets and increased free trade. Such changes bring more companies into the marketplace, adding to the competition. In today's marketplace, major changes are required just to stay in the game. As a result, companies have requested methods for faster business process improvement. Also, companies want breakthrough performance changes, not just incremental changes, and they want this now. Because the rate of change has increased for everyone, few businesses can afford a slow change process. One approach for rapid change and dramatic improvement is business process reengineering (BPR).

BUSINESS PROCESS REENGINEERING (BPR)

An organization must continuously revise and reexamine its decisions, goals, and targets to improve its performance. A bank may have many activities, such as investing, credit cards, loans, and so on, and it may be involved in cross-selling (e.g., insurance) with other preferred vendors in the market. If the credit card department is not functioning in an efficient manner, the bank might reengineer the credit card business process. This activity, **business process reengineering (BPR),** is the analysis and redesign of workflow within and between enterprises. BPR relies on a different school of thought than continuous process improvement. *In the extreme,* BPR assumes the current process is irrelevant, does not work, or is broken and must be overhauled from scratch. Such a clean slate enables business process designers to disassociate themselves from today's process and focus on a new process. It is like the designers projecting themselves into the future and asking: What should the process look like? What do customers want it to look like? What do other employees want it to look like? How do best-in-class companies do it? How can new technology facilitate the process?

Figure B2.4 displays the basic steps in a business process reengineering effort. It begins with defining the scope and objectives of the reengineering project, then goes through a learning process (with customers, employees, competitors, noncompetitors, and new technology). Given this knowledge base, the designers can create a vision for the future and design new business processes by creating a plan of action based on the gap between current processes, technologies, and structures, and process vision. It is then a matter of implementing the chosen solution. The Department of Defense (DoD) is an expert at reengineering business processes. Figure B2.5 highlights the Department of Defense's best-in-class suggestions for a managerial approach to a reengineering effort.

FIGURE B2.3

Continuous Process
Improvement Model

FIGURE B2.4

Business Process
Reengineering Model

FIGURE B2.5

Managerial Approach to
Reengineering Projects

Managerial Approach to Reengineering Projects
1. **Define the scope.** Define functional objectives; determine the management strategy to be followed in streamlining and standardizing processes; and establish the process, data, and information systems baselines from which to begin process improvement.
2. **Analyze.** Analyze business processes to eliminate non-value-added processes; simplify and streamline processes of little value; and identify more effective and efficient alternatives to the process, data, and system baselines.
3. **Evaluate.** Conduct a preliminary, functional, economic analysis to evaluate alternatives to baseline processes and select a preferred course of action.
4. **Plan.** Develop detailed statements of requirements, baseline impacts, costs, benefits, and schedules to implement the planned course of action.
5. **Approve.** Finalize the functional economic analysis using information from the planning data, and present to senior management for approval to proceed with the proposed process improvements and any associated data or system changes.
6. **Execute.** Execute the approved process and data changes, and provide functional management oversight of any associated information system changes.

Business Process Design

After choosing the method of business process improvement that is appropriate for the organization, the process designers must determine the most efficient way to begin revamping the processes. To determine whether each process is appropriately structured, organizations should create a cross-functional team to build process models that display input-output relationships among process-dependent operations and departments. They should create business process models documenting a step-by-step process sequence for the activities that are required to convert inputs to outputs for the specific process.

Business process modeling (or **mapping**) is the activity of creating a detailed flow chart or process map of a work process showing its inputs, tasks, and activities, in a structured sequence. A **business process model** is a graphic description of a process, showing the sequence of process tasks, which is developed for a specific purpose and from a selected viewpoint. A set of one or more process models details the many functions of a system or subject area with graphics and text and its purpose is to:

- Expose process detail gradually and in a controlled manner.
- Encourage conciseness and accuracy in describing the process model.
- Focus attention on the process model interfaces.
- Provide a powerful process analysis and consistent design vocabulary.

A process model typically displays activities as boxes and uses arrows to represent data and interfaces. Process modeling usually begins with a functional process representation of *what* the process problem is or an As-Is process model. **As-Is process models** represent the current state of the operation that has been mapped, without any specific improvements or changes to existing processes. The next step is to build a To-Be process model that displays *how* the process problem will be solved or implemented. **To-Be process models** show the results of applying change improvement opportunities to the current (As-Is) process model. This approach ensures that the process is fully and clearly understood before the details of a process solution are decided. The To-Be process model shows *how* the *what* is to be realized. Figure B2.6 displays the As-Is and To-Be process models for ordering a hamburger.

LO 3. Describe the importance of business process modeling (or mapping) and business process models.

FIGURE B2.6

FIGURE B2.6

As-Is and To-Be Process
Models for Ordering a
Hamburger

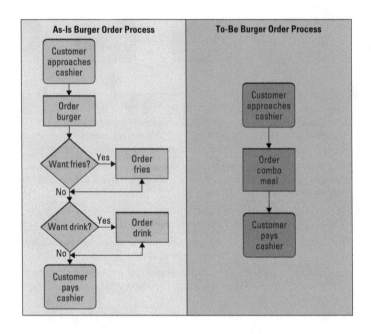

Analyzing As-Is business process models leads to success in business process reengineering since these diagrams are very powerful in visualizing the activities, processes, and data flow of an organization. As-Is and To-Be process models are integral in process reengineering projects. Figure B2.7 illustrates an As-Is process model of an order-filling process developed by a process modeling team representing all departments that contribute to the process. The process modeling team traces the process of converting the input (orders) through all the intervening steps until the final required output (payment) is produced. The map shows how all departments are involved as the order is processed.

It is easy to become bogged down in excessive detail when creating an As-Is process model. The objective is to aggressively eliminate, simplify, or improve the To-Be processes. Successful process improvement efforts result in positive answers to the key process design or improvement question: Is this the most efficient and effective process for accomplishing the process goals? This process modeling structure allows the team to identify all the critical interfaces, overlay the time to complete various processes, start to define the opportunities for process simulation, and identify disconnects (illogical, missing, or extraneous steps) in the processes. Figure B2.8 displays sample disconnects in the order filling process in Figure B2.7.

The team then creates a To-Be process model, which reflects a disconnect-free order fulfillment process (see Figure B2.9). Disconnects fixed by the new process include

- Direct order entry by sales, eliminating sales administration.
- Parallel order processing and credit checking.
- Elimination of multiple order-entry and order-logging steps.

The consulting firm KPMG Peat Marwick uses process modeling as part of its business reengineering practice. Recently the firm helped a large financial services company slash costs and improve productivity in its Manufactured Housing Finance Division. Turnaround time for loan approval was reduced by half, using 40 percent fewer staff members.

Modeling helped the team analyze the complex aspects of the project. "In parts of the loan origination process, a lot of things happen in a short period of time," according to team leader Bob Karrick of KPMG. "During data capture, information is pulled from a number of different sources, and the person doing the risk assessment has to make judgment calls at different points throughout the process. There is often a need to stop, raise

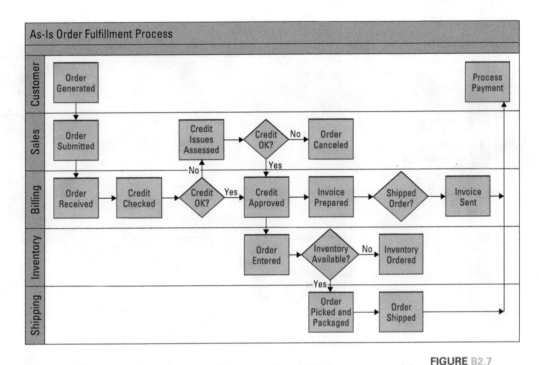

As-Is Order Fulfillment Process

FIGURE B2.7

As-Is Process Model for Order Entry

questions, make follow-up calls, and so on and then continue with the process model-ing effort. Modeling allows us to do a thorough analysis that takes into account all these decision points and variables."

Business Process Management (BPM)

LO 4. Explain business process management along with the reason for its importance to an organization.

A key advantage of technology is its ability to improve business processes. Working faster and smarter has become a necessity for companies. Initial emphasis was given to areas such as production, accounting, procurement, and logistics. The next big areas to discover technology's value in business process were sales and marketing automation, customer relationship management, and supplier relationship manage-ment. Some of these processes involve several departments of the company and some are the result of real-time interaction of the company with its suppliers, customers, and other business partners. The latest area to discover the power of technology in automating and reengineering business process is business process management. *Business process management (BPM)* integrates all of an organization's business process to make individual processes more efficient. BPM can be used to solve a sin-gle glitch or to create one unifying system to consolidate a myriad of processes.

Many organizations are unhappy with their current mix of software applications and dealing with business processes that are subject to constant change. These organizations

Issues in the As-Is Order Process Model
■ Sales representatives take too long to submit orders.
■ There are too many process steps.
■ Sales administration slows down the process by batch-processing orders.
■ Credit checking is performed for both old and new customers.
■ Credit checking holds up the process because it is done before (rather than concurrently with) order picking.

FIGURE B2.8

Issues in the As-Is Process Model for Order Entry

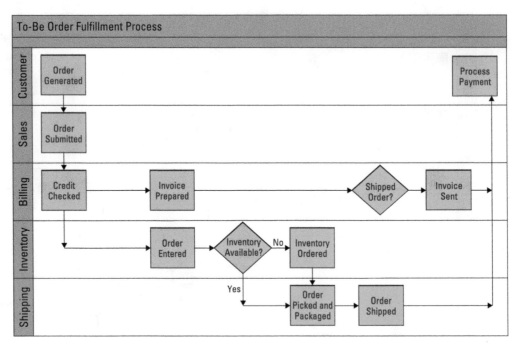

FIGURE B2.9

To-Be Process Model for Order Entry

are turning to BPM systems that can flexibly automate their processes and glue their enterprise applications together. Figure B2.10 displays the key reasons organizations are embracing BPM technologies.

BPM technologies effectively track and orchestrate the business process. BPM can automate tasks involving information from multiple systems, with rules to define the sequence in which the tasks are performed as well as responsibilities, conditions, and other aspects of the process (see Figure B2.11 for BPM benefits). BPM not only allows a business process to be executed more efficiently, but also provides the tools to measure performance and identify opportunities for improvement—as well as to easily make changes in processes to act upon those opportunities such as:

- Bringing processes, people, and information together.
- Identifying the business processes is relatively easy. Breaking down the barriers between business areas and finding owners for the processes are difficult.

FIGURE B2.10

Key Reasons for BPM

- Managing business processes within the enterprise and outside the enterprise with suppliers, business partners, and customers.
- Looking at automation horizontally instead of vertically.

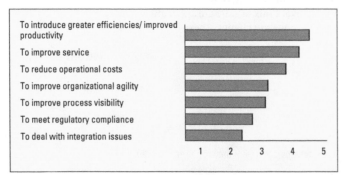

Scale 1 to 5 where 1 = not important and 5 = very important

IS BPM FOR BUSINESS OR IT?

A good BPM solution requires two great parts to work together as one. Since BPM solutions cross application and system boundaries, they often need to be sanctioned and implemented by the IT organization, while at the same time BPM products are business tools that business managers need to own. Therefore, confusion often arises in companies as to whether business or IT managers should be responsible for driving the selection of a new BPM solution.

The key requirement for BPM's success in an organization is the understanding that it is a collaboration of business and IT, and thus both parties need to be involved in evaluating, selecting, and implementing a BPM solution. IT managers need to understand the business drivers behind the processes, and business managers need to understand the impact the BPM solution may have on the infrastructure. Generally, companies that have successfully deployed BPM solutions are those whose business and IT groups have worked together as a cohesive team.

All companies can benefit from a better understanding of their key business processes, analyzing them for areas of improvement and implementing improvements. BPM applications have been successfully developed to improve complex business issues of some medium- to large-sized companies. Like many large-scale implementation projects, BPM solutions are most successful in companies with a good understanding of their technology landscape and management willing to approach business in a new way. BPM solutions are truly driven by the business process and the company's owners.

Effective BPM solutions allow business owners to manage many aspects of the technology through business rules they develop and maintain. Companies that cannot support or manage cultural and organizational changes may lack positive BPM results.

BPM Benefits
■ Update processes in real time
■ Reduce overhead expenses
■ Automate key decisions
■ Reduce process maintenance cost
■ Reduce operating cost
■ Improve productivity
■ Improve process cycle time
■ Improve forecasting
■ Improve customer service

FIGURE B2.11

Benefits of BPM

BPM TOOLS

Business process management tools are used to create an application that is helpful in designing business process models and also helpful in simulating, optimizing, monitoring, and maintaining various processes that occur within an organization. Many tasks are involved in achieving a goal, and these tasks are done either manually or with the help of software systems. For example, if an organization needs to buy a software application that costs $6 million, then a request has to be approved by several authorities and managers. The request approval may be done manually. However, when a person applies for a loan of $300,000, several internal and external business processes are triggered to find out details about that person before approving the loan. For these activities the BPM tool creates an application that coordinates the manual and automated tasks. Figure B2.12 displays several popular BPM tools.

BPM RISKS AND REWARDS

If an organization is considering BPM, it must be aware of the risks involved in implementing these systems. One factor that commonly derails a BPM project has nothing to do with technology and everything to do with people. BPM projects involve cultural and organizational changes that companies must make to support the new management approach required for success. Where 10 area leaders once controlled 10 pieces of an end-to-end process, now a new group is involved in implementing a BPM solution across all these areas. Suddenly the span of control is consolidated and all are accountable to the whole process, not just one piece of the puzzle.

The added benefit of BPM is not only a technology solution, but also a business solution. BPM is a new business architecture and approach to managing the process and enabling proactive, continuous improvement. The new organizational structure and roles created to support BPM help maximize the continuous benefits to ensure success.

An IT director from a large financial services company gave this feedback when asked about his experience in using a BPM solution to improve the company's application help desk process. "Before BPM, the company's

FIGURE B2.12

Popular BPM Tools

Tool Name	Company Name
BPM Suite	Ultimus
Process Suite	Stalfware
Business Manager	Savvion
Pega Rules Process Commander	PegaSystem
E Work Vision	MetaStorm
Team Works	Lombardi Software
Intalio	Intalio
Bizflow	Handysoft
FugeoBPM	Fugeo
Business Process Manager	Filenet

application help desk was a manual process, filled with inefficiencies, human error, and no personal accountability. In addition, the old process provided no visibility into the process. There was absolutely no way to track requests, since it was all manual. Business user satisfaction with the process was extremely low. A BPM solution provided a way for the company to automate, execute, manage, and monitor the process in real time. The biggest technical challenge in implementation was ensuring that the user group was self-sufficient. While the company recognized that the IT organization is needed, it wanted to be able to maintain and implement any necessary process changes with little reliance on IT. It views process management as empowering the business users to maintain, control, and monitor the process. BPM goes a long way to enable this process."

CRITICAL SUCCESS FACTORS

In a publication for the National Academy of Public Administration, Dr. Sharon L. Caudle identified six critical success factors that ensure government BPM initiatives achieve the desired results (see Figure B2.13).

FIGURE B2.13

Critical Success Factors for BPM Projects

Critical Success Factors for BPM Projects

1. **Understand reengineering.**
   - Understand business process fundamentals.
   - Know what reengineering is.
   - Differentiate and integrate process improvement approaches.

2. **Build a business and political case.**
   - Have necessary and sufficient business (mission delivery) reasons for reengineering.
   - Have the organizational commitment and capacity to initiate and sustain reengineering.
   - Secure and sustain political support for reengineering projects.

3. **Adopt a process management approach.**
   - Understand the organizational mandate and set mission strategic directions and goals cascading to process-specific goals and decision making across and down the organization.
   - Define, model, and prioritize business processes important for mission performance.
   - Practice hands-on senior management ownership of process improvement through personal involvement, responsibility, and decision making.
   - Adjust organizational structure to better support process management initiatives.
   - Create an assessment program to evaluate process management.

4. **Measure and track performance continuously.**
   - Create organizational understanding of the value of measurement and how it will be used.
   - Tie performance management to customer and stakeholder current and future expectations.

5. **Practice change management and provide central support.**
   - Develop human resource management strategies to support reengineering.
   - Build information resources management strategies and a technology framework to support process change.
   - Create a central support group to assist and integrate reengineering efforts and other improvement efforts across the organization.
   - Create an overarching and project-specific internal and external communication and education program.

6. **Manage reengineering projects for results.**
   - Have a clear criterion to select what should be reengineered.
   - Place the project at the right level with a defined reengineering team purpose and goals.
   - Use a well-trained, diversified, expert team to ensure optimum project performance.
   - Follow a structured, disciplined approach for reengineering.

Business Process Modeling Examples

A picture is worth a thousand words. Just ask Wayne Kendrick, a system analyst for Mobil Oil Corporation in Dallas, Texas. Kendrick, whose work involves planning and designing complex processes, was scheduled to make a presentation to familiarize top management with a number of projects his group was working on. "I was given 10 minutes for my presentation, and I had 20 to 30 pages of detailed documentation to present. Obviously, I could not get through it all in the time allocated." Kendrick turned to business process models to help communicate his projects. "I think people can relate to pictures better than words," Kendrick said. He applied his thinking to his presentation by using Microsoft's Visio to create business process models and graphs to represent the original 30 pages of text. "It was an effective way to get people interested in my projects and to quickly see the importance of each project," he stated. The process models worked and Kendrick received immediate approval to proceed with all of his projects. Figures B2.14 through B2.20 offer examples of business process models.

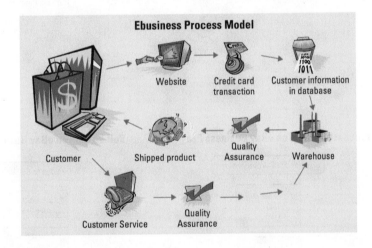

FIGURE B2.14

Ebusiness Process Model

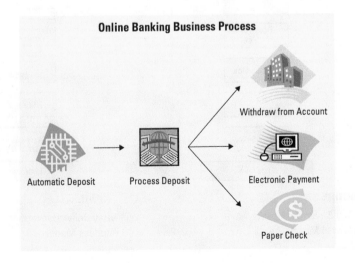

FIGURE B2.15

Online Banking Business Process Model

FIGURE B2.16

Customer Order Business
Process Model

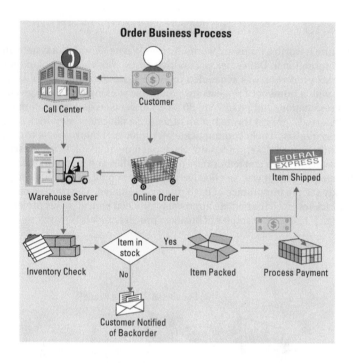

Order Business Process

Call Center

Customer

Warehouse Server

Online Order

Item Shipped

FEDERAL EXPRESS

Inventory Check

Item in stock

Yes

No

Item Packed

Process Payment

Customer Notified
of Backorder

Purchase an Item on eBay Business Process

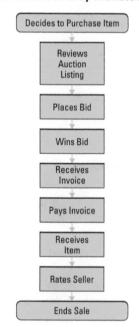

Decides to Purchase Item

Reviews
Auction
Listing

Places Bid

Wins Bid

Receives
Invoice

Pays Invoice

Receives
Item

Rates Seller

Ends Sale

Sell an Item on eBay Business Process

Decides to Sell Item

Lists Item
on eBay

Sets Initial
Price

Sets Auction
Length

Invoices
Winning Bid

Receives
Payment

Ships Item

Rates Buyer

Ends Sale

FIGURE B2.17

eBay Buyer Business
Process Model

FIGURE B2.18

eBay Seller Business
Process Model

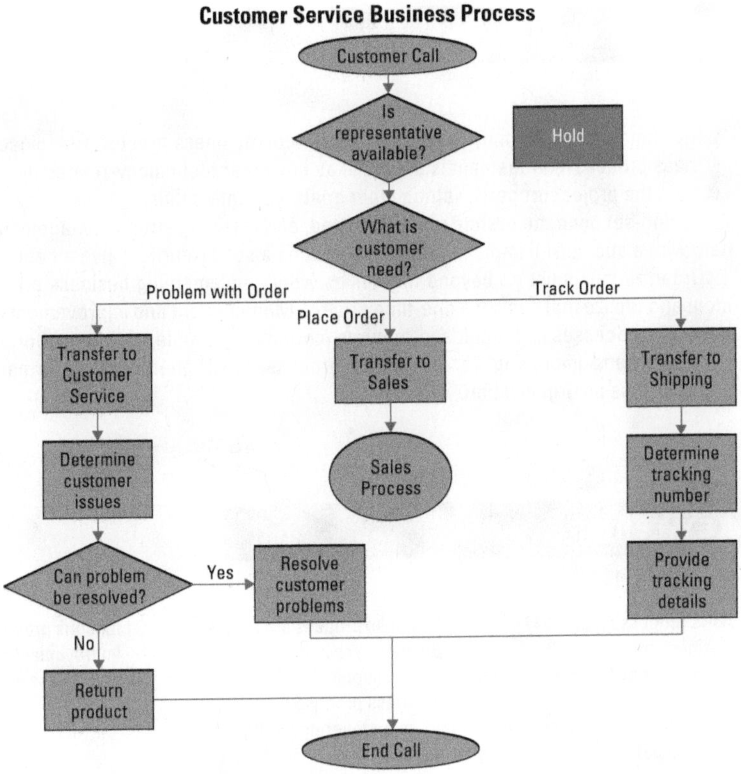

Customer Service Business Process

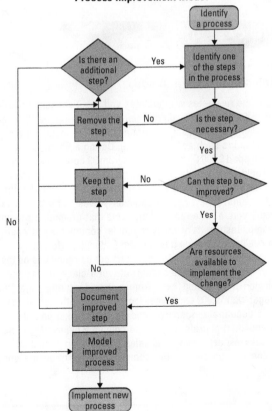

FIGURE B2.19

Customer Service
Business Process Model

Process Improvement Model

FIGURE B2.20

Business Process
Improvement Model

✳ PLUG-IN SUMMARY

Investment in continuous process improvement, business process reengineering, or business process management is the same as any other technology-related investment. Planning the project properly, setting clear goals, educating those people who have to change their mind-set once the system is implemented, and retaining strong management support will help with a successful implementation generating a solid return on investment.

Organizations must go beyond the basics when implementing business process improvement and realize that it is not a one-time project. Management and improvement of end-to-end business processes is difficult and requires more than a simple, one-time effort. Continuously monitoring and improving core business processes will guarantee performance improvements across an organization.

✳ KEY TERMS

As-Is process model, 347
Business process, 342
Business process management (BPM), 349
Business process management tool, 351

Business process model, 347
Business process modeling (or mapping), 347
Business process reengineering (BPR), 346

Continuous process improvement model, 345
To-Be process model, 347

✳ CLOSING CASE ONE

Streamlining Processes at Adidas

The Adidas name resonates with athletes and retail consumers worldwide. Registered as a company in 1949, the company differentiated itself during the 1960s by supporting all athletes who were committed to raising performance levels, including athletes in what some considered fringe sports such as high jumping. During a banner year in 1996, the "three stripes company" equipped 6,000 Olympic athletes from 33 countries. Those athletes won 220 medals, including 70 gold, and helped increase immediate apparel sales by 50 percent.

In 1997, Adidas acquired the Salomon Group, which included the Salomon, Taylor Made, and Bonfire brands. Today, Adidas-Salomon strives to be the global leader in the sporting goods industry with a wide range of products that promote a passion for competition and a sports-oriented lifestyle. Its strategy is simple: continuously strengthen its brands and products to improve its competitive position and financial performance.

Adidas-Salomon competes in an environment as relentless as that of the Olympics. Staying in the forefront requires the support of world-class technology. Over the past 15 years, Adidas-Salomon transformed itself from a manufacturing organization to a global sports brand manager with 14,000 employees located around the world. Previously, Adidas-Salomon operated in a decentralized manner, and each operating unit chose software that suited its geography and internal preferences. The company believed that implementing and creating common processes, especially in its sales organization, would help it establish global direction. With common processes, the company could streamline and automate its business operations—improving flexibility, scalability, and visibility across the extended enterprise. Overall, system integration would translate into faster time to market, higher revenue, and lower costs.

Adidas-Salomon reviewed its IT systems and associated information. One finding was that the company needed to develop a better solution for business process integration and establish an easy way to automate new applications throughout the enterprise. Such an infrastructure required Adidas-Salomon to impose a common business process platform that would allow the company's operating units to remain flexible in meeting their own particular needs and goals.

Adidas-Salomon identified several major business requirements for the project. First, it wanted to automate business events and reduce the manual effort required to exchange data between internal and external parties. Second, Adidas-Salomon needed to develop a cost-effective solution that would be simple to use, maintain, and update in the future. Last, the company wanted to enable real-time data exchange among the key Adidas-Salomon business processes.

"We considered many metrics, and it was clear that TIBCO Software had the breadth and depth of product offering backed by a strong reputation," said Garry Semetka, head of development and integration services in global application development at Adidas-Salomon. With its desired infrastructure in place, Adidas-Salomon standardized on TIBCO products and moved toward real-time business process management of its internal supply chain. The company now publishes and makes the most of events when they occur on key systems, giving the most current, valuable information to business processes and decision makers.

Questions

1. Describe business processes and their importance for Adidas-Salomon.
2. How could Adidas-Salomon use continuous process improvement and business process reengineering to remain competitive?
3. How can a business process management tool help Adidas-Salomon remain at the top of its game?

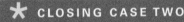

★ CLOSING CASE TWO

3Com Optimizes Product Promotion Processes

Product promotions, such as rebates or subsidized promotional items, can serve as excellent marketing and sales tools to drive increased revenues by providing incentives for customers to purchase select items. However, when you are a leading global networking provider like 3Com that serves thousands of channel partners and customers, such promotions must be easily managed and executed.

To gain better control over the creation and execution of its product promotions, 3Com used Savvion's business process automation and management platform to build a web-based system that streamlines the approval and management workflow of product promotions offered to distributors and resellers. "We needed to ensure that our product promotions were attractive to our channel partners while also being manageable in terms of execution," said Ari Bose, CIO at 3Com. "Using Savvion BusinessManager, we were able to quickly put a process in place that speeds approval and enhances awareness of product promotions to generate opportunities for increased revenue."

Promoting Effective Promotions

The Savvion BusinessManager-based promotions system provides significant time and cost savings by replacing former inefficient and uncontrollable email processes. Instead of informally sending promotion ideas around for approval, employees now use the automated system as a centralized location to manage the workflow involved in proposing new promotions and ensuring all needed approvals are in place before promotion details are shared on the 3Com partner and reseller website.

The promotions system automatically routes proposed promotions to each department that is required to sign off on the promotion, including marketing, promotions communications, and claims administration. The streamlined system also immediately notifies all key parties once new promotions are approved, increasing visibility and revenue opportunities through improved communication with 3Com sales representatives, distributors, and resellers.

Adding Muscle to Management

An important feature of the new system is the automatic auditing of each step taken. The company can easily establish an audit trail, increasing accountability as approvals are given. The structured process also ensures that approved promotions are manageable from an administrative perspective.

In addition, the system tracks promotion fulfillment, enforcing associated terms and conditions such as purchasing limits or available supplies—tracking that was previously almost impossible to do, creating numerous management headaches. The promotions system is also integrated with another BusinessManager-developed process that generates special price quotes (SPQs) for 3Com channel partners, creating built-in checks and balances to prevent the approval of an SPQ while a promotion is being offered for the same product.

The system also provides extensive reporting capabilities that 3Com now uses to gain a better understanding of all offered promotions, authorizations, and potential financial impacts. These online reports replace manually created Excel spreadsheets, enabling departments to generate reports on the fly for enhanced strategic planning.

Bottom-Line Benefits

Greater visibility of product promotions is yielding significant opportunities for increased revenue at 3Com. Sales representatives are immediately notified when promotions are approved, improving internal communications and enabling representatives to share promotion details with resellers and distributors more quickly to foster increased sales. Other business benefits delivered by the automated promotions system include the following:

- Real-time monitoring features enable 3Com employees to check the status of a promotion's approval at any time.
- Greater efficiency in the approval cycle and streamlined communications increase employee productivity, providing significant time and cost savings.
- Claims processing is also more effective because of the structured approval process, delivering additional savings.
- Increased visibility enables 3Com to reduce reserve spending by having a clearer idea of channel response to each promotion.
- Order and efficiency come to previously chaotic manual processes.

Questions

1. Describe business processes and their importance to 3Com's business model.
2. How can 3Com use continuous process improvement to become more efficient?
3. How can 3Com use business process reengineering to become more efficient?
4. Describe the importance of business process modeling (or mapping) and business process models for 3Com.
5. How did 3Com use business process management software to revamp its business?

★ MAKING BUSINESS DECISIONS

1. Discovering Reengineering Opportunities

In an effort to increase efficiency, your college has hired you to analyze its current business processes for registering for classes. Analyze the current business processes from paying tuition to registering for classes and determine which steps in the process are:

- Broken
- Redundant
- Antiquated

Be sure to define how you would reengineer the processes for efficiency.

2. Modeling a Business Process

Do you hate waiting in line at the grocery store? Do you find it frustrating when you go to the movie store and cannot find the movie you wanted to rent? Do you get annoyed when the pizza delivery person brings you the wrong order? This is your chance to reengineer the annoying process that drives you crazy. Choose a problem you are currently experiencing and reengineer the process to make it more efficient. Be sure to provide an As-Is and To-Be process model.

3. Revamping Business Processes

The following is the sales order business process for MusicMan. Draw the As-Is process model based on the following narrative:

1. A customer submits an order for goods to MusicMan, a music retailer, through an online mechanism such as a browser-based order form. The customer supplies his or her name, the appropriate email address, the state to which the order will be shipped, the desired items (IDs and names), and the requested quantities.
2. The order is received by a processing system, which reads the data and appends an ID number to the order.
3. The order is forwarded to a customer service representative, who checks the customer's credit information.
4. If the credit check fails, the customer service representative is assigned the task of notifying the customer to obtain correct credit information, and the process becomes manual from this point on.
5. If the credit check passes, the system checks a database for the current inventory of the ordered item, according to the item ID, and it compares the quantity of items available with the quantity requested.
6. If the amount of stock is not sufficient to accommodate the order, the order is placed on hold until new inventory arrives. When the system receives notice of new incoming inventory, it repeats step 5 until it can verify that the inventory is sufficient to process the order.
7. If the inventory is sufficient, the order is forwarded simultaneously to a shipping agent who arranges shipment and an accounting agent who instructs the system to generate an invoice for the order.
8. If the system encounters an error in processing the input necessary to calculate the total price for the invoice, including state sales tax, the accounting agent who initiated the billing process is notified and prompted to provide the correct information.

9. The system calculates the total price of the order.

10. The system confirms that the order has been shipped and notifies the customer via email.

11. At any point in the transaction before shipping, the order can be canceled by notification from the customer.

4. Revamping Accounts

The accounting department at your company deals with the processing of critical documents. These documents must arrive at their intended destination in a secure and efficient manner. Such documents include invoices, purchase orders, statements, purchase requisitions, financial statements, sales orders, and quotes.

The current processing of documents is done manually, which causes a negative ripple effect. Documents tend to be misplaced or delayed through the mailing process. Unsecured documents are vulnerable to people making changes or seeing confidential documents. In addition, the accounting department incurs costs such as preprinted forms, inefficient distribution, and storage. Explain BPM and how it can be used to revamp the accounting department.

CHAPTER **17**

Developing Software to Streamline Operations

17.1. Describe the seven phases of the systems development life cycle.

17.2. Explain why software problems are business problems.

LO 17.1 Describe the seven phases of the systems development life cycle.

The Systems Development Life Cycle (SDLC)

The multimillion-dollar Nike SCM system failure is legendary as Nike CEO Philip Knight famously stated, "This is what we get for our $400 million?" Nike partnered with i2 to implement an SCM system that never came to fruition. i2 blamed the failed implementation on the fact that Nike failed to use the vendor's implementation methodology and templates. Nike blamed the failure on faulty software.[2]

It is difficult to get an organization to work if its systems do not work. In the information age, software success, or failure, can lead directly to business success, or failure. Companies rely on software to drive business operations and ensure work flows throughout the company. As more and more companies rely on software to operate, so do the business-related consequences of software successes and failures.

The potential advantages of successful software implementations provide firms with significant incentives to manage software development risks. However, an alarmingly high number of software development projects come in late or over budget, and successful projects tend to maintain fewer features and functions than originally specified. Understanding the basics of software development, or the systems development life cycle, will help organizations avoid potential software development pitfalls and ensure that software development efforts are successful.

Before jumping into software development, it is important to understand a few key terms. A *legacy system* is an old system that is fast approaching or beyond the end of its useful life within an organization. *Conversion* is the process of transferring information from a legacy system to a new system. *Software customization* modifies software to meet specific user or business requirements. *Off-the-shelf application software* supports general business processes and does not require any specific software customization to meet the organization's needs.

The *systems development life cycle (SDLC)* is the overall process for developing information systems, from planning and analysis through implementation and maintenance. The SDLC is the foundation for all systems development methods, and hundreds of different activities are associated with each phase. These activities typically include determining budgets, gathering system requirements, and writing detailed user documentation.

The SDLC begins with a business need, proceeds to an assessment of the functions a system must have to satisfy the need, and ends when the benefits of the system no longer outweigh its maintenance costs. This is why it is referred to as a life cycle. The SDLC is comprised of seven distinct phases: planning, analysis, design, development, testing, implementation, and maintenance (see Figure 17.1).

FIGURE 17.1

The SDLC and Its
Associated Activities

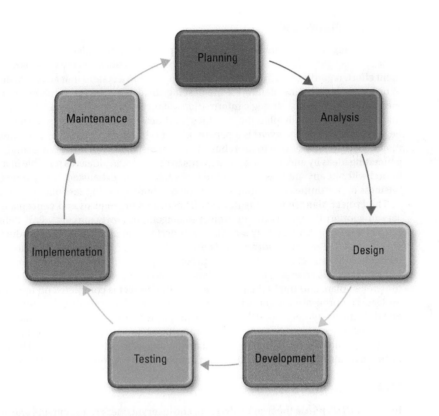

Phase	Associated Activity
Planning	■ Brainstorm issues and identify opportunities for the organization ■ Prioritize and choose projects for development ■ Set the project scope ■ Develop the project plan
Analysis	■ Gather the business requirement for the system ■ Define any constraints associated with the system
Design	■ Design the technical architecture required to support the system ■ Design the system models
Development	■ Build the technical architecture ■ Build the database ■ Build the applications
Testing	■ Write the test conditions ■ Perform system testing
Implementation	■ Write detailed user documentation ■ Provide training for the system users
Maintenance	■ Build a help desk to support the system users ■ Provide an environment to support system changes

PHASE 1: PLANNING

The *planning phase* establishes a high-level plan of the intended project and determines project goals. Planning is the first and most critical phase of any systems development effort, regardless of whether the effort is to develop a system that allows customers to order products online, determine the best logistical structure for warehouses around the world, or develop a strategic information alliance with another organization. Organizations must carefully plan the activities (and determine why they are necessary) to be successful. A *change agent* is a person or event that is the catalyst for implementing major changes for a system to meet business changes. *Brainstorming* is a technique for generating ideas by encouraging participants to offer as many ideas as possible in a short period without any analysis until all the ideas have been exhausted. Many times, new business opportunities are found as the result of a brainstorming session.

The Project Management Institute (PMI) develops procedures and concepts necessary to support the profession of project management (www.pmi.org). PMI defines a *project* as a temporary activity a company undertakes to create a unique product, service, or result. *Project management* is the application of knowledge, skills, tools, and techniques to project activities to meet project requirements. A *project manager* is an individual who is an expert in project planning and management, defines and develops the project plan, and tracks the plan to ensure the project is completed on time and on budget. The project manager is the person responsible for executing the entire project and defining the project scope that links the project to the organization's overall business goals. The *project scope* describes the business need (the problem the project will solve) and the justification, requirements, and current boundaries for the project. The *project plan* is a formal, approved document that manages and controls the entire project.

PHASE 2: ANALYSIS

In the *analysis phase* the firm analyzes its end-user business requirements and refines project goals into defined functions and operations of the intended system. *Business requirements* are the specific business requests the system must meet to be successful, so the analysis phase is critical because business requirements drive the entire systems development effort. A sample business requirement might state, "The CRM system must track all customer inquiries by product, region, and sales representative." The business requirement will state what the system must accomplish to be considered successful.

Gathering business requirements is basically conducting an investigation in which users identify all the organization's business needs and take measurements of these needs. Figure 17.2 displays a number of ways to gather business requirements. *Requirements management* is the process of managing changes to the business requirements throughout the project. Projects are typically dynamic in nature, and change should be expected and anticipated for successful project completion. A *requirements definition document* prioritizes all of the business requirements by order of importance to the company. *Sign-off* consists of the users' actual signatures indicating they approve all of the business requirements. If a system does not meet the business requirements, it will be deemed

FIGURE 17.2

Methods for Gathering
Business Requirements

Methods for Gathering Business Requirements
Perform a *joint application development (JAD)* session where employees meet, sometimes for several days, to define or review the business requirements for the system.
Interview individuals to determine current operations and current issues.
Compile questionnaires to survey employees to discover issues. ·
Make observations to determine how current operations are performed.
Review business documents to discover reports, policies, and how information is used throughout the organization.

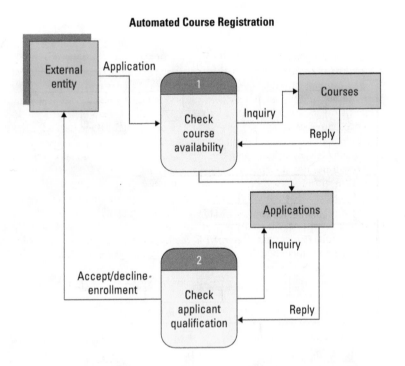

Automated Course Registration

FIGURE 17.3

Sample Data Flow Diagram

a failed project. For this reason, the organization must spend as much time, energy, and resources as necessary to gather accurate and detailed business requirements.

Once a business analyst takes a detailed look at how an organization performs its work and its processes, the analyst can recommend ways to improve these processes to make them more efficient and effective. ***Process modeling*** involves graphically representing the processes that capture, manipulate, store, and distribute information between a system and its environment. One of the most common diagrams used in process modeling is the data flow diagram. A ***data flow diagram (DFD)*** illustrates the movement of information between external entities and the processes and data stores within the system (see Figure 17.3). Process models and data flow diagrams establish the specifications of the system. ***Computer-aided software engineering (CASE)*** tools are software suites that automate systems analysis, design, and development. Process models and data flow diagrams can provide the basis for the automatic generation of the system if they are developed using a CASE tool.

PHASE 3: DESIGN

The ***design phase*** establishes descriptions of the desired features and operations of the system, including screen layouts, business rules, process diagrams, pseudo code, and other documentation. During the analysis phase, end users and MIS specialists work together to gather the detailed business requirements for the proposed project from a logical point of view. That is, during analysis, business requirements are documented without respect to technology or the technical infrastructure that will support the system. Moving into the design phase turns the project focus to the physical or technical point of view, defining the technical architecture that will support the system, including data models, screen designs, report layouts, and database models. (see Figure 17.4). The ***graphical user interface (GUI)*** is the interface to an information system. GUI screen design is the ability to model the information system screens for an entire system using icons, buttons, menus, and submenus. Data models represent a formal way to express data relationships to a database management system (DBMS). Entity relationship diagrams document the relationships between entities in a database environment (see Figure 17.5).

FIGURE 17.4

Sample Technical
Architecture

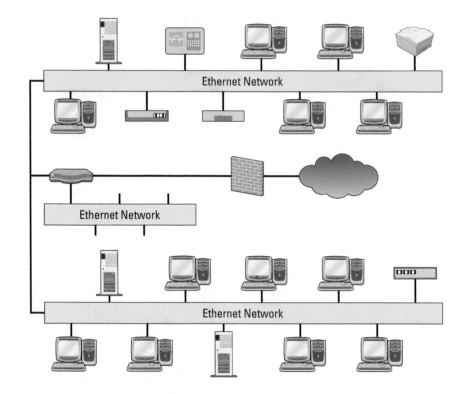

PHASE 4: DEVELOPMENT

The ***development phase*** takes all the detailed design documents from the design phase and transforms them into the actual system. In this phase, the project transitions from preliminary designs to actual physical implementation. During development, the company purchases and implements the equipment necessary to support the architecture. ***Software engineering*** is a disciplined approach for constructing information systems through the use of common methods, techniques, or tools. Software engineers use computer-aided software engineering (CASE) tools, which provide automated support for the development of the system. ***Control objects for information and related technology (COBIT)*** is a set of best practices that helps an organization to maximize the benefits of an information system, while at the same time establishing appropriate controls to ensure minimum errors.

During development, the team defines the programming language it will use to build the system. A ***scripting language*** is a programming method that provides for interactive modules to a website. ***Object-oriented languages*** group data and corresponding processes into objects. ***Fourth-generation languages (4GL)*** are programming languages that look similar to human languages. For example, a typical 4GL command might state, "FIND ALL RECORDS WHERE NAME IS "SMITH"." Programming languages are displayed in Figure 17.6.

PHASE 5: TESTING

The ***testing phase*** brings all the project pieces together into a special testing environment to eliminate errors and bugs and verify that the system meets all the business requirements defined in the analysis phase. ***Bugs*** are defects in the code of an information system. ***Test conditions*** detail the steps the system must perform along with the expected result of each step. Figure 17.7 displays several test conditions for testing user

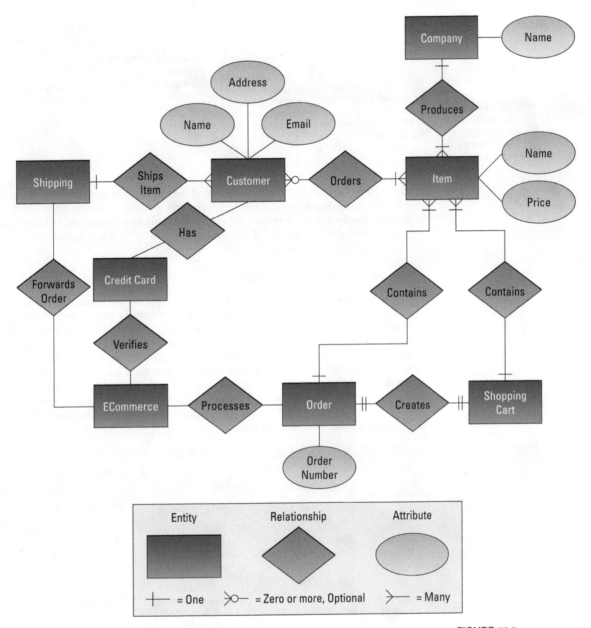

FIGURE 17.5

Sample Entity Relationship Diagram

log-on functionality in a system. The tester will execute each test condition and compare the expected results with the actual results in order to verify that the system functions correctly. Notice in Figure 17.7 how each test condition is extremely detailed and states the expected results that should occur when executing each test condition. Each time the actual result is different from the expected result, a "bug" is generated and the system goes back to development for a bug fix. Test condition 6 in Figure 17.7 displays a different actual result than the expected result because the system failed to allow the user to log on. After this test condition fails, it is obvious that the system is not functioning correctly, and it must be sent back to development for a bug fix.

A typical system development effort has hundreds or thousands of test conditions. Every single test condition must be executed to verify that the system performs as

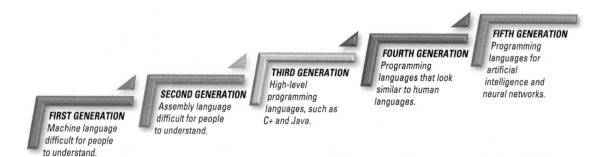

FIRST GENERATION
Machine language
difficult for people
to understand.

SECOND GENERATION
Assembly language
difficult for people
to understand.

THIRD GENERATION
High-level
programming
languages, such as
C+ and Java.

FOURTH GENERATION
Programming
languages that look
similar to human
languages.

FIFTH GENERATION
Programming
languages for
artificial
intelligence and
neural networks.

FIGURE 17.6

Overview of Programming
Languages

expected. Writing all the test conditions and performing the actual testing of the software takes a tremendous amount of time and energy. After reviewing the massive level of effort required to test a system, it becomes obvious why this is a critical step in successful development. Figure 17.8 displays the different types of tests typically included in a systems development effort.

PHASE 6: IMPLEMENTATION

In the **implementation phase,** the organization places the system into production so users can begin to perform actual business operations with it. In this phase, the detailed **user documentation** is created that highlights how to use the system and how to troubleshoot issues or problems. Training is also provided for the system users and can take place online or in a classroom. **Online training** runs over the Internet or on a CD or DVD, and employees complete the training on their own time at their own pace. **Workshop training** is held in a classroom environment and led by an instructor. One of the best ways to support users is to create a **help desk** or a group of people who respond to users' questions. Figure 17.9 displays the different implementation methods an organization can choose to ensure success.

FIGURE 17.7

Sample Test Conditions

Test Condition Number	Date Tested	Tested	Test Condition	Expected Result	Actual Result	Pass/Fail
1	1/1/17	Emily Hickman	Click on System Start Button	Main Menu appears	Same as expected result	Pass
2	1/1/17	Emily Hickman	Click on Log-on Button in Main Menu	Log-on Screen appears asking for User name and Password	Same as expected result	Pass
3	1/1/17	Emily Hickman	Type Emily Hickman in the User Name Field	Emily Hickman appears in the User Name Field	Same as expected result	Pass
4	1/1/17	Emily Hickman	Type Zahara123 in the password field	XXXXXXXXX appears in the password field	Same as expected result	Pass
5	1/1/17	Emily Hickman	Click on OK button	User log-on request is sent to database and user name and password are verified	Same as expected result	Pass
6	1/1/17	Emily Hickman	Click on Start	User name and password are accepted and the system main menu appears	Screen appeared stating log-on failed and user name and password were incorrect	Fail

FIGURE 17.8

Different Forms of System Testing

PHASE 7: MAINTENANCE

Maintaining the system is the final sequential phase of any systems development effort. In the *maintenance phase,* the organization performs changes, corrections, additions, and upgrades to ensure the system continues to meet business goals. This phase continues for the life of the system because the system must change as the business evolves and its needs change, which means conducting constant monitoring, supporting the new system with frequent minor changes (for example, new reports or information capturing), and reviewing the system to be sure it is moving the organization toward its strategic goals. *Corrective maintenance* makes system changes to repair design flaws, coding errors, or implementation issues. *Preventive maintenance* makes system changes to reduce the chance of future system failure. During the maintenance phase, the system will generate reports to help users and MIS specialists ensure it is functioning correctly (see Figure 17.10).

Software Problems Are Business Problems

LO 17.2 Explain why software problems are business problems.

MIS project failures can cost companies financially and even ruin business reputations. The primary reasons for project failure are:

- Unclear or missing business requirements.
- Skipping SDLC phases.

FIGURE 17.9

System Implementation Methods

Parallel Implementation
Uses both the legacy system and new system until all users verify that the new system functions correctly

Plunge Implementation
Discards the legacy system and immediately migrates all users to the new system

Pilot Implementation
Assigns a small group of people to use the new system until it is verified that it works correctly; then the remaining users migrate to the new system

Phased Implementation
Installs the new system in phases (for example, by department) until it is verified that it works correctly

Report	Examples
Internal report	Presents data that are distributed inside the organization and intended for employees within an organization. Internal reports typically support day-to-day operations monitoring that supports managerial decision making.
Detailed internal report	Presents information with little or no filtering or restrictions of the data.
Summary internal report	Organizes and categorizes data for managerial perusal. A report that summarizes total sales by product for each month is an example of a summary internal report. The data for a summary report are typically categorized and summarized to indicate trends and potential problems.
Exception reporting	Highlights situations occurring outside of the normal operating range for a condition or standard. These internal reports include only exceptions and might highlight accounts that are unpaid or delinquent or identify items that are low in stock.
Information system control report	Ensures the reliability of information, consisting of policies and their physical implementation, access restrictions, or record keeping of actions and transactions.
Information systems audit report	Assesses a company's information system to determine necessary changes and to help ensure the information systems' availability, confidentiality, and integrity.
Post-implementation report	Presents a formal report or audit of a project after it is up and running.

FIGURE 17.10

Examples of System Reports

- Failure to manage project scope.
- Failure to manage project plan.
- Changing technology.

UNCLEAR OR MISSING BUSINESS REQUIREMENTS

The most common reason systems fail is because the business requirements are either missing or incorrectly gathered during the analysis phase. The business requirements drive the entire system. If they are not accurate or complete, the system will not be successful.

It is important to discuss the relationship between the SDLC and the cost for the organization to fix errors. An error found during the analysis and design phase is relatively inexpensive to fix. All that is typically required is a change to a Word document. However, exactly the same error found during the testing or implementation phase is going to cost the organization an enormous amount to fix because it has to change the actual system. Figure 17.11 displays how the cost to fix an error grows exponentially the later the error is found in the SDLC.

FIGURE 17.11

The Cost of Finding Errors

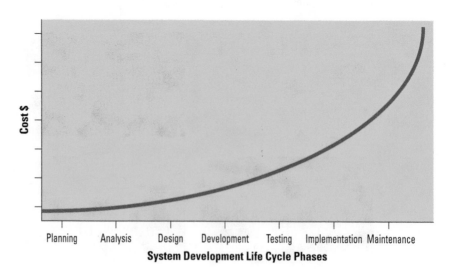

SKIPPING SDLC PHASES

The first thing individuals tend to do when a project falls behind schedule is to start skipping phases in the SDLC. For example, if a project is three weeks behind in the development phase, the project manager might decide to cut testing down from six weeks to three weeks. Obviously, it is impossible to perform all the testing in half the time. Failing to test the system will lead to unfound errors, and chances are high that the system will fail. It is critical that an organization perform all phases in the SDLC during every project. Skipping any of the phases is sure to lead to system failure.

FAILURE TO MANAGE PROJECT SCOPE

As the project progresses, the project manager must track the status of each activity and adjust the project plan if an activity is added or taking longer than expected. Scope creep and feature creep are difficult to manage and can easily cause a project to fall behind schedule.

FAILURE TO MANAGE PROJECT PLAN

Managing the project plan is one of the biggest challenges during systems development. The project plan is the road map the organization follows during the development of the system. Developing the initial project plan is the easiest part of the project manager's job. Managing and revising the project plan is the hard part. The project plan is a living document since it changes almost daily on any project. Failing to monitor, revise, and update the project plan can lead to project failure.

CHANGING TECHNOLOGY

Many real-world projects have hundreds of business requirements, take years to complete, and cost millions of dollars. Gordon Moore, co-founder of Intel Corporation, observed in 1965 that chip density doubles every 18 months. This observation, known as Moore's law, simply means that memory sizes, processor power, and so on, all follow the same pattern and roughly double in capacity every 18 months. As Moore's law states, technology changes at an incredibly fast pace; therefore, it is possible to have to revise an entire project plan in the middle of a project as a result of a change in technology. Technology changes so fast that it is almost impossible to deliver an information system without feeling the pain of changing technology.

OPENING CASE STUDY QUESTIONS

1. Which phase in the systems development life cycle is the most critical when building a social networking website?

2. Which phase in the systems development life cycle is the least critical when building a social networking website?

3. Why is the cost of finding errors important to a business when developing software?

Chapter Seventeen Case: Reducing Ambiguity in Business Requirements

The number one reason projects fail is bad business requirements. Business requirements are considered "bad" because of ambiguity or insufficient involvement of end users during analysis and design.

A requirement is unambiguous if it has the same interpretation for all parties. Different interpretations by different participants will usually result in unmet expectations. Here is an example of an ambiguous requirement and an example of an unambiguous requirement:

- **Ambiguous requirement:** The financial report must show profits in local and U.S. currencies.
- **Unambiguous requirement:** The financial report must show profits in local and U.S. currencies using the exchange rate printed in *The Wall Street Journal* for the last business day of the period being reported.

Ambiguity is impossible to prevent completely because it is introduced into requirements in natural ways. For example:

- Requirements can contain technical implications that are obvious to the IT developers but not to the customers.
- Requirements can contain business implications that are obvious to the customer but not to the IT developers.
- Requirements may contain everyday words whose meanings are "obvious" to everyone, yet different for everyone.
- Requirements are reflections of detailed explanations that may have included multiple events, multiple perspectives, verbal rephrasing, emotion, iterative refinement, selective emphasis, and body language—none of which are captured in the written statements.

Tips for Reviewing Business Requirements

When reviewing business requirements always look for the following words to help dramatically reduce ambiguity:

- **"And"** and **"or"** have well-defined meanings and ought to be completely unambiguous, yet they are often understood only informally and interpreted inconsistently. For example, consider the statement "The alarm must ring if button T is pressed and if button F is pressed." This statement may be intended to mean that to ring the alarm, both buttons must be pressed or it may be intended to mean that either one can be pressed. A statement like this should never appear in a requirement because the potential for misinterpretation is too great. A preferable approach is to be very explicit, for example, "The alarm must ring if both buttons T and F are pressed simultaneously. The alarm should not ring in any other circumstance."
- **"Always"** might really mean "most of the time," in which case it should be made more explicit. For example, the statement "We always run reports A and B together" could be challenged with "In other words, there is never any circumstance where you would run A without B and B without A?" If you build a system with an "always" requirement, then you are actually building the system to never run report A without report B. If a user suddenly wants report B without report A, you will need to make significant system changes.
- **"Never"** might mean "rarely," in which case it should be made more explicit. For example, the statement "We never run reports A and B in the same month" could be challenged

with, "So that means that if I see that A has been run, I can be absolutely certain that no one will want to run B." Again, if you build a system that supports a "never" requirement then the system users can never perform that requirement. For example, the system would never allow a user to run reports A and B in the same month, no matter what the circumstances.

- **Boundary conditions** are statements about the line between true and false and do and do not. These statements may or may not be meant to include end points. For example, "We want to use method X when there are up to 10 pages, but method Y otherwise." If you were building this system, would you include page 10 in method X or in method Y? The answer to this question will vary causing an ambiguous business requirement.

Questions

1. Why are ambiguous business requirements the leading cause of system development failures?

2. Why do the words *and* and *or* tend to lead to ambiguous requirements?

3. Research the web and determine other reasons for "bad" business requirements.

4. What is wrong with the following business requirement: "The system must support employee birthdays since every employee always has a birthday every year."

18

Methodologies for Supporting Agile Organizations

LEARNING OUTCOMES

18.1. Summarize the different software development methodologies.

LO 18.1 Summarize the different software development methodologies.

Software Development Methodologies

Today, systems are so large and complex that teams of architects, analysts, developers, testers, and users must work together to create the millions of lines of custom-written code that drive enterprises. For this reason, developers have created a number of different systems development life cycle methodologies. A ***methodology*** is a set of policies, procedures, standards, processes, practices, tools, techniques, and tasks that people apply to technical and management challenges. Firms use a methodology to manage the deployment of technology with work plans, requirements documents, and test plans, for instance. A formal methodology can include coding standards, code libraries, development practices, and much more.

The oldest and the best known is the ***waterfall methodology,*** a sequence of phases in which the output of each phase becomes the input for the next (see Figure 18.1). In the SDLC, this means the steps are performed one at a time, in order, from planning through implementation and maintenance. The traditional waterfall method no longer

FIGURE 18.1

The Traditional Waterfall Methodology

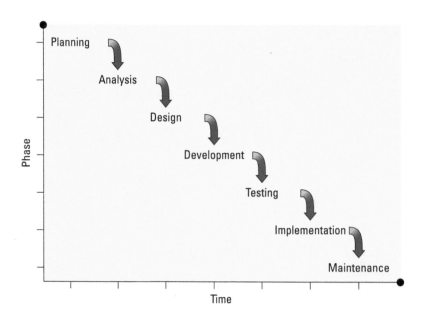

FIGURE 18.2

Disadvantages of the
Waterfall Methodology

Issues Related to the Waterfall Methodology	
The business problem	Any flaws in accurately defining and articulating the business problem in terms of what the business users actually require flow onward to the next phase.
The plan	Managing costs, resources, and time constraints is difficult in the waterfall sequence. What happens to the schedule if a programmer quits? How will a schedule delay in a specific phase impact the total cost of the project? Unexpected contingencies may sabotage the plan.
The solution	The waterfall methodology is problematic in that it assumes users can specify all business requirements in advance. Defining the appropriate IT infrastructure that is flexible, scalable, and reliable is a challenge. The final IT infrastructure solution must meet not only current but also future needs in terms of time, cost, feasibility, and flexibility. Vision is inevitably limited at the head of the waterfall.

serves most of today's development efforts, however; it is inflexible and expensive, and it requires rigid adherence to the sequence of steps. Its success rate is only about 1 in 10. Figure 18.2 explains some issues related to the waterfall methodology.

Today's business environment is fierce. The desire and need to outsmart and outplay competitors remains intense. Given this drive for success, leaders push internal development teams and external vendors to deliver agreed-upon systems faster and cheaper so they can realize benefits as early as possible. Even so, systems remain large and complex. The traditional waterfall methodology no longer serves as an adequate systems development methodology in most cases. Because this development environment is the norm and not the exception anymore, development teams use a new breed of alternative development methods to achieve their business objectives.

Prototyping is a modern design approach where the designers and system users use an iterative approach to building the system. *Discovery prototyping* builds a small-scale representation or working model of the system to ensure it meets the user and business requirements. The advantages of prototyping include:

- Prototyping encourages user participation.

- Prototypes evolve through iteration, which better supports change.

- Prototypes have a physical quality allowing users to see, touch, and experience the system as it is developed.

- Prototypes tend to detect errors earlier.

- Prototyping accelerates the phases of the SDLC, helping to ensure success.

It is common knowledge that the smaller the project, the greater the success rate. The iterative development style is the ultimate in small projects. Basically, *iterative development* consists of a series of tiny projects. It has become the foundation of multiple agile methodologies. Figure 18.3 displays an iterative approach.

An *agile methodology* aims for customer satisfaction through early and continuous delivery of useful software components developed by an iterative process using the bare minimum requirements. Agile methodology is what it sounds like: fast and efficient, with lower costs and fewer features. Using agile methods helps refine feasibility and supports the process for getting rapid feedback as functionality is introduced. Developers can adjust as they move along and better clarify unclear requirements.

One key to delivering a successful product or system is to deliver value to users as soon as possible—give them something they want and like early to create buy-in, generate enthusiasm, and, ultimately, reduce scope. Using agile methodologies helps maintain accountability and helps to establish a barometer for the satisfaction of end users. It

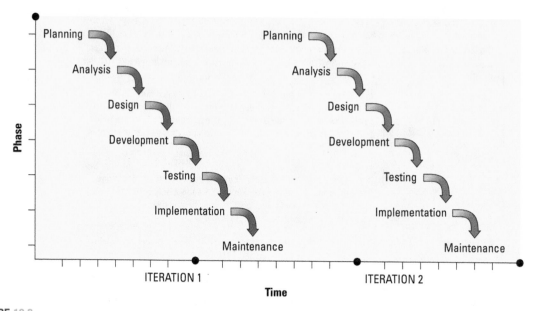

FIGURE 18.3

The Iterative Approach

does no good to accomplish something on time and on budget if it does not satisfy the end user. The primary forms of agile methodologies include:

- Rapid prototyping or rapid application development methodology.
- Extreme programming methodology.
- Rational unified process (RUP) methodology.
- Scrum methodology.

It is important not to get hung up on the names of the methodologies—some are proprietary brand names, others are generally accepted names. It is more important to know how these alternative methodologies are used in today's business environment and the benefits they can deliver.

RAPID APPLICATION DEVELOPMENT (RAD) METHODOLOGY

In response to the faster pace of business, rapid application development has become a popular route for accelerating systems development. *Rapid application development (RAD) methodology* (also called *rapid prototyping*) emphasizes extensive user involvement in the rapid and evolutionary construction of working prototypes of a system, to accelerate the systems development process. Figure 18.4 displays the fundamentals of RAD.

EXTREME PROGRAMMING METHODOLOGY

Extreme programming (XP) methodology, like other agile methods, breaks a project into four phases, and developers cannot continue to the next phase until the previous phase is complete. The delivery strategy supporting XP is that the quicker the feedback

FIGURE 18.4

Fundamentals of RAD

Fundamentals of RAD
Focus initially on creating a prototype that looks and acts like the desired system.
Actively involve system users in the analysis, design, and development phases.
Accelerate collecting the business requirements through an interactive and iterative construction approach.

the more improved the results. XP has four basic phases: planning, designing, coding, and testing. Planning can include user interviews, meetings, and small releases. During design, functionality is not added until it is required or needed. During coding, the developers work together soliciting continuous feedback from users, eliminating the communication gap that generally exists between developers and customers. During testing, the test requirements are generated before any code is developed. Extreme programming saves time and produces successful projects by continuously reviewing and revamping needed and unneeded requirements.

Customer satisfaction is the primary reason XP finds success as developers quickly respond to changing business requirements, even late in the life cycle. XP encourages managers, customers, and developers to work together as a team to ensure the delivery of high-quality systems. XP is similar to a puzzle; there are many small pieces and individually the pieces make no sense, but when they are pieced together they can create a new system.

RATIONAL UNIFIED PROCESS (RUP) METHODOLOGY

The *rational unified process (RUP) methodology,* owned by IBM, provides a framework for breaking down the development of software into four "gates." Each gate consists of executable iterations of the software in development. A project stays in a gate waiting for the stakeholder's analysis, and then it either moves to the next gate or is cancelled. The gates include:

- **Gate one: inception.** This phase ensures all stakeholders have a shared understanding of the proposed system and what it will do.
- **Gate two: elaboration.** This phase expands on the agreed-upon details of the system, including the ability to provide an architecture to support and build it.
- **Gate three: construction.** This phase includes building and developing the product.
- **Gate four: transition.** Primary questions answered in this phase address ownership of the system and training of key personnel.

Because RUP is an iterative methodology, the user can reject the product and force the developers to go back to gate one. RUP helps developers avoid reinventing the wheel and focuses on rapidly adding or removing reusable chunks of processes addressing common problems.

SCRUM METHODOLOGY

Another agile methodology, *scrum methodology,* uses small teams to produce small pieces of software using a series of "sprints," or 30-day intervals, to achieve an appointed goal. In rugby, a scrum is a team pack and everyone in the pack works together to move the ball down the field. In scrum methodology, each day ends or begins with a stand-up meeting to monitor and control the development effort.

OPENING CASE STUDY QUESTION

If you were consulting to a business that wanted to build a social networking website, which development methodology would you recommend and why?

Chapter Eighteen Case: Getting Your Project on Track

June is the perfect time of year to reflect on the current state of all the key projects that were approved in January. At this stage, you and your management team should have enough data to know if each initiative will successfully meet its objectives. You may already know there are projects in your organization that are not positioned to succeed, yet they still receive funding and staff. When you assess the current state of your projects, do you see any of the following signs:

- Critical issues keep opening up, but they're not getting resolved.
- Project scope is constantly changing.
- The project is consistently behind its plan, despite efforts to get it back on schedule.
- Competing deliverables are distracting your attention.

If all of these signs appear, it may be time to cut your losses and cut the project—or at least radically restructure it. You know better than anyone that throwing good money after the bad will not save the project because it doesn't address the root cause of the project's woes. To determine a course of action, ask yourself the following questions about the project:

- What can be salvaged?
- What can be delivered with the time and budget that are left?
- Do you have the right leadership in place to complete the project successfully?
- Is the plan for the initiative sound and realistic?
- Am I and my management team doing everything we can to support the initiative?

If part of or the entire project can be salvaged and delivered on time and with the remaining budget, if the right leaders are present to steer the project, if the new plan is solid, and if management will continue to support the project, the following four steps will help you regain control and deliver the revised project successfully. These steps are basic blocking and tackling, but the detail behind the plan—and more importantly, the execution and focus the project team brings to the effort—will determine whether the project recovery effort will succeed.

Step One: Assess the Situation

Get as much information about the current state of the project as possible. Use that data to make informed decisions about what needs to happen next. Don't be afraid if, at this stage, there are more questions than answers; that is normal. The key is to ask the right question to obtain as accurate a picture of the project's status as possible. The following questions address key data points you need to collect:

- How critical is the delivery date?
- What functionality is exactly required by the delivery date?
- What has been completed and what is still outstanding?
- How willing will people be to change scope, dates, and budget?

The last question about change is critical because it touches on the people and political issues that are present in any project and any organization. Even when faced with sure failure, people find it hard to change unless there is a direct benefit to them and their team. For recovery to have a chance, expectations need to change, especially those of the key stakeholders.

When gathering data about the current state of the project, remember to ask the current team for their opinions on what went wrong. It can be easy to ignore their input since they're associated with the current failure. In fact, each individual can provide great insight into why the project arrived in its current state. Reach out to key team members and get their suggestions for correcting the situation.

Step Two: Prepare the Team for Recovery

Everyone involved in the project—from executive management to stakeholders to project team members—needs to accept that the current project is broken and needs to be fixed. They also need to accept that the existing project plan and approach to delivering the project is flawed and needs to be restructured. If they don't accept these facts, they will likely resist the steps needed for recovery.

Once everyone has accepted the need to change course, define realistic expectations for what can be delivered given the current state and time frame. Also establish metrics for success and control of the recovery. If you had metrics at the outset of the project, you may need to establish new ones, or you may simply need to hold yourself and others accountable to them.

Both management and the project manager in charge of the recovery need to develop a supportive environment for team members. Giving them realistic goals and providing them with the needed space, equipment, and training will position them for success.

Finally, take advantage of the new momentum associated with the recovery and involve all the key parties in the status of the project. This involvement will keep everyone focused and engaged. It will assure project team members and stakeholders that they're needed for more than just executing tasks.

Step Three: Develop a Game Plan for Recovery

Think of the recovery as a new project, separate from the old one. This new project requires its own scope of work to make the expectations around what is being delivered and the new criteria for judging success crystal clear. The new scope may require you to determine if you have the right resources on the project team or if you need to re-staff some team members.

Based on the new project scope, the project manager and project team should lay out a clear and realistic road map to achieve the objectives. The main difference in the plan this time is that it must not fail. It will also be under much greater scrutiny by management. Consequently, it will be critical to make sure the milestones are shorter in duration to demonstrate success and to allow for course correction if needed. The shorter milestones will provide valuable data points to determine the health of the project early.

Step Four: Execute the Game Plan

With the new plan in hand, it's time to get down to business. Remember that during execution, it is not just the project team members who are accountable. Everyone from management on down is on the hook. All facets of the project, from environment to support, need to be in sync at all times, and everyone needs to know they are accountable for the project recovery to succeed.

To make sure everyone is on the same page during the recovery, the project communication needs to be clear, informative, and frequent. Clearly define in your communication plan how information will be disseminated, how urgent items will be addressed, and how key decisions will be made.

Given the added level of scrutiny on the plan and the project, being able to provide the latest on the metrics to show the improved control over the project will be key. The data will also allow you to quickly make corrections when any sign of trouble surfaces.

Getting a flailing project back on track is not easy. It requires sustained effort, focus, commitment, and objectivity. During the project recovery there is no time for personal agendas. The ability to see and do what is best for the project is required from every team member.

It is also important to not lose sight of the pressure that everyone is under. Make sure there is a positive focus on people. The team needs to have the ability to bond, release a little steam, and be focused on the task at hand.

When the project has been successfully delivered, celebrate and recognize the effort of each and every team member. Finally, learn from this successful project recovery so that you and your organization can avoid having to recover a project again. Pay attention to the warning signs and act swiftly and decisively to make corrections early in the project's life cycle so that successful delivery is ensured the first time.[1]

Questions

1. What signs identify if a current project is experiencing issues?

2. Which software development methodology would you choose to build a new accounting system? Explain why.

3. Which software development methodology would you choose to build a personal website? Explain why.

CHAPTER **14** Ebusiness

14.1. Compare the four categories of ebusiness models.

14.2. Describe the six ebusiness tools for connecting and communicating.

14.3. Identify the four challenges associated with ebusiness.

LO 14.1 **Compare the four categories of ebusiness models.**

Ebusiness Models

A **business model** is a plan that details how a company creates, delivers, and generates revenues. Some models are quite simple: A company produces a good or service and sells it to customers. If the company is successful, sales exceed costs and the company generates a profit. Other models are less straightforward, and sometimes it's not immediately clear who makes money and how much. Radio and network television are broadcast free to anyone with a receiver, for instance; advertisers pay the costs of programming.

The majority of online business activities consist of the exchange of products and services either between businesses or between businesses and consumers. An **ebusiness model** is a plan that details how a company creates, delivers, and generates revenues on the Internet. Ebusiness models fall into one of the four categories: (1) business-to-business, (2) business-to-consumer, (3) consumer-to-business, and (4) consumer-to-consumer (see Figure 14.1).

BUSINESS-TO-BUSINESS (B2B)

Business-to-business (B2B) applies to businesses buying from and selling to each other over the Internet. Examples include medical billing service, software sales and licensing, and virtual assistant businesses. B2B relationships represent 80 percent of all online business and are more complex with greater security needs than the other types.

FIGURE 14.1

Ebusiness Models

Ebusiness Term	Definition
Business-to-business (B2B)	Applies to businesses buying from and selling to each other over the Internet.
Business-to-consumer (B2C)	Applies to any business that sells its products or services to consumers over the Internet.
Consumer-to-business (C2B)	Applies to any consumer that sells a product or service to a business over the Internet.
Consumer-to-consumer (C2C)	Applies to sites primarily offering goods and services to assist consumers interacting with each other over the Internet.

	Business	Consumer
Business	B2B	B2C
Consumer	C2B	C2C

Brick-and-Mortar Business
A business that operates in
a physical store without an
Internet presence.
Example: T.J. Maxx

Click-and-Mortar Business
A business that operates
in a physical store and on
the Internet.
Example: Barnes & Noble

Pure-Play (Virtual) Business
A business that operates on
the Internet only without a
physical store.
Example: Google

Electronic marketplaces, or emarketplaces, are interactive business communities providing a central market where multiple buyers and sellers can engage in ebusiness activities. By tightening and automating the relationship between the two parties, they create structures for conducting commercial exchange, consolidating supply chains, and creating new sales channels.

FIGURE 14.2

Forms of Business-to-
Consumer Operations

BUSINESS-TO-CONSUMER (B2C)

Business-to-consumer (B2C) applies to any business that sells its products or services directly to consumers online. Carfax offers car buyers detailed histories of used vehicles for a fee. An *eshop,* sometimes referred to as an *estore* or *etailer,* is an online version of a retail store where customers can shop at any hour. It can be an extension of an existing store such as The Gap or operate only online such as Amazon.com. There are three ways to operate as a B2C: brick-and-mortar, click-and-mortar, and pure play (see Figure 14.2).

CONSUMER-TO-BUSINESS (C2B)

Consumer-to-business (C2B) applies to any consumer who sells a product or service to a business on the Internet. One example is customers of Priceline.com, who set their own prices for items such as airline tickets or hotel rooms and wait for a seller to decide whether to supply them. The demand for C2B ebusiness will increase over the next few years due to customers' desire for greater convenience and lower prices.

CONSUMER-TO-CONSUMER (C2C)

Consumer-to-consumer (C2C) applies to customers offering goods and services to each other on the Internet. A good example of C2C is an auction where buyers and sellers solicit consecutive bids from each other and prices are determined dynamically. EBay, the Internet's most successful C2C online auction website, links like-minded buyers and sellers for a small commission. Other types of online auctions include forward auctions, where sellers market to many buyers and the highest bid wins, and reverse auctions, where buyers select goods and services from the seller with the lowest bid.

EBUSINESS FORMS AND REVENUE-GENERATING STRATEGIES

As more and more companies began jumping on the ebusiness bandwagon, new forms of ebusiness began to emerge (see Figure 14.3). Many of the new forms of ebusiness went to market without clear strategies on how they were going to generate revenue.

FIGURE 14.3

Ebusiness Forms

Form	Description	Examples
Content providers	Generate revenues by providing digital content such as news, music, photos, or videos.	Netflix.com, iTunes.com, CNN.com
Infomediaries	Provide specialized information on behalf of producers of goods and services and their potential customers	Edmunds.com, BizRate.com, Bloomberg.com, Zillow.com
Online marketplaces	Bring together buyers and sellers of products and services.	Amazon.com, eBay.com, Priceline.com
Portals	Operate central website for users to access specialized content and other services.	Google.com, Yahoo.com, MSN.com
Service providers	Provide services such as photo sharing, video sharing, online backup and storage.	Flickr.com, Mapquest.com, YouTube.com
Transaction brokers	Process online sales transactions.	Etrade.com, Charlesschwab.com, Fidelity.com

Google is an excellent example of an ebusiness that did not figure out a way to generate profits until many years after its launch.[1]

Google's primary line of business is its search engine; however, the company does not generate revenue from people using its site to search the Internet. It generates revenue from the marketers and advertisers that pay to place their ads on the site. About 200 million times each day, people from all over the world access Google to perform searches.

FIGURE 14.4

Different Forms of Searching

AdWords, a part of the Google site, allows advertisers to bid on common search terms. The advertisers simply enter in the keywords they want to bid on and the maximum amounts they want to pay per click per day. Google then determines a price and a search ranking for those keywords based on how much other advertisers are willing to pay for the same terms. Pricing for keywords can range from 5 cents to $10 a click. Paid search is the ultimate in targeted advertising because consumers type in exactly what they want. A general search term such as *tropical vacation* costs less than a more specific term such as *Hawaiian vacation*. Whoever bids the most for a term appears in a sponsored advertisement link either at the top or along the side of the search-results page.[2]

A *search engine* is website software that finds other pages based on keyword matching similar to Google. *Search engine ranking* evaluates variables that search engines use to determine where a URL appears on the list of search results. *Search engine optimization (SEO)* combines art along with science to determine how to make URLs more attractive to search engines resulting in higher search engine ranking (see Figure 14.4). The better the SEO, the higher the ranking for a website in the list of search engine results. SEO is critical because most people view only the first few pages of a search result. After that a person is more inclined to begin a new search than review pages and pages of search results. Websites can generate revenue through:

- *Pay-per-click:* generates revenue each time a user clicks on a link to a retailer's website.
- *Pay-per-call:* generates revenue each time a user clicks on a link that takes the user directly to an online agent waiting for a call.
- *Pay-per-conversion:* generates revenue each time a website visitor is converted to a customer.

FIGURE 14.5

Ebusiness Revenue
Models

Ebusiness Revenue Model	Benefits	Challenges
Advertising fees	■ Well-targeted advertisements can be perceived as value-added content by trading participants. ■ Easy to implement	■ Limited revenue potential ■ Overdone or poorly targeted advertisements can be disturbing elements on the website.
License fees	■ Creates incentives to do many transactions ■ Customization and back-end integration lead to lock-in of participants.	■ Up-front fee is a barrier to entry for participants. ■ Price differentiation is complicated.
Subscription fees	■ Creates incentives to do transactions ■ Price can be differentiated. ■ Possibility to build additional revenue from new user groups	■ Fixed fee is a barrier to entry for participants.
Transaction fees	■ Can be directly tied to savings (both process and price savings) ■ Important revenue source when high level of liquidity (transaction volume) is reached	■ If process savings are not completely visible, use of the system is discouraged (incentive to move transactions offline). ■ Transaction fees likely to decrease with time
Value-added services fees	■ Service offering can be differentiated. ■ Price can be differentiated. ■ Possibility to build additional revenue from established and new user groups (third parties)	■ Cumbersome process for customers to continually evaluate new services

Ebusinesses must have a revenue model, or a model for making money. For instance, will they accept advertising, or sell subscriptions or licensing rights? Figure 14.5 lists the different benefits and challenges of various ebusiness revenue models.[3]

Ebusiness Tools for Connecting and Communicating

LO 14.2 Describe the six ebusiness tools for connecting and communicating.

As firms began to move online, more MIS tools were created to support ebusiness processes and requirements. The tools supporting and driving ebusiness are highlighted in Figure 14.6 and covered below in detail.

EMAIL

Email, short for electronic mail, is the exchange of digital messages over the Internet. No longer do business professionals have to wait for the mail to receive important documents as email single-handedly increased the speed of business by allowing the transfer of documents with the same speed as the telephone. Its chief business advantage is the ability to inform and communicate with many people simultaneously, immediately, and with ease. There are no time or place constraints, and users can check, send, and view emails whenever they require.

An *Internet service provider (ISP)* is a company that provides access to the Internet for a monthly fee. Major ISPs in the United States include AOL, AT&T, Comcast, Earthlink, and Netzero, as well as thousands of local ISPs including regional telephone companies.

FIGURE 14.6

Ebusiness Tools

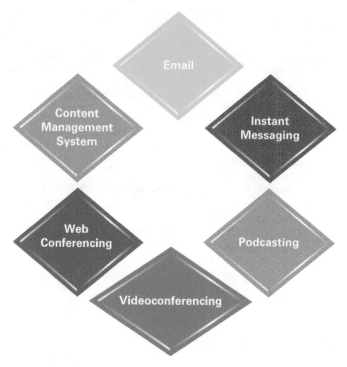

INSTANT MESSAGING

Real-time communication occurs when a system updates information at the same rate it receives it. Email was a great advancement over traditional communication methods such as the U.S. mail, but it did not operate in real time. ***Instant messaging (IMing)*** is a service that enables instant or real-time communication between people. Businesses immediately saw what they could do:

- Answer simple questions quickly and easily.
- Resolve questions or problems immediately.
- Transmit messages as fast as naturally flowing conversation.
- Easily hold simultaneous IM sessions with multiple people.
- Eliminate long-distance phone charges.
- Quickly identify which employees are at their computers.

PODCASTING

Podcasting converts an audio broadcast to a digital music player. Podcasts can increase marketing reach and build customer loyalty. Companies use podcasts as marketing communication channels discussing everything from corporate strategies to detailed product overviews. The senior executive team can share weekly or monthly podcasts featuring important issues or expert briefings on new technical or marketing developments.

VIDEOCONFERENCING

A videoconference allows people at two or more locations to interact via two-way video and audio transmissions simultaneously as well as share documents, data, computer displays, and whiteboards. Point-to-point videoconferences connect two people, and multipoint conferences connect more than two people at multiple locations.

   Videoconferences can increase productivity because users participate without leaving their offices. They can improve communication and relationships, because participants see each other's facial expressions and body language, both important aspects of communication that are lost with a basic telephone call or email. They also reduce travel expenses, a big win for firms facing economic challenges. Of course, nothing can replace meeting someone face-to-face and shaking hands, but videoconferencing offers a viable and cost-effective alternative.

WEB CONFERENCING

Web conferencing, or a *webinar,* blends videoconferencing with document sharing and allows the user to deliver a presentation over the web to a group of geographically dispersed participants. Regardless of the type of hardware or software the attendees are running, every participant can see what is on anyone else's screen. Schools use web conferencing tools such as Illuminate Live to deliver lectures to students, and businesses use tools such as WebEx to demonstrate products. Web conferencing is not quite like being there, but professionals can accomplish more sitting at their desks than in an airport waiting to make travel connections.

CONTENT MANAGEMENT SYSTEMS

In the fourth century BC Aristotle catalogued the natural world according to a systematic organization, and the ancient library at Alexandria was reportedly organized by subject, connecting like information with like. Today *content management systems (CMS)* help companies manage the creation, storage, editing, and publication of their website content. CMSs are user-friendly; most include web-based publishing, search, navigation, and indexing to organize information; and they let users with little or no technical expertise make website changes.

A search is typically carried out by entering a keyword or phrase (query) into a text field and clicking a button or a hyperlink. Navigation facilitates movement from one web page to another. Content management systems play a crucial role in getting site visitors to view more than just the home page. If navigation choices are unclear, visitors may hit the "Back" button on their first (and final) visit to a website. One rule of thumb to remember is that each time a user has to click to find search information, there is a 50 percent chance the user will leave the website instead. A key principle of good website design, therefore, is to keep the number of clicks to a minimum.

Taxonomy is the scientific classification of organisms into groups based on similarities of structure or origin. Taxonomies are also used for indexing the content on the website into categories and subcategories of topics. For example, car is a subtype of vehicle. Every car is a vehicle, but not every vehicle is a car; some vehicles are vans, buses, and trucks. Taxonomy terms are arranged so that narrower/more specific/"child" terms fall under broader/more generic/"parent" terms. *Information architecture* is the set of ideas about how all information in a given context should be organized. Many companies hire information architects to create their website taxonomies. A well-planned taxonomy ensures search and navigation are easy and user-friendly. If the taxonomy is confusing, the site will soon fail.

The Challenges of Ebusiness

LO 14.3 **Identify the four challenges associated with ebusiness.**

Although the benefits of ebusiness are enticing, developing, deploying, and managing ebusiness systems is not always easy. Figure 14.7 lists the challenges facing ebusiness.

IDENTIFYING LIMITED MARKET SEGMENTS

The main challenge of ebusiness is the lack of growth in some sectors due to product or service limitations. The online food sector has not grown in sales, in part because food products are perishable and consumers prefer to buy them at the supermarket as needed. Other sectors with limited ebusiness appeal include fragile or consumable goods and highly sensitive or confidential businesses such as government agencies.

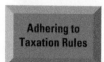

FIGURE 14.7

Challenges Facing Ebusiness

MANAGING CONSUMER TRUST

Trust in the ebusiness exchange deserves special attention. The physical separation of buyer and seller, the physical separation of buyer and merchandise, and customer perceptions about the risk of doing business online provide unique challenges. Internet marketers must develop a trustworthy relationship to make that initial sale and generate customer loyalty. A few ways to build trust when working online include being accessible and available to communicate in person with your customers; using customers' testimonials that link to your client website or to provide their contact information; accepting legitimate forms of payment such as credit cards.

ENSURING CONSUMER PROTECTION

An organization that wants to dominate with superior customer service as a competitive advantage must not only serve but also protect its customers, guarding them against unsolicited goods and communication, illegal or harmful goods, insufficient information about goods and suppliers, invasion of privacy and misuse of personal information, and online fraud. System security, however, must not make ebusiness websites inflexible or difficult to use.

ADHERING TO TAXATION RULES

Many believe that U.S. tax policy should provide a level playing field for traditional retail businesses, mail-order companies, and online merchants. Yet the Internet marketplace remains mostly free of traditional forms of sales tax, partly because ecommerce law is vaguely defined and differs from state to state. For now, companies that operate online must obey a patchwork of rules about which customers are subject to sales tax on their purchases and which are not.

OPENING CASE STUDY QUESTIONS

1. What is the ebusiness model implemented by Pinterest?
2. What is the revenue model implemented by Pinterest?

Chapter Fourteen Case: eBiz

Amazing things are happening on the Internet, things nobody would believe. Here are two stories that demonstrate how innovation, creativity, and a great idea can turn the Internet into a cash cow.

A Million Dollar Homepage

The Million Dollar Homepage is a website conceived by Alex Tew, a 21-year-old student from Cricklade, Wiltshire, England, to help raise money for his university education. Launched on August 26, 2005, the website is said to have generated a gross income of $1,037,100 and has a current Google PageRank of 7.

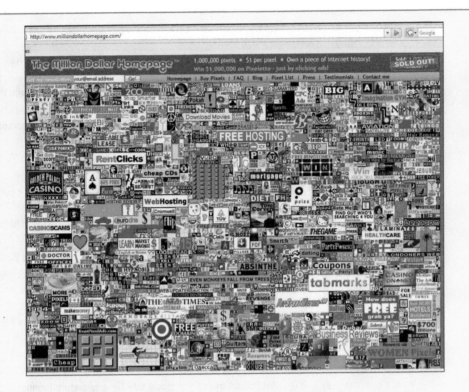

The index page of the site consists of a 1000 by 1000 pixel grid (1 million pixels), on which he sells image-based links for $1 per pixel, in minimum 10 by 10 blocks. A person who buys one or more of these pixel blocks can design a tiny image that will be displayed on the block, decide which URL the block will link to, and write a slogan that appears when the cursor hovers over the link. The aim of the site was to sell all of the pixels in the image, thus generating $1 million of income for the creator, which seems to have been accomplished. On January 1, 2006, the final 1,000 pixels left were put up for auction on eBay. The auction closed on January 11 with the winning bid of $38,100. This brought the final tally to $1,037,100 in gross income. The Million Dollar Homepage is shown above.

One Red Paperclip

The website One Red Paperclip was created by Kyle MacDonald, a Canadian blogger who bartered his way from a single paper clip to a house in a series of trades spanning almost one year. MacDonald began with one red paper clip on July 14, 2005. By July 5, 2006, a chain of bartering had ultimately led to trading a movie role for a two-story farmhouse in Kipling, Saskatchewan. On July 7, 2006—almost exactly one year after MacDonald began his experiment—the deed to the house was signed. In September, at the housewarming party where 12 of the 14 traders were present, he proposed to his girlfriend and she accepted. The wedding ring was made from the original red paper clip he got back from the first woman to have agreed to trade with him.

Following is the timeline, based on the website and as summarized by the BBC:

- On July 14, 2005, MacDonald went to Vancouver and traded the paper clip for a fish-shaped pen.
- MacDonald then traded the pen the same day for a hand-sculpted doorknob from Seattle, Washington, which he nicknamed Knob-T.
- On July 25, 2005, MacDonald traveled to Amherst, Massachusetts, with a friend to trade the Knob-T for a Coleman camp stove (with fuel).

- On September 24, 2005, he went to San Clemente, California, and traded the camp stove for a Honda generator, from a U.S. Marine.

- On November 16, 2005, MacDonald made a second (and successful) attempt (after having the generator confiscated by the New York City Fire Department) in Maspeth, Queens, to trade the generator for an "instant party": an empty keg, an IOU for filling the keg with the beer of the holder's choice, and a neon Budweiser sign.

- On December 8, 2005, he traded the "instant party" to Quebec comedian and radio personality Michel Barrette for a Ski-doo snowmobile.

- Within a week of that, MacDonald traded the snowmobile for a two-person trip to Yahk, British Columbia, in February 2006.

- On or about January 7, 2006, the second person on the trip to Yahk traded MacDonald a cube van for the privilege.

- On or about February 22, 2006, he traded the cube van for a recording contract with Metal Works in Toronto.

- On or about April 11, 2006, MacDonald traded the recording contract to Jody Gnant for a year's rent in Phoenix, Arizona.

- On or about April 26, 2006, he traded the one year's rent in Phoenix, Arizona, for one afternoon with Alice Cooper.

- On or about May 26, 2006, MacDonald traded the one afternoon with Alice Cooper for a KISS motorized snow globe.

- On or about June 2, 2006, he traded the KISS motorized snow globe to Corbin Bernsen for a role in the film *Donna on Demand*.

- On or about July 5, 2006, MacDonald traded the movie role for a two-story farmhouse in Kipling, Saskatchewan.[4]

Questions

1. How else can you use the Internet to raise money?
2. What types of businesses could benefit from trading on the Internet?
3. Can you think of any other disruptive or nontraditional ways that you could use the Internet?

PLUG-IN

B11 Global Information Systems

1. Explain the cultural, political, and geoeconomic challenges facing global businesses.
2. Describe the four global IT business drivers that should be included in all IT strategies.
3. Describe governance and compliance and the associated frameworks an organization can implement.
4. Identify why an organization would need to understand global enterprise architectures when expanding operations abroad.
5. Explain the many different global information issues an organization might encounter as it conducts business abroad.
6. Identify global system development issues organizations should understand before building a global system.

Introduction

Whether they are in Berlin or Bombay, Kuala Lumpur or Kansas City, San Francisco or Seoul, organizations around the globe are developing new business models to operate competitively in a digital economy. These models are structured, yet agile; global, yet local; and they concentrate on maximizing the risk-adjusted return from both knowledge and technology assets.

Globalization and working in an international global economy are integral parts of business today. Fortune 500 companies to mom-and-pop shops are now competing globally, and international developments affect all forms of business.

LO 1. Explain the cultural, political, and geoeconomic challenges facing global businesses.

Globalization

According to Thomas Friedman, the world is flat! Businesses are strategizing and operating on a global playing field. Traditional forms of business are simply not good enough in a global environment. Recall the way the Internet is changing business

FIGURE B11.1

Examples of How
the Internet Is Changing
Business

Industry	Business Changes Due to Technology
Travel	Travel site Expedia.com is now the biggest leisure-travel agency, with higher profit margins than even American Express. Thirteen percent of traditional travel agencies closed in 2002 because of their inability to compete with online travel.
Entertainment	The music industry has kept Napster and others from operating, but $35 billion annual online downloads are wrecking the traditional music business. U.S. music unit sales are down 20 percent since 2000. The next big entertainment industry to feel the effects of ebusiness will be the $67 billion movie business.
Electronics	Using the Internet to link suppliers and customers, Dell dictates industry profits. Its operating margins rose from 7.3 percent in 2002 to 8 percent in 2003, even as it took prices to levels where rivals couldn't make money.
Financial services	Nearly every public efinance company remaining makes money, with online mortgage service LendingTree growing 70 percent a year. Processing online mortgage applications is now 40 percent cheaper for customers.
Retail	Less than 5 percent of retail sales occur online, but eBay was on track in 2003 to become one of the nation's top 15 retailers, and Amazon.com will join the top 40. Walmart's ebusiness strategy is forcing rivals to make heavy investments in technology.
Automobiles	The cost of producing vehicles is down because of SCM and web-based purchasing. Also, eBay has become the leading U.S. used-car dealer, and most major car sites are profitable.
Education and training	Cisco saved $133 million in 2002 by moving training sessions to the Internet, and the University of Phoenix online college classes please investors.

FIGURE B11.1

Examples of How
the Internet Is Changing
Business

by reviewing Figure B11.1. To succeed in a global business environment, cultural, political, and geoeconomic (geographic and economic) business challenges must be confronted.

CULTURAL BUSINESS CHALLENGES

Cultural business challenges include differences in languages, cultural interests, religions, customs, social attitudes, and political philosophies. Global businesses must be sensitive to such cultural differences. McDonald's, a truly global brand, has created several minority-specific websites in the United States: McEncanta for Hispanics, 365Black for African Americans, and i-am-asian for Asians. But these minority groups are not homogenous. Consider Asians: There are East Asian, Southeast Asian, Asian Indian, and, within each of these, divisions of national, regional, and linguistic nature. No company has the budget to create a separate website for every subsegment, but to assume that all Asian Americans fit into a single room—even a virtual room—risks a serious backlash. A company should ask a few key questions when creating a global website:

■ Will the site require new navigational logic to accommodate cultural preferences?

■ Will content be translated? If so, into how many languages?

■ Will multilingual efforts be included in the main site or will it be a separate site, perhaps with a country-specific domain?

■ Which country will the server be located in to support local user needs?

■ What legal ramifications might occur by having the website targeted at a particular country, such as laws on competitive behaviors, treatment of children, or privacy?

FIGURE B11.2

Global IT Business
Management Areas

POLITICAL BUSINESS CHALLENGES

Political business challenges include the numerous rules and regulations surrounding data transfers across national boundaries, especially personal information, tax implications, hardware and software importing and exporting, and trade agreements. The protection of personal information is a real concern for all countries. For example, evidence from a national survey about citizen satisfaction with the Canadian government online services speaks to the importance of paying attention to privacy concerns. This highly publicized survey, known as Citizens First, was administered by the Institute for Citizen-Centered Service (ICCS) and the Institute for Public Administration in Canada (IPCA). Results from the survey indicate that although other factors help promote citizen satisfaction with the Internet, such as ease of finding information, sufficient information, site navigation, and visual appeal, the key driver that directly impacts whether citizens will conduct online transactions is their concerns over information security and privacy.

For security, there are high levels of concerns over information storage, transmission, and access and identity verification. For privacy and the protection of personal information, there are even stronger concerns about consolidation of information, unauthorized access, and sharing without permission.

GLOBAL GEOECONOMIC BUSINESS CHALLENGES

Geoeconomic refers to the effects of geography on the economic realities of international business activities. Even with the Internet, telecommunications, and air travel, the sheer physical distances across the globe make it difficult to operate multinational business. Flying IT specialists into remote sites is costly, communicating in real-time across the globe's 24 time zones is challenging, and finding quality telecommunication services in every country is difficult. Skilled labor supplies, cost of living, and labor costs also differ among the various countries. When developing global business strategies, all of these geoeconomic challengés must be addressed.

Understanding the cultural, political, and geoeconomic business challenges is a good start to understanding global business, but the problems facing managers run far deeper. The remainder of this plug-in focuses on business management issues that are central to all global business. Business managers must understand four primary areas—global IT business strategies, global enterprise architectures, global information issues, and global systems development—when running multinational companies (see Figure B11.2).

LO 2. Describe the four global IT business drivers that should be included in all IT strategies.

Global IT Business Strategies

Global IT business strategies must include detailed information on the application of information technology across the organization. IT systems depend on global business drivers such as the nature of the industry, competitive factors, and environmental forces. For example, airlines and hotels have global customers who travel extensively and expect the same service regardless of location. Organizations require global IT systems that can provide fast, convenient service to all international employees who are servicing these customers. When a high-end hotel customer checks into a hotel in Asia she expects to receive the same high-end service as when she is checking into a hotel in Chicago or London. Figure B11.3 displays the global IT business drivers that should be included in all IT strategies.

Many global IT systems, such as finance, accounting, and operations management, have been in operation for years. Most multinational companies have global financial

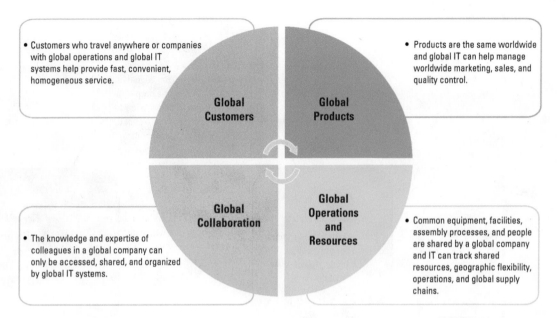

- Customers who travel anywhere or companies with global operations and global IT systems help provide fast, convenient, homogeneous service.

Global Customers

- Products are the same worldwide and global IT can help manage worldwide marketing, sales, and quality control.

Global Products

Global Collaboration

Global Operations and Resources

- The knowledge and expertise of colleagues in a global company can only be accessed, shared, and organized by global IT systems.

- Common equipment, facilities, assembly processes, and people are shared by a global company and IT can track shared resources, geographic flexibility, operations, and global supply chains.

FIGURE B11.3

Global IT Business Drivers

budgeting and cash management. As global operations expand and global competition heats up, pressure increases for companies to install global ebusiness applications for customers, suppliers, and employees. Examples include portals and websites geared toward customer service and supply chain management. In the past, such systems relied almost exclusively on privately constructed or government-owned telecommunications networks. But the explosive business use of the Internet, intranets, and extranets for electronic commerce has made such applications more feasible for global companies.

GOVERNANCE AND COMPLIANCE

One fast-growing key area for all global business strategies is governance and compliance. *Governance* is a method or system of government for management or control. *Compliance* is the act of conforming, acquiescing, or yielding. A few years ago the ideas of governance and compliance were relatively obscure. Today, the concept of formal IT governance and compliance is a must for virtually every company, both domestic and global. Key drivers for governance and compliance include financial and technological regulations as well as pressure from shareholders and customers.

Organizations today are subject to many regulations governing data retention, confidential information, financial accountability, and recovery from disasters. By implementing IT governance, organizations have the internal controls they need to meet the core guidelines of many of these regulations, such as the Sarbanes-Oxley Act of 2002.

IT governance essentially places structure around how organizations align IT strategy with business strategy, ensuring that companies stay on track to achieve their strategies and goals, and implementing good ways to measure IT's performance. Governance makes sure that all stakeholders' interests are considered and that processes provide measurable results. IT governance should answer key questions including how the IT department is functioning overall, what key metrics management requires, and what return the business is getting from its IT investment. Figure B11.4 displays the five key areas of focus according to the IT Governance Institute.

Organizations can follow a few different IT governance frameworks, including:

■ **CoBIT:** *Information Systems Audit and Control Association (ISACA)* is a set of guidelines and supporting tools for IT governance that is accepted worldwide and generally used by auditors and companies as a way to integrate technology to implement controls and meet specific business objectives.

LO 3. Describe governance and compliance and the associated frameworks an organization can implement.

FIGURE B11.4

IT Governance Institute
Five Focus Areas

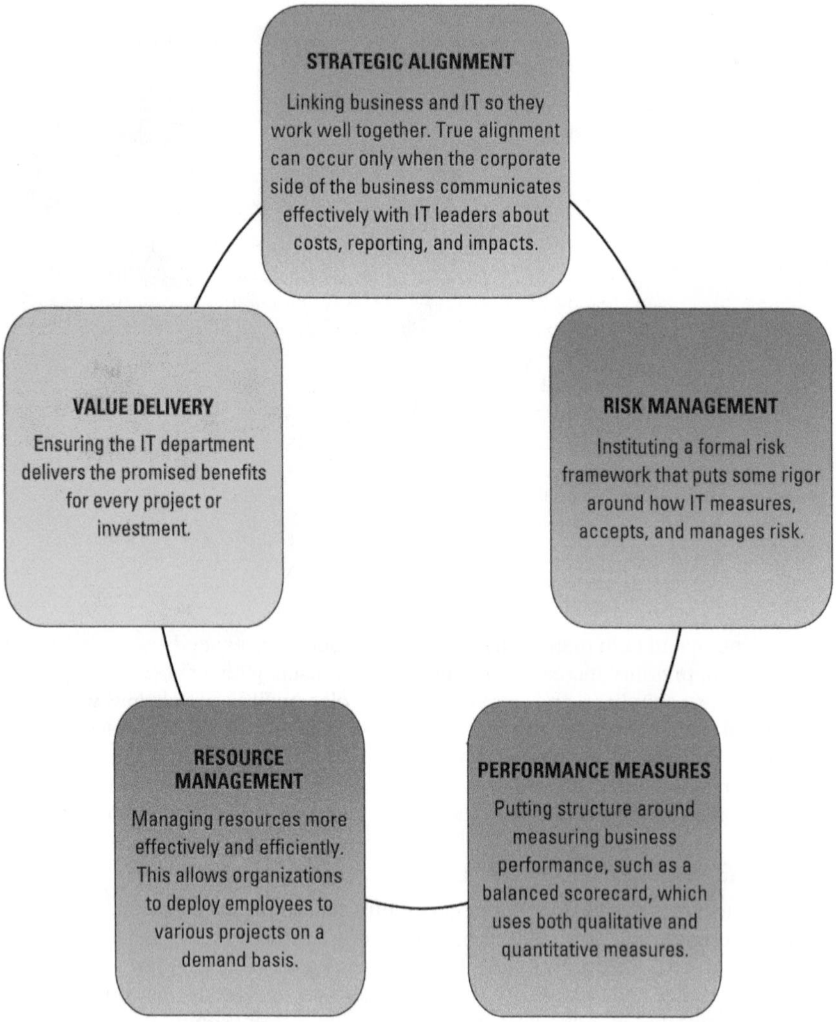

STRATEGIC ALIGNMENT

Linking business and IT so they work well together. True alignment can occur only when the corporate side of the business communicates effectively with IT leaders about costs, reporting, and impacts.

VALUE DELIVERY

Ensuring the IT department delivers the promised benefits for every project or investment.

RISK MANAGEMENT

Instituting a formal risk framework that puts some rigor around how IT measures, accepts, and manages risk.

RESOURCE MANAGEMENT

Managing resources more effectively and efficiently. This allows organizations to deploy employees to various projects on a demand basis.

PERFORMANCE MEASURES

Putting structure around measuring business performance, such as a balanced scorecard, which uses both qualitative and quantitative measures.

- **ITIL:** The *Information Technology Infrastructure Library (ITIL)* is a framework provided by the government of the United Kingdom and offers eight sets of management procedures: (1) service delivery, (2) service support, (3) service management, (4) Information and Communication Technology (ICT) infrastructure management, (5) software asset management, (6) business perspective, (7) security management, and (8) application management. ITIL is a good fit for organizations concerned about operations.

- **COSO:** The framework developed by the *Committee of Sponsoring Organizations (COSO)* is key for evaluating internal controls such as human resources, logistics, information technology, risk, legal, marketing and sales, operations, financial functions, procurement, and reporting. This is a more business-general framework that is less IT-specific.

- **CMMI:** Created by a group from government, industry, and Carnegie Mellon's Software Engineering Institute, the *Capability Maturity Model Integration method (CMMI)* is a process improvement approach that contains 22 process areas. It is divided into appraisal, evaluation, and structure. CMMI is particularly well-suited to organizations that need help with application development, life cycle issues, and improving the delivery of products throughout the life cycle.

Global Enterprise Architectures

An *enterprise architecture* includes the plans for how an organization will build, deploy, use, and share its data, processes, and IT assets. An organization must manage its global enterprise architecture to support its global business operations. Management of a global enterprise architecture not only is technically complex, but also has major political and cultural implications. For example, hardware choices are difficult in some countries because of high prices, high tariffs, import restrictions, long lead times for government approvals, lack of local service or replacement parts, and lack of documentation tailored to local conditions. Software choices also present issues; for example, European data standards differ from American or Asian standards, even when purchased from the same vendor. Some software vendors also refuse to offer service and support in countries that disregard software licensing and copyright agreements.

The Internet and the World Wide Web are critical to international business. This interconnected matrix of computers, information, and networks that reaches tens of millions of users in hundreds of countries is a business environment free of traditional boundaries and limits. Linking to online global businesses offers companies unprecedented potential for expanding markets, reducing costs, and improving profit margins at a price that is typically a small percentage of the corporate communications budget. The Internet provides an interactive channel for direct communication and data exchange with customers, suppliers, distributors, manufacturers, product developers, financial backers, information providers—in fact, with all parties involved in an international organization.

The Paris-based organization Reporters Without Borders notes that 45 countries restrict their citizens' access to the Internet. "At its most fundamental, the struggle between Internet censorship and openness at the national level revolves around three main means: controlling the conduits, filtering the flows, and punishing the purveyors. In countries such as Burma, Libya, North Korea, Syria, and the countries of Central Asia and the Caucasus, Internet access is either banned or subject to tight limitations through government-controlled ISPs. These countries face a lose-lose struggle against the information age. By denying or limiting Internet access, they stymie a major engine of economic growth. But by easing access, they expose their citizenry to ideas potentially destabilizing to the status quo. Either way, many people will get access to the electronic information they want. In Syria, for example, people go to Lebanon for the weekend to retrieve their email," said Virgini Locussol, Reporters Without Borders desk officer for the Middle East and North Africa.

Figure B11.5 displays the top 10 international telecommunication issues as reported by the IT executives at 300 Fortune 500 multinational companies. Political issues dominate the listing over technology issues, clearly emphasizing their importance in the management of global enterprise architectures.

Estimating the operational expenses associated with international IT operations is another global challenge. Companies with global business operations usually establish or contract with systems integrators for additional IT facilities for their subsidiaries in other countries. These IT facilities must meet local and regional computing needs, and even help balance global computing workloads through communications satellite links. However, offshore IT facilities can pose major problems in headquarters' support, hardware and software acquisition, maintenance, and security. This is why many global companies prefer to outsource these facilities to application service providers or systems integrators such as IBM or Accenture to manage overseas operations. Managing global enterprise architectures, including Internet, intranet, extranet, and other telecommunication networks, is a key global IT challenge for the 21st century.

LO 4. Identify why an organization would need to understand global enterprise architectures when expanding operations abroad.

FIGURE B11.5

Top 10 International
Telecommunication Issues

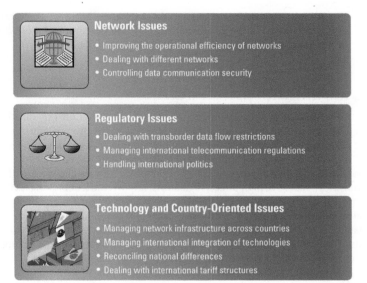

LO 5. Explain the many different
global information issues an
organization might encounter as
it conducts business abroad.

Global Information Issues

While many consumer gadgets and software applications can benefit a company—for instance, by helping employees get their jobs done more efficiently—the security implications are legion, said Ken Silva, chief security officer at VeriSign, which specializes in network security software. "When we bolt those things onto corporate networks, we open up holes in the environment." Drugmaker Pfizer found this out the hard way. An employee's spouse loaded file-sharing software onto a Pfizer laptop at home, creating a security hole that appears to have compromised the names and Social Security numbers of 17,000 current and former Pfizer employees, according to a letter Pfizer sent to state attorneys general. Pfizer's investigation showed that 15,700 of those employees actually had their data accessed and copied.

Rather than fight the trend, some companies are experimenting with giving employees more choice regarding the technology they use—so long as they accept more responsibility for it. In 2005, BP began a pilot project that gives employees about $1,000 to spend on productivity-enhancing tools in addition to standard-issue equipment, according to a report from the Leading Edge Forum. But before they can participate, employees must pass a test of their computer literacy skills.

The company takes other steps to give employees free rein while mitigating risk. BP cordons off its network by letting employees link to the Internet via consumer connections, from outside the firewall, in the case of its 18,000 laptops. At the same time it beefs up security on those machines. This lets employees safely experiment with software such as Amazon's on-demand computing and storage services.

Deperimeterization occurs when an organization moves employees outside its firewall, a growing movement to change the way corporations address technology security. In a business world where many employees are off-site or on the road, or where businesses increasingly must collaborate with partners and customers, some say it's not practical to rely on a hardened perimeter of firewalls. Instead, proponents of deperimeterization say companies should focus on beefing up security in end-user devices and organizations' critical information assets.

INFORMATION PRIVACY

For many years, global data access issues have been the subject of political controversy and technology barriers in global business environments. These issues have become more prevalent with the growth of the Internet and the expansion of ebusinesses. **Transborder data flows (TDF)** occur when business data flows across international boundaries over the telecommunications networks of global information systems. Many countries view TDF as violating their national sovereignty because transborder data flows avoid customs duties and regulations for the import or export of goods and services. Others view transborder data flows as violating their laws to protect the local IT industry from competition or their labor regulations from protecting local jobs. In many cases, the data flow issues that seem particularly politically sensitive are those that affect the movement out of a country of personal data in ebusiness and human resource applications.

Many countries, especially those in the European Union (EU), may view transborder data flows as a violation of their privacy legislation since, in many cases, data about individuals are being moved out of the country without stringent privacy safeguards. Figure B11.6 highlights the key provisions of a data privacy agreement between the United States and the European Union. The agreement exempts U.S. companies engaging in international ebusiness from EU data privacy sanctions if they join a self-regulatory program that provides EU consumers with basic information about, and control over, how their personal data are used. Thus, the agreement is said to provide a "safe harbor" for such companies from the requirements of the EU's Data Privacy Directive, which bans the transfer of personal information on EU citizens to countries that do not have adequate data privacy protection.

Information privacy concerns the legal right or general expectation of individuals, groups, or institutions to determine for themselves when and to what extent information about them is communicated to others. In essence, information privacy is about how personal information is collected and shared. To facilitate information privacy, many countries have established legislation to protect the collection and sharing of personal information. However, this legislation varies greatly around the globe.

EUROPE

On one end of the spectrum lie European nations with their strong information privacy laws. Most notably, all member countries of the European Union adhere to a directive on the protection of personal data. A directive is a legislative act of the European Union that requires member states to achieve a particular result without dictating the means of how to achieve that result.

The directive on the protection of personal data grants European Union members the following rights:

■ The right to know the source of personal data processing and the purposes of such processing.

■ The right to access and/or rectify inaccuracies in one's own personal data.

■ The right to disallow the use of personal data.

These rights are based on key principles pertaining to the collection or storage of personal data. The directive defines personal data to cover both facts and opinions about an individual. Any organization processing personal data of a person living in the European Union must comply with these key principles as outlined in the directive; these state that the data must be:

■ Fairly and lawfully processed.

■ Processed for limited purposes.

■ Adequate, relevant, and not excessive.

■ Accurate.

FIGURE B11.6

U.S.–EU Data Privacy Requirements

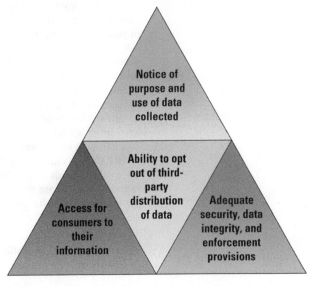

- Not kept longer than necessary.
- Processed in accordance with the data subject's rights.
- Not transferred to countries without adequate protection.

This last right restricts the flow of personal information outside the European Union by permitting its transfer to only countries that provide an "adequate" level of privacy protection—adequate in the sense that these other countries have to offer a level of privacy protection equivalent to that of the European Union. When first implemented, this part of the directive caused some concerns since countries outside the EU had much weaker privacy protection laws. Organizations in the United States were greatly concerned because they were at a legal risk if the personal data of EU citizens were transferred to computer servers in the United States—a likely scenario in today's global world of ebusiness. This led to extensive negotiations. The result was the establishment of a "safe harbor" program in the United States. This program provides a framework for U.S. organizations to show evidence of compliance with the EU directive. In this way, American companies can self-declare their compliance with the key principles of the directive and do business with EU nations without worrying about EU citizens suing them.

THE UNITED STATES

On the other end of the spectrum lies the United States. Information privacy is not highly legislated or regulated. There is no all-encompassing law that regulates the use of personal data or information. In many cases, access to public information is considered culturally acceptable, such as obtaining credit reports for employment or housing purposes. The reason for this may be historical. In the United States, the first amendment protects free speech, and in many instances the protection of privacy might conflict with this amendment.

There are some exceptions. Though very few states recognize an individual's right to privacy, California's constitution protects an inalienable right to privacy. The California legislature has enacted several pieces of legislation aimed at protecting citizen information privacy. For example, California's Online Privacy Protection Act, established in 2003, requires commercial websites or online services that collect personal information of California residents to clearly post a privacy policy on the website or online service and to comply with this policy. Other nationwide exceptions include the Children's Online Privacy Protection Act (COPPA) and the Health Insurance Portability and Accountability Act (HIPAA).

COPPA is a federal law established in 1998 that applies to the collection of personal information from American children who are under 13 years of age. The act outlines what a website should include in its privacy policy, how to seek consent from a parent or guardian, and the responsibilities a website operator has to protect children's online safety and privacy. This law applies to any website that is perceived to be targeting American children. For example, if a toy company established in Canada wanted to sell toys in the United States, the company's website should have to comply with the collection and use of information as outlined in COPPA. To show compliance requires a substantial amount of paperwork. As a result, many websites disallow underage users to join online communities and websites. Not complying with COPPA can be costly. In September 2006, the website Xanga, an online community, was fined $1 million for violating COPPA legislation.

HIPAA was enacted by the U.S. Congress in 1996. Provisions in HIPPA establish national standards for the electronic data interchange of health care-related transactions between health care providers, insurance plans, and employers. Embedded in these standards are rules for the handling and protection of personal health care information.

CANADA

Canada's privacy laws follow very closely the European model. Canada as a nation is quite concerned about protecting the personal information of its citizens. Its primary privacy law is the Personal Information Protection and Electronic Document Act (PIPEDA). The purpose of PIPEDA is to provide Canadians with a right of privacy with respect to how their personal information is collected, used, or disclosed by an organization. This is most important today, especially in the private sector, when information technology increasingly facilitates the collection and free flow of information.

Its precursor was the Privacy Act established in 1983 that restricted the handling of personal information within federal government departments and agencies only. This information concerned such things as pension and employment insurance files, medical records, tax records, and military records.

PIPEDA took effect in January 2001 and, like the Privacy Act, applied only to federally regulated organizations. By January 2004, PIPEDA's reach extended beyond government borders and applied to all other types of organizations, including commercial businesses. By doing so, Canada's PIPEDA law brought Canada into compliance with the European Union's directive on the protection of personal data. Hence, since January 2004, Canada no longer needed to implement safe harbor provisions for organizations wishing to collect and store personal information on European Union citizens.

Global Systems Development

LO 6. Identify global system development issues organizations should understand before building a global system.

It is extremely difficult to develop a domestic information system, but the added complexity of developing a global information system quadruples the effort. Global information systems must support a diverse base of customers, users, products, languages, currencies, laws, and so on. Developing efficient, effective, and responsive information systems for multiple countries, differing cultures, and global ebusinesses is an enormous challenge for any organization. Managers should expect conflicts over local versus global system requirements and difficulties agreeing on common system features. For the project to succeed, the development environment should promote involvement and ownership by all local system users.

One of the most important global information systems development issues is the global standardization of data definitions. Common data definitions are necessary for sharing information among the parts of an international business. Differences in language, culture, and technology platforms can make global data standardization quite difficult. For example, what Americans call a "sale" may be called "an order booked" in the United Kingdom, an "order scheduled" in Germany, and an "order produced" in France. These are all referring to the exact same business event, but could cause problems if global employees have different versions of the data definition. Businesses are moving ahead to standardize data definitions and business processes. Many organizations are implementing corporate wikis where all global employees can post and maintain common business definitions.

Organizations can use several strategies to solve some of the problems that arise in global information systems development. First is transforming and customizing an information system used by the home office into a global application. This ensures the system uses the established business processes and supports the primary needs of the end users. Second is setting up a multinational development team with key people from several subsidiaries to ensure that the system design meets the needs of all local sites as well as corporate headquarters. Third, an organization could use centers of excellence where an entire system might be assigned for development to a particular subsidiary based on its expertise in the business or technical dimensions needed for successful development. A final approach that has rapidly become a major development option is to outsource the development work to global or offshore development countries that have the required skills and experience to build global information systems. All of these approaches require development team collaboration and managerial oversight to meet the global needs of the business.

✳ PLUG-IN SUMMARY

Whether you aspire to be an entrepreneur, manager, or other type of business leader, it is increasingly important to think globally in planning your career. As this plug-in points out, global markets offer many opportunities yet are laced with significant challenges and complexities including cultural, political, and geoeconomic issues, such as:

- Global business strategies.
- Global enterprise architectures.
- Global information issues.
- Global systems development.

✳ KEY TERMS

Capability Maturity Model
    Integration method
    (CMMI) 492
Committee of Sponsoring
    Organizations (COSO) 492
Compliance 491
Deperimeterization 494

Enterprise architecture 493
Geoeconomic 490
Governance 491
Information privacy 495
Information Systems Audit
    and Control Association
    (ISACA) 491

Information Technology
    Infrastructure Library
    (ITIL) 492
Transborder data flows
    (TDF) 495

✳ CLOSING CASE ONE

Tata's Nano $2,500 Car

The announcement by Tata Motors of its newest car, the Nano, priced at $2,500, was revealing on many levels. The announcement generated extensive coverage and commentary, but just about everyone missed the Nano's real significance, which goes far beyond the car itself.

At about $2,500 retail, the Nano is the most inexpensive car in the world. Its closest competitor, the Maruti 800, made in India by Maruti Udyog, sells for roughly twice as much. To put this in perspective, the price of the entire Nano car is roughly equivalent to the price of a DVD player option in a luxury Western car. The low price point has left other auto companies scrambling to catch up.

Thinking Outside the Patent Box

How could Tata Motors make a car so inexpensively? It started by looking at everything from scratch, applying what some analysts have described as "Gandhian engineering" principles—deep frugality with a willingness to challenge conventional wisdom. A lot of features that Western consumers take for granted—air conditioning, power brakes, radios, etc.—are missing from the entry-level model.

More fundamentally, the engineers worked to do more with less. The car is smaller in overall dimensions than the Maruti, but it offers about 20 percent more seating capacity as a result of design choices such as putting the wheels at the extreme edges of the car. The Nano is also much lighter than comparable models as a result of efforts to reduce the amount of steel in the car (including the use of an aluminum engine) and the use of lightweight steel where possible. The car currently meets all Indian emission, pollution, and safety standards, though it only attains a maximum speed of about 65 mph. The fuel efficiency is attractive—50 miles to the gallon.

Hearing all this, many Western executives doubt that this new car represents real innovation. Too often, when they think of innovation, they focus on product innovation using breakthrough technologies; often, specifically, on patents. Tata Motors has filed for 34 patents associated with the design of the Nano, which contrasts with the roughly 280 patents awarded to General Motors (GM) every year. Admittedly that figure tallies all of GM's research efforts, but if innovation is measured only in terms of patents, no wonder the Nano is not of much interest to Western executives. Measuring progress solely by patent creation misses a key dimension of innovation: Some of the most valuable innovations take existing, patented components and remix them in ways that more effectively serve the needs of large numbers of customers.

A Modular Design Revolution

But even this broader perspective fails to capture other significant dimensions of innovation. In fact, Tata Motors itself did not draw a lot of attention to what is perhaps the most innovative aspect of the Nano: its modular design. The Nano is constructed of components that can be built and shipped separately to be assembled in a variety of locations. In effect, the Nano is being sold in kits that are distributed, assembled, and serviced by local entrepreneurs. As Ratan Tata, chairman of the Tata group of companies, observed in an interview with *The Times* of London: "A bunch of entrepreneurs could establish an assembly operation and Tata Motors would train their people, would oversee their quality assurance and they would become satellite assembly operations for us. So we would create entrepreneurs across the country that would produce the car. We would produce the mass items and ship it to them as kits. That is my idea of dispersing wealth. The service person would be like an insurance agent who would be trained, have a cell phone and scooter and would be assigned to a set of customers."

In fact, Tata envisions going even further, providing the tools for local mechanics to assemble the car in existing auto shops or even in new garages created to cater to remote rural customers. With the exception of Manjeet Kripalani, *BusinessWeek*'s India bureau chief, few have focused on this breakthrough element of the Nano innovation.

This is part of a broader pattern of innovation emerging in India in a variety of markets, ranging from diesel engines and agricultural products to financial services. While most of the companies pursuing this type of innovation are Indian, the U.S. engineering firm Cummins (CMI) demonstrates that Western companies can also harness this approach and apply it effectively. In 2000 Cummins designed innovative "gensets" (generation sets) to enter the lower end of the power generator market in India. These modular sets were explicitly designed to lower distribution costs and make it easy for distributors and customers to tailor the product for highly variable customer environments. Using this approach, Cummins captured a leading position in the Indian market and now actively exports these new products to Africa, Latin America, and the Middle East.

Lessons Executives Should Learn

What are the broader lessons that Western executives should learn from this innovation story? Emerging markets are a fertile ground for innovation. The challenge of reaching dispersed, low-income consumers in emerging markets often spurs significant innovation. Western executives should be careful about compartmentalizing the impact of these innovations on the edge of the global economy. These innovations will become the basis for "attacker" strategies that can be used to challenge incumbents in more developed economies. What is initially on the edge soon comes to the core.

■ Find ways to help customers and others on the edge to tinker with your products. Modular and open product designs help engage large numbers of motivated users in tailoring and pushing the performance boundaries of your products, leading to significant insight into unmet customer needs and creative approaches to addressing those needs.

- Pay attention to institutional innovation. Western executives often become too narrowly focused on product or process innovation. Far higher returns may come from investing in institutional innovation—redefining the roles and relationships that bring together independent entities to deliver more value to the market. Tata is innovating in all three dimensions simultaneously.

- Rethink distribution models. In our relentless quest for operating efficiency, we have gone for more standardization and fewer business partners in our efforts to reach customers. As customers gain more power, they will demand more tailoring and value-added service to meet their needs. Companies that innovate on this dimension are likely to be richly rewarded.

Questions

1. How can cultural and political issues affect Tata Motors' Nano car?
2. How would governance and compliance affect Tata Motors?
3. Identify the different global system development issues Tata Motors might encounter as it deploys its Nano.

✳ CLOSING CASE TWO

Global Governance

Tarun Khanna, a Harvard professor, states that Indian companies exhibit corporate governance superior to their Chinese rivals. Khanna has just released a new book, *Billions of Entrepreneurs: How China and India Are Reshaping Their Future and Yours*. However, Khanna believes that Chinese organizations might not require world-class governance to emerge as fierce competitors. Here are edited excerpts from a recent conversation between Khanna and *BusinessWeek*'s William J. Holstein:

Much as their societies and political systems are different, are Indian and Chinese companies complete opposites when it comes to corporate governance?
Absolutely. Indian companies are so much better governed. India is sort of a noisier version of the U.S. system, which is that you have to be accountable to shareholders and all the other stakeholders. The principles are the same, but the information acquisition is a little bit more problematic in India compared to the U.S. It's not so easy to figure out everything you need to. But there's a very vibrant, credible business media. No opinion is forbidden to be expressed. Information is noisy and unbiased—no one is willfully distorting the truth.

China is the opposite—it is noise-free but biased. You get a clean story but the story is not always right. There are views that cannot be expressed.

Which country has more independent boards of directors?
In India, there is a spectrum of companies, such as Infosys, which on some dimensions is better governed than companies in the West in terms of how quickly it discloses things and how quickly it complies with Nasdaq norms. At the other end of the spectrum you have companies that are still the fiefdoms of families, many of which are badly governed. But even those companies are accountable to the market. Market pressures will force them to clean up their act to some extent. The equity markets function so well that it's hard to believe you could be a continuous violator of norms of good governance and still have access to the equity markets.

In China, none of that matters because the financial markets still do not work in the sense that we think of them working in the U.S. In China, all stock prices move together. They move up on a given day or they move down. There is no company-specific information embodied in the stock price. You cannot possibly decide that a company is good or bad because the market isn't working in that sense. What you see is aggregate enthusiasm, or lack thereof, for China Inc. The market is not putting pressure on managers to behave in ways that approximate corporate governance in the West.

Are companies in India and China making progress in developing talent in the same way that Western multinationals do?
They are both making progress. But Indian companies are significantly further along, partly because India never had a Cultural Revolution as China did, which wiped out much of the business class. It had a residue of corporations already in existence. Some companies are 100 or 150 years old and they have an established way of doing things.

Where are the Chinese when it comes to managing multiculturally?
Utterly zero. It is hard to blame them because there is a language barrier also. A lot of the internal tensions were about language and cultural barriers, and questions like, Can a Frenchman report to a Chinese? And what if the French guy makes more than the Chinese guy?

How do companies of the two countries compare when it comes to corruption?
Here, I am not positive on India at all. Transparency International puts out these indices, and India and China are both close to the bottom of that list. China does a little bit better than India. In China, there is corruption, but it is constructive corruption. You, as a bureaucrat, get to be corrupt but only after you generate some value for society. You get a piece of it.

In India, there is corruption but it is not constructive. You are not fostering new bridges or highways. It is just shuffling stuff back and forth. I do not think we have cracked that in India at all. I am very sorry about that.

In the final analysis, does it matter that Indian companies, on the whole, have an edge over the Chinese in reaching international standards of governance? The Chinese have huge capital at their disposal because of their $1.5 trillion in foreign exchange reserves. Could not they still be fearsome competitors?
I think that is right. Corporate governance matters because you want to reassure the providers of inputs—whether it is time and talent, or ideas, or capital—that their rights will be respected and they will get a return on it. But if you are already sitting on hundreds of billions of dollars of capital, and you do not need to reassure anybody else because you already have your capital, why have good corporate governance?

The reason the Chinese feel less pressured to do something about it is not because they do not know how to do it—far from it, they have the best technical help from Hong Kong and other places. It is because they make a reasoned judgment that it is not worth their while.

Questions

1. Explain governance and compliance and why they are important to any company looking to perform global business.

2. How can an organization use governance and compliance to help protect itself from global security breaches?

3. If you were choosing between outsourcing to India or China, based on this case, which country would you choose and why?

4. What types of ethical dilemmas might an organization face when dealing with IT governance in India or China?

★ **MAKING BUSINESS DECISIONS**

1. Transforming an Organization

Your college has asked you to help develop the curriculum for a new course titled "Building a 21st Century Organization." Use the materials in this text, the Internet, and any other resources to outline the curriculum that you would suggest the course cover. Be sure to include your reasons why the material should be covered and the order in which it should be covered.

2. Connecting Components

Components of a solid enterprise architecture include everything from documentation to business concepts to software and hardware. Deciding which components to implement and how to implement them can be a challenge. New IT components are released daily, and business needs continually change. An enterprise architecture that meets your organization's needs today may not meet those needs tomorrow. Building an enterprise architecture that is scalable, flexible, available, accessible, and reliable is key to your organization's success.

You are the enterprise architect for a large clothing company called Xedous. You are responsible for developing the initial enterprise architecture. Create a list of questions you will need answered to develop your architecture. Below is an example of a few questions you might ask.

- What are the company's growth expectations?
- Will systems be able to handle additional users?
- How long will information be stored in the systems?
- How much customer history must be stored?
- What are the organization's business hours?
- What are the organization's backup requirements?

3. IT Gets Its Say

CIOs need to speak the language of business to sell IT's strategic benefits. It is no secret that the most successful companies today are the ones that deliver the right products and services faster, more efficiently, more securely, and more cost-effectively than their competitors, and the key to that is a practical implementation of enterprise technology to improve business performance. IT executives and managers therefore must speak the language of business to articulate how technology can solve business problems.

CIOs of tomorrow will focus on a number of changing dynamics: enabling the business to grow versus just optimizing performance, saying yes instead of no; allowing open innovation rather than closed, traditional R&D practices; creating a culture of strategic growth and innovation; and empowering the customer to make decisions that drive a heightened value proposition for both the customer and supplier. You have been charged with creating a slogan for your company that explains the correlation of business and IT. A few examples include:

- IT should no longer be viewed as just an enabler of somebody else's business strategy.
- The distinction between technology and business is antediluvian – it's gone.

Create a slogan that you can use to explain to your employees the importance of business and IT.

4. Mom-and-Pop Multinationals

Global outsourcing is no longer just for big corporations as small businesses jump into the multisourcing game. Increasingly, Main Street businesses from car dealers to advertising agencies are finding it easier to farm out software development, accounting, support services, and design work to distant lands. For example, Randy and Nicola Wilburn run a micro-multinational organization right from their home. The Wilburns run real estate, consulting, design, and baby food companies from their home by taking outsourcing to the extreme. Professionals from around the globe are at their service. For $300, an Indian artist designed the cute logo of an infant peering over the words "Baby Fresh Organic Baby Foods" and Nicola's letterhead. A London freelancer wrote promotional materials. Randy has hired "virtual assistants" in Jerusalem to transcribe voice mail, update his website, and design PowerPoint graphics. Retired brokers in Virginia and Michigan handle real estate paperwork.

Elance, an online-services marketplace, boasts 48,500 small businesses as clients—up 70 percent in the past year—posting 18,000 new projects a month. Other online-services marketplaces such as Guru.com, Brickwork India, DoMyStuff.com, and RentACoder also report fast growth. You have decided to jump in the micro-multinational game and start your own online-services marketplace. Research the following as you compile your start-up business plan.

1. To compete in this market what types of services would you offer?
2. What types of cultural, political, and geoeconomic challenges would your business experience?
3. How would governance and compliance fit into your business strategy?
4. What types of global information issues might your company experience?
5. What types of customers would you want to attract and what vehicle would you use to find your customers?
6. What types of global systems development issues would your company experience?
7. What types of information security and ethical dilemmas should you anticipate?

B6

Information Security

LEARNING OUTCOMES

1. Describe the relationships and differences between hackers and viruses.
2. Describe the relationship between information security policies and an information security plan.
3. Provide an example of each of the three primary information security areas: (1) authentication and authorization, (2) prevention and resistance, and (3) detection and response.

LO 1. Describe the relationships and differences between hackers and viruses.

Security Threats Caused by Hackers and Viruses

Hackers are experts in technology who use their knowledge to break into computers and computer networks, either for profit or just motivated by the challenge. Smoking is not just bad for a person's health; it seems it is also bad for company security as hackers regularly use smoking entrances to gain building access. Once inside they pose as employees from the MIS department and either ask for permission to use an employee's computer to access the corporate network, or find a conference room where they simply plug-in their own laptop. *Drive-by hacking* is a computer attack where an attacker accesses a wireless computer network, intercepts data, uses network services, and/or sends attack instructions without entering the office or organization that owns the network. Figure B6.1 lists the various types of hackers for organizations to be aware of, and Figure B6.2 shows how a virus is spread.

FIGURE B6.1

Types of Hackers

Common Types of Hackers
■ **Black-hat hackers** break into other people's computer systems and may just look around or may steal and destroy information.
■ **Crackers** have criminal intent when hacking.
■ **Cyberterrorists** seek to cause harm to people or to destroy critical systems or information and use the Internet as a weapon of mass destruction.
■ **Hactivists** have philosophical and political reasons for breaking into systems and will often deface the website as a protest.
■ **Script kiddies** or **script bunnies** find hacking code on the Internet and click-and-point their way into systems to cause damage or spread viruses.
■ **White-hat hackers** work at the request of the system owners to find system vulnerabilities and plug the holes.

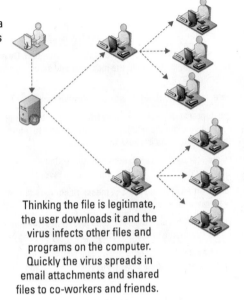

A hacker creates a
virus and attaches
it to a program,
document, or
website.

Thinking the file is legitimate,
the user downloads it and the
virus infects other files and
programs on the computer.
Quickly the virus spreads in
email attachments and shared
files to co-workers and friends.

One of the most common forms of computer vulnerabilities is a virus. A ***virus*** is software written with malicious intent to cause annoyance or damage. Some hackers create and leave viruses causing massive computer damage. Figure B6.3 provides an overview of the most common types of viruses. Two additional computer vulnerabilities include adware and spyware. ***Adware*** is software that, while purporting to serve some useful function and often fulfilling that function, also allows Internet advertisers to display advertisements without the consent of the computer user. ***Spyware*** is a special class of adware that collects data about the user and transmits it over the Internet without the user's knowledge or permission. Spyware programs collect specific data about the user, ranging from general demographics such as name, address, and browsing habits to credit card numbers, Social Security numbers, and user names and passwords. Not all adware programs are spyware and used correctly it can generate revenue for a company allowing users to receive free products. Spyware is a clear threat to privacy. Figure B6.4 displays a few additional weapons hackers use for launching attacks.[1]

Organizational information is intellectual capital. Just as organizations protect their tangible assets—keeping their money in an insured bank or providing a safe working

Backdoor programs open a way into the network for future attacks.

Denial-of-service attack (DoS) floods a website with so many requests for service that it slows down or crashes the site.

Distributed denial-of-service attack (DDoS) attacks from multiple computers that flood a website with so many requests for service that it slows down or crashes. A common type is the Ping of Death, in which thousands of computers try to access a website at the same time, overloading it and shutting it down.

Polymorphic viruses and worms change their form as they propagate.

Trojan-horse virus hides inside other software, usually as an attachment or a downloadable file.

Worm spreads itself, not only from file to file, but also from computer to computer. The primary difference between a virus and a worm is that a virus must attach to something, such as an executable file, to spread. Worms do not need to attach to anything to spread and can tunnel themselves into computers.

FIGURE B6.3

Common Forms of Viruses

Elevation of privilege is a process by which a user misleads a system into granting unauthorized rights, usually for the purpose of compromising or destroying the system. For example, an attacker might log onto a network by using a guest account and then exploit a weakness in the software that lets the attacker change the guest privileges to administrative privileges.

Hoaxes attack computer systems by transmitting a virus hoax, with a real virus attached. By masking the attack in a seemingly legitimate message, unsuspecting users more readily distribute the message and send the attack on to their co-workers and friends, infecting many users along the way.

Malicious code includes a variety of threats such as viruses, worms, and Trojan horses.

Packet tampering consists of altering the contents of packets as they travel over the Internet or altering data on computer disks after penetrating a network. For example, an attacker might place a tap on a network line to intercept packets as they leave the computer. The attacker could eavesdrop or alter the information as it leaves the network.

A **sniffer** is a program or device that can monitor data traveling over a network. Sniffers can show all the data being transmitted over a network, including passwords and sensitive information. Sniffers tend to be a favorite weapon in the hacker's arsenal.

Spoofing is the forging of the return address on an email so that the message appears to come from someone other than the actual sender. This is not a virus but rather a way by which virus authors conceal their identities as they send out viruses.

Splogs (spam blogs) are fake blogs created solely to raise the search engine rank of affiliated websites. Even blogs that are legitimate are plagued by spam, with spammers taking advantage of the Comment feature by posting comments with links to spam sites.

Spyware is software that comes hidden in free downloadable software and tracks online movements, mines the information stored on a computer, or uses a computer's CPU and storage for some task the user knows nothing about.

FIGURE B6.4

Hacker Weapons

environment for employees—they must also protect their intellectual capital, everything from patents to transactional and analytical information. With security breaches and viruses on the rise and computer hackers everywhere, an organization must put in place strong security measures to survive.

LO 2. Describe the relationship between information security policies and an information security plan.

The First Line of Defense—People

Organizations today are able to mine valuable information such as the identity of the top 20 percent of their customers, who usually produce 80 percent of revenues. Most organizations view this type of information as intellectual capital and implement security measures to prevent it from walking out the door or falling into the wrong hands. At the same time, they must enable employees, customers, and partners to access needed information electronically. Organizations address security risks through two lines of defense; the first is people, the second technology.

Surprisingly, the biggest problem is people as the majority of information security breaches result from people misusing organizational information. *Insiders* are legitimate users who purposely or accidentally misuse their access to the environment and cause some kind of business-affecting incident. For example, many individuals freely give up their passwords or write them on sticky notes next to their computers, leaving the door wide open for hackers. Through *social engineering,* hackers use their social skills to trick people into revealing access credentials or other valuable information. *Dumpster diving,* or looking through people's trash, is another way hackers obtain information.

Information security policies identify the rules required to maintain information security, such as requiring users to log off before leaving for lunch or meetings, never sharing passwords with anyone, and changing passwords every 30 days. An *information security plan* details how an organization will implement the information security policies. The best way a company can safeguard itself from people is by implementing and communicating its information security plan. This becomes even more important with Web 2.0 and as the use of mobile devices, remote workforce, and contractors are growing. A few details managers should consider surrounding people and information security policies include defining the best practices for[2]

- Applications allowed to be placed on the corporate network, especially various file sharing applications (Kazaz), IM software, and entertainment or freeware created by unknown sources (iPhone applications).

- Corporate computer equipment used for personal reason on personal networks.

- Password creation and maintenance including minimum password length, characters to be included while choosing passwords, and frequency for password changes.

- Personal computer equipment allowed to connect to the corporate network.

- Virus protection including how often the system should be scanned and how frequently the software should be updated. This could also include if downloading attachments is allowed and practices for safe downloading from trusted and untrustworthy sources.

The Second Line of Defense—Technology

Once an organization has protected its intellectual capital by arming its people with a detailed information security plan, it can begin to focus on deploying technology to help combat attackers. **Destructive agents** are malicious agents designed by spammers and other Internet attackers to farm email addresses off websites or deposit spyware on machines. Figure B6.5 displays the three areas where technology can aid in the defense against attacks.

PEOPLE: AUTHENTICATION AND AUTHORIZATION

Identity theft is the forging of someone's identity for the purpose of fraud. The fraud is often financial, because thieves apply for and use credit cards or loans in the victim's name. Two means of stealing an identity are phishing and pharming. **Information secrecy** is the category of computer security that addresses the protection of data from unauthorized disclosure and confirmation of data source authenticity. **Phishing** is a technique to gain personal information for the purpose of identity theft, usually by means of fraudulent emails that look as though they came from legitimate businesses. The messages appear to be genuine, with official-looking formats and logos, and typically ask for verification of important information such as passwords and account numbers, ostensibly for accounting or auditing purposes. Since the emails look authentic, up to one in five recipients responds with the information and subsequently becomes a victim of identity theft and other fraud. Figure B6.6 displays a phishing scam attempting to gain information for Bank of America; you should never click on emails asking you to verify your identity as companies will never contact you directly asking for your user name or password.[3] **Phishing expedition** is a masquerading attack that combines spam with spoofing. The perpetrator sends millions of spam emails that appear to be from a respectable company. The emails contain a link to a website that is designed to look exactly like the company's website. The victim is encouraged to enter his or her username, password, and sometimes credit card information. **Spear phishing** is a phishing expedition in which

LO 3. **Provide an example of each of the three primary information security areas: (1) authentication and authorization, (2) prevention and resistance, and (3) detection and response.**

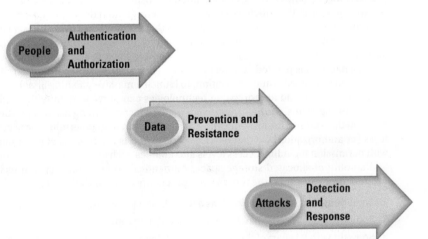

FIGURE B6.5

Three Areas of Information Security

FIGURE B6.6
Bank of America Phishing Scam

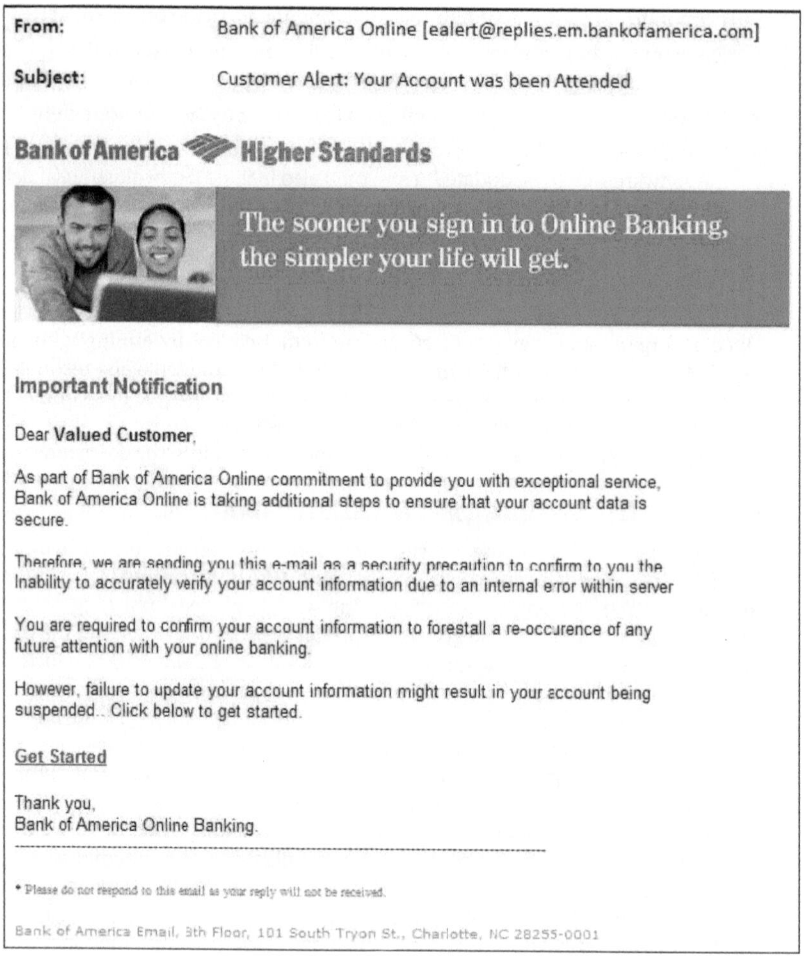

From: Bank of America Online [ealert@replies.em.bankofamerica.com]

Subject: Customer Alert: Your Account was been Attended

Important Notification

Dear **Valued Customer**,

As part of Bank of America Online commitment to provide you with exceptional service, Bank of America Online is taking additional steps to ensure that your account data is secure.

Therefore, we are sending you this e-mail as a security precaution to confirm to you the Inability to accurately verify your account information due to an internal error within server

You are required to confirm your account information to forestall a re-occurence of any future attention with your online banking.

However, failure to update your account information might result in your account being suspended.. Click below to get started.

Get Started

Thank you,
Bank of America Online Banking.

* Please do not respond to this email as your reply will not be received.

Bank of America Email, 3th Floor, 101 South Tryon St., Charlotte, NC 28255-0001

the emails are carefully designed to target a particular person or organization. ***Vishing*** (or ***voice phishing***) is a phone scam that attempts to defraud people by asking them to call a bogus telephone number to "confirm" their account information.

Pharming reroutes requests for legitimate websites to false websites. For example, if you were to type in the URL to your bank, pharming could redirect to a fake site that collects your information. A ***zombie*** is a program that secretly takes over another computer for the purpose of launching attacks on other computers. Zombie attacks are almost impossible to trace back to the attacker. A ***zombie farm*** is a group of computers on which a hacker has planted zombie programs. A ***pharming attack*** uses a zombie farm, often by an organized crime association, to launch a massive phishing attack.

Authentication and authorization technologies can prevent identity theft, phishing, and pharming scams. ***Authentication*** is a method for confirming users' identities. Once a system determines the authentication of a user, it can then determine the access privileges (or authorization) for that user. ***Authorization*** is the process of providing a user with permission including access levels and abilities such as file access, hours of access, and amount of allocated storage space. Authentication and authorization techniques fall into three categories; the most secure procedures combine all three:

1. Something the user knows, such as a user ID and password.
2. Something the user has, such as a smart card or token.
3. Something that is part of the user, such as a fingerprint or voice signature.

Something the User Knows Such as a User ID and Password

The first type of authentication, using something the user knows, is the most common way to identify individual users and typically consists of a unique user ID and password. However, this is actually one of the most *ineffective* ways for determining authentication because passwords are not secure. All it typically takes to crack one is enough time. More than 50 percent of help-desk calls are password related, which can cost an organization significant money, and a social engineer can coax a password from almost anybody.

Something the User Has Such as a Smart Card or Token

The second type of authentication, using something the user has, offers a much more effective way to identify individuals than a user ID and password. Tokens and smart cards are two of the primary forms of this type of authentication. *Tokens* are small electronic devices that change user passwords automatically. The user enters his or her user ID and token-displayed password to gain access to the network. A *smart card* is a device about the size of a credit card, containing embedded technologies that can store information and small amounts of software to perform some limited processing. Smart cards can act as identification instruments, a form of digital cash, or a data storage device with the ability to store an entire medical record.

Something That Is Part of the User Such as a Fingerprint or Voice Signature

The third kind of authentication, something that is part of the user, is by far the best and most effective way to manage authentication. *Biometrics* (narrowly defined) is the identification of a user based on a physical characteristic, such as a fingerprint, iris, face, voice, or handwriting. Unfortunately, biometric authentication can be costly and intrusive.

DATA: PREVENTION AND RESISTANCE

Prevention and resistance technologies stop intruders from accessing and reading data by means of content filtering, encryption, and firewalls. *Time bombs* are computer viruses that wait for a specific date before executing their instructions. *Content filtering* occurs when organizations use software that filters content, such as emails, to prevent the accidental or malicious transmission of unauthorized information. Organizations can use content filtering technologies to filter email and prevent emails containing sensitive information from transmitting, whether the transmission was malicious or accidental. It can also filter emails and prevent any suspicious files from transmitting such as potential virus-infected files. Email content filtering can also filter for spam, a form of unsolicited email.

   Encryption scrambles information into an alternative form that requires a key or password to decrypt. If there were a security breach and the stolen information were encrypted, the thief would be unable to read it. Encryption can switch the order of characters, replace characters with other characters, insert or remove characters, or use a mathematical formula to convert the information into a code. Companies that transmit sensitive customer information over the Internet, such as credit card numbers, frequently use encryption. To *decrypt* information is to decode it and is the opposite of *encrypt*. *Cryptography* is the science that studies encryption, which is the hiding of messages so that only the sender and receiver can read them. The National Institute of Standards and Technology (NIST) introduced an *advanced encryption standard (AES)* designed to keep government information secure.

   Some encryption technologies use multiple keys. *Public key encryption (PKE)* uses two keys: a public key that everyone can have and a private key for only the recipient (see Figure B6.7). The organization provides the public key to all customers, whether end consumers or other businesses, who use that key to encrypt their information and send it via the Internet. When it arrives at its destination, the organization uses the private key to unscramble it.

FIGURE B6.7

Public Key Encryption
(PKE)

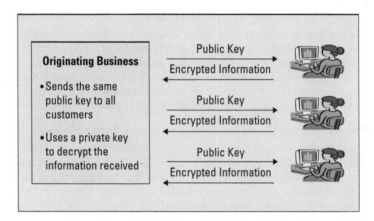

Public keys are becoming popular to use for authentication techniques consisting of digital objects in which a trusted third party confirms correlation between the user and the public key. A ***certificate authority*** is a trusted third party, such as VeriSign, that validates user identities by means of digital certificates. A ***digital certificate*** is a data file that identifies individuals or organizations online and is comparable to a digital signature.

A ***firewall*** is hardware and/or software that guard a private network by analyzing incoming and outgoing information for the correct markings. If they are missing, the firewall prevents the information from entering the network. Firewalls can even detect computers communicating with the Internet without approval. As Figure B6.8 illustrates, organizations typically place a firewall between a server and the Internet. Think of a firewall as a gatekeeper that protects computer networks from intrusion by providing a filter and safe transfer points for access to and from the Internet and other networks. It screens all network traffic for proper passwords or other security codes and allows only authorized transmissions in and out of the network.

Firewalls do not guarantee complete protection, and users should enlist additional security technologies such as antivirus software and antispyware software. ***Antivirus software*** scans and searches hard drives to prevent, detect, and remove known viruses, adware, and spyware. Antivirus software must be frequently updated to protect against newly created viruses.

FIGURE B6.8

Sample Firewall
Architecture Connecting
Systems Located in
Chicago, New York, and
Boston

ATTACK: DETECTION AND RESPONSE

Cyberwar is an organized attempt by a country's military to disrupt or destroy information and communication systems for another country. ***Cyberterrorism*** is the use

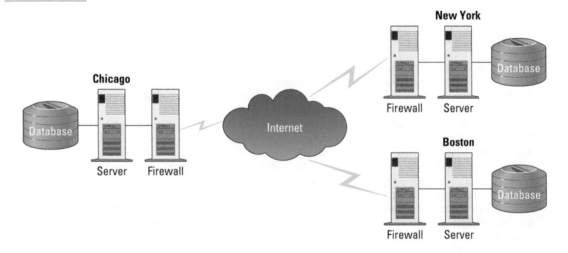

of computer and networking technologies against persons or property to intimidate or coerce governments, individuals, or any segment of society to attain political, religious, or ideological goals. With so many intruders planning computer attacks, it is critical that all computer systems are protected. The presence of an intruder can be detected by watching for suspicious network events such as bad passwords, the removal of highly classified data files, or unauthorized user attempts. ***Intrusion detection software (IDS)*** features full-time monitoring tools that search for patterns in network traffic to identify intruders. IDS protects against suspicious network traffic and attempts to access files and data. If a suspicious event or unauthorized traffic is identified, the IDS will generate an alarm and can even be customized to shut down a particularly sensitive part of a network. After identifying an attack, an MIS department can implement response tactics to mitigate the damage. Response tactics outline procedures such as how long a system under attack will remain plugged in and connected to the corporate network, when to shut down a compromised system, and how quickly a backup system will be up and running.

Guaranteeing the safety of organization information is achieved by implementing the two lines of defense: people and technology. To protect information through people, firms should develop information security policies and plans that provide employees with specific precautions they should take in creating, working with, and transmitting the organization's information assets. Technology-based lines of defense fall into three categories: authentication and authorization; prevention and resistance; and detection and response.

PLUG-IN SUMMARY

Implementing information security lines of defense through people first and through technology second is the best way for an organization to protect its vital intellectual capital. The first line of defense is securing intellectual capital by creating an information security plan detailing the various information security policies. The second line of defense is investing in technology to help secure information through authentication and authorization, prevention and resistance, and detection and response.

KEY TERMS

Advanced encryption
    standard (AES), 415
Adware, 411
Antivirus software, 416
Authentication, 414
Authorization, 414
Biometrics, 415
Certificate authority, 416
Content filtering, 415
Cryptography, 415
Cyberterrorism, 416
Cyberwar, 416
Decrypt, 415
Destructive agents, 413
Digital certificate, 416

Dumpster diving, 412
Drive-by hacking, 410
Encryption, 415
Firewall, 416
Hackers, 410
Identity theft, 413
Information secrecy, 413
Information security plan, 412
Information security
    policies, 412
Insiders, 412
Intrusion detection software
    (IDS), 417
Pharming, 414
Pharming attack, 414

Phishing, 413
Phishing expedition, 413
Public key encryption
    (PKE), 415
Smart card, 415
Social engineering, 412
Spear phishing, 413
Spyware, 411
Time bombs, 415
Tokens, 415
Virus, 411
Vishing (or voice
    phishing), 414
Zombie, 414
Zombie farm 414

CLOSING CASE ONE

Thinking Like the Enemy

David and Barry Kaufman, the founders of the Intense School, recently added several security courses, including the five-day "Professional Hacking Boot Camp" and "Social Engineering in Two Days."

Information technology departments must know how to protect organizational information. Therefore, organizations must teach their IT personnel how to protect their systems, especially in light of the many new government regulations, such as the Health Insurance Portability and Accountability Act (HIPAA), that demand secure systems. The concept of sending IT professionals to a hacking school seems counterintuitive; it is somewhat similar to sending accountants to an Embezzling 101 course. The Intense School does not strive to breed the next generation of hackers, however, but to teach its students how to be "ethical" hackers: to use their skills to build better locks, and to understand the minds of those who would attempt to crack them.

The main philosophy of the security courses at the Intense School is simply "To know thy enemy." In fact, one of the teachers at the Intense School is none other than Kevin Mitnick, the famous hacker who was imprisoned from 1995 to 2000. Teaching security from the hacker's perspective, as Mitnick does, is more difficult than teaching hacking itself: A hacker just needs to know one way into a system, David Kaufman notes, but a security professional needs to know *all* of the system's vulnerabilities. The two courses analyze those vulnerabilities from different perspectives.

The hacking course, which costs $3,500, teaches ways to protect against the mischief typically associated with hackers: worming through computer systems through vulnerabilities that are susceptible to technical, or computer-based, attacks. Mitnick's $1,950 social engineering course, by contrast, teaches the more frightening art of worming through the vulnerabilities of the people using and maintaining systems—getting passwords and access through duplicity, not technology. People that take this class, or read Mitnick's book, *The Art of Deception,* never again think of passwords or the trash bin the same way.

So how does the Intense School teach hacking? With sessions on dumpster diving (the unsavory practice of looking for passwords and other bits of information on discarded papers), with field trips to case target systems, and with practice runs at the company's in-house "target range," a network of computers set up to thwart and educate students.

One feature of the Intense School that raises a few questions is that the school does not check on morals at the door: Anyone paying the tuition can attend the school. Given the potential danger that an unchecked graduate of a hacking school could represent, it is surprising that the FBI does not collect the names of the graduates. But perhaps it gets them anyhow—several governmental agencies have sent students to the school.[4]

Questions

1. How could an organization benefit from attending one of the courses offered at the Intense School?
2. What are the two primary lines of security defense and how can organizational employees use the information taught by the Intense School when drafting an information security plan?
3. Determine the differences between the two primary courses offered at the Intense School, "Professional Hacking Boot Camp" and "Social Engineering in Two Days." Which course is more important for organizational employees to attend?
4. If your employer sent you to take a course at the Intense School, which one would you choose and why?
5. What are the ethical dilemmas involved with having such a course offered by a private company?

CLOSING CASE TWO

Hacker Hunters

Hacker hunters are the new breed of crime-fighter. They employ the same methodology used to fight organized crime in the 1980s—informants and the cyberworld equivalent of wiretaps. Daniel Larking, a 20-year veteran who runs the FBI's Internet Crime Complaint Center, taps online service providers to help track down criminal hackers. Leads supplied by the FBI and eBay helped Romanian police round up 11 members of a gang that set up fake eBay accounts and auctioned off cell phones, laptops, and cameras they never intended to deliver.

On October 26, 2004, the FBI unleashed Operation Firewall, targeting the ShadowCrew, a gang whose members were schooled in identity theft, bank account pillage, and selling illegal goods on the Internet. ShadowCrew's 4,000 gang members lived in a dozen countries and across the United States. For months, agents had been watching their every move through a clandestine gateway into their website, shadowcrew.com. One member turned informant called a group meeting, ensuring the members would be at home on their computers during a certain time. At 9 p.m. the Secret Service issued orders to move in on the gang. The move was synchronized around the globe to prevent gang members from warning each other via instant messages. Twenty-eight gang members in eight states and six countries were arrested, most still at their computers. Authorities seized dozens of computers and found 1.7 million credit card numbers and more than 18 million email accounts.

ShadowCrew's Operations

The alleged ringleaders of ShadowCrew included Andres Mantovani, 23, a part-time community college student in Arizona, and David Appleyard, 45, a former New Jersey mortgage broker. Mantovani and Appleyard allegedly were administrators in charge of running the website and recruiting members. The site created a marketplace for over 4,000 gang members who bought and sold hot information and merchandise. The website was open for business 24 hours a day, but since most of the members held jobs, the busiest time was from 10 p.m. to 2 a.m. on Sundays. Hundreds of gang members would meet online to trade credit card information, passports, and even equipment to make fake identity documents. Platinum credit cards cost more than gold ones and discounts were offered for package deals. One member known as "Scarface" sold 115,695 stolen credit card numbers in a single trade. Overall, the gang made more than $4 million in credit card purchases over two years. ShadowCrew was equivalent to an eBay for the underworld. The site even posted crime tips on how to use stolen credit cards and fake IDs at big retailers.

The gang stole credit card numbers and other valuable information through clever tricks. One of the favorites was sending millions of phishing emails—messages that appeared to be from legitimate companies such as Yahoo!—designed to steal passwords and credit card numbers. The gang also hacked into corporate databases to steal account data. According to sources familiar with the investigation, the gang cracked the networks of 12 unidentified companies that were not even aware their systems had been breached.

Police Operations

Brian Nagel, an assistant director at the Secret Service, coordinated the effort to track the ShadowCrew. Allies included Britain's National High-Tech Crimes unit, the Royal Canadian Mounted Police, and the Bulgarian Interior Ministry. Authorities turned one of the high-ranking members of the gang into a snitch and had the man help the Secret Service set up a new electronic doorway for ShadowCrew members to enter their website. The snitch spread the word that the new gateway was a more secure way to the website. It was the first-ever tap of a private computer network. "We became shadowcrew.com," Nagel said.[5]

Questions

1. What types of technology could big retailers use to prevent identity thieves from purchasing merchandise?

2. What can organizations do to protect themselves from hackers looking to steal account data?

3. Authorities frequently tap online service providers to track down hackers. Do you think it is ethical for authorities to tap an online service provider and read people's email? Why or why not?

4. Do you think it was ethical for authorities to use one of the high-ranking members to trap other gang members? Why or why not?

5. In a team, research the Internet and find the best ways to protect yourself from identity theft.

✳ MAKING BUSINESS DECISIONS

1. Firewall Decisions

You are the CEO of Inverness Investments, a medium-sized venture capital firm that specializes in investing in high-tech companies. The company receives more than 30,000 email messages per year. On average, there are two viruses and three successful hackings against the company each year, which result in losses to the company of about $250,000. Currently, the company has antivirus software installed but does not have any firewalls.

Your CIO is suggesting implementing 10 firewalls for a total cost of $80,000. The estimated life of each firewall is about three years. The chances of hackers breaking into the system with the firewalls installed are about 3 percent. Annual maintenance costs on the firewalls are estimated around $15,000. Create an argument for or against supporting your CIO's recommendation to purchase the firewalls.

2. Drafting an Information Security Plan

Making The Grade is a nonprofit organization that helps students learn how to achieve better grades in school. The organization has 40 offices in 25 states and more than 2,000 employees. The company is currently building a website to offer its services online. You have recently been hired by the CIO as the director of information security. Your first assignment is to develop a document discussing the importance of creating information security policies and an information security plan. Be sure to include the following:

- The importance of educating employees on information security.
- A few samples of employee information security policies.
- Other major areas the information security plan should address.
- Signs the company should look for to determine if the new site is being hacked.
- The major types of attacks the company should expect to experience.

3. Discussing the Three Areas of Security

Great Granola Inc. is a small business operating out of northern California. The company specializes in selling unique homemade granola, and its primary sales vehicle is through its website. The company is growing exponentially and expects its revenues to triple this year to $12 million. The company also expects to hire 60 additional employees to support its growing number of customers. Joan Martin, the CEO, is aware that if her competitors discover the recipe for her granola, or who her primary customers are, it could easily ruin her business. Joan has hired you to draft a document discussing the different areas of information security, along with your recommendations for providing a secure ebusiness environment.

4. College Security

Computer and online security is a growing concern for businesses of all sizes. Computer security issues range from viruses to automated Internet attacks to outright theft, the result of which is lost information and lost time. Security issues pop up in news articles daily, and most business owners understand the need to secure their businesses. Your college is no different from any other business when it comes to information security. Draft a document identifying the questions you should ask your college's CIO to ensure information security across your campus.

CHAPTER 19   # Managing Organizational Projects

19.1. Explain project management and identify the primary reasons projects fail.

19.2. Identify the primary project planning diagrams.

19.3. Identify the three different types of outsourcing along with their benefits and challenges.

Using Project Management to Deliver Successful Projects

LO 19.1 Explain project management and identify the primary reasons projects fail.

No one would think of building an office complex by turning loose 100 different construction teams to build 100 different rooms with no single blueprint or agreed-upon vision of the completed structure. Yet this is precisely the situation in which many large organizations find themselves when managing information technology projects. Organizations routinely overschedule their resources (human and otherwise), develop redundant projects, and damage profitability by investing in nonstrategic efforts that do not contribute to the organization's bottom line. Business leaders face a rapidly moving and unforgiving global marketplace that will force them to use every possible tool to sustain competitiveness; project management is one of those tools. For this reason, business personnel must anticipate being involved in some form of project management during their career. Figure 19.1 displays a few examples of the different types of projects organizations encounter.

FIGURE 19.1

Types of Organizational Projects

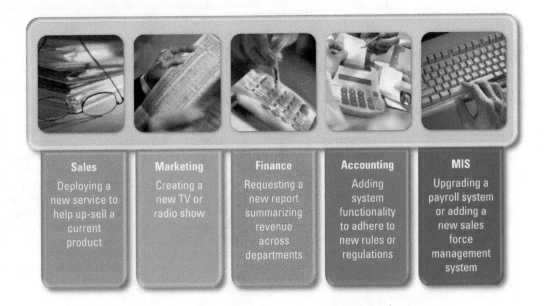

Sales	Marketing	Finance	Accounting	MIS
Deploying a new service to help up-sell a current product	Creating a new TV or radio show	Requesting a new report summarizing revenue across departments	Adding system functionality to adhere to new rules or regulations	Upgrading a payroll system or adding a new sales force management system

FIGURE 19.2

Examples of Tangible
and Intangible
Benefits

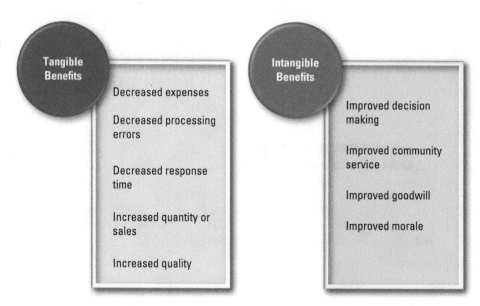

Tangible Benefits

Decreased expenses

Decreased processing errors

Decreased response time

Increased quantity or sales

Increased quality

Intangible Benefits

Improved decision making

Improved community service

Improved goodwill

Improved morale

Tangible benefits are easy to quantify and typically measured to determine the success or failure of a project. *Intangible benefits* are difficult to quantify or measure (see Figure 19.2 for examples). One of the most difficult decisions managers make is identifying the projects in which to invest time, energy, and resources. An organization must choose what it wants to do—justifying it, defining it, and listing expected results—and how to do it, including project budget, schedule, and analysis of project risks. *Feasibility* is the measure of the tangible and intangible benefits of an information system. Figure 19.3 displays several types of feasibility studies business analysts can use to determine the projects that best fit business goals.

With today's volatile economic environment, many businesses are being forced to do more with less. Businesses today must respond quickly to a rapidly changing business environment by continually innovating goods and services. Effective project management provides a controlled way to respond to changing market conditions, to foster global communications, and to provide key metrics to enable managerial decision making.

BALANCE OF THE TRIPLE CONSTRAINT

Figure 19.4 displays the relationships among the three primary and interdependent variables in any project—time, cost, and scope. All projects are limited in some way by these three constraints. The Project Management Institute calls the framework for evaluating these competing demands *the triple constraint.*

The relationship among these variables is such that if any one changes, at least one other is likely to be affected. For example, moving up a project's finish date could mean either increasing costs to hire more staff or decreasing the scope to eliminate features or functions. Increasing a project's scope to include additional customer requests could extend the project's time to completion or increase the project's cost—or both—to accommodate the changes. Project quality is affected by the project manager's ability to balance these competing demands. High-quality projects deliver the agreed upon product or service on time and on budget. Project management is the science of making intelligent trade-offs between time, cost, and scope. Benjamin Franklin's timeless advice—*by failing to prepare, you prepare to fail*—applies to many of today's software development projects.

The Project Management Institute created the *Project Management Body of Knowledge (PMBOK)* for the education and certification of project managers. Figure 19.5 summarizes the key elements of project planning according to *PMBOK.*

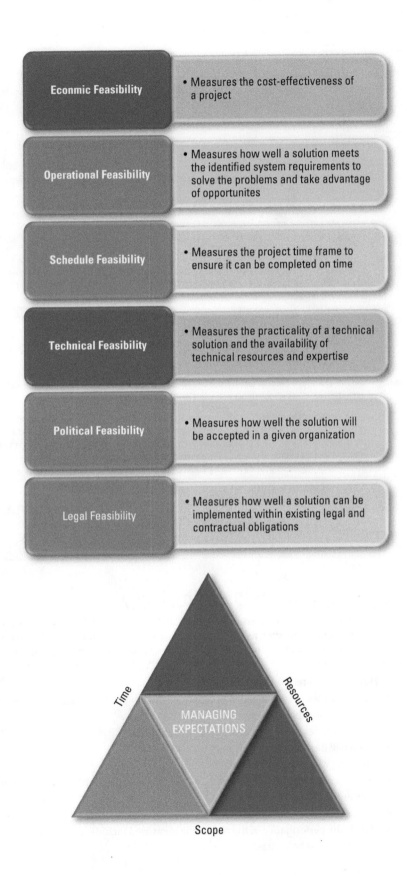

FIGURE 19.3

Types of Feasibility Studies

FIGURE 19.4

The Triple Constraint:
Changing One Changes All

Tool	Description
Communication plan	Defines the how, what, when, and who regarding the flow of project information to stakeholders and is key for managing expectations.
Executive sponsor	The person or group who provides the financial resources for the project.
Project assumption	Factors considered to be true, real, or certain without proof or demonstration. Examples include hours in a workweek or time of year the work will be performed.
Project constraint	Specific factors that can limit options, including budget, delivery dates, available skilled resources, and organizational policies.
Project deliverable	Any measurable, tangible, verifiable outcome, result, or item that is produced to complete a project or part of a project. Examples of project deliverables include design documents, testing scripts, and requirements documents.
Project management office (PMO)	An internal department that oversees all organizational projects. This group must formalize and professionalize project management expertise and leadership. One of the primary initiatives of the PMO is to educate the organization on techniques and procedures necessary to run successful projects.
Project milestone	Represents key dates when a certain group of activities must be performed. For example, completing the planning phase might be a project milestone. If a project milestone is missed, then chances are the project is experiencing problems.
Project objectives	Quantifiable criteria that must be met for the project to be considered a success.
Project requirements document	Defines the specifications for product/output of the project and is key for managing expectations, controlling scope, and completing other planning efforts.
Project scope statement	Links the project to the organization's overall business goals. It describes the business need (the problem the project will solve) and the justification, requirements, and current boundaries for the project. It defines the work that must be completed to deliver the product with the specified features and functions, and it includes constraints, assumptions, and requirements—all components necessary for developing accurate cost estimates.
Project stakeholder	Individuals and organizations actively involved in the project or whose interests might be affected as a result of project execution or project completion.
Responsibility matrix	Defines all project roles and indicates what responsibilities are associated with each role.
Status report	Periodic reviews of actual performance versus expected performance.

FIGURE 19.5

PMBOK Elements of Project Management

LO 19.2 **Identify the primary project planning diagrams.**

Primary Project Planning Diagrams

Project planning is the process of detailed planning that generates answers to common operational questions such as why are we doing this project or what is the project going to accomplish for the business? Some of the key questions project planning can help answer include:

- How are deliverables being produced?
- What activities or tasks need to be accomplished to produce the deliverables?
- Who is responsible for performing the tasks?
- What resources are required to perform the tasks?
- When will the tasks be performed?
- How long will it take to perform each task?
- Are any tasks dependent upon other tasks being completed before they can begin?
- How much does each task cost?
- What skills and experience are required to perform each task?
- How is the performance of the task being measured including quality?
- How are issues being tracked?

- How is change being addressed?
- How is communication occurring and when?
- What risks are associated with each task?

The project objectives are among the most important areas to define because they are essentially the major elements of the project. When an organization achieves the project objectives, it has accomplished the major goals of the project and the project scope is satisfied. Project objectives must include metrics so that the project's success can be measured. The metrics can include cost, schedule, and quality metrics. Figure 19.6 lists the SMART criteria—useful reminders about how to ensure the project has created understandable and measurable objectives.

The project plan is a formal, approved document that manages and controls project execution. The project plan should include a description of the project scope, a list of activities, a schedule, time estimates, cost estimates, risk factors, resources, assignments, and responsibilities. In addition to these basic components, most project professionals also include contingency plans, review and communications strategies, and a **kill switch**—a trigger that enables a project manager to close the project before completion.

A good project plan should include estimates for revenue and strategic necessities. It also should include measurement and reporting methods and details as to how top leadership will engage in the project. It also informs stakeholders of the benefits of the project and justifies the investment, commitment, and risk of the project as it relates to the overall mission of the organization.

Managers need to continuously monitor projects to measure their success. If a project is failing, the manager must cancel the project and save the company any further project costs. Canceling a project is not necessarily a failure as much as it is successful resource management as it frees resources that can be used on other projects that are more valuable to the firm.

The most important part of the plan is communication. The project manager must communicate the plan to every member of the project team and to any key stakeholders and executives. The project plan must also include any project assumptions and be detailed enough to guide the execution of the project. A key to achieving project success is earning consensus and buy-in from all key stakeholders. By including key stakeholders in project plan development, the project manager allows them to have ownership of the plan. This often translates to greater commitment, which in turn results in enhanced motivation and productivity. The two primary diagrams most frequently used in project planning are PERT and Gantt charts.

A **PERT (Program Evaluation and Review Technique) chart** is a graphical network model that depicts a project's tasks and the relationships between them. A **dependency** is a logical relationship that exists between the project tasks, or between a project task and a milestone. PERT charts define dependency between project tasks before those tasks are scheduled (see Figure 19.7). The boxes in Figure 19.7 represent project tasks, and the project manager can adjust the contents of the boxes to display various project attributes such as schedule and actual start and finish times. The arrows indicate that a task depends on the start or the completion of a different task. The **critical path** estimates the shortest path through the project ensuring all critical tasks are completed from start to finish. The red line in Figure 19.7 displays the critical path for the project.

A **Gantt chart** is a simple bar chart that lists project tasks vertically against the project's time frame, listed horizontally. A Gantt chart works well for representing the project schedule. It also shows actual progress of tasks against the planned duration. Figure 19.8 displays a software development project using a Gantt chart.

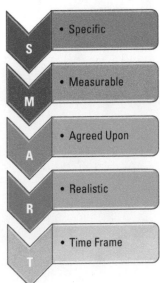

FIGURE 19.6

SMART Criteria for Successful Objective Creation

Outsourcing Projects

LO 19.3 **Identify the three different types of outsourcing along with their benefits and challenges.**

In the high-speed global business environment, an organization needs to increase profits, grow market share, and reduce costs. Two basic options are available to organizations wishing to develop and maintain their information systems—in-sourcing or outsourcing.

FIGURE 19.7

PERT Chart Expert, a PERT Chart Example

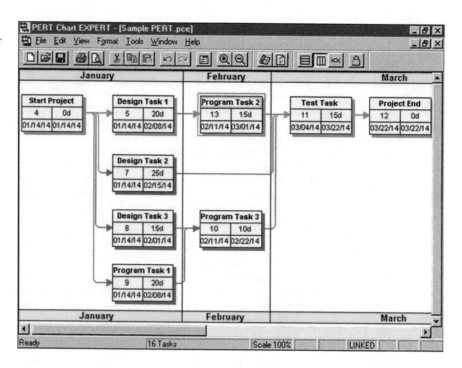

FIGURE 19.8

Microsoft Project, a Gantt Chart Example

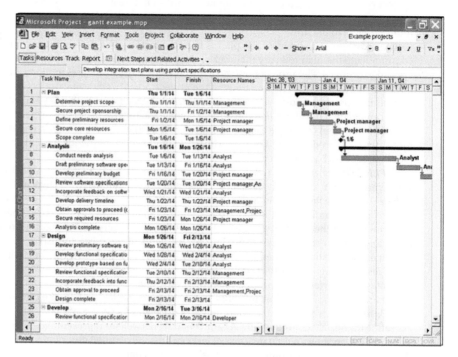

In-sourcing (in-house development) uses the professional expertise within an organization to develop and maintain its information technology systems. In-sourcing has been instrumental in creating a viable supply of IT professionals and in creating a better quality workforce combining both technical and business skills.

Outsourcing is an arrangement by which one organization provides a service or services for another organization that chooses not to perform them in-house. In some cases, the entire MIS department is outsourced, including planning and business analysis as well as the design, development, and maintenance of equipment and projects. Outsourcing can range from a large contract under which an organization such as IBM manages all MIS services for another company, to hiring contractors and temporary staff on an individual basis. Common reasons companies outsource include:

- **Core competencies.** Many companies have recently begun to consider outsourcing as a way to acquire best-practices and the business process expertise of highly skilled technology resources for a low cost. Technology is advancing at such an accelerated rate that companies often lack the technical resources required to keep current.

- **Financial savings.** It is far cheaper to hire people in China and India than pay the required salaries for similar labor in the United States.

- **Rapid growth.** Firms must get their products to market quickly and still be able to react to market changes. By taking advantage of outsourcing, an organization can acquire the resources required to speed up operations or scale to new demand levels.

- **The Internet and globalization.** The pervasive nature of the Internet has made more people comfortable with outsourcing abroad as India, China, and the United States become virtual neighbors.

Outsourcing MIS enables organizations to keep up with market and technology advances—with less strain on human and financial resources and more assurance that the IT infrastructure will keep pace with evolving business priorities (see Figure 19.9). The three forms of outsourcing options available for a project are:

1. *Onshore outsourcing*—engaging another company within the same country for services.

2. *Nearshore outsourcing*—contracting an outsourcing arrangement with a company in a nearby country. Often this country will share a border with the native country.

3. *Offshore outsourcing*—using organizations from developing countries to write code and develop systems. In offshore outsourcing the country is geographically far away.

Since the mid-1990s, major U.S. companies have been sending significant portions of their software development work offshore—primarily to vendors in India, but also to vendors in China, eastern Europe (including Russia), Ireland, Israel, and the Philippines. The big selling point for offshore outsourcing is inexpensive but good work. The overseas counterpart to an American programmer who earns as much as $63,000 per year is paid as little as $5,000 per year (see Figure 19.10). Developing countries in Asia and South Africa offer some outsourcing services but are challenged by language difference, inadequate telecommunication equipment, and regulatory obstacles. India is the largest offshore marketplace because it promotes English along with a technologically advanced population. Infosys, NIIT, Mahindra Satyam, Tata Consultancy Services, and Wipro are among the biggest Indian outsourcing service providers, each of which has a large presence in the United States.[1]

OUTSOURCING BENEFITS

The many benefits associated with outsourcing include:

- Increased quality and efficiency of business processes.

- Reduced operating expenses for head count and exposure to risk for large capital investments.

- Access to outsourcing service provider's expertise, economies of scale, best practices, and advanced technologies.

- Increased flexibility for faster response to market changes and less time to market for new products or services.

FIGURE 19.9

Outsourcing Models

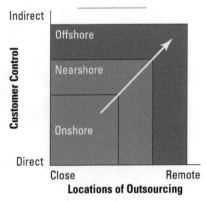

FIGURE 19.10

Typical Salary Ranges for
Computer Programmers

Country	Salary Range Per Year
China	$5,000–$9,000
India	6,000–10,000
Philippines	6,500–11,000
Russia	7,000–13,000
Ireland	21,000–28,000
Canada	25,000–50,000
United States	60,000–90,000

OUTSOURCING CHALLENGES

Outsourcing comes with several challenges. These arguments are valid and should be considered when a company is thinking about outsourcing. Many challenges can be avoided with proper research. The challenges include:

- **Length of contract.** Most companies look at outsourcing as a long-term solution with a time period of several years. Training and transferring resources around the globe is difficult and expensive, hence most companies pursuing offshore outsourcing contract for multiple years of service. A few of the challenges facing the length of the contract include:
  1. It can be difficult to break the contract.
  2. Forecasting business needs for the next several years is challenging and the contract might not meet future business needs.
  3. Re-creating an internal MIS department if the outsource provider fails is costly and challenging.

- **Threat to competitive advantage.** Many businesses view MIS as a competitive advantage and view outsourcing as a threat because the outsourcer could share the company's trade secrets.

- **Loss of confidentiality.** Information on pricing, products, sales, and customers can be a competitive asset and often critical for business success. Outsourcing could place confidential information in the wrong hands. Although confidentiality clauses contained in the contracts are supposed to protect the company, the potential risk and costs of a breach must be analyzed.

Every type of organization in business today relies on software to operate and solve complex problems or create exciting opportunities. Software built correctly can support nimble organizations and transform with them as they and their businesses transform. Software that effectively meets employee needs will help an organization become more productive and enhance decision making. Software that does not meet employee needs might have a damaging effect on productivity and can even cause a business to fail. Employee involvement in software development, along with the right implementation, is critical to the success of an organization.

OPENING CASE STUDY QUESTIONS

1. What are the three interdependent variables shaping project management? Why are these variables important to a social media software development project?

2. What are the ethical and security issues associated with outsourcing the development of a social media system?

Chapter 19 Case: Death March

Edward Yourdon's book *Death March* describes the complete software developer's guide to surviving "mission impossible" projects. MIS projects are challenging, and project managers are expected to achieve the impossible by pulling off a successful project even when pitted against impossible challenges. In *Death March,* infamous software developer Edward Yourdon presents his project classification displayed here. Yourdon measures projects based on the level of pain and chances for success.

■ **Mission Impossible Project:** This project has a great chance of success and your hard work will pay off as you find happiness and joy in the work. For example, this is the type of project where you work all day and night for a year and become the project hero as you complete the mission impossible and reap a giant promotion as your reward.

■ **Ugly Project:** This project has a high chance of success but is very painful and offers little happiness. For example, you work day and night to install a new accounting system and although successful, you hate accounting and dislike the company and its products.

■ **Kamikaze Project:** This is a project that has little chance of success but you are so passionate about the content that you find great happiness working on the project. For example, you are asked to build a website to support a cancer foundation, a cause near to your heart, but the company is nonprofit and doesn't have any funds to help buy the software you need to get everything working. You patch the system together and implement many manual work-arounds just to keep the system functioning.

■ **Suicide Project:** This project has no chance of success and offers you nothing but pain. This is the equivalent of your worst nightmare project. Word of caution, avoid suicide projects![2]

Questions

1. Analyze your school and work projects and find a project that would fit in each box in the accompanying figure.
2. What could you have done differently on your suicide project to ensure its success?
3. What can you do to avoid being placed on a suicide project? Given the choice, which type of project would you choose to work on and why?

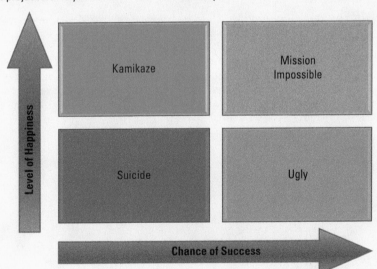

CHAPTER 9

Enabling the Organization—Decision Making

9.1. Explain the importance of decision making for managers at each of the three primary organization levels along with the associated decision characteristics.

9.2. Classify the different operational support systems, managerial support systems, and strategic support systems, and explain how managers can use these systems to make decisions and gain competitive advantages.

9.3. Describe artificial intelligence, and identify its five main types.

Making Business Decisions

Porter's strategies outlined in Unit 1 suggest entering markets with a competitive advantage in either overall cost leadership, differentiation, or focus. To achieve these results, managers must be able to make decisions and forecast future business needs and requirements. The most important and most challenging question confronting managers today is how to lay the foundation for tomorrow's success while competing to win in today's business environment. A company will not have a future if it is not cultivating strategies for tomorrow. The goal of this section is to expand on Porter's Five Forces Model, three generic strategies, and value chain analysis to demonstrate how managers can learn the concepts and practices of business decision making to add value. It will also highlight how companies heading into the 21st century are taking advantage of advanced MIS capable of generating significant competitive advantages across the value chain.

As we discussed in Unit 1, decision making is one of the most important and challenging aspects of management. Decisions range from routine choices, such as how many items to order or how many people to hire, to unexpected ones such as what to do if a key employee suddenly quits or needed materials do not arrive. Today, with massive volumes of information available, managers are challenged to make highly complex decisions—some involving far more information than the human brain can comprehend—in increasingly shorter time frames. Figure 9.1 displays the three primary challenges managers face when making decisions.

THE DECISION-MAKING PROCESS

The process of making decisions plays a crucial role in communication and leadership for operational, managerial, and strategic projects. *Analytics* is the science of fact-based decision making. There are numerous academic decision-making models; Figure 9.2 presents just one example.[2]

DECISION-MAKING ESSENTIALS

A few key concepts about organizational structure will help our discussion of MIS decision-making tools. The structure of a typical organization is similar to a pyramid,

LO 9.1 Explain the importance of decision making for managers at each of the three primary organization levels along with the associated decision characteristics.

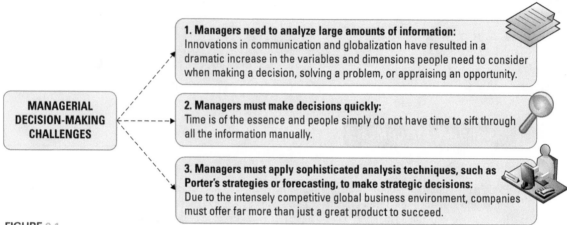

MANAGERIAL DECISION-MAKING CHALLENGES

1. **Managers need to analyze large amounts of information:** Innovations in communication and globalization have resulted in a dramatic increase in the variables and dimensions people need to consider when making a decision, solving a problem, or appraising an opportunity.

2. **Managers must make decisions quickly:** Time is of the essence and people simply do not have time to sift through all the information manually.

3. **Managers must apply sophisticated analysis techniques, such as Porter's strategies or forecasting, to make strategic decisions:** Due to the intensely competitive global business environment, companies must offer far more than just a great product to succeed.

FIGURE 9.1

Managerial Decision-Making Challenges

and the different levels require different types of information to assist in decision making, problem solving, and opportunity capturing (see Figure 9.3).

Operational

At the *operational level,* employees develop, control, and maintain core business activities required to run the day-to-day operations. Operational decisions are considered *structured decisions,* which arise in situations where established processes offer potential solutions. Structured decisions are made frequently and are almost repetitive in nature; they affect short-term business strategies. Reordering inventory and creating the

FIGURE 9.2

The Six-Step Decision-Making Process

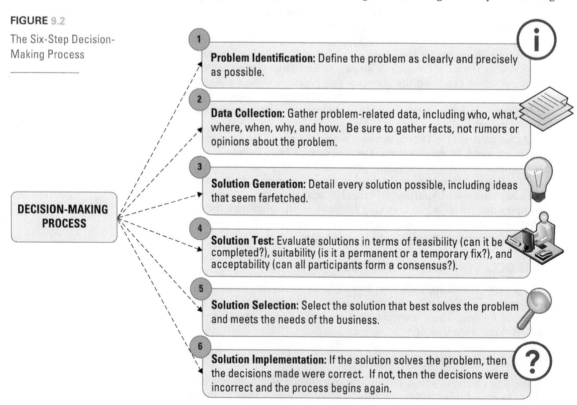

DECISION-MAKING PROCESS

1. **Problem Identification:** Define the problem as clearly and precisely as possible.

2. **Data Collection:** Gather problem-related data, including who, what, where, when, why, and how. Be sure to gather facts, not rumors or opinions about the problem.

3. **Solution Generation:** Detail every solution possible, including ideas that seem farfetched.

4. **Solution Test:** Evaluate solutions in terms of feasibility (can it be completed?), suitability (is it a permanent or a temporary fix?), and acceptability (can all participants form a consensus?).

5. **Solution Selection:** Select the solution that best solves the problem and meets the needs of the business.

6. **Solution Implementation:** If the solution solves the problem, then the decisions made were correct. If not, then the decisions were incorrect and the process begins again.

FIGURE 9.3

Common Company
Structure

employee staffing and weekly production schedules are examples of routine structured decisions. Figure 9.4 highlights the essential elements required for operational decision making. All the elements in the figure should be familiar, except metrics which are discussed in detail below.

Managerial

At the ***managerial level,*** employees are continuously evaluating company operations to hone the firm's abilities to identify, adapt to, and leverage change. A company that has a

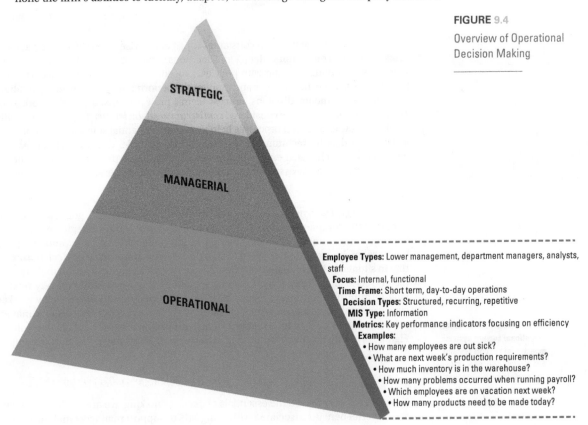

FIGURE 9.4

Overview of Operational
Decision Making

Employee Types: Lower management, department managers, analysts, staff
Focus: Internal, functional
Time Frame: Short term, day-to-day operations
Decision Types: Structured, recurring, repetitive
MIS Type: Information
Metrics: Key performance indicators focusing on efficiency
Examples:
• How many employees are out sick?
• What are next week's production requirements?
• How much inventory is in the warehouse?
• How many problems occurred when running payroll?
• Which employees are on vacation next week?
• How many products need to be made today?

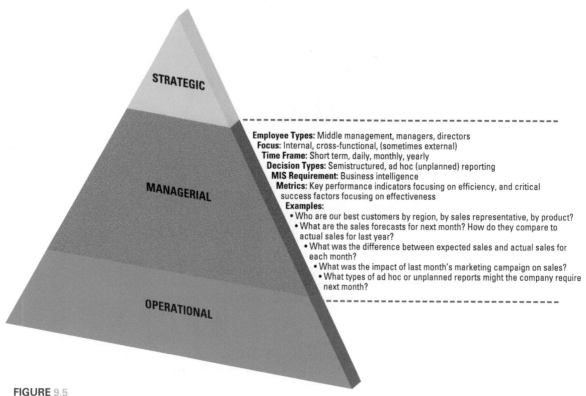

Employee Types: Middle management, managers, directors
Focus: Internal, cross-functional, (sometimes external)
Time Frame: Short term, daily, monthly, yearly
Decision Types: Semistructured, ad hoc (unplanned) reporting
MIS Requirement: Business intelligence
Metrics: Key performance indicators focusing on efficiency, and critical success factors focusing on effectiveness
Examples:
• Who are our best customers by region, by sales representative, by product?
• What are the sales forecasts for next month? How do they compare to actual sales for last year?
• What was the difference between expected sales and actual sales for each month?
• What was the impact of last month's marketing campaign on sales?
• What types of ad hoc or unplanned reports might the company require next month?

FIGURE 9.5

Overview of Managerial Decision Making

competitive advantage needs to constantly adjust and revise its strategy to remain ahead of fast-following competitors. Managerial decisions cover short- and medium-range plans, schedules, and budgets along with policies, procedures, and business objectives for the firm. They also allocate resources and monitor the performance of organizational subunits, including departments, divisions, process teams, project teams, and other work groups. These types of decisions are considered *semistructured decisions;* they occur in situations in which a few established processes help to evaluate potential solutions, but not enough to lead to a definite recommended decision. For example, decisions about producing new products or changing employee benefits range from unstructured to semistructured. Figure 9.5 highlights the essential elements required for managerial decision making.

Strategic

At the *strategic level,* managers develop overall business strategies, goals, and objectives as part of the company's strategic plan. They also monitor the strategic performance of the organization and its overall direction in the political, economic, and competitive business environment. Strategic decisions are highly *unstructured decisions,* occurring in situations in which no procedures or rules exist to guide decision makers toward the correct choice. They are infrequent, extremely important, and typically related to long-term business strategy. Examples include the decision to enter a new market or even a new industry over, say, the next three years. In these types of decisions, managers rely on many sources of information, along with personal knowledge, to find solutions. Figure 9.6 highlights the essential elements required for strategic decision making.

LO 9.2 Classify the different operational support systems, managerial support systems, and strategic support systems, and explain how managers can use these systems to make decisions and gain competitive advantages.

Support: Enhancing Decision Making with MIS

Now that we've reviewed the essentials of decision making, we are ready to understand the powerful benefits associated with using MIS to support managers making decisions.

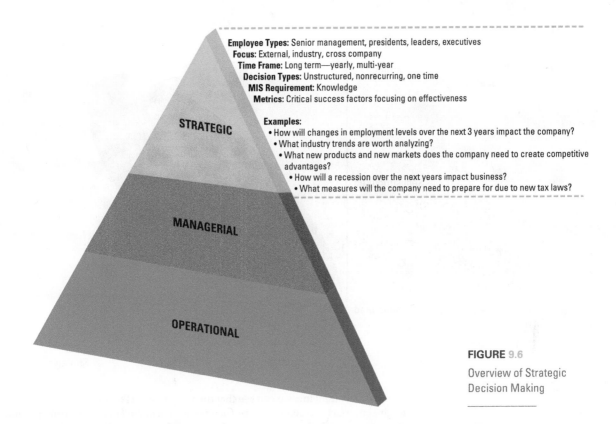

Employee Types: Senior management, presidents, leaders, executives
Focus: External, industry, cross company
Time Frame: Long term—yearly, multi-year
Decision Types: Unstructured, nonrecurring, one time
MIS Requirement: Knowledge
Metrics: Critical success factors focusing on effectiveness

Examples:
• How will changes in employment levels over the next 3 years impact the company?
• What industry trends are worth analyzing?
• What new products and new markets does the company need to create competitive advantages?
• How will a recession over the next years impact business?
• What measures will the company need to prepare for due to new tax laws?

STRATEGIC

MANAGERIAL

OPERATIONAL

FIGURE 9.6

Overview of Strategic Decision Making

A **model** is a simplified representation or abstraction of reality. Models help managers calculate risks, understand uncertainty, change variables, and manipulate time to make decisions. MIS support systems rely on models for computational and analytical routines that mathematically express relationships among variables. For example, a spreadsheet program, such as Microsoft Office Excel, might contain models that calculate market share or ROI. MIS have the capability and functionality to express far more complex modeling relationships that provide information, business intelligence, and knowledge. Figure 9.7 highlights the three primary types of management information systems available to support decision making across the company levels.

OPERATIONAL SUPPORT SYSTEMS

Transactional information encompasses all the information contained within a single business process or unit of work, and its primary purpose is to support the performance of daily operational or structured decisions. Transactional information is created, for example, when customers are purchasing stocks, making an airline reservation, or withdrawing cash from an ATM. Managers use transactional information when making structured decisions at the operational level, such as when analyzing daily sales reports to determine how much inventory to carry.

Online transaction processing (OLTP) is the capture of transaction and event information using technology to (1) process the information according to defined business rules, (2) store the information, and (3) update existing information to reflect the new information. During OLTP, the organization must capture every detail of transactions and events. A *transaction processing system (TPS)* is the basic business system that serves the operational level (analysts) and assists in making structured decisions. The most common example of a TPS is an operational accounting system such as a payroll system or an order-entry system.

FIGURE 9.7

Primary Types of MIS
Systems for Decision
Making

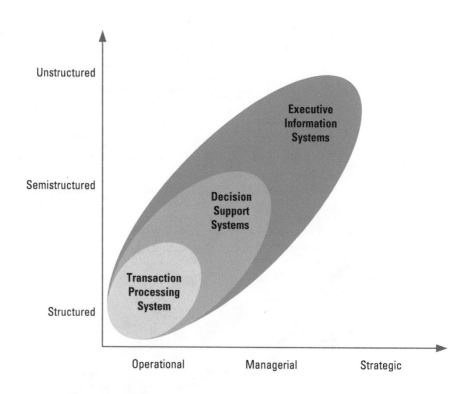

Using systems thinking, we can see that the inputs for a TPS are *source documents,* the original transaction record. Source documents for a payroll system can include time sheets, wage rates, and employee benefit reports. Transformation includes common procedures such as creating, reading, updating, and deleting (commonly referred to as CRUD) employee records, along with calculating the payroll and summarizing benefits. The output includes cutting the paychecks and generating payroll reports. Figure 9.8 demonstrates the systems thinking view of a TPS.[3]

MANAGERIAL SUPPORT SYSTEMS

Analytical information encompasses all organizational information, and its primary purpose is to support the performance of managerial analysis or semistructured decisions.

FIGURE 9.8

Systems Thinking Example
of a TPS

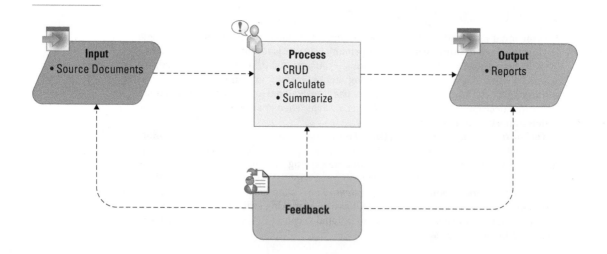

Analytical information includes transactional information along with other information such as market and industry information. Examples of analytical information are trends, sales, product statistics, and future growth projections. Managers use analytical information when making important semistructured decisions, such as whether the organization should build a new manufacturing plant or hire additional sales reps.

Online analytical processing (OLAP) is the manipulation of information to create business intelligence in support of strategic decision making. *Decision support systems (DSSs)* model information using OLAP, which provides assistance in evaluating and choosing among different courses of action. DSSs enable high-level managers to examine and manipulate large amounts of detailed data from different internal and external sources. Analyzing complex relationships among thousands or even millions of data items to discover patterns, trends, and exception conditions is one of the key uses associated with a DSS. For example, doctors may enter symptoms into a decision support system so it can help diagnose and treat patients. Insurance companies also use a DSS to gauge the risk of providing insurance to drivers who have imperfect driving records. One company found that married women who are homeowners with one speeding ticket are rarely cited for speeding again. Armed with this business intelligence, the company achieved a cost advantage by lowering insurance rates to this specific group of customers. The following are common DSS analysis techniques.

What-If Analysis

What-if analysis checks the impact of a change in a variable or assumption on the model. For example, "What will happen to the supply chain if a hurricane in South Carolina reduces holding inventory from 30 percent to 10 percent?" A user would be able to observe and evaluate any changes that occurred to the values in the model, especially to a variable such as profits. Users repeat this analysis with different variables until they understand all the effects of various situations.

Sensitivity Analysis

Sensitivity analysis, a special case of what-if analysis, is the study of the impact on other variables when one variable is changed repeatedly. Sensitivity analysis is useful when users are uncertain about the assumptions made in estimating the value of certain key variables. For example, repeatedly changing revenue in small increments to determine its effects on other variables would help a manager understand the impact of various revenue levels on other decision factors.

Goal-Seeking Analysis

Goal-seeking analysis finds the inputs necessary to achieve a goal such as a desired level of output. It is the reverse of what-if and sensitivity analysis. Instead of observing how changes in a variable affect other variables, goal-seeking analysis sets a target value (a goal) for a variable and then repeatedly changes other variables until the target value is achieved. For example, goal-seeking analysis could determine how many customers must purchase a new product to increase gross profits to $5 million.

Optimization Analysis

Optimization analysis, an extension of goal-seeking analysis, finds the optimum value for a target variable by repeatedly changing other variables, subject to specified constraints. By changing revenue and cost variables in an optimization analysis, managers can calculate the highest potential profits. Constraints on revenue and cost variables can be taken into consideration, such as limits on the amount of raw materials the company can afford to purchase and limits on employees available to meet production needs.

Figure 9.9 shows the common systems view of a DSS. Figure 9.10 shows how TPSs supply transactional data to a DSS. The DSS then summarizes and aggregates the information from the different TPSs, which assist managers in making semistructured decision.

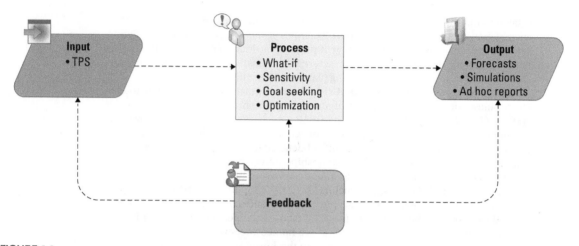

FIGURE 9.9

Systems Thinking Example of a DSS

STRATEGIC SUPPORT SYSTEMS

Decision making at the strategic level requires both business intelligence and knowledge to support the uncertainty and complexity associated with business strategies. An *executive information system (EIS)* is a specialized DSS that supports senior-level executives and unstructured, long-term, nonroutine decisions requiring judgment, evaluation, and insight. These decisions do not have a right or wrong answer, only efficient and effective answers. Moving up through the organizational pyramid, managers deal less with the details ("finer" information) and more with meaningful aggregations of information ("coarser" information). *Granularity* refers to the level of detail in the model or the decision-making process. The greater the granularity, the deeper the level of detail or fineness of data (see Figure 9.11).

A DSS differs from an EIS in that an EIS requires data from external sources to support unstructured decisions (see Figure 9.12). This is not to say that DSSs never use data from external sources, but typically DSS semistructured decisions rely on internal data only.

Visualization produces graphical displays of patterns and complex relationships in large amounts of data. Executive information systems use visualization to deliver specific key information to top managers at a glance, with little or no interaction with

FIGURE 9.10

Interaction Between TPS and DSS to Support Semistructured Decisions

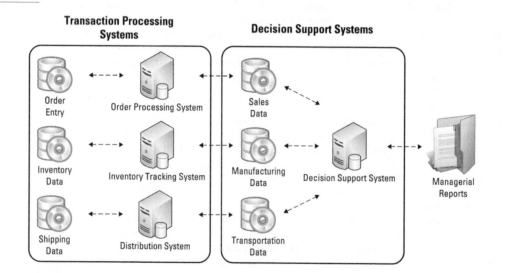

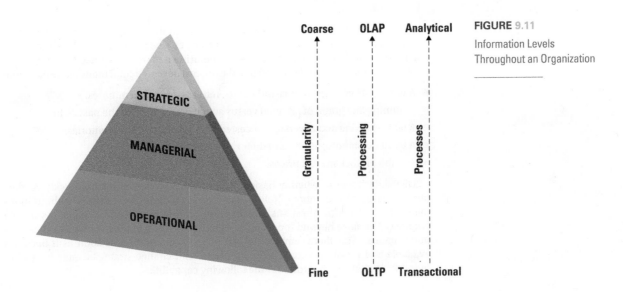

FIGURE 9.11

Information Levels
Throughout an Organization

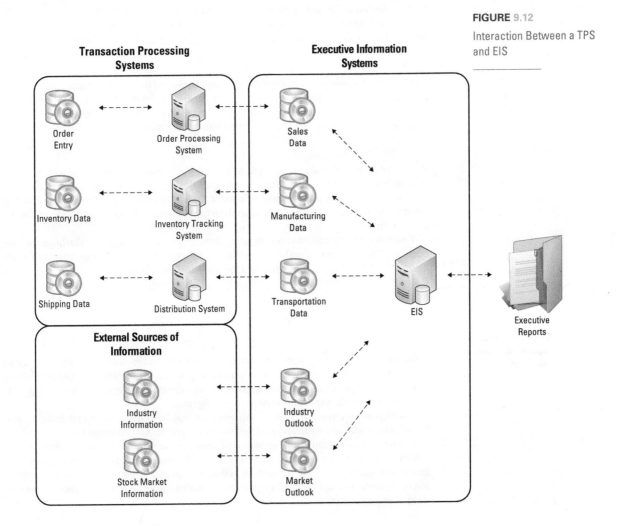

FIGURE 9.12

Interaction Between a TPS
and EIS

the system. A common tool that supports visualization is a ***digital dashboard,*** which tracks key performance indicators (KPIs) and critical success factors (CSFs) by compiling information from multiple sources and tailoring it to meet user needs. Following is a list of potential features included in a dashboard designed for a manufacturing team:

- A hot list of key performance indicators, refreshed every 15 minutes.
- A running line graph of planned versus actual production for the past 24 hours.
- A table showing actual versus forecasted product prices and inventories.
- A list of outstanding alerts and their resolution status.
- A graph of stock market prices.

Digital dashboards, whether basic or comprehensive, deliver results quickly. As they become easier to use, more employees can perform their own analyses without inundating MIS staff with questions and requests for reports. Digital dashboards enable employees to move beyond reporting to using information to directly increase business performance. With them, employees can react to information as soon as it becomes available and make decisions, solve problems, and change strategies daily instead of monthly. Digital dashboards offer the following capabilities:

Consolidation

Consolidation is the aggregation of data from simple roll-ups to complex groupings of interrelated information. For example, data for different sales representatives can then be rolled up to an office level, then a state level, then a regional sales level.

Drill-Down

Drill-down enables users to view details, and details of details, of information. This is the reverse of consolidation; a user can view regional sales data and then drill down all the way to each sales representative's data at each office. Drill-down capability lets managers view monthly, weekly, daily, or even hourly information.

Slice-and-Dice

Slice-and-dice is the ability to look at information from different perspectives. One slice of information could display all product sales during a given promotion. Another slice could display a single product's sales for all promotions. Slicing and dicing is often performed along a time axis to analyze trends and find time-based patterns in the information.

One thing to remember when making decisions is the old saying, "Garbage in, garbage out." If the transactional data used in the support system are wrong, then the managerial analysis will be wrong and the DSS will simply assist in making a wrong decision faster. Managers should also ask, "What is the DSS *not* telling me before I make my final decision?"

The Future: Artificial Intelligence

LO 9.3 Describe artificial intelligence, and identify its five main types.

Executive information systems are starting to take advantage of artificial intelligence to facilitate unstructured strategic decision making. ***Artificial intelligence (AI)*** simulates human thinking and behavior, such as the ability to reason and learn. Its ultimate goal is to build a system that can mimic human intelligence.

Intelligent systems are various commercial applications of artificial intelligence. They include sensors, software, and devices that emulate and enhance human capabilities, learn or understand from experience, make sense of ambiguous or contradictory information, and even use reasoning to solve problems and make decisions effectively. Intelligent systems perform such tasks as boosting productivity in factories by monitoring equipment and signaling when preventive maintenance is required. They are beginning to show up everywhere:

- At Manchester Airport in England, the Hefner AI Robot Cleaner alerts passengers to security and nonsmoking rules while it scrubs up to 65,600 square feet of floor per day. Laser scanners and ultrasonic detectors keep it from colliding with passengers.

- Shell Oil's SmartPump keeps drivers in their cars on cold, wet winter days. It can service any automobile built after 1987 that has been fitted with a special gas cap and a windshield-mounted transponder that tells the robot where to insert the pump.

- Matsushita's courier robot navigates hospital hallways, delivering patient files, X-ray films, and medical supplies.

- The FireFighter AI Robot can extinguish flames at chemical plants and nuclear reactors with water, foam, powder, or inert gas. The robot puts distance between human operators and the fire.[4]

AI systems increase the speed and consistency of decision making, solve problems with incomplete information, and resolve complicated issues that cannot be solved by conventional computing. There are many categories of AI systems; five of the most familiar are (1) expert systems, (2) neural networks, (3) genetic algorithms, (4) intelligent agents, and (5) virtual reality (see Figure 9.13).

EXPERT SYSTEMS

Expert systems are computerized advisory programs that imitate the reasoning processes of experts in solving difficult problems. Typically, they include a knowledge base containing various accumulated experience and a set of rules for applying the knowledge base to each particular situation. Expert systems are the most common form of AI in the business arena because they fill the gap when human experts are difficult to find or retain or are too expensive. The best-known systems play chess and assist in medical diagnosis.

NEURAL NETWORKS

A *neural network,* also called an artificial neural network, is a category of AI that attempts to emulate the way the human brain works. Neural networks analyze large quantities of information to establish patterns and characteristics in situations where the logic or rules are unknown. Neural networks' many features include:

- Learning and adjusting to new circumstances on their own.
- Lending themselves to massive parallel processing.

FIGURE 9.13

Examples of Artificial Intelligence

Artificial Intelligence

Expert Systems
Example:
Playing chess.

Neural Networks
Example: Credit card companies checking for fraud.

Genetic Algorithms
Example:
Investment companies in trading decisions.

Intelligent Agents
Example:
Environmental scanning and competitive intelligence.

Virtual Reality
Example:
Working virtually around the globe.

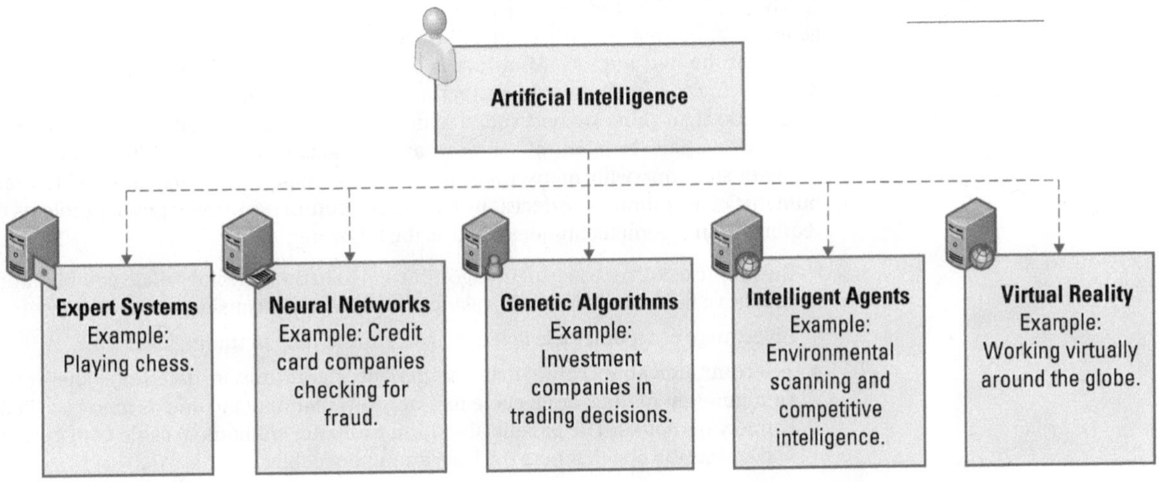

- Functioning without complete or well-structured information.
- Coping with huge volumes of information with many dependent variables.
- Analyzing nonlinear relationships in information (they have been called fancy regression analysis systems).

The finance industry is a veteran in the use of neural network technology and has been relying on various forms for over two decades. It uses neural networks to review loan applications and create patterns or profiles of applications that fall into two categories—approved or denied. Here are some examples of neural networks in finance:

- Citibank uses neural networks to find opportunities in financial markets. By carefully examining historical stock market data with neural network software, Citibank financial managers learn of interesting coincidences or small anomalies (called market inefficiencies). For example, it could be that whenever IBM stock goes up, so does Unisys stock, or that a U.S. Treasury note is selling for 1 cent less in Japan than in the United States. These snippets of information can make a big difference to Citibank's bottom line in a very competitive financial market.
- Visa, MasterCard, and many other credit card companies use a neural network to spot peculiarities in individual accounts and follow up by checking for fraud. MasterCard estimates neural networks save it $50 million annually.
- Insurance companies along with state compensation funds and other carriers use neural network software to identify fraud. The system searches for patterns in billing charges, laboratory tests, and frequency of office visits. A claim for which the diagnosis was a sprained ankle but treatment included an electrocardiogram would be flagged for the account manager.[5]

Fuzzy logic is a mathematical method of handling imprecise or subjective information. The basic approach is to assign values between 0 and 1 to vague or ambiguous information. Zero represents information not included, while 1 represents inclusion or membership. For example, fuzzy logic is used in washing machines that determine by themselves how much water to use or how long to wash (they continue washing until the water is clean). In accounting and finance, fuzzy logic allows people to analyze information with subjective financial values (intangibles such as goodwill) that are very important considerations in economic analysis. Fuzzy logic and neural networks are often combined to express complicated and subjective concepts in a form that makes it possible to simplify the problem and apply rules that are executed with a level of certainty.

GENETIC ALGORITHMS

A *genetic algorithm* is an artificial intelligence system that mimics the evolutionary, survival-of-the-fittest process to generate increasingly better solutions to a problem. A genetic algorithm is essentially an optimizing system: It finds the combination of inputs that gives the best outputs. *Mutation* is the process within a genetic algorithm of randomly trying combinations and evaluating the success (or failure) of the outcome.

Genetic algorithms are best suited to decision-making environments in which thousands, or perhaps millions, of solutions are possible. Genetic algorithms can find and evaluate solutions with many more possibilities, faster and more thoroughly than a human. Organizations face decision-making environments for all types of problems that require optimization techniques, such as the following:

- Business executives use genetic algorithms to help them decide which combination of projects a firm should invest in, taking complicated tax considerations into account.
- Investment companies use genetic algorithms to help in trading decisions.
- Telecommunication companies use genetic algorithms to determine the optimal configuration of fiber-optic cable in a network that may include as many as 100,000 connection points. The genetic algorithm evaluates millions of cable configurations and selects the one that uses the least amount of cable.

INTELLIGENT AGENTS

An *intelligent agent* is a special-purpose knowledge-based information system that accomplishes specific tasks on behalf of its users. Intelligent agents usually have a graphical representation, such as "Sherlock Holmes" for an information search agent.

One of the simplest examples of an intelligent agent is a shopping bot. A *shopping bot* is software that will search several retailer websites and provide a comparison of each retailer's offerings including price and availability. Increasingly, intelligent agents handle the majority of a company's Internet buying and selling and complete such processes as finding products, bargaining over prices, and executing transactions. Intelligent agents also have the capability to handle all supply chain buying and selling.

Another application for intelligent agents is in environmental scanning and competitive intelligence. For instance, an intelligent agent can learn the types of competitor information users want to track, continuously scan the web for it, and alert users when a significant event occurs.

Multiagent Systems and Agent-Based Modeling

What do cargo transport systems, book distribution centers, the video game market, and a flu epidemic have in common with an ant colony? They are all complex adaptive systems. By observing parts of Earth's ecosystem, like ant colonies, artificial intelligence scientists can use hardware and software models that incorporate insect characteristics and behavior to (1) learn how people-based systems behave, (2) predict how they will behave under a given set of circumstances, and (3) improve human systems to make them more efficient and effective. This process of learning from ecosystems and adapting their characteristics to human and organizational situations is called biomimicry.

In the past few years, AI research has made much progress in modeling complex organizations as a whole with the help of multiagent systems. In a multiagent system, groups of intelligent agents have the ability to work independently and to interact with each other. Agent-based modeling is a way of simulating human organizations using multiple intelligent agents, each of which follows a set of simple rules and can adapt to changing conditions.

Agent-based modeling systems are being used to model stock market fluctuations, predict the escape routes people seek in a burning building, estimate the effects of interest rates on consumers with different types of debt, and anticipate how changes in conditions will affect the supply chain, to name just a few.

VIRTUAL REALITY

Virtual reality is a computer-simulated environment that can be a simulation of the real world or an imaginary world. Virtual reality is a fast-growing area of artificial intelligence that had its origins in efforts to build more natural, realistic, multisensory human-computer interfaces. Virtual reality enables telepresence where users can be anywhere in the world and use virtual reality systems to work alone or together at a remote site. Typically, this involves using a virtual reality system to enhance the sight and touch of a human who is remotely manipulating equipment to accomplish a task. Examples range from virtual surgery, where surgeon and patient may be on opposite sides of the globe, to the remote use of equipment in hazardous environments such as chemical plants and nuclear reactors. *Augmented reality* is the viewing of the physical world with computer-generated layers of information added to it.

Virtual Workforce

At Microsoft's headquarters in Redmond, Washington, traffic congestion occurs daily for the 35,000 commuters. To alleviate the congestion Microsoft is offering its employees the ability to work virtually from home. Over 42 percent of IBM's 330,000 employees work virtually, saving over $100 million per year in real estate-related expenses. Working virtually offers several advantages such as fewer cars on the road, increases in worker productive, and decreased real estate expenses. Drawbacks include the fear among workers that they will jeopardize their careers by working from home, and some workers need a busy environment to stay productive. Virtual workers also tend to feel alone, secluded, and deprived of vital training and mentoring.

OPENING CASE STUDY QUESTIONS

1. Define the three primary types of decision-making systems, and explain how a customer of Actionly might use them to find business intelligence.

2. Describe the difference between transactional and analytical information, and determine which types Actionly uses to create a customer's digital dashboard.

3. Identify the five different types of artificial intelligence systems, and create an example of each for Actionly.

Chapter Nine Case: Defense Advanced Research Projects Agency (DARPA) Grand Challenge

The goal of the DARPA Grand Challenge is to save lives by making one-third of ground military forces autonomous or driverless vehicles by 2015. Created in response to a congressional and U.S. Department of Defense (DoD) mandate, the DARPA Grand Challenge brings together individuals and organizations from industry, the research and development (R&D) community, government, the armed services, and academia and includes students, backyard inventors, and automotive enthusiasts.

The DARPA Grand Challenge 2004

The DARPA Grand Challenge 2004 field test of autonomous ground vehicles ran from Barstow, California, to Primm, Nevada, and offered a $1 million prize. From the qualifying round at the California Speedway, 15 finalists emerged to attempt the Grand Challenge. However, the prize went unclaimed when no vehicles were able to complete the difficult desert route.

The DARPA Grand Challenge 2005

The DARPA Grand Challenge 2005 was held in the Mojave Desert and offered a $2 million prize to the team that completed the 132-mile course in the shortest time under 10 hours. The race, over desert terrain, included narrow tunnels, sharp turns, and a winding mountain pass with a sheer drop-off on one side and a rock face on the other. Five teams completed the course, and "Stanley," the Stanford Racing Team's car, won the $2 million prize with a time of 6 hours, 53 minutes.

The DARPA Grand Challenge 2007

The third DARPA Grand Challenge was an urban challenge on the site of the now-closed George Air Force Base in Victorville, California. It offered a $2 million prize to the autonomous vehicle that could cover the 60-mile course in less than 6 hours. The vehicles had to obey stop lights, navigate around other vehicles, and even merge into heavy traffic. Tartan Racing, a collaborative effort by Carnegie Mellon University and General Motors Corporation, won the prize with "Boss," a Chevy Tahoe. The Stanford Racing Team's "Junior," a 2006 Volkswagen Passat, won second prize of $1 million. "Victor Tango," a 2005 Ford Escape hybrid from Virginia Tech, won third place along with a $500,000 prize.[6]

Questions

1. How is the DoD using AI to improve its operations and save lives?

2. Why would the DoD use an event like the DARPA Grand Challenge to further technological innovation?

3. Describe how autonomous vehicles could be used by organizations around the world to improve business efficiency and effectiveness.

4. Research the Internet and determine if DARPA achieved its goal of creating one-third of ground military forces autonomous or driverless vehicles by 2015.

PLUG-IN

T2

Basic Skills Using Excel 2010

1. Describe how to open, close, and save an Excel workbook.
2. Explain how to insert and delete an Excel worksheet.
3. Describe how to insert, delete, merge, and split cells in an Excel worksheet.
4. Explain how to set up a worksheet in Excel for printing.
5. Describe how to insert and delete rows and columns in an Excel worksheet.
6. Explain how to create and edit formulas in Excel using the formula bar.
7. Describe how to create a chart using Excel.

Introduction to Excel

Microsoft Excel is a spreadsheet program that enables you to enter, manipulate, calculate, and chart data. An Excel file is referred to as a *workbook*, which is a collection of worksheets. Each *worksheet* is comprised of rows and columns of data that you can perform calculations on. It is these calculations that make Excel such a powerful tool.

You can use Excel for a wide variety of purposes, from calculating payments for a personal loan, to creating a personal budget, to tracking employee sales and calculating bonuses for your business.

This plug-in introduces the basics of using Excel 2010. It is designed to show you the nuts and bolts, along with a few fancy features, to get you off to a good start using the program. Additional material, animated tutorials, and simulated practice files that go beyond what we cover in the text can be found at https://misource.simnetonline.com. Figure T2.1 displays many of the tasks and lessons that are provided from this Web site. This plug-in will focus on the following six areas:

1. Workbooks and worksheets.
2. Working with cells and cell data.
3. Printing worksheets.
4. Formatting worksheets.
5. Formulas.
6. Working with charts and graphics.

MISource CD **Microsoft Excel Lessons**	
Introduction to Excel 2010 ■ Introduction to Excel 2010 ■ Creating a New Blank Workbook ■ Creating Workbooks Using Templates	**Setting up Workbooks for Printing** ■ Setting and Clearing the Print Area ■ Previewing a Print Area ■ Scaling Worksheets for Printing ■ Changing Worksheet Orientation ■ Setting Up Margins for Printing ■ Using Page Breaks ■ Printing Titles ■ Printing Selections, Worksheets, and Workbooks
Managing Workbooks ■ Inserting Worksheets ■ Deleting Worksheets ■ Hiding and Unhiding Worksheets ■ Moving and Copying Worksheets ■ Changing the Color of Tabs ■ Naming Worksheets ■ Arranging Workbooks ■ Splitting Workbooks ■ Changing Worksheet Views	**Working with Cells and Cell Data** ■ Entering Data in Cells ■ Editing Data in Cells ■ Inserting Data Using AutoFill ■ Clearing Cell Content ■ Cutting, Copying and Pasting Cells ■ Applying Cell Styles ■ Applying Number Formats ■ Wrapping Text in Cells ■ Changing Text Orientation ■ Converting Text to Columns ■ Changing Cell Borders
Organizing Data ■ Highlighting Cells with Conditional Formatting ■ Applying Conditional Formatting ■ Creating New Conditional Formatting Rules ■ Converting Data into Tables ■ Formatting Tables ■ Sorting Data ■ Using AutoFilter ■ Using Advanced Filter ■ Creating an Outline ■ Adding Subtotals to Worksheets ■ Adding Data Validation Criteria to Cells ■ Removing Duplicate Rows ■ Naming Ranges of Cells ■ Working with Named Ranges	**Working with Charts and Graphs** ■ Inserting a Chart ■ Changing the Chart Type ■ Changing the Chart Design ■ Changing the Chart Layout ■ Moving a Chart ■ Adding Graphics

FIGURE T2.1

MISource Excel Lessons

(*Continued*)

FIGURE T2.1

(*Continued*)

MISource CD **Microsoft Excel Lessons**	
Working with Formulas and Functions	**Formatting Worksheets**
■ Entering Simple Formulas	■ Inserting Cells
■ Using Absolute and Relative References	■ Deleting Cells
■ Creating Formulas Referencing Data in Another Worksheet	■ Merging and Splitting Cells
■ Creating Formulas Using the SUM Function	■ Inserting and Deleting Rows and Columns
■ Creating Formulas Using the AVERAGE Function	■ Hiding and Unhiding Rows and Columns
■ Creating Formulas Using the COUNT Function	■ Freezing and Unfreezing Rows and Columns
■ Creating Formulas Using the MIN and MAX Functions	■ Modifying Row Heights and Column Widths
■ Formatting Text by Using Formulas	■ Applying Themes
■ Using Financial Functions in Formulas	■ Showing and Hiding Gridlines
■ Using Conditional Logic in Formulas	■ Formatting Worksheet Backgrounds
■ Using Lookup and Reference Functions	■ Adding Headers and Footers
■ Checking Formulas for Errors	■ Working with Others
■ Troubleshooting Formulas	
	Sharing Workbooks
	■ Locking Cells and Protecting Worksheets
	■ Tracking Changes in Workbooks
	■ Adding Comments to Workbooks
	■ Setting Workbook Properties

Excel 2010 has been redesigned so that you can find and use program capabilities more easily (see Figure T2.2). The overall look and feel has been streamlined from previous versions. New technologies have been introduced that give you the ability to "browse, pick, and click" rather than select from complicated dialog boxes. You can also produce better results faster by taking advantage of the rich feature sets presented in the application's new user interface.

Workbooks and Worksheets

Opening a file retrieves it from storage and displays it on your computer screen. To open an existing workbook:

1. Open Excel.
2. Click the **File** tab, and scroll down and click **Open.**
3. The **Open** dialog box appears; make sure the location in the **Look in:** box is correct.
4. Select the workbook name in the large list box.
5. Click the **Open** button in the dialog box (see Figure T2.3).

Closing a workbook removes it from your computer screen and stores the last saved version for future use. If you have not saved your latest changes, Excel prevents you from losing work by displaying a dialog box that asks if you want to save

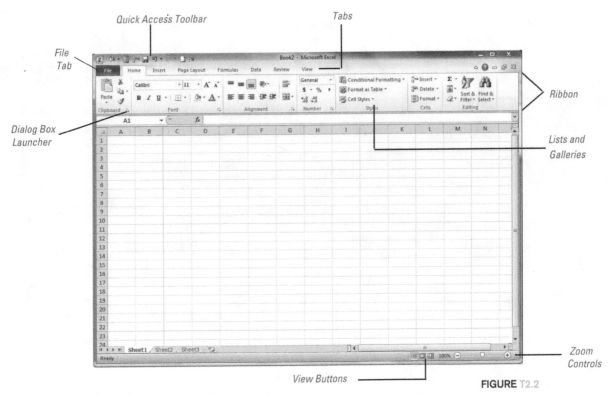

Quick Access Toolbar

File Tab

Tabs

Dialog Box Launcher

Ribbon

Lists and Galleries

Zoom Controls

View Buttons

FIGURE T2.2

Viewing the Excel Window

the changes you made before closing. To close a workbook and save your latest changes:

1. Click the **File** tab.

2. Scroll down and then select **Close Window.**

FIGURE T2.3

Opening a Workbook

If the Open dialog box appears, the last location you used appears as the default location in the box. If this is not the location of the workbook you want, click the **up one level button** to the right of the Look in: box until the correct location is displayed (you may have to double-click a different folder or drive). Another method is to click the arrow on the Look in: box to open the drop-down list, which displays different drives. Next, click the desired drive and double-click folders until you see your workbook name in the large list box.

If you have made no changes since the last time you saved the workbook, it will close immediately. If changes have been made, Excel displays a dialog box asking if you want to save the changes you made before closing. Click **Yes** to save the changes. Click **No** to close the workbook without saving your latest changes. Click **Cancel** to keep the workbook open.

CREATING WORKBOOKS USING TEMPLATES

A *template* is a file with predefined settings that you can use as a starting point for your workbook. An Excel template makes creating a new workbook easy and results in a professional appearance. Some examples of workbook templates are Balance Sheet, Sales Invoice, and Loan Amortization.

Verify the location in the Look in: box.

Click the workbook in the list box.

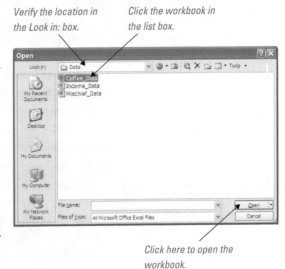

Click here to open the workbook.

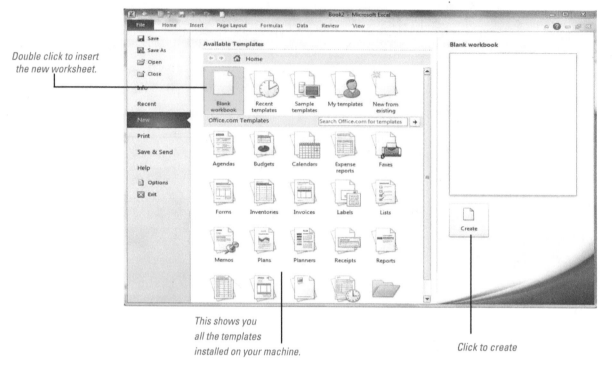

Double click to insert the new worksheet.

This shows you all the templates installed on your machine.

Click to create

FIGURE T2.4

Workbook Template

To create a workbook using a template:

1. Click the **File** tab, and then click **New.**
2. Click the templete you want under **Available Templates.**
3. Click **Create** (see Figure T2.4).

SAVING A WORKBOOK

Sometimes when you are saving a workbook, you will want to create a new folder, where you can later save other, similar workbooks. You can create this new folder at the same time you save the workbook.

To create a new folder:

1. Click the **File** tab and select **Save As,** and then select **Excel Workbook** from the Save as type: drop-down list.
2. Click the **Create New Folder** button to the right of the Save in: box.
3. Enter the name for the new folder in the dialog box that appears.
4. Click **OK.**
5. Enter the name for the file in the **File name:** box.
6. Click the **Save** button.

You can also use the Save As dialog box to save the workbook with a new name (refer to Figure T2.5):

1. Click the **File** tab, select **Save As,** and then select **Excel Workbook** from the Save as type: drop-down list.
2. Click in the **File name:** box.

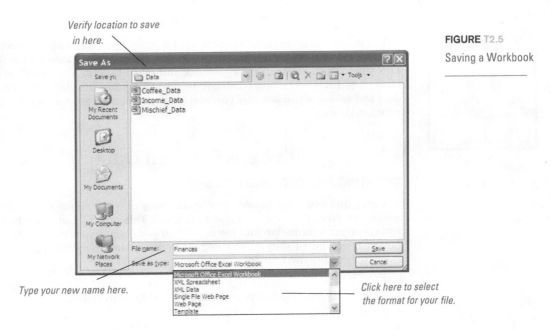

Verify location to save in here.

Type your new name here.

Click here to select the format for your file.

FIGURE T2.5

Saving a Workbook

3. Type in the new file name.

4. Click the **Save** button in the Save As dialog box.

INSERTING AND DELETING WORKSHEETS

When you create a new workbook, it contains three worksheets. However, a workbook can contain as many worksheets as you need.

To add a worksheet:

1. Right-click on any Worksheet tab.

2. Select **Insert** from the shortcut menu.

  a. To insert a simple worksheet, click the **Worksheet** icon in the dialog box.

  b. To insert a formatted worksheet, click the **Spread-sheet Solutions** tab, and click any of the template icons.

3. Click **OK** (see Figure T2.6).

> *** SHORTCUT** - *Click the Insert Worksheet button at the right edge after the last worksheet tab.*

Insert worksheet.

You can insert more than one worksheet at once. First, select the number of worksheets you want to add, by clicking on one Worksheet tab, then holding down the **CTRL** key and selecting as many more tabs as you want worksheets. Next, right-click and select **Insert.** Click the **Worksheet** icon, and click **OK.**

Sometimes you may need only one worksheet in your workbook. Limiting the worksheets in your workbook to those that contain information can make your workbook appear organized and professional.

To delete a worksheet:

1. Right-click on a Worksheet tab.

2. Select **Delete** from the menu.

FIGURE T2.6

Inserting a New Worksheet

Click the Worksheet icon.

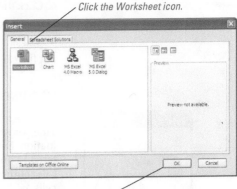

Click here to insert the new worksheet.

FIGURE T2.7

Inserting a New Cell

You can delete more than one worksheet at once. First, select all the sheet tabs you want to remove by holding the **CTRL** key down and clicking on the **Sheet tabs** you wish to delete. Next, right-click and select **Delete.** If a worksheet contains data, Excel will display a dialog box, warning that the sheet may contain data and asking if you are sure you want to permanently remove that data from your workbook.

Working with Cells and Cell Data

INSERTING AND DELETING CELLS

You may find you want to add some extra space or more information into your worksheet. To do this, you must insert a new cell. This new cell can be left blank, or you can enter information into the cell. When you insert a new cell, you have the option to shift the existing data to the right or down, allowing you to place the new cell exactly where you want it.

To insert a cell:

1. Select the cell or cells where you want to insert the new cell(s).
2. Click the **Home** tab.
3. Click the **Insert** button arrow, and then click **Insert Cells.**
4. Click the **Shift cells right** or **Shift cells down** radio button (see Figure T2.7).
5. Click **OK.**

You can customize your workbook and change the layout of data by deleting cells. Deleting cells not only deletes the information and formatting in the cell, but it also shifts the layout of the workbook. By deleting an empty cell, you shift all the surrounding cells as well.

To delete a cell:

1. Select the cell or cells that you want to delete.
2. Click the **Home** tab.
3. Click the **Delete** button arrow, and then click **Delete Cells.**
4. Click the **Shift cells left** or **Shift cells up** radio button (see Figure T2.8).
5. Click **OK.**

Pressing the **Delete** key on the keyboard will delete the contents of the cell but not the cell itself.

MERGING AND SPLITTING CELLS

FIGURE T2.8

Deleting a Cell

Merging and splitting cells is one way to control the appearance of your worksheet. Titles of worksheets are typically centered across the top of the columns of information. Excel allows you to merge and center cells to create a title that appears centered in one cell across the top of your workbook. Excel also allows you to reverse this action by splitting the cell. Splitting a cell converts a merged cell back to several cells, with the information displayed in the uppermost left cell.

To center and merge cells:

1. Select the cells you want to merge, making sure the text you want centered is in the uppermost left cell.
2. Click the **Home** tab.
3. Click the **Merge & Center** button (see Figure T2.9).

Select the cells you want to merge and center.

Click the Merge & Center button from the Home tab.

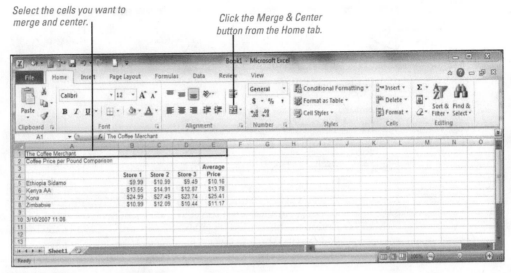

FIGURE T2.9

Merging Cells

To split merged cells:

1. Select the merged cell you want to split into several cells.

2. Click the **Home** tab.

3. Click the **Merge & Center** button arrow, and then click **Unmerge Cells.**

When you select cells to be merged, Excel will center only the data in the upper-most left cell. All other data will be lost.

CUTTING, COPYING, AND PASTING CELLS

The *Cut, Copy, and Paste commands* are used to move data and other items within a workbook and between applications. Data that are cut are removed from the document and placed on the Clipboard for later use. The Copy command places a duplicate of the selected data on the Clipboard without changing the workbook. The Paste command is used to insert items from the Clipboard into a workbook.

To cut or copy data within a workbook:

1. Select the cell or cells you want to cut or copy.

2. Click the **Home** tab.

3. Click the appropriate toolbar button:

   a. **Cut** or

   b. **Copy**

   c. The cell appears with a flashing dotted line around it.

4. Place the cursor where you want to insert data from the Clipboard.

5. Click the **Paste** toolbar button (see Figure T2.10).

When you cut or copy items, they are placed on the Clipboard. The Clipboard can store up to 24 items for use in the current document or any other application. You can view the contents of the Clipboard at any time by selecting **Clipboard** from the **Home** tab. The icons in the Clipboard identify the type of document from which each item originated (Word, Excel, Paint, etc.). A short description of an item will appear when you select it or move the cursor over its icon.

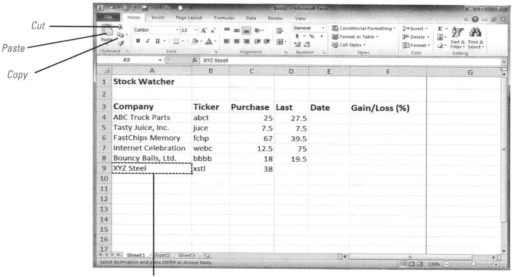

Cut

Paste

Copy

*A cell that you have copied
appears with a dotted line around it.*

FIGURE T2.10

Copying and Pasting Cells

ENTERING TEXT IN CELLS

Without text headers, descriptions, and instructions, your workbook would consist of numbers and formulas without any structure. Adding text headers to your rows and columns creates the structure for you to enter data into your workbook.

To add text to your workbook:

1. Click in the cell in which you want to add text.
2. Type your text.
3. Click outside the cell to have your entry accepted.

APPLYING NUMBER FORMATS

Formatting your numbers changes the appearance of the data in your worksheet, but does not change their value. The formatted number is displayed in the cell, and the actual value is displayed in the formula bar. Excel provides several numeric formats for you to use in your workbook, including Currency, Percentage, Date, Time, and Accounting.

To format numbers:

1. Select the cells you want to format.
2. Click the **Home** tab.
3. Click the **Number** list arrow, and then click the number format from the list (see Figure T2.11).

Under each number category, you can choose predefined formatting or create and edit formats of your own.

The Formatting toolbar allows you to add default number styles. Select the cell you want to format, and then do one of the following:

- To add the default currency style, click the **Currency Style** button on the **Home** tab.
- To add the default percent style, click the **Percent Style** button on the **Home** tab.
- To add the default comma style, click the **Comma Style** button on the **Home** tab.

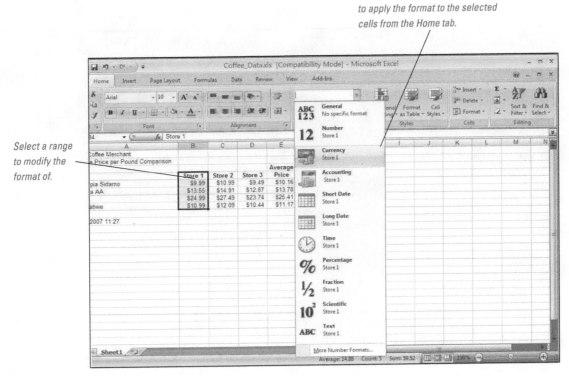

Click the Currency button to apply the format to the selected cells from the Home tab.

Select a range to modify the format of.

FIGURE T2.11

Applying Number Formats

APPLYING STYLES

A *style* is the combination of effects that can be applied at one time. Styles can include formatting such as character effects, background color, typefaces, and number formatting. Excel comes with predefined styles including Currency, Comma, and Percent styles, but also gives you the ability to create your own styles in the Style dialog box.

To apply a basic style:

1. Select the cells you want to format.

2. Click the **Home** tab.

3. Click the **Cell Styles** button, and then click the cell style that you want to apply (see Figure T2.12).

Printing Worksheets

SETTING UP THE PAGE FOR PRINTING

You may find that your worksheet is too wide to print on one sheet of paper, even with landscape orientation. Excel allows you to adjust how your worksheet will print. In the dialog box, you can adjust the scale of your worksheet, making it smaller and forcing it to fit on one page, or you can print your worksheet across multiple pages.

To set up a page to print:

1. Click the **Page Layout** tab.

- To change the page orientation click the **Orientation** button. Click **Portrait** or **Landscape** from the submenu.

- To change the page size, click the **Size** button from the submenu.

Click on Cell Styles
from the Home tab.

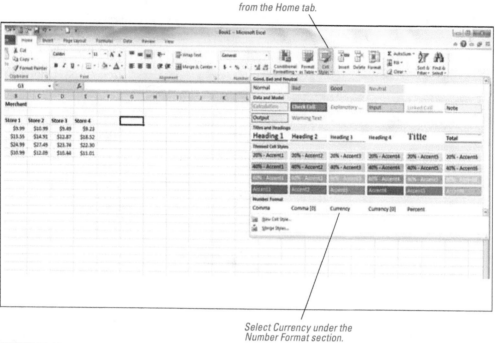

Select Currency under the
Number Format section.

FIGURE T2.12

Applying Styles

2. Click the **File** tab, select **Print,** the right side of the screen will display your print preview to review. (see Figure T2.13)
3. Click the **Print** button.

SETTING MARGINS FOR PRINTING

Margins are the blank spaces at the top, bottom, left, and right of a printed page. Excel's default margins are typically 1 inch for the top and bottom, and 0.75 inches forthe left and right. Using the Page Setup dialog box, you can easily adjust these margins.

To adjust the margins for a document:

1. Click the **Page Layout** tab.
2. Click the **Margins** button and then click **Custom Margins.**
3. Click the arrows to adjust the top, bottom, left, and right margins.
4. The Preview box shows you which part of the page you are changing (see Figure T2.14).
5. Click **OK.**

The Margins tab also allows you to adjust the placement of the header and footer. Further, you can choose to horizontally and/or vertically center the information on the printed page.

Click File Tab to modify
the print settings.

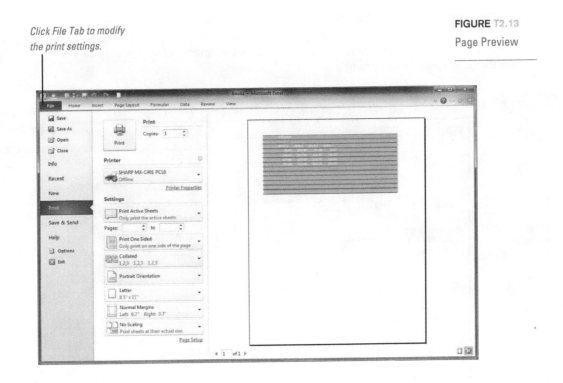

PREVIEWING A PRINT AREA

The *File Tab* gives you the option to check printer settings, orientation, margins, and see a print preview all on the same screen. Always check your layout in Print Preview before you print. Use this view to see how your information fits on each page and to verify such things as placement of page numbers, headers, and column and row labels.

Click these arrows to adjust
left and right margins.

Click these arrows to
adjust top and bottom
margins.

View your changes in
the Preview box.

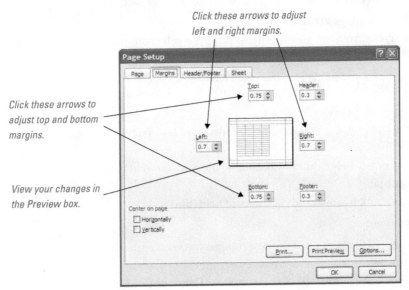

PRINTING SELECTIONS, WORKSHEETS, AND WORKBOOKS

With Excel 2010, the print preview and the print options are all accessible from the same screen, the File Tab. You can choose your printer, check your settings, and scaling all from the same screen before printing.

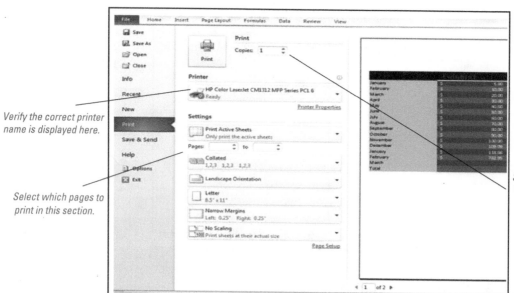

FIGURE T2.16

File Tab,

Print Options Screen

Verify the correct printer name is displayed here.

Select which pages to print in this section.

Select the number of copies to print here.

You can select the number of pages you want to print in the **Print range** section. if you have set a Print Area, then only that part of your worksheet will print.
To check your print settings and print:

1. Click the **File tab,** scroll down to **Print,** then click the **Print** button.

2. Verify that the correct printer name is displayed in the **Printer** section.

3. Verify the correct **Settings** are selected to print.

In the File tab screen, you can also specify to print the selection, the entire workbook, or just the active worksheet.

Formatting Worksheets

INSERTING ROWS AND COLUMNS

You may need to add *rows* or *columns* of new information into your worksheet.
To insert a row:

1. Click the row immediately below the location of the row you want to insert.
2. Click the **Home** tab.
3. Click the **Insert** button arrow, and click **Insert Sheet Rows.**

To insert a column:

1. Click to the right of the location of the new column you want to insert.
2. Click the **Home** tab.
3. Click the **Insert** button arrow, and click **Insert Sheet Columns** (see Figure T2.17).

FIGURE T2.17

Inserting a Row or Column

*Click rows or columns
from the Insert button.*

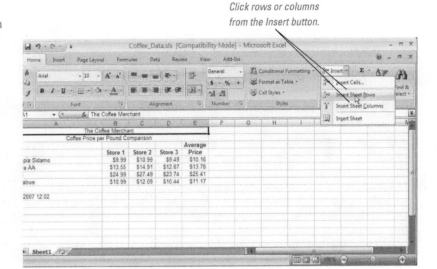

FIGURE T2.17

Inserting a Row or Column

When you insert a row or column, a smart tag will appear. Click the smart tag to choose formatting options—Format Same As Left, Format Same As Right, or Clear Formatting.

DELETING ROWS AND COLUMNS

When you delete a row or column, you are removing all of those cells from your workbook. Once you have deleted the row or column, it disappears and the rest of the columns and rows move to replace it.

To delete a row or column:

1. Select the row header or column header you want to delete.

2. Click the **Home** tab (see Figure T2.18).

3. Click the **Delete** button arrow and then click **Delete Sheet Rows** or **Delete Sheet Columns.**

Be careful. If you delete a row or column containing data, that data will be lost.

FIGURE T2.18

Delete a Row or Column

Click the row you want to delete.

*Click Delete Sheet Rows
from the Delete button.*

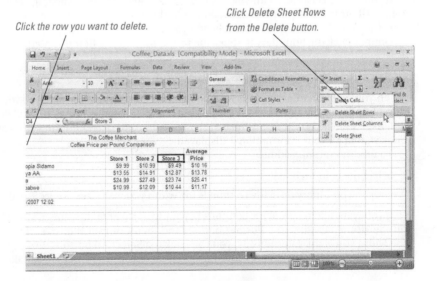

As you drag, a ToolTip indicates the current height.

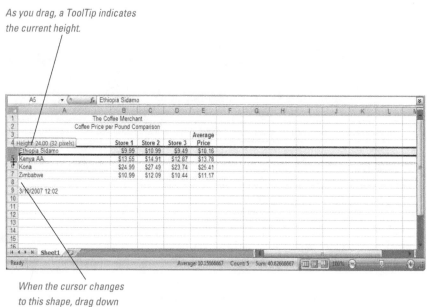

When the cursor changes to this shape, drag down to desired height.

MODIFYING ROW HEIGHTS

When you first enter data in your workbook, Excel automatically sets the rows of your worksheet according to preferences. You may want to make rows a different height from this default setting.

To modify row heights:

1. Select the row or rows you want to change.

2. Drag the *boundary* (the physical line that separates each column and row) until the row is the height you want (see Figure T2.19).

If you want to change all the rows in your worksheet to the same height, click the **Select All** button (the gray box above Row 1 and to the left of Column A) and then drag the boundary of any row to the height you want.

Double-click the boundary to make the row automatically fit the contents.

MODIFYING COLUMN WIDTHS

When you first enter data in your workbook, Excel automatically sets the widths of the columns. As you type data into multiple columns, you may find that Excel does not display all the text in a cell. You can change the widths of columns in your workbook so that all your information is displayed.

To modify column widths:

1. Select the column or columns you want to change.

2. Drag the boundary until the column is the width you want (see Figure T2.20).

If you want to change all the columns in your worksheet to the same width, click on the **Home** tab, then the **Format** button, and then **Column Width,** and type in the width you want. Alternatively, you can click the **Select All** button (the gray box above Row 1 and to the left of Column A) and then drag the boundary. To make the

FIGURE T2.20

Modifying Column Widths

_____

When the cursor changes to this shape, drag across to desired width.

As you drag, a ToolTip indicates the current width.

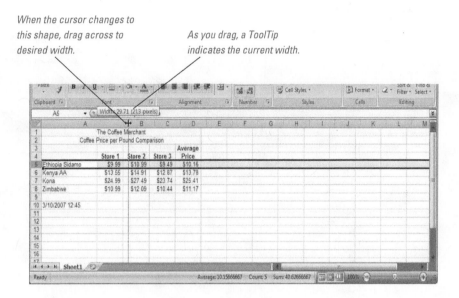

column automatically fit the contents of the selected cell, double-click the boundary to the right of the column.

Formulas

ENTERING FORMULAS

A *formula* is an equation that performs calculations between cells in a worksheet or table. A formula always begins with an equal sign. A simple formula may contain cell references and operators.

To enter a formula:

1. Click the cell in which you want to enter the formula.
2. Type = (an equal sign).
3. Type the formula.
4. Click outside the cell or press **Enter** (see Figure T2.21).

If a formula has more than one operator, Excel will perform mathematical operations in this order:

- Exponentiation.
- Multiplication and division.
- Addition and subtraction.

Adding parentheses around an operation will override this order, forcing Excel to perform calculations within the parentheses first.

USING THE FORMULA BAR

To enter a formula in the formula bar:

1. Select the cell in which you want to add the formula.
2. In the formula bar, type = (an equal sign).

Every formula begins with an equal sign.

Cell references provide the values to be used.

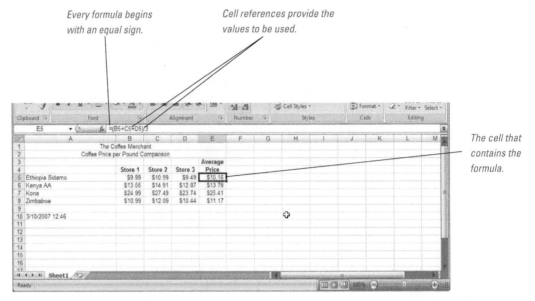

The cell that contains the formula.

Entering a Formula

3. Enter the formula (including any functions, operators, references, and/or constants).

4. Click the **Enter Formula** button (see Figure T2.22).

Formulas can be complex equations. Often when you first enter a formula, you will not get the result you intended. This may be because a cell reference has changed, or because the operations are being performed in an undesired order. Use the formula bar when you need to edit a formula.

Click the Enter Formula button when you are done.

Click inside the formula bar to edit the formula.

FIGURE T2.22

Using the Formula Bar

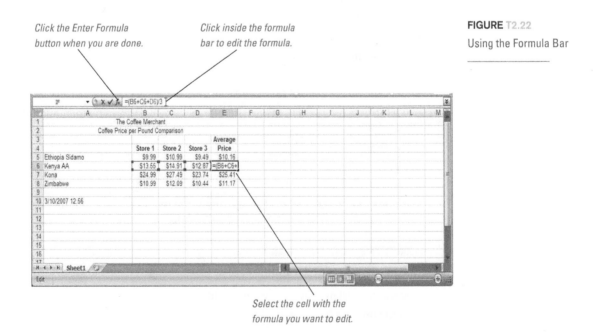

Select the cell with the formula you want to edit.

FIGURE T2.23

Using Absolute and
Relative References

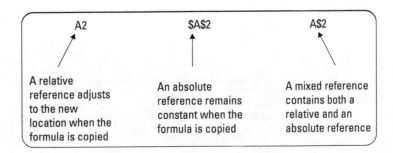

To edit a formula using the formula bar:

1. Select the cell containing the formula you want to change.
2. Click inside the formula bar.
3. Click and drag to highlight the part of the formula you want to change.
4. Make the changes to the formula.
5. Click the **Enter Formula** button.

USING ABSOLUTE AND RELATIVE REFERENCES

Cell references can be relative, absolute, or mixed. A *relative reference* is a reference that adjusts to the new location in the worksheet when the formula is copied. An *absolute reference* is a reference whose location remains constant when the formula is copied. A *mixed reference* is a reference that contains both a relative and an absolute reference. Figure T2.23 displays an example of each.

To enter an absolute or relative reference:

1. Select the cell to enter a formula.
2. Type the = (equal sign) and the *name of the cell.*
   - To enter an absolute reference, type a **$,** *the column name*, another **$,** and *the row name* (e.g., $A$1).
   - To enter a mixed reference, type a *relative reference* and an *absolute reference* in the cell reference (e.g., A$1 or A1$).

By default, formulas use relative references. If you want your formula to have an absolute reference, you must change the reference to absolute.

USING THE SUM FUNCTION

The *SUM mathematical function* is used to add several cells together. Instead of writing a formula with several references separated by a plus sign, you can sum a range of cells. A SUM function looks like this: =**SUM(A3:A6).**

To use the SUM function:

1. Select the cell in which you want to enter the function.
2. Click the **Insert Function** button *(fx)* to the left of the formula bar (view in Figure T2.21).
3. Click **SUM** from the list of **Most Recently Used** in the **Or select a category:** drop-down box, and click **OK.**
4. Enter the range of cells that you want to add.
5. Click **OK** (see Figure T2.24).

FIGURE T2.24

Insert Functions

Search for a function.

Choose the function that you want from the dialog box.

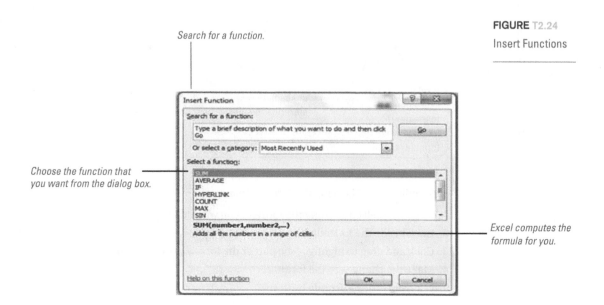

Excel computes the formula for you.

When you click an *argument box,* a description of the argument appears below the description of the function. An *argument* is a name for a value, expression, or cell reference that is passed to the function for its use in calculating an answer. As you enter arguments, the dialog box will display the results of your formula.

If the SUM function is not in your list of most recently used functions, click the arrow next to the **Or select a category:** box, click **Math & Trig,** and select **SUM** from that list of functions.

USING THE MIN AND MAX FUNCTIONS

The *MIN (minimum) statistical function* will give you the smallest value in a range of values. The *MAX (maximum) statistical function* will give you the largest value in a range of values. These functions look like this:

MIN function: =MIN(A3:A6)

MAX function: =MAX(A3:A6)

To use the MIN and MAX functions:

1. Select the cell in which you want to enter the function.
2. Click the **Insert Function** button on the formula bar.
3. Click **MIN** or **MAX** from the list of **Most Recently Used** functions and click **OK.**
4. If necessary, enter the range of cells.
5. Click **OK** (see Figure T2.25).

If the MIN or MAX functions are not in your list of **Most Recently Used** functions, click the arrow next to the **Or select a category:** box, click **Statistical,** and select **MIN** or **MAX** from that list of functions.

When you click an argument box, a description of the argument appears below the description of the function. As you enter arguments, the dialog box will display the results of your formula. By default, Excel will enter a range of contiguous cells for you.

FIGURE T2.25

Using the MIN and MAX
Function

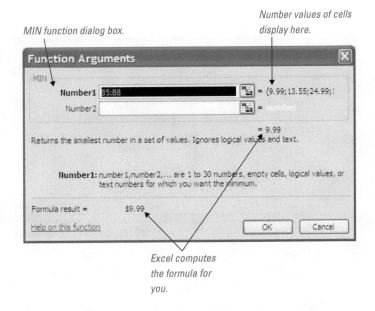

MIN function dialog box.

Number values of cells display here.

Excel computes the formula for you.

USING THE DATE OR NOW FUNCTION

Use the *Date & Time function* or the *NOW function* to insert the date and time into your workbook. The date and time will be displayed at all times, but will only be updated when the worksheet is calculated. The NOW function looks like this:

=**NOW**()

To use the NOW function:

1. Select the cell in which you want to enter the function.
2. Click the **Insert Function** button on the formula bar.
3. Click **NOW** from the list of **Most Recently Used** or **Date & Time** functions and click **OK.**
4. The NOW function takes no arguments.
5. Click **OK** (see Figure T2.26).

The NOW function uses the computer's system clock to determine the date and time.

Working with Charts and Graphics

CREATING A CHART

A *chart* is a visual representation of data from your workbook. Charts add a visual element to your workbook and help convey the information in a simple, easy-to-understand manner (see Figure T2.27).

To create a chart:

1. Select the data you want to use to create a chart.
2. Click the **Insert** tab.
3. Use one of the following methods:

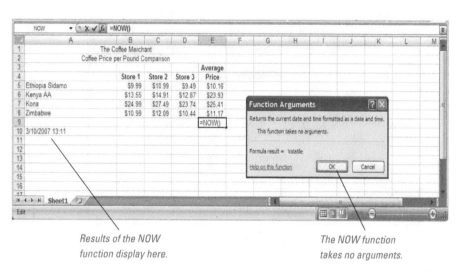

*Results of the NOW
function display here.*

*The NOW function
takes no arguments.*

- **Basic Chart Types.** Click a **chart button** (Column, Line, Pie, Bar, Area, Scatter, Other Charts) in the Charts group, and then click the chart type you want.
- **All Chart Types.** Click the **Charts Dialog Box Launcher,** click a **category** in the left pane, click a **chart,** and then click **OK.**

*Cells A5 : A8 and
B4 : B8 are selected.*

*Cells B5 : B8 display
as bars in the chart.*

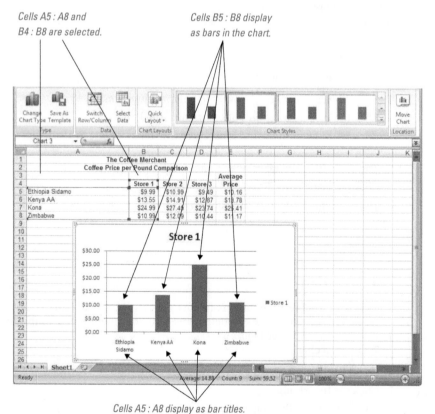

Cells A5 : A8 display as bar titles.

FIGURE T2.28

Modifying Charts

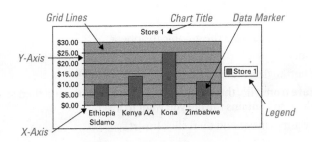

MODIFYING CHARTS

When you modify a chart, you can change any of the options that belong to that chart type. Modifying a chart allows you to change the text of the chart and how it appears on the chart. This includes titles, legends, axes, data labels, and data tables (refer to Figure T2.28).

To change chart elements:

1. Select the chart you want to modify and click the **Design** tab under **Chart Tools.**

   ■ To change a chart type, click the **Change Chart Type** button.

   ■ To change a chart layout and style, click the scroll-up or -down arrow, or click the **More** list arrow in the **Chart Layouts** group, and then click the layout you want.

   ■ To change the chart title, click the **Chart Titles** button.

   ■ To change the chart labels, click the **Legend** button.

To delete a chart, select the chart and press the **Delete** key.

MOVING A CHART

When you create a chart, Excel places the chart in the middle of the worksheet. However, the chart may be covering data that you want to view. You can move a chart by selecting it and then dragging it anywhere on the worksheet.

To move a chart by dragging:

1. Select the chart you want to move.
2. Click in the chart area margin.
3. With your left mouse depressed, drag the chart to the new location on the worksheet.
4. Release the mouse button.

ADDING GRAPHICS

A *graphic* is a drawing or illustration that can be added to your workbooks. You can add drawing objects such as AutoShapes from the Drawing toolbar. You can also insert clip art and other graphic files into your workbook. These images are embedded objects, meaning they become part of the new document.

To add a graphic to a workbook:

1. Place your cursor where you want the graphic to appear.
2. Click the **Insert** tab.
3. Click the **Picture** button (see Figure T2.29).
4. Select **Insert Picture from File,** then click the **Look in:** list arrow, and then select the drive and folder that contains the file you want to insert.
5. Click the file you want to insert and then click **Insert.**

Point to Picture from the Insert tab.

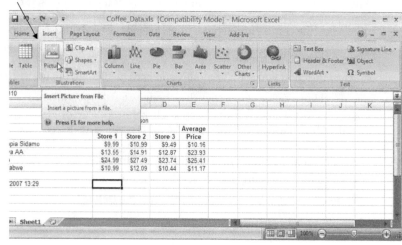

★ PLUG-IN SUMMARY

Microsoft Excel 2010 is a general-purpose electronic spreadsheet used to organize, calculate, and analyze data. The tasks you can perform with Excel range from preparing a simple invoice to managing an accounting ledger for a business. Six areas in Excel were covered in this plug-in:

1. Workbooks and worksheets.
2. Working with cells and cell data.
3. Printing worksheets.
4. Formatting worksheets.
5. Formulas.
6. Working with charts and graphics.

★ MAKING BUSINESS DECISIONS

1. Stock Watcher

Mark Martin has created a basic stock watcher worksheet that he uses to report on gains or losses from when he purchased the stock and the last recorded date and price. Mark has given you a snapshot of his spreadsheet (see Figure T2.30) that you can use to re-create this spreadsheet for yourself. Here are some basic steps to follow:

1. Create a new workbook.
2. Enter all the information provided in Figure T2.30.

FIGURE T2.30

Stock Watcher Data

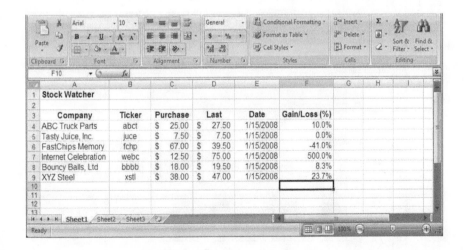

3. Apply the Currency format to the respective columns.

4. The date should be entered as a function. **Hint:** Use the NOW function.

5. Enter a formula for the **Gain/Loss (%)** column. **Hint:** You should subtract the **Last** column from the **Purchase** column, and then divide by the **Purchase** column.

6. Format for percent in the **Gain/Loss (%)** column.

2. Total Mischief

Mischief, Inc., is a regional pet toy supplier that tracks its business sales in a spreadsheet. The owner, Lisa Derrick, has provided you with a skeleton worksheet, **T2_TotalMischief_ Data.xls,** with the totals for each quarter by sales region. Lisa needs you to total each column and row, and then provide her with a clustered column chart of each region by quarter. See Figure T2.31 for a sample of what Lisa would like you to do.

3. Recycling Can

For the past 10 years, five Colorado cities have held a recycling contest to see which city does the best job of recycling plastic, glass, and aluminum. Those participating in this year's contest are Arvada, Centennial, Lakewood, Highlands Ranch, and Parker.

To make the contest fair for both large and small cities, the winning city will be the one that recycles the largest number of cans per capita—the number of cans recycled divided by the number of city residents.

FIGURE T2.31

Total Mischief Spreadsheet

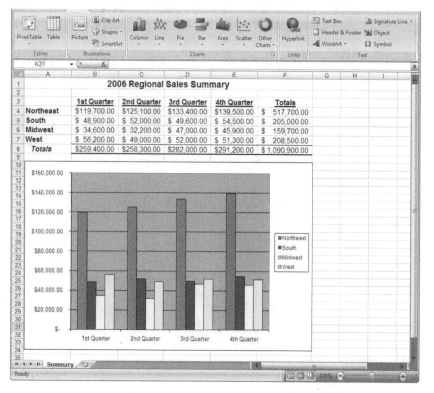

FIGURE T2.32

Recycling Can Contest
Worksheet

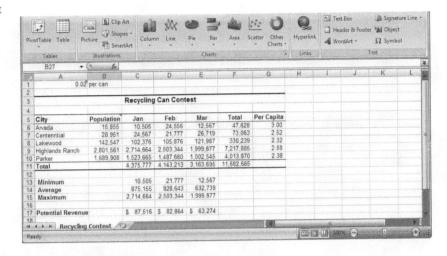

You have been asked to help the coordinator, Jill Slater, to compile the numbers in an Excel worksheet and create the formulas to compute the total recycling by city each month, total recycling for all cities each month, and the per capita recycling value that determines the contest winner. In addition, Jill wants to know a few statistics about the monthly recycling efforts, including the minimum, average, and maximum number of cans recycled. Jill has provided you with sample data, **T2_RecyclingCans_Data.xls.** Figure T2.32 shows a sample of what Jill would like to see as a completed worksheet.

4. MusicPlayerz Sales Projections

MusicPlayerz is a wholesale MP3 distributor headquartered in Morrison, Colorado. Corporate buyers for the retail stores contract with MusicPlayerz to supply and ship MP3s to warehouses scattered throughout the western United States. MusicPlayerz chief procurement officer Julianne Beekman oversees the purchase and distribution operations for all divisions from the Morrison office.

MusicPlayerz also maintains a small Web site from which it sells to consumers. While the online store is not a large part of the revenue stream, it is an essential and growing part of MusicPlayerz's business. Julianne has developed a sales report for the coming year, using the previous year's figures as the basis of the projection. Julianne wants to investigate sales predictions based on the assumption that next year's wholesale sales will increase by 10 percent for each product included in the projection.

Julianne has asked you to complete the worksheet she has provided you, **T2_Music-Playerz_Data.xls,** for her presentation at the annual board meeting next month. You will have to calculate the following:

- Projected 2008 sales (this is 10 percent more than 2007 figures).
- Gross sales (this is the projected 2008 sales times the price).
- Profit.
- Percent of sales.

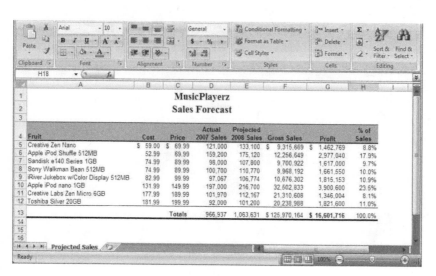

Fruit	Cost	Price	Actual 2007 Sales	Projected 2008 Sales	Gross Sales	Profit	% of Sales
Creative Zen Nano	$ 59.00	$ 69.99	121,000	133,100	$ 9,315,669	$ 1,462,769	8.8%
Apple iPod Shuffle 512MB	52.99	69.99	159,200	175,120	12,256,649	2,977,040	17.9%
Sandisk e140 Series 1GB	74.99	89.99	98,000	107,800	9,700,922	1,617,000	9.7%
Sony Walkman Bean 512MB	74.99	89.99	100,700	110,770	9,968,192	1,661,550	10.0%
iRiver Jukebox w/Color Display 512MB	82.99	99.99	97,067	106,774	10,676,302	1,815,153	10.9%
Apple iPod nano 1GB	131.99	149.99	197,000	216,700	32,502,833	3,900,600	23.5%
Creative Labs Zen Micro 6GB	177.99	189.99	101,970	112,167	21,310,608	1,346,004	8.1%
Toshiba Silver 20GB	181.99	199.99	92,000	101,200	20,238,988	1,821,600	11.0%
		Totals	966,937	1,063,631	$ 125,970,164	$ 16,601,716	100.0%

Figure T2.33 shows a sample of what Julianne would like to see as a completed work-sheet.

PLUG-IN

T3

Problem Solving Using Excel 2010

1. Describe how to create and sort a list using Excel.
2. Explain why you would use conditional formatting using Excel.
3. Describe the use of AutoFilter using Excel.
4. Explain how to use the Subtotal command using Excel.
5. Describe the use of a PivotTable using Excel.

Introduction

If you routinely track large amounts of information, such as customer mailing lists, phone lists, product inventories, sales transactions, and so on, you can use the extensive list-management capabilities of Excel to make your job easier.

In this plug-in you will learn how to create a list in a workbook, sort the list based on one or more fields, locate important records by using filters, organize and analyze entries by using subtotals, and create summary information by using pivot tables and pivot charts. The lists that you create will be compatible with Microsoft Access 2010, and if you are not already familiar with Access, the techniques that you learn here will give you a head start on learning several database commands and terms. Plug-In T6, "Basic Skills and Tools Using Access 2010," will provide detail on many of the Access database commands and terms.

There are five areas in this plug-in:

1. Lists.
2. Conditional formatting.
3. AutoFilter.
4. Subtotals.
5. PivotTables.

Lists

A *list* is a collection of rows and columns of consistently formatted data adhering to somewhat stricter rules than an ordinary worksheet. To build a list that works with all of Excel's list-management commands, you need to follow a few guidelines.

When you create a list, keep the following in mind:

- Maintain a fixed number of columns (or categories) of information; you can alter the number of rows as you add, delete, or rearrange records to keep your list up to date.
- Use each column to hold the same type of information.
- Don't leave blank rows or columns in the list area; you can leave blank cells, if necessary.
- Make your list the only information in the worksheet so that Excel can more easily recognize the data as a list.
- Maintain your data's integrity by entering identical information consistently. For example, don't enter an expense category as *Ad* in one row, *Adv* in another, and *Advertising* in a third if all belong to the same classification.

To create a list in Excel, you would follow these steps:

1. Open a new workbook or a new sheet in an existing workbook.
2. Create a column heading for each field in the list, format the headings in **bold** type, and adjust their alignment.
3. Format the cells below the column headings for the data that you plan to use. This can include number formats (such as currency or date), alignment, or any other formats.
4. Add new records (your data) below the column headings, taking care to be consistent in your use of words and titles so that you can organize related records into groups later. Enter as many rows as you need, making sure that there are no empty rows in your list, not even between the column headings and the first record. See Figure T3.1 for a sample list.

SORTING ROWS AND COLUMNS

Once your records are organized into a list, you can use several commands on the Data menu to rearrange and analyze the data. The *Sort* command allows you to

FIGURE T3.1

An Excel List

Each column represents a field containing one type of information.

Each row represents a record in the list.

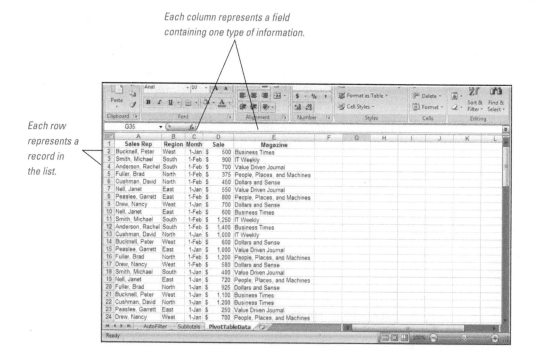

FIGURE T3.2

A Sorted List

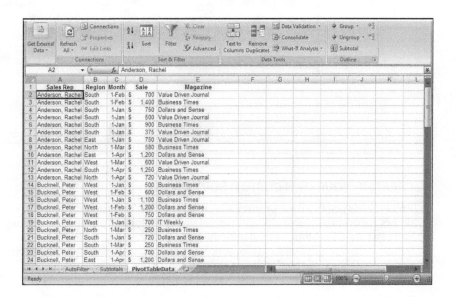

arrange the records in a different order based on the values in one or more columns. You can sort records in ascending or descending order or in a custom order, such as by days of the week, months of the year, or job title.

To sort a list based on one column, follow these steps:

1. Select the **SortData** worksheet from the **T3_ProblemSolving_Data.xls** workbook that accompanies this textbook.
2. Click any cell in the **Sales Rep** column; you want to use this column as the basis for sorting the list.
3. Click the **Data** tab.
4. Click the **Ascending** button to specify the order to sort by (A to Z, lowest to highest, earliest date to latest).

Your screen will look similar to Figure T3.2.

SORTING MORE THAN ONE COLUMN

If you have records in your list that have identical entries in the column you are sorting, you can specify additional sorting criteria to further organize your list.

To sort a list based on two or three columns follow these steps:

1. Click any cell in the **Sales Rep** column.
2. Click the **Data** tab, and then click the **Sort** button. The **Sort** dialog box opens.
3. Click the **Column** list arrow, and then select the **Sales Rep** in the **Sort by** drop-down list. Click the **Order** list arrow and specify **A to Z** order for that column.
4. Click the **Add Level** button, then click **Magazine** in the **Then by** drop-down list. Specify **A to Z** order for the second sort.
5. Click the **Add Level** button, then click **Sale** for the sort. Specify **Smallest to Largest** order for the third sort. The Sort dialog box should look like Figure T3.3 when you are done.
6. Click **OK** to run the sort.

Figure T3.4 shows how the sort looks based on the options you selected above.

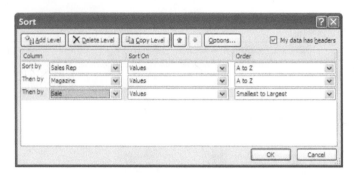

FIGURE T3.3

Sort Dialog Box with
Multiple Records

CREATING YOUR OWN CUSTOM SORT ORDER

Excel allows you to create custom sort orders so that you can rearrange lists that
do not follow predictable alphanumerical or chronological patterns. For example,
you can create a custom sort order for the regions of the country (West, North, East,
South). When you define a custom sort order, it appears in the Options dialog box
and is available to all the workbooks on your computer.

To create a custom sort order, follow these steps:

1. Click the **File** tab, scroll down to the **Options** button. A box will open, choose
   Advanced. Scroll down to the bottom of the dialog box that opens. Click the box
   Edit Custom Lists.

2. Click the line **NEW LIST** under the **Custom Lists** section, and the text pointer
   appears in the **List entries:** list box. This is where you will type the items in your
   custom list.

FIGURE T3.4

Data Sort Using More
than One Column

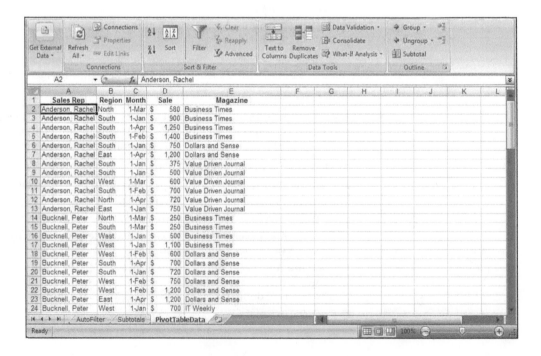

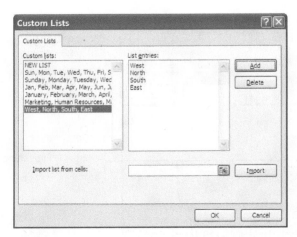

FIGURE T3.5

Creating a Custom Sort
Order

_____

3. Type **West, North, South, East,** and then click **Add.**
   You can either separate each value with a comma
   or type each one on a separate line. The new custom order appears in the Custom Lists list box, as
   shown in Figure T3.5.

4. Click **OK** to close the Custom Lists dialog box, and
   again for the Excel Options box.

   To use a custom sort order, follow these steps:

1. Click any cell in your list.

2. Click the **Home** tab, then under the Editing group
   click **Sort & Filter,** and then click **Custom Sort.**

3. Under **Column,** in the **Sort by** drop-down box,
   select the **Region** field.

4. Under **Order,** select **Custom List.**

5. In the **Custom Lists** dialog box, select **West, North, South, East,** as shown in
   Figure T3.6.

6. Click **OK** to run the sort. Your list appears sorted with the custom criteria you
   specified.

Creating Conditional Formatting

Excel gives you the ability to add *conditional formatting*—formatting that automatically adjusts depending on the contents of cells—to your worksheet. This
means you can highlight important trends in your data, such as the rise in a stock
price, a missed milestone, or a sudden
spurt in your college expenses, based on
conditions you set in advance using the
Conditional Formatting dialog box. With
this feature, an out-of-the-ordinary number jumps out at anyone who routinely
uses the worksheet.

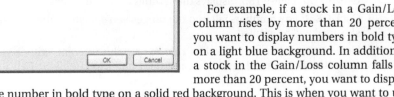

FIGURE T3.6

Sort Options Dialog Box

_____

For example, if a stock in a Gain/Loss
column rises by more than 20 percent,
you want to display numbers in bold type
on a light blue background. In addition, if
a stock in the Gain/Loss column falls by
more than 20 percent, you want to display
the number in bold type on a solid red background. This is when you want to use
conditional formatting.

To create such a conditional format, complete the following steps:

1. If the workbook **T3_ProblemSolving_Data.xls** is closed, open it.

2. Select the worksheet **ConditionalFormatting.**

3. Select the column **Sale.** (Note that each cell can maintain its own, unique conditional formatting, so that you can set up several different conditions.)

4. Click the **Home** tab.

5. In the **Styles** section, click the **Conditional Formatting** button, and then point
   to **Highlight Cell Rules** and click **Between. . . .**

6. In the first text box, type the number **1000.**

7. In the second text box, type the number **1200.**

8. In the third text box, use the drop-down arrow to select **Green Fill with Dark Green Text.** Figure T3.7 displays the settings for this example.

9. Click **OK.** If any numbers fall into the ranges you specified, the formatting you specified will be applied.

10. Now you need to add another rule to supply different criteria. Click the **Conditional Formatting** button, and then point to **Highlight Cell Rules** and click **Greater Than....**

11. Type **1250** in the first box and select **Red Fill with Dark Red Text** using the drop-down arrow from the second box.

12. Click **OK.**

13. If any numbers fall into the ranges you identified, the formatting you specified will be applied. Figure T3.8 shows the conditional formatting you entered for this example.

Using AutoFilter to Find Records

When you want to hide all the records (rows) in your list except those that meet certain criteria, you can use the AutoFilter command on the Filter submenu of the Data menu. The *AutoFilter* command places a drop-down list at the top of each column in your list (in the heading row). To display a particular group of records,

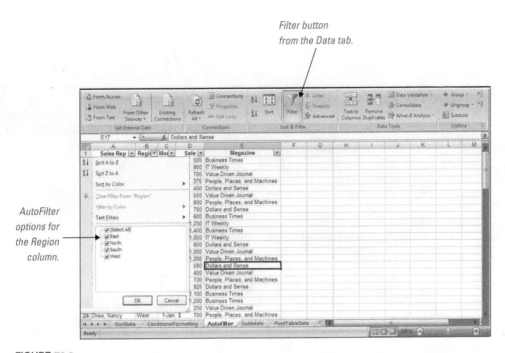

Filter button
from the Data tab.

AutoFilter
options for
the Region
column.

FIGURE T3.9

AutoFilter Options

select the criteria that you want in one or more of the drop-down lists. For example, to display the sales history for all employees that had $1,000 orders in January, you could select **January** in the **Month** column drop-down list and **$1,000** in the **Sale** drop-down list.

To use the AutoFilter command to find records, follow these steps:

1. If the workbook **T3_ProblemSolving_Data.xls** is closed, open it.

2. Select the worksheet **AutoFilter.**

3. Click any cell in the list.

4. Click the **Data** tab and then click the **Filter** button in the **Sort & Filter** section. Each column head now displays a list arrow.

5. Click the list arrow next to the **Region** heading. A list box that contains filter options appears, as shown in Figure T3.9.

If a column in your list contains one or more blank cells, you will also see (Blanks) and (NonBlanks) options at the bottom of the list. The *(Blanks)* option displays only the records containing an empty cell (blank field) in the filter column, so that you can locate any missing items quickly. The *(NonBlanks)* option displays the opposite—all records that have an entry—in the filter column.

6. Select only **East** to use for this filter (you will have to uncheck the other entries). Excel hides the entries that don't match the criterion you specify and highlights the active filter arrow. Figure T3.10 shows the results of using East as the criterion in the Region column.

7. You can use more than one filter arrow to further narrow your list, which is useful if your list is many records long. To continue working with AutoFilter but also redisplay all your records, click the list arrow next to **Region** and check **Show All.** Excel displays all your records again.

8. To remove the AutoFilter drop-down lists, unselect the **AutoFilter** command on the **Filter** submenu.

Filter button
from the Data tab.

Active filter
icon.

Rows that fit
the filter
criteria.

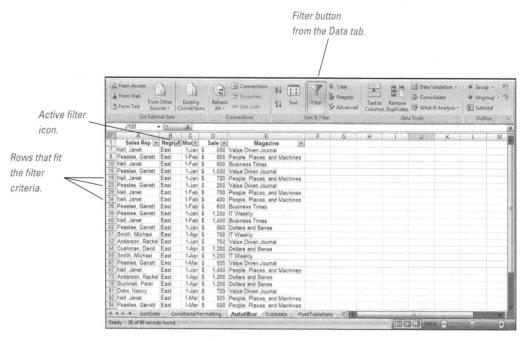

FIGURE T3.10

AutoFilter Output

CREATING A CUSTOM AUTOFILTER

When you want to display a numeric range of data or customize a column filter in other ways, choose **Custom Filter . . .** from the **Number Filters** option to display the **Custom AutoFilter** dialog box. The dialog box contains two relational list boxes and two value list boxes that you can use to build a custom range for the filter. For example, you could display all sales greater than $1,000 or all sales between $500 and $800.

To create a custom AutoFilter, follow these steps:

1. Click any cell in the list.
2. Click the **Data** tab and then click the **Filter** button.
3. Click the list arrow next to the heading **Sale** and select **Number Filters,** then click on **Custom Filter. . . .** The **Custom AutoFilter** dialog box opens.
4. Click the first list box and select **is greater than or equal to** and then click the value list box and select **$500.**
5. Click the **And** radio button to indicate that the records must meet both criteria, then specify **is less than or equal to** in the second list box and select **$800** in the second value list box. Figure T3.11 shows the Custom AutoFilter dialog box with two range criteria specified.
6. Click **OK** to apply the custom AutoFilter. The records selected by the filter are displayed in your worksheet.

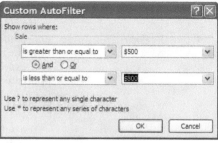

FIGURE T3.11

Custom AutoFilter

Analyzing a List with the Subtotals Command

The *Subtotals* command in the Outline section of the Data menu helps you organize and analyze a list by displaying records in groups and inserting summary information, such as subtotals, averages, maximum values, or minimum values.

FIGURE T3.12

Subtotal Settings

The Subtotals command can also display a grand total at the top or bottom of your list, letting you quickly add up columns of numbers. As a bonus, Subtotals displays your list in *Outline view* so that you can expand or shrink each section in the list simply by clicking.

To add subtotals to a list, follow these steps:

1. If the workbook **T3_ProblemSolving_Data.xls** is closed, open it.

2. Select the worksheet **Subtotals.**

3. Arrange the list so that the records for each group are located together. To do this, sort the list by **Sales Rep.**

4. Click the **Data** tab, then click the **Subtotal** button in the **Outline** section. Excel opens the **Subtotal** dialog box and selects the list.

5. In the **At each change in:** list box, choose **Sales Rep.** Each time this value changes, Excel inserts a row and computes a subtotal for the numeric fields in this group of records.

6. In the **Use function:** list box, choose **Sum.**

7. In the **Add subtotal to:** list box, choose **Sale,** which is the column to use in the subtotal calculation. Figure T3.12 shows the settings for this example.

8. Click **OK** to add the subtotals to the list. You will see a screen similar to the one in Figure T3.13, complete with subtotals, outlining, and a grand total.

When you use the Subtotals command in Excel to create outlines, you can examine different parts of a list by clicking buttons in the left margin. Click the numbers at the top of the left margin to choose how many levels of data you

FIGURE T3.13

Subtotals, Outline, and
Grand Total

*Subtotal button
from the Data tab.*

*Total for
Rachel
Anderson.*

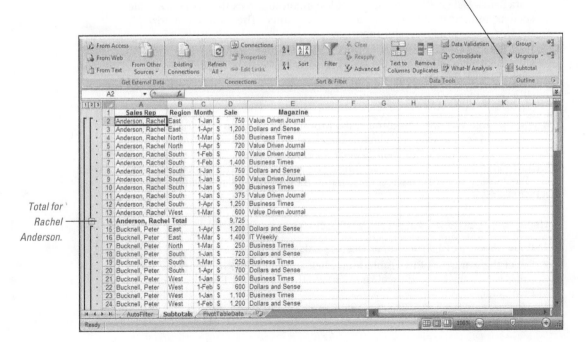

want to see. Click the plus or minus button to expand or collapse specific sub-groups of data.

You can choose the Subtotals command as often as necessary to modify your groupings or calculations. When you are finished using the Subtotals command, click **Remove All** in the **Subtotal** dialog box.

PivotTables

A powerful built-in data-analysis feature in Excel is the PivotTable. A *PivotTable* analyzes, summarizes, and manipulates data in large lists, databases, worksheets, or other collections. It is called a PivotTable because fields can be moved within the table to create different types of summary lists, providing a "pivot." PivotTables offer flexible and intuitive analysis of data.

Although the data that appear in PivotTables look like any other worksheet data, the data in the data area of the PivotTable cannot be directly entered or changed. The PivotTable is linked to the source data; the output in the cells of the table are read-only data. The formatting (number, alignment, font, etc.) can be changed as well as a variety of computational options such as SUM, AVERAGE, MIN, and MAX.

PIVOTTABLE TERMINOLOGY

Some notable PivotTable terms are:

■ **Row field**—Row fields have a row orientation in a PivotTable report and are displayed as row labels. These appear in the ROW area of a PivotTable report layout.

■ **Column field**—Column fields have a column orientation in a PivotTable report and are displayed as column labels. These appear in the COLUMN area of a PivotTable report layout.

■ **Data field**—Data fields from a list or table contain summary data in a PivotTable, such as numeric data (e.g., statistics, sales amounts). These are summarized in the DATA area of a PivotTable report layout.

■ **Page field**—Page fields filter out the data for other items and display one page at a time in a PivotTable report.

BUILDING A PIVOTTABLE

The PivotTable Wizard steps through the process of creating a PivotTable, allowing a visual breakdown of the data in the Excel list or database. When the wizard steps are complete, a diagram, such as Figure T3.14, with the labels PAGE, COLUMN, ROW, and DATA appears. The next step is to drag the field buttons onto the PivotTable grid. This step tells Excel about the data needed to be analyzed with a PivotTable.

Using the PivotTable Feature

1. If the workbook **T3_ProblemSolving_Data.xls** is closed, open it.

2. Select the worksheet **PivotTableData.** Click any cell in the list. Now the active cell is within the list, and Excel knows to use the data in the Excel list to create a PivotTable.

3. Click the **Insert** tab, then click the **PivotTable** button in the **Tables** group, and click on **PivotTable.**

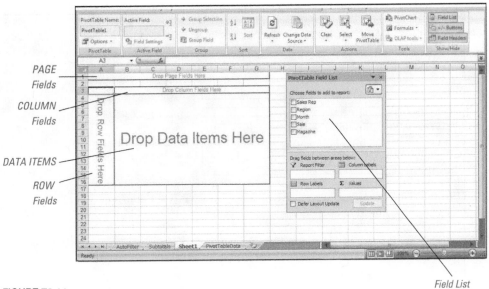

Field List

FIGURE T3.14

The PivotTable, PivotTable Toolbar, and PivotTable Field List

4. The **Create PivotTable** dialog box opens. In the **Select a table or range** box, make sure you see **$A$1:$E$97.**

5. Click **OK.** Your spreadsheet will now look like Figure T3.14.

6. Using the **PivotTable Field List,** drag the **Month** button to the **PAGE** area. The page field operates like the row and column fields but provides a third dimension to the data. It allows another variable to be added to the PivotTable without necessarily viewing all its values at the same time.

7. Drag the **Region** button to the **COLUMN** area. The column field is another variable used for comparison.

8. Drag the **Magazine** button to the **ROW** area. A row field in a PivotTable is a variable that takes on different values.

9. Drag the **Sale** button to the **DATA** area. The data field is the variable that the Pivot Table summarizes. Your PivotTable should now look like Figure T3.15.

MODIFYING A PIVOTTABLE VIEW

After a PivotTable is built, modifications can be done at any time. For example, examining the sales for a particular region would mean that the Region field would need to be changed. Use the drop-down list to the right of the field name. Select a region and click **OK.** The grand total dollar amounts by region are at the bottom of each item, which have been recalculated according to the selected region (or regions).

This report can be used in various ways to analyze the data. For instance, click the **Clear** button on the PivotTable ribbon, click **Clear All,** then arrange the fields like this:

1. **Magazine** in the **PAGE** area.

2. **Month** in the **COLUMN** area.

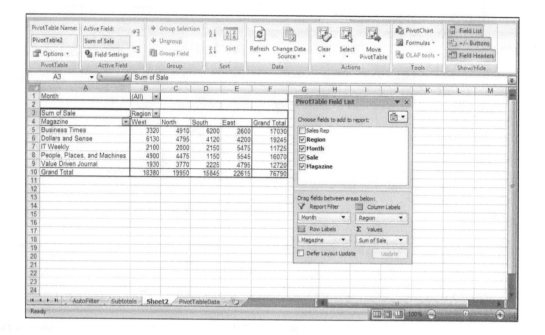

FIGURE T3.15

The PivotTable with Data,
PivotTable Toolbar, and
PivotTable Field List

3. **Sales Rep** in the **ROW** area.

4. **Sale** in the **DATA** area.

The completed PivotTable dialog box should look like the one in Figure T3.16 on the next page. The PivotTable now illustrates the sales by month for each salesperson, along with the total amount for the sales for each sales representative.

BUILDING A PIVOTCHART

A *PivotChart* is a column chart (by default) that is based on the data in a PivotTable. The chart type can be changed if desired. To build a PivotChart:

1. Click the **PivotChart** button in the **Tools** section of the PivotTable ribbon.

2. The **Insert Chart** dialog box appears. Select the **Stacked Column** chart and click **OK.**

3. The chart appears in your PivotTable worksheet. Click the **Move Chart** button on the PivotTable ribbon (on the **Design** tab, in the **Location** group) and select **New sheet** from the **Move Chart** dialog box.

4. The PivotChart should look like Figure T3.17.

Note: Whatever changes are selected on the PivotChart are also made to the PivotTable, as the two features are linked dynamically.

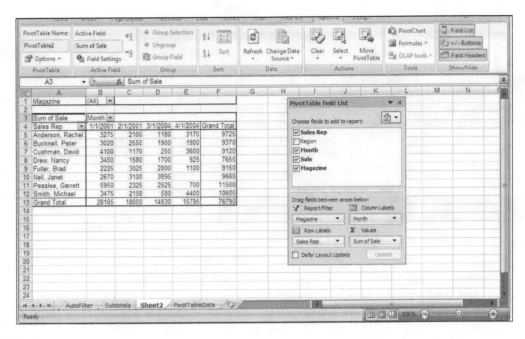

FIGURE T3.16

Rearranged Data in the
PivotTable

FIGURE T3.17

PivotChart

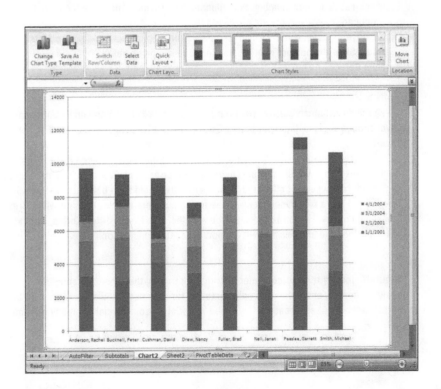

✻ PLUG-IN SUMMARY

If you routinely track large amounts of information, you can use several Excel tools for problem solving. A *list* is a table of data stored in a worksheet, organized into columns of fields and rows of records. Excel gives you the ability to add *conditional formatting*—formatting that automatically adjusts depending on the contents of cells—to your worksheet. The *AutoFilter* command places a drop-down list at the top of each column in your list (in the heading row). The *Subtotals* command on the Data menu helps you organize and analyze a list by displaying records in groups and inserting summary information, such as subtotals, averages, maximum values, or minimum values. A *PivotTable* analyzes, summarizes, and manipulates data in large lists, databases, worksheets, or other collections.

✻ MAKING BUSINESS DECISIONS

1. Production Errors

Established in 2002, t-shirts.com has rapidly become the place to find, order, and save on T-shirts. One huge selling factor is that the company manufactures its own T-shirts. However, the quality manager for the production plant, Kasey Harnish, has noticed an unacceptable number of defective T-shirts being produced. You have been hired to assist Kasey in understanding where the problems are concentrated. He suggests using a PivotTable to perform an analysis and has provided you with a data file, **T3_TshirtProduction_Data.xls.** The following is a brief definition of the information within the data file:

A. **Batch:** A unique number that identifies each batch or group of products produced.
B. **Product:** A unique number that identifies each product.
C. **Machine:** A unique number that identifies each machine on which products are produced.
D. **Employee:** A unique number that identifies each employee producing products.
E. **Batch Size:** The number of products produced in a given batch.
F. **Num Defect:** The number of defective products produced in a given batch.

2. Coffee Trends

College chums Hannah Baltzan and Tyler Phillips are working on opening a third espresso drive-through stand in Highlands Ranch, Colorado, called Brewed Awakening. Their original drive-through stand, Jitters, and their second espresso stand, Bean Scene, have done well in their current locations in Englewood, Colorado, five miles away. Since Hannah and Tyler want to start with low overhead, they need assistance analyzing the data from the past year on the different types of coffee and amounts that they sold from both stands. Hannah and Tyler would like a recommendation of the four top sellers to start offering when Brewed Awakening opens. They have provided you with the data file **T3_JittersCoffee_Data.xls** for you to perform the analysis that will support your recommendation.

3. Filtering SecureIT Data

SecureIT, Inc., is a small computer security contractor that provides computer security analysis, design, and software implementation for commercial clients. Almost all of SecureIT work requires access to classified material or confidential company documents.

Consequently, all of the security personnel have clearances of either Secret or Top Secret. Some have even higher clearances for work that involves so-called black box security work.

While most of the personnel information for SecureIT resides in database systems, a basic employee worksheet is maintained for quick calculations and ad hoc report generation. Because SecureIT is a small company, it can take advantage of Excel's excellent list management facilities to satisfy many of its personnel information management needs. You have been provided with a sample worksheet, **T3_Employee_Data.xls,** to assist SecureIT with producing several worksheet summaries. Here is what is needed:

1. One worksheet that is sorted by last name and hire data.
2. One worksheet that uses a custom sort by department in this order: Marketing, Human Resources, Management, and Engineering.
3. One worksheet that uses a filter to display only those employees in the Engineering department with a clearance of Top Secret (TS).
4. One worksheet that uses a custom filter to display only those employees born between 1960 and 1969 (inclusive).
5. One worksheet that totals the salaries by department and the grand total of all department salaries. This worksheet should be sorted by department name first.

4. Filtering RedRocks Consulting Contributions

RedRocks Consulting is a large computer consulting firm in Denver, Colorado. Don McCubbrey, the CEO and founder of the firm, is well-known for his philanthropic efforts. He believes that many of his employees also contribute to nonprofit organizations and wants to reward them for their efforts while encouraging others to contribute to charities. He started a program in which RedRocks Consulting matches 50 percent of each donation an employee makes to the charity of his or her choice. The only guidelines are that the charity must be a nonprofit organization and the firm's donation per employee may not exceed $500 a year.

Don has started an Excel file, **T3_RedRocks_Data.xls,** to record the firm's donations. Included in this file are the dates the request for a donation was submitted, the employee's name and ID number, the name of the charity, the dollar amount contributed by the firm, and the date the contribution was sent. Don wants you to help him create several worksheets with the following criteria:

1. One worksheet that sorts the list alphabetically by organization and then by employee's last name.
2. One worksheet that totals the contribution made per employee for the month of December.
3. One worksheet that sorts the list by donation value by lowest amount to highest amount.

Decision Making Using Excel 2010

LEARNING OUTCOMES

1. Describe the use of the IF function.
2. Compare the functions of Goal Seek and Solver.
3. List the advantages of using the Scenario Manager.

Introduction

Most of the decision-analysis tools on the market focus on one specific analytical technique, like simulation or decision trees. They may be tailored to a specific industry need, such as insurance claims modeling. Furthermore, the cost of these tools can run into the tens of thousands, even millions, of dollars—such as SAS and Cognos. One integrated set of tools that combines the best analytical methods, can be applied to different problems, and is reasonably priced is Microsoft Excel 2010.

The measure of any business intelligence solution is its ability to derive knowledge from data, as discussed in the core units of this book. This plug-in will examine a few of the advanced business-analysis tools that have the capability to identify patterns, trends, and rules and create "what-if" analyses. There are four areas in this plug-in:

1. The *IF* function is used to conduct conditional tests on values and formulas.
2. The *Goal Seek* function is used to find an unknown value that produces a desired result.
3. The *Solver* function is used to calculate an optimum solution based on several variables and constraints.
4. The *Scenario Manager* function is used to create and evaluate a collection of "what-if" scenarios containing multiple input values.

Creating Formulas Using the IF Function

The *IF* logical function will return one value if a condition is TRUE and another value if the condition is FALSE. Use the IF function when you want to compare two items in your workbook. The IF function looks like this:

=IF(logical_test,value_if_true,value_if_false)

- **Logical_test** is any value or expression that can be evaluated to TRUE or FALSE. For example, A10 = 100 is a logical expression; if the value in cell A10 is equal to 100, the expression evaluates to TRUE. Otherwise, the expression evaluates to FALSE. This argument can use any comparison calculation operator.

- **Value_if_true** is the value that is returned if the logical_test is TRUE. For example, if this argument is the text string "Within budget" and the logical_test argument evaluates to TRUE, then the IF function displays the text "Within budget." **Note:** Value_if_true can be another formula.

- **Value_if_false** is the value that is returned if the logical_test is FALSE. For example, if this argument is the text string "Over budget" and the logical_test argument evaluates to FALSE, then the IF function displays the text "Over budget." **Note:** Value_if_false can be another formula.

Logical operators are used to compare numbers in two or more cells to a constant.	
=	Equal to
<	Less than
>	Greater than
≤	Less than or equal to
≥	Greater than or equal to
≠	Not equal to
NOT	Logical Not
AND	Logical And
OR	Logical Or

FIGURE T4.1

Logical Operators

To use the IF function follow these steps:

1. Select the cell in which you want to enter the function.
2. Click the **Formulas** tab, then click the **Insert Function** button.
3. Click **IF** from the list of **Logical** functions and click **OK.**
4. In the **Function Arguments** dialog box that opens, enter the **Logical_test** argument. This argument states the condition you want to test for. Use cell references and/or values with logical operators. Figure T4.1 displays the list of logical operators.
5. Enter the **Value_if_true** argument. This is the text string or value that will be displayed if the logical_test argument is true.
6. Enter the **Value_if_false** argument. This is the text string or value that will be displayed if the logical_test argument is false.
7. Click **OK.**

For example, in a loan analysis worksheet, you want to write a conditional expression that examines the ratio of a loan amount to a purchase price. The logic for solving this is if the ratio is greater than 0.8, then there is an assessment fee of $300. Otherwise, the assessment fee is $0.

To create a conditional expression, complete the following steps:

1. Open the workbook **T4_LoanAnalysis_Data.xls** that accompanies this textbook.
2. Click cell **B14,** the cell that will display **Assessment** if the ratio of loan amount to purchase price is greater than 0.8—the same criteria for displaying (or not) an assessment fee of $300.
3. Type **=IF(B13/B4 > 0.8,300,0)** and press **Enter.** The cell displays **300** because the loan-to-price ratio is 0.875.

When you are unsure of a function and want help writing it, you can use the Insert Function command. Executing the Insert Function command opens a dialog box that lists functions by categories and helps you build the function.

To write an IF function using the Insert Function complete the following steps:

1. Click cell **B16** to make it active.
2. Click the **Formulas** tab, then click the **Logical** button and select **IF.** The **Function Arguments** dialog box opens (see Figure T4.2).
3. Click the **Logical_test** box and type **B13/B4 > 0.8** (there are no spaces in this line). Notice that the moment you type 0.8, the label TRUE appears to the right of the value. That indicates the current value of the expression based on the condition you just completed.

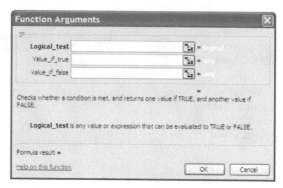

4. Click the **Value-if-true** box and type **300,** which is the value to return if the condition is true.

5. Click the **Value-if-false** box and type **0,** which is the value to return if the condition is false (see Figure T4.3).

6. Click **OK** to complete the function. Excel places the completed IF function into cell B16, calculates the value of the function, and displays 300.00 because the ratio of the down payment to the purchase price is greater than 0.8.

Goal Seek

Goal Seek is an analytical function that allows a value in a formula to be adjusted to reach a desired result or answer. Goal Seek can eliminate unnecessary calculations that can be used to determine a single variable value in a formula. For example, a salesperson might participate in a bonus program that pays 3 percent of all sales dollars. The salesperson wants to receive a bonus of at least $2,500 and needs to know the target sales dollar amount needed.

Create a worksheet with the following information (see Figure T4.4 for a layout design):

Label	Cell Address	Value
Sales Dollars	B1	(unknown—leave blank)
Bonus Percentage	B2	3%
Bonus Amount	B3	=B1*B2

When the Goal Seek command starts to run, it repeatedly tries new values in the variable cell to find a solution to the problem. This process is called *iteration,* and it continues until Excel has run the problem 100 times or has found an answer within .001 of the target value specified. The iteration settings can be adjusted by clicking the **Office** button, then clicking **Excel Options,** clicking the **Formulas** button, and adjusting the **Maximum Iteration** options. It calculates so fast, the Goal Seek command can save significant time and effort over the brute force method of trying one number after another in a formula.

USING THE GOAL SEEK COMMAND

The Goal Seek feature is used to fill in the target value of the cell containing the *Sales Dollars* amount. The Goal Seek values read "Set cell = B3, To value = 2500, By changing cell = $B$1."

To use the Goal Seek command:

1. Click the **Data** tab. In the **Data Tools** group click **What-If Analysis** and then click **Goal Seek.**

2. In the **Goal Seek** dialog box, specify the cell that contains the desired value in the **Set cell:** box. Type in or select **B3.**

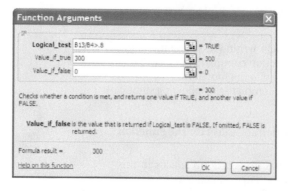

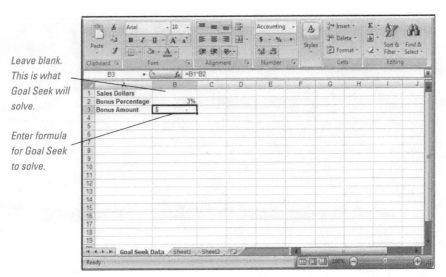

FIGURE T4.4

Goal Seek Worksheet

Leave blank.
This is what
Goal Seek will
solve.

Enter formula
for Goal Seek
to solve.

3. Enter the desired value or answer in the **To value:** box. Type in 2500.

4. Enter the cell whose value will be changed in the **By changing cell:** box. Type in or select **$B$1.**

5. The Goal Seek dialog box should look like Figure T4.5.

6. Choose **OK.**

   a. If a solution is found, the **Goal Seek Status** dialog box appears.
   b. The results are shown in Figure T4.6.

7. Select **OK.**

   Goal Seek is used to adjust a single variable in a formula. Use the Solver feature to adjust multiple variables in a formula, as described in the next section.

FIGURE T4.5

Goal Seek Function

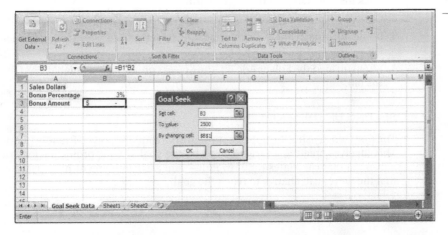

FIGURE T4.6

Goal Seek Results

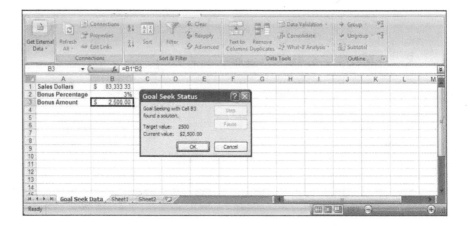

Solver

Solver is part of a suite of functions sometimes called *what-if analysis tools* used for optimizing problems that contain more than one variable. The Solver add-in utility is needed to analyze the scenarios in decision-making situations that involve consideration of values and constraints for several variables simultaneously. This powerful function uses multiple changing variables and constraints to find the optimal solution to solve a problem.

For example, consider a coffee shop that currently sells three beverages: (1) regular fresh-brewed coffee, (2) premium caffe latte, and (3) premium caffe mocha. The current price for regular coffee is set at $1.25, caffe latte at $2.00, and caffe mocha at $2.25, but the revenue potential is uncertain. What special emphasis (or marketing) should be given to each of the beverages to maximize revenue? Although the premium coffees bring in more money, their ingredients are more expensive and they take more time to make than regular coffee. Making some basic calculations by hand is easy, but there needs to be some structure to the sales data in a worksheet so that periodic changes can be made and analyzed.

INSTALLING SOLVER

Solver comes with the standard Excel package, but it has to be installed. To install Solver, do the following:

1. Click the **File** tab, and then click **Options.**
2. Click **Add-Ins,** and then, in the **Manage** box, select **Excel Add-ins.** Click **Go.**
3. In the **Add-Ins Available** box, select the **Solver Add-in** check box, and then click **OK.**
4. After you load the Solver Add-in, the Solver command is available from the **Add-Ins** tab.

SETTING UP THE PROBLEM

The first step in using the Solver command is to build a "Solver-friendly" worksheet. This involves creating a target cell to be the goal of your problem—for example, a formula that calculates total revenue—and assigning one or more variable cells that the Solver can change to reach the goal.

The Total Revenue is the sum of D6, D10, and D14.

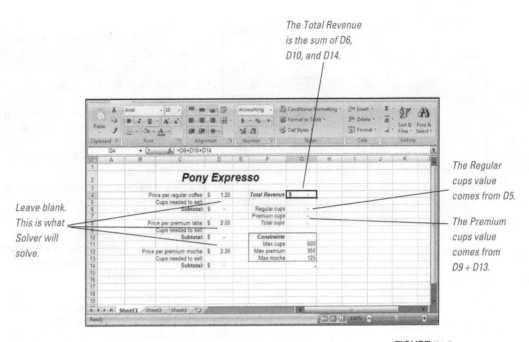

Leave blank. This is what Solver will solve.

The Regular cups value comes from D5.

The Premium cups value comes from D9 + D13.

FIGURE T4.7

Coffee Sales Data Sheet for Solver

To use Solver, complete the following:

1. Set up a worksheet similar to Figure T4.7 (this will follow the scenario presented above).

2. The three variable cells in the worksheet are cells **D5, D9,** and **D13.** These are the cells whose values Solver needs to determine to maximize the weekly revenue.

3. In the bottom-right corner of the table is a list of constraints to use for forecasting.

4. The worksheet must contain cells **(G6 through G8)** that include the formulas used as constraints. The limiting values for the constraints are listed in cells **G11 through G13:**

   ■ No more than **500** total cups of coffee (both regular and premium).
   ■ No more than **350** cups of premium coffee (both caffe latte and caffe mocha).
   ■ No more than **125** caffe mochas.

5. The subtotals for cells **D6, D10, D14** need to be calculated, as well as the **Total Revenue** (sum of D6, D10, and D14) in **G4.**

6. The value for cell **G6** should equal the value that will be calculated for D5, and the value for cell **G7** will be the sum of the values from D9 and D13. The calculation of **G8** equals the sum of D5, D9, and D13.

7. Click the target cell **G4**—the one containing the formula that is based on the variable cells you want Solver to determine.

8. Click on the **Add-Ins** tab and then click the **Solver** button. The Solver Parameters dialog box opens, as shown in Figure T4.8. Select the **Set Target Cell:** box (unless it already contains the correct reference),

FIGURE T4.8

Solver Parameters Dialog Box

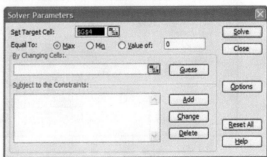

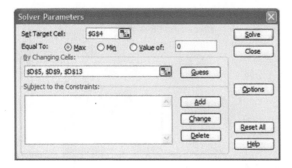

FIGURE T4.9

By Changing Cells Values
in Solver Parameters
Dialog Box

_____

and then click cell **G4** to insert **$G$4** as the target cell. The **Equal To:** option button, **Max,** is already selected. Do not change this since the problem requests the maximum value for the target cell.

9. Select the **By Changing Cells:** box. Click the Collapse Dialog button to the right of the box to collapse the dialog box. Select each of the variable cells by holding down the **CTRL** key and clicking **D5, D9,** and **D13.** This places commas between the three cell entries in the box: **$D$5, $D$9, $D$13** (refer to Figure T4.9).

10. This problem has three constraints. Click **Add,** in the **Subject to the Constraints:** section, to add the first constraint in the **Add Constraint** dialog box.

   a. The first constraint is the coffee shop can sell only 500 cups of coffee in one week. To enter this constraint, after clicking in the **Cell Reference:** box, click cell **G8,** click <= in the operator drop-down list, and with the insertion point in the **Constraint:** box, type or click cell **G11.**

   b. Click **Add** to enter the first constraint and begin the second constraint—the coffee shop can sell only 350 premium coffees in one week. With the insertion point in the **Cell Reference:** box, click cell **G7,** click <= in the operator drop-down list, and in the **Constraint:** box, type or click cell **G12.**

   c. Click **Add** to enter the second constraint and begin the third—the coffee shop can sell only 125 caffe mochas in one week. Click cell **D13,** click <= in the operator drop-down list, and in the **Constraint:** box, type or click cell **G13.**

   d. Click **OK** to add all three constraints to the Solver Parameters dialog box as shown in Figure T4.10.

11. Click **Solve** to calculate the result.

12. Solver displays a dialog box describing the results of the analysis. If Solver runs into a problem, an error message will be displayed. If Solver finds a solution, a Solver Results dialog box like Figure T4.11 will appear.

13. To display the new solution in the worksheet, click the **Keep Solver Solution** option button in the Solver Results dialog box, and then click **OK.** Solver places an optimum value in the target cell and fills the variable cells with the solutions that satisfy the constraints specified and provide the optimal result, as shown in Figure T4.12.

FIGURE T4.10

Solver Parameters with
Constraints

_____

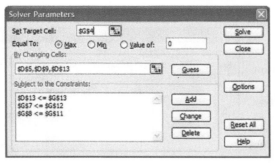

EDITING A SOLVER FORECAST

The Solver tool is very useful in modifying the constraints to evaluate new goals and possibilities. For example, if a coffee shop wants to earn exactly $800 per week from coffee drinks, use Solver to "solve" for the optimum combination of drinks. Setting a target value in Solver is a little like using the Goal Seek command to determine a value for an unknown variable, although Solver can use more than one variable. To edit the Solver forecast to find the variables to reach a specific goal, follow these steps:

1. Select the **Add-Ins** tab then select **Solver.** The **Solver Parameters** dialog box appears, still displaying the variables and constraints of the last

Solver problem. These will be adjusted to compute a new forecasting goal.

2. Click the **Value of:** option button and type **800** in the box to the right. The Value of: option button sets the target cell to a particular goal to determine the variable mix needed to reach the milestone. The dialog box should look similar to Figure T4.13.

3. Click **Solve** to find a solution to the problem. When Solver has finished, click **OK** to display the new solution.

4. Figure T4.14 shows the new solution that Solver generates.

Note: The results presented in Figure T4.14 are one possible solution that Solver may return.

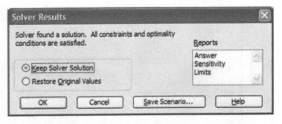

FIGURE T4.11

Solver Results Dialog Box

Scenario Manager

A *scenario* is a set of input values and corresponding results from calculations that Excel can save and report as needed. A worksheet can be used to conduct a "what-if" analysis on a particular set of data. Several input values in a worksheet might change depending on different situations or circumstances. Values that produce different results can be stored as scenarios.

Excel's *Scenario Manager* allows 32 different scenarios or groups of values to be defined. The Scenario Manager can then be used to selectively display the desired values or scenario in the worksheet. The Scenario Manager eliminates the need to have multiple copies of the same worksheet representing different situations. For each group of input values a scenario must be named and stored before it can be used.

FIGURE T4.12

Optimum Revenue for Solver Results

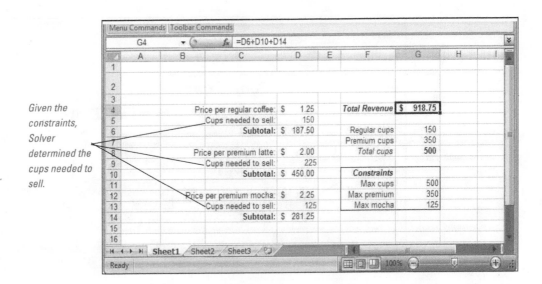

Given the constraints, Solver determined the cups needed to sell.

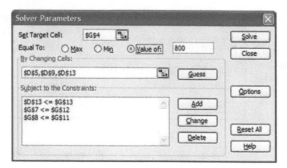

FIGURE T4.13

Editing Solver Forecast

SETTING UP SCENARIOS

Each group of input values or scenarios must be named and stored before it can be used. Scenarios are stored with the worksheet. To set up a scenario:

1. Open the file **T4_Scenario_Data.xls** that accompanies this text (see Figure T4.15).

2. Click on the **Data** tab, click the **What-If Analysis** button, and then select **Scenario Manager.**

3. Click **Add** to display the **Add Scenario** dialog box.

4. Enter **Original** in the **Scenario name:** box.

5. In the **Changing cells:** box, type **D9:D11** or use the Collapse Dialog button at the right side of the box to manually select the cells that hold the Number of **Technicians, Regular Hours,** and **OverTime Hours** values.

6. Choose **OK.** The **Scenario Values** dialog box appears.

7. The Scenario Values dialog box will display the values for cells **D9, D10,** and **D11** as **1, 300,** and **0,** respectively, as shown in Figure T4.16. Click **OK.** You will return to the **Scenario Manager** dialog box.

8. Once the original values have been saved, the what-if scenarios need to be created.

9. Click **Add.** In the **Add Scenario** dialog box, type **Single Contractor Overtime.**

10. Click **OK.** In the Scenario Values dialog box for cell **D11,** enter **40.** The values in cells **D9** and **D10** remain at **1** and **300,** respectively.

11. Click **OK.** Ensure that the **Single Contractor Overtime** scenario is selected, and click **Show.** Excel reports that this project will need an additional $3,000, as shown in Figure T4.17.

FIGURE T4.14

Solver Solution

Modifying the constraints, Solver adjusted the cups needed to sell.

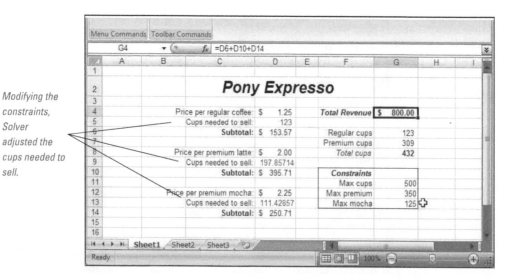

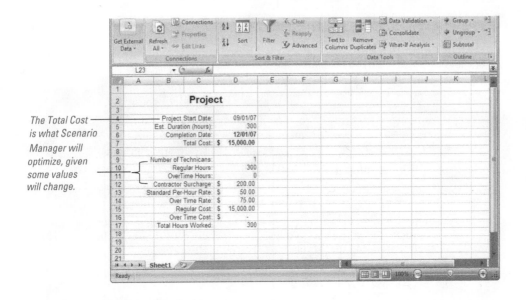

The Total Cost is what Scenario Manager will optimize, given some values will change.

12. Create one more scenario. In the **Scenario Manager** dialog box, click **Add** again.

13. The **Add Scenario** dialog box appears. In the **Scenario name:** box, type **Two Contractors No Overtime.**

14. The **Changing cells: (D9:D11)** should already appear in the proper boxes; if not, enter that range. Click **OK** to invoke the **Scenario Values** dialog box.

15. Two outside contractors are brought in (by charging $200 for each additional technician). Enter **2** in the box for cell **D9** and **0** in the box for cell **D11.** In cell **D10's** box, type **=300/2** since there will be two technicians to split the time. Click **OK.** A message box like that shown in Figure T4.18 will say that Excel converted the formula into a value.

16. Click **OK** to dismiss the message, and Excel returns you to the **Scenario Manager** dialog box.

17. Select **Two Contractors No Overtime** and click **Show.** Excel displays **150** in cell **D10** even though the total hours are 300. This scenario gives a completion cost of $15,200.

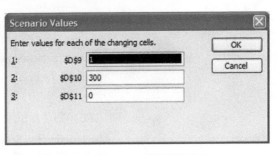

FIGURE T4.16

Scenario Values Dialog Box Values

Compare the Scenarios

Compare each scenario to determine the best solution, such as:

Scenario	Cost
Original	$15,000
Single Contractor Overtime	$18,000
Two Contractors No Overtime	$15,200

FIGURE T4.17

Single Contractor
Overtime Scenario

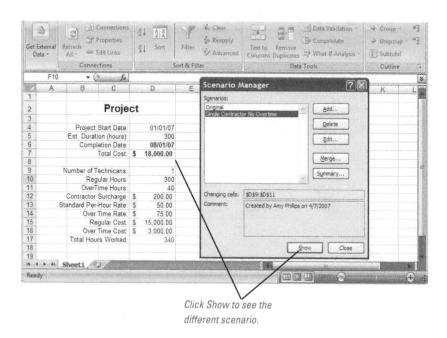

Click Show to see the
different scenario.

MODIFYING A SCENARIO

Once scenarios have been defined, the data values in the scenarios can be modified, as needed. To modify a scenario:

1. Click on the **Data** tab, click the **What-If Analysis** button, and then select **Scenario Manager.**
2. Select the desired scenario name.
3. Click the **Edit** button.
4. Modify the scenario information as desired.
5. Close the Scenario Manager dialog box.

CREATING A SCENARIO SUMMARY REPORT

Included in the Scenario Manager is a feature called the *Summary Report* that creates a report that summarizes the result cells that are affected by a scenario. The Summary Report appears in the form of a summary table that is placed on a new worksheet, which can be printed.

FIGURE T4.18

Message Dialog Box

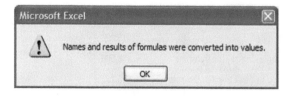

To create a Scenario Summary Report:

1. Click on the **Data** tab, click the **What-If Analysis** button, and then select **Scenario Manager.**
2. Click the **Summary . . .** button. The **Scenario Summary** dialog box appears.
3. Choose **Scenario summary** in the **Report type** group box.
4. In the **Result cells:** box, type in **D7,D12,D15,D16,D17.** Result cells are the cells affected by the specified scenario.
5. Choose **OK.**
6. Excel produces a Scenario Summary Report like Figure T4.19.

*All three constraints you
defined are represented here.*

FIGURE T4.19

Scenario Summary Report

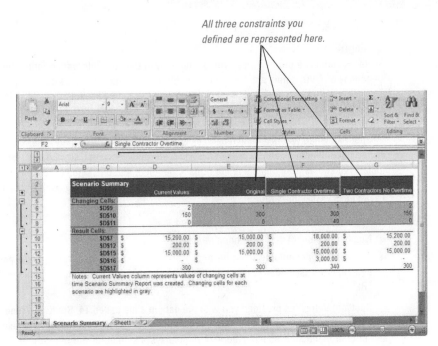

Technology can and does play a vitally important role in both supporting decision making and, in some instances, actually making decisions or recommendations. Microsoft Excel 2010 spreadsheet software has an integrated set of tools combining the analytical methods that can be applied to different problems. The If function, Goal Seek, Solver, and Scenario Manager analysis tools have the capability to identify patterns, trends, and rules and create *"what-if"* analyses.

⁕ **MAKING BUSINESS DECISIONS**

1. Spotlight Video Rentals

Spotlight Video is a premier video rental company in Denver, Colorado, offering the latest selections on DVD, game, and VHS releases. After DVDs and VHS tapes have been viewed a certain number of times, their quality deteriorates to the point that Spotlight Video considers them to be defective. Furthermore, some customers own DVD and VHS players that are defective and can ruin Spotlight Video's merchandise.

Spotlight Video wants to maintain an inventory of DVDs and VHS tapes that are at least 85 percent acceptable, although 95 percent is preferable. However, since it can't keep customers' machines from damaging the rentals, Spotlight Video has had to relax its criterion a little. You have been hired to create a spreadsheet that will evaluate each DVD and VHS based on the following criteria:

- Number of times each title has been rented.
- Number of defects that have been reported.
- The percent acceptable must be above 85 percent based on usage. If the percentage reported is below 85 percent, then Spotlight Video wants to flag this video as "REPLACE."

Spotlight Video has provided you with the data in a file called **T4_SpotlightVideo_Data. xls.** You will want to create an IF function to write a conditional expression that examines the criteria mentioned above. Figure T4.20 displays a sample of the output that Spotlight Video needs.

2. Scheduling Solver

AirPlains Airline is a new airline company that maintains a schedule of two daily flights each way between Salt Lake City, Denver, and Chicago. AirPlains Airline must strategically position itself as a low-cost provider in a volatile industry. Therefore, it must work toward finding a minimum cost for assigning flight crews to a given flight schedule while satisfying restrictions dictated by the Federal Aviation Administration.

Using Excel Solver, determine all the possible crew rotations based on the flight schedule below. You will want to find an approximate expected cost of each combination and then solve the original crew scheduling problem by using these costs. Second, you will want to calculate the crew constraints to determine the decision variables, constraints, and objectives.

FIGURE T4.20

Spotlight Video Report
Sample

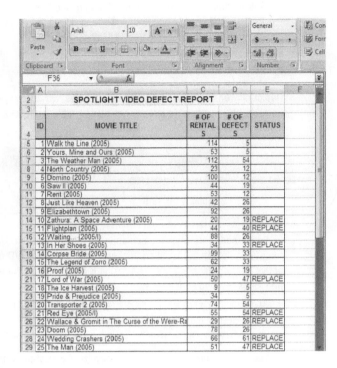

The AirPlains Airline flight schedule is as follows:

From	To	Departure	Arrival
Salt Lake City	Denver	9:00AM	12:00PM
Salt Lake City	Denver	2:00PM	5:00PM
Salt Lake City	Chicago	10:00AM	2:00PM
Salt Lake City	Chicago	3:00PM	7:00PM
Denver	Salt Lake City	8:00AM	11:00AM
Denver	Salt Lake City	2:00PM	5:00PM
Denver	Chicago	9:00AM	11:00AM
Denver	Chicago	3:00PM	5:00PM
Chicago	Salt Lake City	8:00AM	12:00PM
Chicago	Salt Lake City	2:00PM	6:00PM
Chicago	Denver	10:00AM	12:00PM
Chicago	Denver	4:00PM	6:00PM

Apply the following business rules (constraints) to your model:

1. A crew that leaves a city in the morning has to return to the same city at night.
2. The crew can return on another airplane. There are six airplanes in use.
3. When a crew is flying, the cost is $200 per hour.
4. When a crew is waiting or returning, the cost is $75 per hour.

3. DVD Sales

Hans Hultgren, the sales manager for DVD Sales, wants to maximize his profit on the sale of portable DVD players. He already has two portable models he plans to sell:

Products	Retail Price	Wholesale Cost
Panasonic DVD–LS50	$349.95	$192.47
Mintek MDP–1810	$199.95	$109.99

Hans needs your help in calculating his maximum profit. First, he would like you to use the Web to locate the retail price of two other portable DVD players not listed in the table above. The wholesale price of each unit is 55 percent of the retail price for both units you find. Hans has two constraints:

1. Hans has $200,000 to purchase new DVD players. The total wholesale cost of the four types of DVD units must be less than $200,000.
2. Hans must purchase a minimum of 100 units of each player from his wholesaler.

You want to use Excel Solver to maximize the total profit for Hans with the constraints mentioned above and limiting the number of units to positive integers.

4. Maximizing Profit

HotSprings Spas manufactures and sells two spa models: the Steamboat and the Classic. HotSprings Spas receives spa bodies from another manufacturer and then adds a pump and tubing to circulate the water. The Steamboat model demands 15.5 hours of labor and 14.5 feet of tubing. The Classic model requires 10.5 hours of labor and uses 20 feet of tubing. Based on selling patterns, the owner, Deborah Liebson, has determined that the Steamboat model generates a profit of $400 per unit, and each Classic model generates $345 profit. While Deborah would like a large labor capacity and sufficient tubing and motors to build any number of spas, her resources are limited. For the next production period, Deborah has 2,650 labor hours, 3,450 feet of tubing, and 231 pumps available. Deborah needs assistance in figuring out how many Steamboat and Classic models to build in order to maximize her profit. Given the constraints above, use Solver to assist Deborah in her what-if analysis.

Deborah has provided you with a screen shot of a template you can use to get started (see Figure T4.21).

FIGURE T4.21

HotSprings Spa
Template

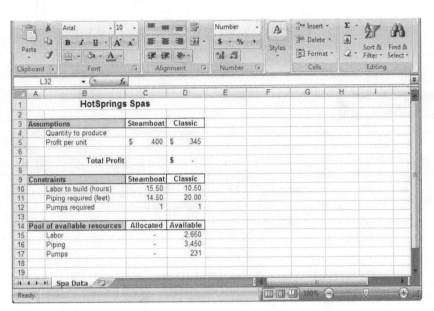

5. Budget Constraints

Joanne Krol wants to purchase a newer model automobile to replace her rusty 1989 car. The bank where Joanne has a checking account, US Bank, is advertising an annual interest rate of 6.75 percent for a three-year loan on used cars. By selling her old car and using some cash she has accumulated, Joanne has $3,000 available as a down payment. Under her current budget, Joanne figures that the maximum monthly loan payment she can afford is $300. She wants to find out the maximum car price she can afford and keep the monthly payment no higher than $300. She cannot alter the interest rate or the three-year term. Use the Excel Goal Seek command to figure out the highest purchase price Joanne can afford.

7

Storing Organizational Information—Databases

7.1. Describe a database, a database management system, and the relational database model.

7.2. Identify the business advantages of a relational database.

7.3. Explain the business benefits of a data-driven website.

7.4. Explain why an organization would want to integrate its databases.

LO 7.1 Describe a database, a database management system, and the relational database model.

Storing Information Using a Relational Database Management System

The core component of any system, regardless of size, is a database and a database management system. Broadly defined, a ***database*** maintains information about various types of objects (inventory), events (transactions), people (employees), and places (warehouses). A ***database management system (DBMS)*** creates, reads, updates, and deletes data in a database while controlling access and security. Managers send requests to the DBMS, and the DBMS performs the actual manipulation of the data in the database. Companies store their information in databases, and managers access these systems to answer operational questions such as how many customers purchased Product A in December or what were the average sales by region. There are two primary tools available for retrieving information from a DBMS. First is a ***query-by-example (QBE) tool*** that helps users graphically design the answer to a question against a database. Second is a ***structured query language (SQL)*** that asks users to write lines of code to answer questions against a database. Managers typically interact with QBE tools, and MIS professionals have the skills required to code SQL. Figure 7.1 displays the relationship between a database, a DBMS, and a user. Some of the more popular examples of DBMS include MySQL, Microsoft Access, SQL Server, FileMaker, Oracle, and FoxPro.

A ***data element*** (or ***data field***) is the smallest or basic unit of information. Data elements can include a customer's name, address, email, discount rate, preferred shipping method, product name, quantity ordered, and so on. ***Data models*** are logical data structures that detail the relationships among data elements using graphics or pictures.

FIGURE 7.1

Relationship of Database, DBMS, and User

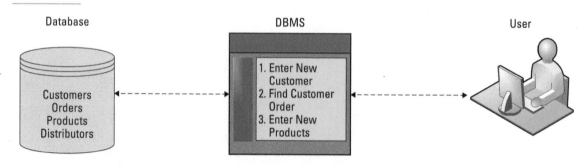

Metadata provides details about data. For example, metadata for an image could include its size, resolution, and date created. Metadata about a text document could contain document length, data created, author's name, and summary. Each data element is given a description, such as Customer Name; metadata is provided for the type of data (text, numeric, alphanumeric, date, image, binary value) and descriptions of potential predefined values such as a certain area code; and finally the relationship is defined. A *data dictionary* compiles all of the metadata about the data elements in the data model. Looking at a data model along with reviewing the data dictionary provides tremendous insight into the database's functions, purpose, and business rules.

DBMS use three primary data models for organizing information—hierarchical, network, and the relational database, the most prevalent. A *relational database model* stores information in the form of logically related two-dimensional tables. A *relational database management system* allows users to create, read, update, and delete data in a relational database. Although the hierarchical and network models are important, this text focuses only on the relational database model.

STORING DATA ELEMENTS IN ENTITIES AND ATTRIBUTES

For flexibility in supporting business operations, managers need to query or search for the answers to business questions such as which artist sold the most albums during a certain month. The relationships in the relational database model help managers extract this information. Figure 7.2 illustrates the primary concepts of the relational database model—entities, attributes, keys, and relationships. An *entity* (also referred to as a table) stores information about a person, place, thing, transaction, or event. The entities, or tables, of interest in Figure 7.2 are *TRACKS, RECORDINGS, MUSICIANS,* and *CATEGORIES.* Notice that each entity is stored in a different two-dimensional table (with rows and columns).

Attributes (also called columns or fields) are the data elements associated with an entity. In Figure 7.2 the attributes for the entity *TRACKS* are *TrackNumber, TrackTitle, TrackLength,* and *RecordingID.* Attributes for the entity *MUSICIANS* are *MusicianID,*

FIGURE 7.2

Primary Concepts of the Relational Database Model

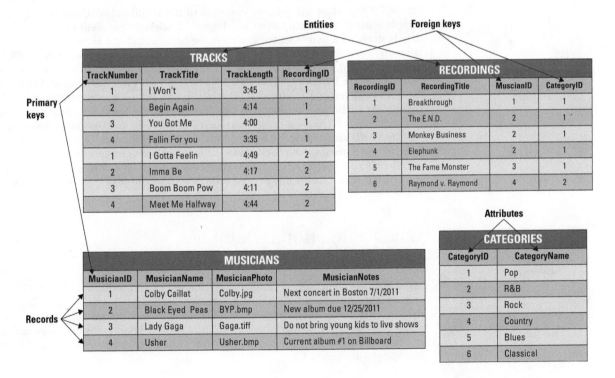

MusicianName, MusicianPhoto, and *MusicianNotes.* A **record** is a collection of related data elements (in the *MUSICIANS* table these include "3, Lady Gaga, gag.tiff, Do not bring young kids to live shows"). Each record in an entity occupies one row in its respective table.

CREATING RELATIONSHIPS THROUGH KEYS

To manage and organize various entities within the relational database model, you use primary keys and foreign keys to create logical relationships. A **primary key** is a field (or group of fields) that uniquely identifies a given record in a table. In the table *RECORDINGS,* the primary key is the field *RecordingID* that uniquely identifies each record in the table. Primary keys are a critical piece of a relational database because they provide a way of distinguishing each record in a table; for instance, imagine you need to find information on a customer named Steve Smith. Simply searching the customer name would not be an ideal way to find the information because there might be 20 customers with the name Steve Smith. This is the reason the relational database model uses primary keys to uniquely identify each record. Using Steve Smith's unique ID allows a manager to search the database to identify all information associated with this customer.

A **foreign key** is a primary key of one table that appears as an attribute in another table and acts to provide a logical relationship between the two tables. For instance, Black Eyed Peas in Figure 7.2 is one of the musicians appearing in the *MUSICIANS* table. Its primary key, *MusicianID,* is "2." Notice that *MusicianID* also appears as an attribute in the *RECORDINGS* table. By matching these attributes, you create a relationship between the *MUSICIANS* and *RECORDINGS* tables that states the Black Eyed Peas *(MusicianID 2)* have several recordings including The E.N.D., Monkey Business, and Elepunk. In essence, *MusicianID* in the *RECORDINGS* table creates a logical relationship (who was the musician that made the recording) to the *MUSICIANS* table. Creating the logical relationship between the tables allows managers to search the data and turn it into useful information.

COCA-COLA RELATIONAL DATABASE EXAMPLE

Figure 7.3 illustrates the primary concepts of the relational database model for a sample order of soda from Coca-Cola. Figure 7.3 offers an excellent example of how data is stored in a database. For example, the order number is stored in the *ORDER* table and each line item is stored in the *ORDER LINE* table. Entities include *CUSTOMER, ORDER, ORDER LINE, PRODUCT,* and *DISTRIBUTOR.* Attributes for *CUSTOMER* include *Customer ID, Customer Name, Contact Name,* and *Phone.* Attributes for *PRODUCT* include *Product ID, Description,* and *Price.* The columns in the table contain the attributes. Consider Hawkins Shipping, one of the distributors appearing in the *DISTRIBUTOR* table. Its primary key, *Distributor ID,* is DEN8001. Notice that *Distributor ID* also appears as an attribute in the *ORDER* table. This establishes the fact that Hawkins Shipping (*Distributor ID* DEN8001) was responsible for delivering orders 34561 and 34562 to the appropriate customer(s). Therefore, *Distributor ID* in the *ORDER* table creates a logical relationship (who shipped what order) between *ORDER* and *DISTRIBUTOR.*

LO 7.2 Identify the business advantages of a relational database.

Using a Relational Database for Business Advantages

Many business managers are familiar with Excel and other spreadsheet programs they can use to store business data. Although spreadsheets are excellent for supporting some data analysis, they offer limited functionality in terms of security, accessibility, and flexibility and can rarely scale to support business growth. From a business perspective, relational databases offer many advantages over using a text document or a spreadsheet, as displayed in Figure 7.4.

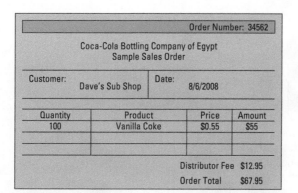

FIGURE 7.3

Potential Relational
Database for Coca-Cola
Bottling Company of Egypt
(TCCBCE)

		Order Number: 34562
Coca-Cola Bottling Company of Egypt		
Sample Sales Order		

Customer: Dave's Sub Shop	Date: 8/6/2008

Quantity	Product	Price	Amount
100	Vanilla Coke	$0.55	$55
		Distributor Fee	$12.95
		Order Total	$67.95

CUSTOMER

Customer ID	Customer Name	Contact Name	Phone
23	Dave's Sub Shop	David Logan	(555)333-4545
43	Pizza Palace	Debbie Fernandez	(555)345-5432
765	T's Fun Zone	Tom Repicci	(555)565-6655

ORDER

Order ID	Order Date	Customer ID	Distributor ID	Distributor Fee	Total Due
34561	7/4/2008	23	DEN8001	$22.00	$145.75
34562	8/6/2008	23	DEN8001	$12.95	$67.95
34563	6/5/2008	765	NY9001	$29.50	$249.50

ORDER LINE

Order ID	Line Item	Product ID	Quantity
34561	1	12345AA	75
34561	2	12346BB	50
34561	3	12347CC	100
34562	1	12349EE	100
34563	1	12345AA	100
34563	2	12346BB	100
34563	3	12347CC	50
34563	4	12348DD	50
34563	5	12349EE	100

DISTRIBUTOR

Distributor ID	Distributor Name
DEN8001	Hawkins Shipping
CHI3001	ABC Trucking
NY9001	Van Distributors

PRODUCT

Product ID	Product Description	Price
12345AA	Coca-Cola	$0.55
12346BB	Diet Coke	$0.55
12347CC	Sprite	$0.55
12348DD	Diet Sprite	$0.55
12349EE	Vanilla Coke	$0.55

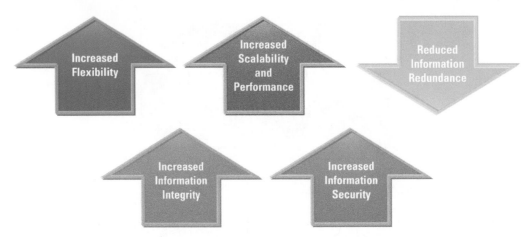

FIGURE 7.4

Business Advantages of
a Relational Database

INCREASED FLEXIBILITY

Databases tend to mirror business structures, and a database needs to handle changes quickly and easily, just as any business needs to be able to do. Equally important, databases need to provide flexibility in allowing each user to access the information in whatever way best suits his or her needs. The distinction between logical and physical views is important in understanding flexible database user views. The *physical view of information* deals with the physical storage of information on a storage device. The *logical view of information* focuses on how individual users logically access information to meet their own particular business needs.

In the database illustration from Figure 7.2, for example, one user could perform a query to determine which recordings had a track length of four minutes or more. At the same time, another user could perform an analysis to determine the distribution of recordings as they relate to the different categories. For example, are there more R&B recordings than rock, or are they evenly distributed? This example demonstrates that while a database has only one physical view, it can easily support multiple logical views that provides for flexibility.

Consider another example—a mail-order business. One user might want a report presented in alphabetical format, in which case last name should appear before first name. Another user, working with a catalog mailing system, would want customer names appearing as first name and then last name. Both are easily achievable, but different logical views of the same physical information.

INCREASED SCALABILITY AND PERFORMANCE

In its first year of operation, the official website of the American Family Immigration History Center, www.ellisisland.org, generated more than 2.5 billion hits. The site offers immigration information about people who entered America through the Port of New York and Ellis Island between 1892 and 1924. The database contains more than 25 million passenger names that are correlated to 3.5 million images of ships' manifests.[1]

The database had to be scalable to handle the massive volumes of information and the large numbers of users expected for the launch of the website. In addition, the database needed to perform quickly under heavy use. Some organizations must be able to support hundreds or thousands of users including employees, partners, customers, and suppliers, who all want to access and share the same information. Databases today scale to exceptional levels, allowing all types of users and programs to perform information-processing and information-searching tasks.

REDUCED INFORMATION REDUNDANCY

Information redundancy is the duplication of data, or the storage of the same data in multiple places. Redundant data can cause storage issues along with data integrity issues, making it difficult to determine which values are the most current or most accurate. Employees become confused and frustrated when faced with incorrect information causing disruptions to business processes and procedures. One primary goal of a database is to eliminate information redundancy by recording each piece of information in only one place in the database. This saves disk space, makes performing information updates easier, and improves information quality.

INCREASED INFORMATION INTEGRITY (QUALITY)

Information integrity is a measure of the quality of information. *Integrity constraints* are rules that help ensure the quality of information. The database design needs to consider integrity constraints. The database and the DBMS ensures that users can never violate these constraints. There are two types of integrity constraints: (1) relational and (2) business critical.

    Relational integrity constraints are rules that enforce basic and fundamental information-based constraints. For example, a relational integrity constraint would not allow someone to create an order for a nonexistent customer, provide a markup percentage that was negative, or order zero pounds of raw materials from a supplier. A *business rule* defines how a company performs certain aspects of its business and typically results in either a yes/no or true/false answer. Stating that merchandise returns are allowed within 10 days of purchase is an example of a business rule. *Business-critical integrity constraints* enforce business rules vital to an organization's success and often require more insight and knowledge than relational integrity constraints. Consider a supplier of fresh produce to large grocery chains such as Kroger. The supplier might implement a business-critical integrity constraint stating that no product returns are accepted after 15 days past delivery. That would make sense because of the chance of spoilage of the produce. Business-critical integrity constraints tend to mirror the very rules by which an organization achieves success.

    The specification and enforcement of integrity constraints produce higher-quality information that will provide better support for business decisions. Organizations that establish specific procedures for developing integrity constraints typically see an increase in accuracy that then increases the use of organizational information by business professionals.

INCREASED INFORMATION SECURITY

Managers must protect information, like any asset, from unauthorized users or misuse. As systems become increasingly complex and highly available over the Internet on many different devices, security becomes an even bigger issue. Databases offer many security features including passwords to provide authentication, access levels to determine who can access the data, and access controls to determine what type of access they have to the information.

    For example, customer service representatives might need read-only access to customer order information so they can answer customer order inquiries; they might not have or need the authority to change or delete order information. Managers might require access to employee files, but they should have access only to their own employees' files, not the employee files for the entire company. Various security features of databases can ensure that individuals have only certain types of access to certain types of information.

    Security risks are increasing as more and more databases and DBMS systems are moving to data centers run in the cloud. The biggest risks when using cloud computing are ensuring the security and privacy of the information in the database. Implementing data governance policies and procedures that outline the data management requirements can ensure safe and secure cloud computing.

LO 7.3 **Explain the business benefits of a data-driven website.**

Driving Websites with Data

A *content creator* is the person responsible for creating the original website content. A *content editor* is the person responsible for updating and maintaining website content. *Static information* includes fixed data incapable of change in the event of a user action. *Dynamic information* includes data that change based on user actions. For example, static websites supply only information that will not change until the content editor changes the information. Dynamic information changes when a user requests information. A dynamic website changes information based on user requests such as movie ticket availability, airline prices, or restaurant reservations. Dynamic website information is stored in a *dynamic catalog,* or an area of a website that stores information about products in a database.

Websites change for site visitors depending on the type of information they request. Consider, for example, an automobile dealer. The dealer would create a database containing data elements for each car it has available for sale including make, model, color, year, miles per gallon, a photograph, and so on. Website visitors might click on Porsche and then enter their specific requests such as price range or year made. Once the user hits "go" the website automatically provides a custom view of the requested information. The dealer must create, update, and delete automobile information as the inventory changes.

A *data-driven website* is an interactive website kept constantly updated and relevant to the needs of its customers using a database. Data-driven capabilities are especially useful when a firm needs to offer large amounts of information, products, or services. Visitors can become quickly annoyed if they find themselves buried under an avalanche of information when searching a website. A data-driven website can help limit the amount of information displayed to customers based on unique search requirements. Companies even use data-driven websites to make information in their internal databases available to customers and business partners.

There are a number of advantages to using the web to access company databases. First, web browsers are much easier to use than directly accessing the database using a custom-query tool. Second, the web interface requires few or no changes to the database model. Finally, it costs less to add a web interface in front of a DBMS than to redesign and rebuild the system to support changes. Additional data-driven website advantages include:

- **Easy to manage content:** Website owners can make changes without relying on MIS professionals; users can update a data-driven website with little or no training.

- **Easy to store large amounts of data:** Data-driven websites can keep large volumes of information organized. Website owners can use templates to implement changes for layouts, navigation, or website structure. This improves website reliability, scalability, and performance.

- **Easy to eliminate human errors:** Data-driven websites trap data-entry errors, eliminating inconsistencies while ensuring all information is entered correctly.

Zappos credits its success as an online shoe retailer to its vast inventory of nearly 3 million products available through its dynamic data-driven website. The company built its data-driven website catering to a specific niche market: consumers who were tired of finding that their most-desired items were always out of stock at traditional retailers. Zappos' highly flexible, scalable, and secure database helped it rank as the most-available Internet retailer. Figure 7.5 displays Zappos data-driven website illustrating a user querying the database and receiving information that satisfies the user's request.[2]

Companies can gain valuable business knowledge by viewing the data accessed and analyzed from their website. Figure 7.6 displays how running queries or using analytical tools, such as a PivotTable, on the database that is attached to the website can offer insight into the business, such as items browsed, frequent requests, items bought together, and so on.

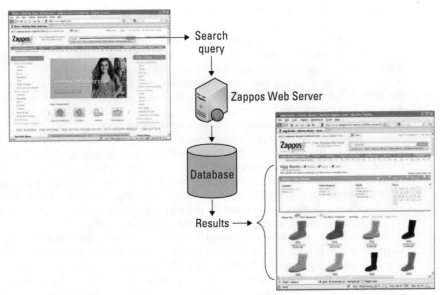

FIGURE 7.5

Zappos.com—
A Data-Driven Website

Integrating Information among Multiple Databases

LO 7.4 Explain why an organization would want to integrate its databases.

Until the 1990s, each department in the United Kingdom's Ministry of Defense (MOD) and Army headquarters had its own systems, each system had its own database, and sharing information among the departments was difficult. Manually inputting the same information multiple times into the different systems was also time consuming and inefficient. In many cases, management could not even compile the information it required to answer questions and make decisions.

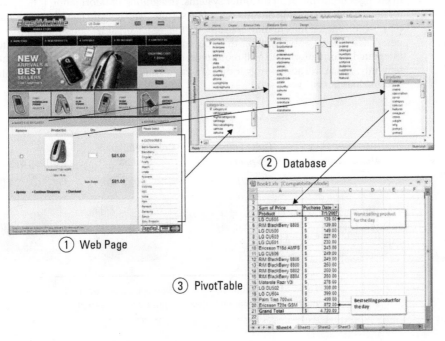

FIGURE 7.6

BI in a Data-Driven Website

The Army solved the problem by integrating its systems, or building connections between its many databases. These integrations allow the Army's multiple systems to automatically communicate by passing information between the databases, eliminating the need for manual information entry into multiple systems because after entering the information once, the integrations send the information immediately to all other databases. The integrations not only enable the different departments to share information, but have also dramatically increased the quality of the information. The Army can now generate reports detailing its state of readiness and other vital issues, nearly impossible tasks before building the integrations among the separate systems.[3]

An *integration* allows separate systems to communicate directly with each other. Similar to the UK's Army, an organization will probably maintain multiple systems, with each system having its own database. Without integrations, an organization will (1) spend considerable time entering the same information in multiple systems and (2) suffer from the low quality and inconsistency typically embedded in redundant information. While most integrations do not completely eliminate redundant information, they can ensure the consistency of it across multiple systems.

An organization can choose from two integration methods. The first is to create forward and backward integrations that link processes (and their underlying databases) in the value chain. A *forward integration* takes information entered into a given system and sends it automatically to all downstream systems and processes. A *backward integration* takes information entered into a given system and sends it automatically to all upstream systems and processes.

Figure 7.7 demonstrates how this method works across the systems or processes of sales, order entry, order fulfillment, and billing. In the order entry system, for example, an employee can update the information for a customer. That information, via the integrations, would be sent upstream to the sales system and downstream to the order fulfillment and billing systems.

Ideally, an organization wants to build both forward and backward integrations, which provide the flexibility to create, update, and delete information in any of the systems. However, integrations are expensive and difficult to build and maintain and most organizations build only forward integrations (sales through billing in Figure 7.7). Building only forward integrations implies that a change in the initial system (sales) will result in changes occurring in all the other systems. Integration of information is not possible for any changes occurring outside the initial system, which again can result in inconsistent organizational information. To address this issue, organizations can enforce business rules that all systems, other than the initial system, have read-only access to the integrated information. This will require users to change information in the initial system only, which will always trigger the integration and ensure that organizational information does not get out of sync.

FIGURE 7.7

A Forward and Backward Customer Information Integration Example

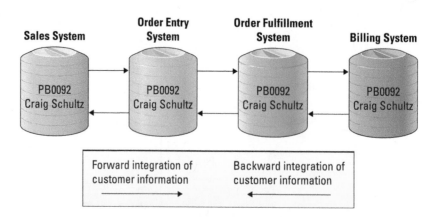

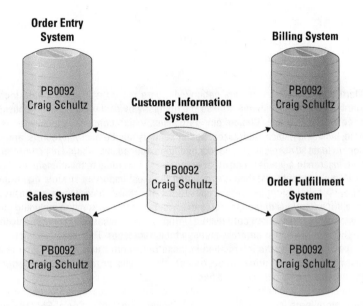

FIGURE 7.8

Integrating Customer
Information among
Databases

The second integration method builds a central repository for a particular type of information. Figure 7.8 provides an example of customer information integrated using this method across four different systems in an organization. Users can create, update, and delete customer information only in the central customer information database. As users perform these tasks on the central customer information database, integrations automatically send the new and/or updated customer information to the other systems. The other systems limit users to read-only access of the customer information stored in them. Again, this method does not eliminate redundancy—but it does ensure consistency of the information among multiple systems.

OPENING CASE STUDY QUESTIONS

1. Explain why database technology is important to a business.

2. Develop a list of some possible entities located in the Hotels.com database.

3. Develop a list of some possible attributes located in the Hotels.com database.

Chapter Seven Case: Keeper of the Keys

More than 145,000 consumers nationwide were placed at risk by a data theft at database giant ChoicePoint. Criminals tricked the company by posing as legitimate businesses to gain access to the various ChoicePoint databases, which contain a treasure trove of consumer data, including names, addresses, Social Security numbers, credit reports, and other information. At least 50 suspicious accounts had been opened in the name of nonexistent debt collectors, insurance agencies, and other companies, according to the company.

Without a doubt, databases are one of the most important IT tools that organizations use today. Databases contain large repositories of detailed data. When a transaction occurs, a sale, for example, a database stores every detail of the transaction including customer name, customer address, credit card number, products purchased, discounts received, and so on.

Organizations must carefully manage their databases. This management function includes properly organizing the information in these repositories in the most efficient way, ensuring that no erroneous information ever enters the databases, and—most important—protecting the information from thieves and hackers.

Information is a valuable commodity, and, sadly, this makes it a target for theft. Organizations store large amounts of customer information including Social Security numbers, credit card numbers, and bank account numbers—just think of the information stored at eBay, Amazon, or the IRS. When someone steals personal information (not necessarily by taking it from the person, but rather stealing it from a company), that person becomes a victim of identity theft. Consider this short list of organizations that have lost information and the huge numbers of customers affected.

- Bank of America: 1.2 million customers.
- CardSystems: 40 million customers.
- Citigroup: 3.9 million customers.
- DSW Shoe Warehouse: 1.4 million customers.
- TJX Companies: 45.6 million customers.
- Wachovia: 676,000 customers.

Adding up the numbers, more than 90 million people had their personal information either stolen or lost through organizations.

Business Accountability in Data Security

Companies may soon face stiff penalties for wayward data security practices. Massachusetts is considering legislation that would require companies to pay for any costs associated with a data breach of their IT systems. This move to protect customer data in Massachusetts comes at a fitting time, as two prominent retailers in the area, TJX Companies and Stop & Shop, wrestle with the aftermath of significant breaches that have exposed some of their customers to fraud.

Much of the expense associated with stopping fraudulent activity, such as canceling or reissuing credit or debit cards, stopping payment, and refunding customers, has been absorbed by the banks issuing credit or debit cards to the victims. The merchant banks that allow businesses such as TJX and Stop & Shop stores to accept credit and debit card transactions are penalized with fines from Visa, MasterCard, and other credit card organizations if the merchants they work with are found to violate the payment card industry's data security standards.

But the businesses that have had customer data stolen have largely suffered only from the costs to offer customers free credit-monitoring services and to repair a tarnished public image. In the case of popular retailers, this tarnish is easily polished away when juicy sales incentives are offered to get customers back.

Massachusetts House Bill 213, sponsored by Rep. Michael Costello, proposes to amend the Commonwealth's general laws to include a section that would require any corporation or other commercial entity whose sensitive customer information is stolen to notify customers about the data breach and also make companies liable to card-issuing banks for the costs those banks incur because of the breach and any subsequent fraudulent activity. This would include making businesses cover the costs to cancel or reissue cards, stop payments or block transactions with respect to any such account, open or reopen an account, and issue any refund or credit made to any customer of the bank as a result of unauthorized transactions.

. The Massachusetts legislation is a key step in compelling companies to invest in better data security. Passage of this bill would put Massachusetts ahead of other states in terms of protecting customer data and spreading out the penalties so that both financial institutions and retailers have incentives to improve security. Security vendors are likely to be watching Massachusetts very closely, because the bill also would create an urgent need for companies doing business in that state to invest in ways to improve their ability to protect customer data. If the companies will not do this on their own, then holding them accountable for their customers' financial losses may be just what is needed to stop the next data breach from occurring.[4]

Questions

1. How many organizations have your personal information, including your Social Security number, bank account numbers, and credit card numbers?

2. What information is stored at your college? Is there a chance your information could be hacked and stolen from your college?

3. What can you do to protect yourself from identity theft?

4. Do you agree or disagree with changing laws to hold the company where the data theft occurred accountable? Why or why not?

5. What impact would holding the company liable where the data theft occurred have on large organizations?

6. What impact would holding the company liable where the data theft occurred have on small businesses?

CHAPTER 8

Accessing Organizational Information—Data Warehouse

8.1. Describe the roles and purposes of data warehouses and data marts in an organization.

8.2. Identify the advantages of using business intelligence to support managerial decision making.

LO 8.1 Describe the roles and purposes of data warehouses and data marts in an organization.

Accessing Organizational Information

Applebee's Neighborhood Grill & Bar posts annual sales in excess of $3.2 billion and is actively using information from its data warehouse to increase sales and cut costs. The company gathers daily information for the previous day's sales into its data warehouse from 1,500 restaurants located in 49 states and seven countries. Understanding regional preferences, such as patrons in Texas preferring steaks more than patrons in New England, allows the company to meet its corporate strategy of being a neighborhood grill appealing to local tastes. The company has found tremendous value in its data warehouse by being able to make business decisions about customers' regional needs. The company also uses data warehouse information to perform the following:

- Base labor budgets on actual number of guests served per hour.
- Develop promotional sale item analysis to help avoid losses from overstocking or understocking inventory.
- Determine theoretical and actual costs of food and the use of ingredients.[1]

History of Data Warehousing

In the 1990s as organizations began to need more timely information about their business, they found that traditional operational information systems were too cumbersome to provide relevant data efficiently and quickly. Operational systems typically include accounting, order entry, customer service, and sales and are not appropriate for business analysis for the following reasons:

- Information from other operational applications is not included.
- Operational systems are not integrated, or not available in one place.
- Operational information is mainly current—does not include the history that is required to make good decisions.
- Operational information frequently has quality issues (errors)—the information needs to be cleansed.
- Without information history, it is difficult to tell how and why things change over time.
- Operational systems are not designed for analysis and decision support.

During the latter half of the 20th century, the numbers and types of databases increased. Many large businesses found themselves with information scattered across multiple platforms and variations of technology, making it almost impossible for any one individual to use information from multiple sources. Completing reporting requests across operational systems could take days or weeks using antiquated reporting tools that were designed to execute the business rather than run the business. From this idea, the data warehouse was born as a place where relevant information could be held for completing strategic reports for management. The key here is the word *strategic* as most executives were less concerned with the day-to-day operations than they were with a more overall look at the model and business functions.

A key idea within data warehousing is to take data from multiple platforms/ technologies (as varied as spreadsheets, databases, and word files) and place them in a common location that uses a common querying tool. In this way operational databases could be held on whatever system was most efficient for the operational business, while the reporting/strategic information could be held in a common location using a common language. Data warehouses take this a step further by giving the information itself commonality by defining what each term means and keeping it standard. An example of this would be gender, which can be referred to in many ways (Male, Female; M/F; 1/0), but should be standardized on a data warehouse with one common way of referring to each sex (M/F).

This design makes decision support more readily available without affecting day-to-day operations. One aspect of a data warehouse that should be stressed is that it is *not* a location for *all* of a business's information, but rather a location for information that is interesting, or information that will assist decision makers in making strategic decisions relative to the organization's overall mission.

Data warehousing is about extending the transformation of data into information. Data warehouses offer strategic level, external, integrated, and historical information so businesses can make projections, identify trends, and decide key business issues. The data warehouse collects and stores integrated sets of historical information from multiple operational systems and feeds them to one or more data marts. It may also provide end-user access to support enterprisewide views of information.

Data Warehouse Fundamentals

A *data warehouse* is a logical collection of information—gathered from many different operational databases—that supports business analysis activities and decision-making tasks. The primary purpose of a data warehouse is to aggregate information throughout an organization into a single repository in such a way that employees can make decisions and undertake business analysis activities. Therefore, while databases store the details of all transactions (for instance, the sale of a product) and events (hiring a new employee), data warehouses store that same information but in an aggregated form more suited to supporting decision-making tasks. Aggregation, in this instance, can include totals, counts, averages, and the like. Because of this sort of aggregation, data warehouses support only analytical processing.

The data warehouse modeled in Figure 8.1 compiles information from internal databases or transactional/operational databases and external databases through *extraction, transformation, and loading (ETL),* which is a process that extracts information from internal and external databases, transforms the information using a common set of enterprise definitions, and loads the information into a data warehouse. The data warehouse then sends subsets of the information to data marts. A *data mart* contains a subset of data warehouse information. To distinguish between data warehouses and data marts, think of data warehouses as having a more organizational focus and data marts as having focused information subsets particular to the needs of a given business unit such as finance or production and operations.

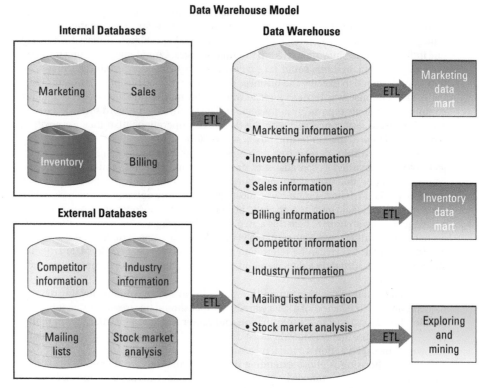

Data Warehouse Model

FIGURE 8.1

Model of a Typical Data
Warehouse

Lands' End created an organizationwide data warehouse so all its employees could access organizational information. Lands' End soon found out that there could be "too much of a good thing." Many of its employees would not use the data warehouse because it was simply too big, too complicated, and had too much irrelevant information. Lands' End knew there was valuable information in its data warehouse, and it had to find a way for its employees to easily access the information. Data marts were the perfect solution to the company's information overload problem. Once the employees began using the data marts, they were ecstatic at the wealth of information. Data marts were a huge success for Lands' End.[2]

MULTIDIMENSIONAL ANALYSIS AND DATA MINING

A relational database contains information in a series of two-dimensional tables. In a data warehouse and data mart, information is multidimensional, meaning it contains layers of columns and rows. For this reason, most data warehouses and data marts are *multidimensional databases*. A *dimension* is a particular attribute of information. Each layer in a data warehouse or data mart represents information according to an additional dimension. A **cube** is the common term for the representation of multidimensional information. Figure 8.2 displays a cube (cube *a*) that represents store information (the layers), product information (the rows), and promotion information (the columns).

Once a cube of information is created, users can begin to slice and dice the cube to drill down into the information. The second cube (cube *b*) in Figure 8.2 displays a slice representing promotion II information for all products, at all stores. The third cube (cube *c*) in Figure 8.2 displays only information for promotion III, product B, at store 2. By using multidimensional analysis, users can analyze information in a number of different ways and with any number of different dimensions. For example, users might

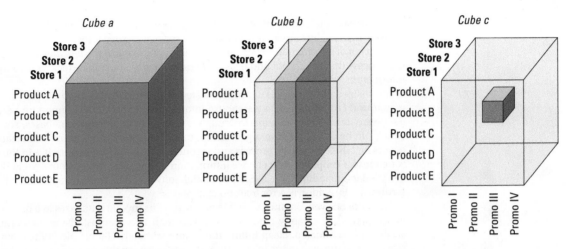

FIGURE 8.2

A Cube of Information for Performing a Multidimensional Analysis on Three Different Stores, for Five Different Products, and Four Different Promotions

want to add dimensions of information to a current analysis including product category, region, and even forecasted versus actual weather. The true value of a data warehouse is its ability to provide multidimensional analysis that allows users to gain insights into their information.

Data warehouses and data marts are ideal for off-loading some of the querying against a database. For example, querying a database to obtain an average of sales for product B at store 2 while promotion III is under way might create a considerable processing burden for a database, essentially slowing down the time it takes another person to enter a new sale into the same database. If an organization performs numerous queries against a database (or multiple databases), aggregating that information into a data warehouse could be beneficial.

Data mining is the process of analyzing data to extract information not offered by the raw data alone. For example, Ruf Strategic Solutions helps organizations employ statistical approaches within a large data warehouse to identify customer segments that display common traits. Marketers can then target these segments with specially designed products and promotions.

Data mining can also begin at a summary information level (coarse granularity) and progress through increasing levels of detail (drilling down), or the reverse (drilling up). To perform data mining, users need data-mining tools. **Data-mining tools** use a variety of techniques to find patterns and relationships in large volumes of information and infer rules from them that predict future behavior and guide decision making. Data-mining tools for data warehouses and data marts include query tools, reporting tools, multidimensional analysis tools, statistical tools, and intelligent agents.

Sega of America, one of the largest publishers of video games, uses a data warehouse and statistical tools to distribute its annual advertising budget of more than $50 million. With its data warehouse, product line specialists and marketing strategists "drill" into trends of each retail store chain. Their goal is to find buying trends that help them determine which advertising strategies are working best and how to reallocate advertising resources by media, territory, and time.[3]

INFORMATION CLEANSING OR SCRUBBING

Maintaining quality information in a data warehouse or data mart is extremely important. The Data Warehousing Institute estimates that low-quality information costs U.S. businesses $600 billion annually. That number may seem high, but it is not. If an organization is using a data warehouse or data mart to allocate dollars across advertising strategies (such as in the case of Sega of America), low-quality information will definitely have a negative impact on its ability to make the right decision.[4]

To increase the quality of organizational information and thus the effectiveness of decision making, businesses must formulate a strategy to keep information clean. This is the concept of information cleansing or scrubbing. ***Information cleansing or scrubbing*** is a process that weeds out and fixes or discards inconsistent, incorrect, or incomplete information.

Specialized software tools use sophisticated algorithms to parse, standardize, correct, match, and consolidate data warehouse information. This is vitally important because data warehouses often contain information from several different databases, some of which can be external to the organization. In a data warehouse, information cleansing occurs first during the ETL process and second on the information once it is in the data warehouse. Companies can choose information cleansing software from several different vendors including Oracle, SAS, Ascential Software, and Group 1 Software. Ideally, scrubbed information is error free and consistent.

Dr Pepper/Seven Up, Inc., was able to integrate its myriad databases in a data warehouse (and subsequently data marts) in less than two months, giving the company access to consolidated, clean information. Approximately 600 people in the company regularly use the data marts to analyze and track beverage sales across multiple dimensions, including various distribution routes such as bottle/can sales, fountain food-service sales, premier distributor sales, and chain and national accounts. The company is now performing in-depth analysis of up-to-date sales information that is clean and error free.[5]

Looking at customer information highlights why information cleansing is necessary. Customer information exists in several operational systems. In each system all details of this customer information could change from the customer ID to contact information (see Figure 8.3). Determining which contact information is accurate and correct for this customer depends on the business process that is being executed.

Figure 8.4 displays a customer name entered differently in multiple operational systems. Information cleansing allows an organization to fix these types of inconsistencies and cleans the information in the data warehouse. Figure 8.5 displays the typical events that occur during information cleansing.

Achieving perfect information is almost impossible. The more complete and accurate an organization wants its information to be, the more it costs (see Figure 8.6). The trade-off for perfect information lies in accuracy versus completeness. Accurate information means it is correct, while complete information means there are no blanks. A birth date of 2/31/10 is an example of complete but inaccurate information (February 31 does not exist). An address containing Denver, Colorado, without a ZIP code is an example of incomplete information that is accurate. For their information, most organizations determine a percentage high enough to make good decisions at a reasonable cost, such as 85 percent accurate and 65 percent complete.

FIGURE 8.3

Contact Information in
Operational Systems

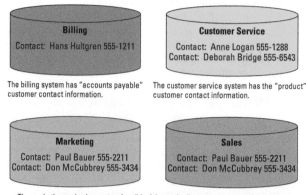

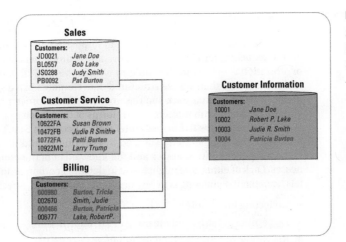

FIGURE 8.4

Standardizing Customer Name from Operational Systems

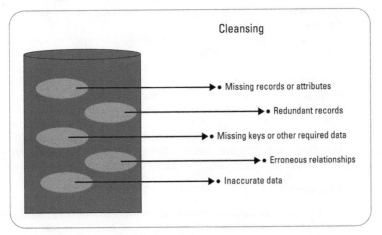

FIGURE 8.5

Information Cleansing Activities

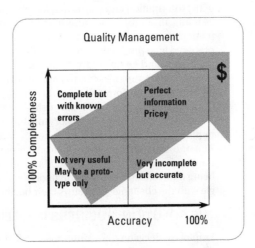

FIGURE 8.6

Accurate and Complete Information

LO 8.2 Identify the advantages of using business intelligence to support managerial decision making.

Supporting Decisions with Business Intelligence

Many organizations today find it next to impossible to understand their own strengths and weaknesses, let alone their biggest competitors, because the enormous volume of organizational data is inaccessible to all but the MIS department. Organization data include far more than simple structured data elements in a database; the set of data also includes unstructured data such as voice mail, customer phone calls, text messages, video clips, along with numerous new forms of data, such as tweets from Twitter.

An early reference to business intelligence occurs in Sun Tzu's book titled *The Art of War*. Sun Tzu claims that to succeed in war, one should have full knowledge of one's own strengths and weaknesses and full knowledge of the enemy's strengths and weaknesses. Lack of either one might result in defeat. A certain school of thought draws parallels between the challenges in business and those of war, specifically:

- Collecting information.
- Discerning patterns and meaning in the information.
- Responding to the resultant information.

Before the start of the information age in the late 20th century, businesses sometimes collected information from nonautomated sources. Businesses then lacked the computing resources to properly analyze the information and often made commercial decisions based primarily on intuition.

As businesses started automating more and more systems, more and more information became available. However, collection remained a challenge due to a lack of infrastructure for information exchange or to incompatibilities between systems. Reports sometimes took months to generate. Such reports allowed informed long-term strategic decision making. However, short-term tactical decision making continued to rely on intuition. In modern businesses, increasing standards, automation, and technologies have led to vast amounts of available information. Data warehouse technologies have set up repositories to store this information. Improved ETL has increased the speedy collecting of information. Business intelligence has now become the art of sifting through large amounts of data, extracting information, and turning that information into actionable knowledge.

THE PROBLEM: DATA RICH, INFORMATION POOR

An ideal business scenario would be as follows: As a business manager on his way to meet with a client reviews historical customer data, he realizes that the client's ordering volume has substantially decreased. As he drills down into the data, he notices the client had a support issue with a particular product. He quickly calls the support team to find out all of the information and learns that a replacement for the defective part can be shipped in 24 hours. In addition, he learns that the client has visited the website and requested information on a new product line. Armed with all this information, the business manager is prepared for a productive meeting with his client. He now understands the client's needs and issues, and he can address new sales opportunities with confidence.

For many companies the above example is simply a pipe dream. Attempting to gather all of the client information would actually take hours or even days to compile. With so much data available, it is surprisingly hard for managers to get information, such as inventory levels, past order history, or shipping details. Managers send their information requests to the MIS department where a dedicated person compiles the various reports. In some situations, responses can take days, by which time the information may be outdated and opportunities lost. Many organizations find themselves in the position of being data rich and information poor. Even in today's electronic world, managers struggle with the challenge of turning their business data into business intelligence.

THE SOLUTION: BUSINESS INTELLIGENCE

Employee decisions are numerous and they include providing service information, offering new products, and supporting frustrated customers. Employees can base their decisions on data, experience, or knowledge and preferably a combination of all three. Business intelligence can provide managers with the ability to make better decisions. A few examples of how different industries use business intelligence include:

- **Airlines:** Analyze popular vacation locations with current flight listings.
- **Banking:** Understand customer credit card usage and nonpayment rates.
- **Health care:** Compare the demographics of patients with critical illnesses.
- **Insurance:** Predict claim amounts and medical coverage costs.
- **Law enforcement:** Track crime patterns, locations, and criminal behavior.
- **Marketing:** Analyze customer demographics.
- **Retail:** Predict sales, inventory levels, and distribution.
- **Technology:** Predict hardware failures.

Figure 8.7 displays how organizations using BI can find the cause to many issues and problems simply by asking "Why?" The process starts by analyzing a report such as sales amounts by quarter. Managers will drill down into the report looking for why sales are up or why sales are down. Once they understand why a certain location or product is experiencing an increase in sales, they can share the information in an effort to raise enterprisewide sales. Once they understand the cause for a decrease in sales, they can take effective action to resolve the issue. Here are a few examples of how managers can use BI to answer tough business questions:

- **Where has the business been?** Historical perspective offers important variables for determining trends and patterns.
- **Where is the business now?** Looking at the current business situation allows managers to take effective action to solve issues before they grow out of control.
- **Where is the business going?** Setting strategic direction is critical for planning and creating solid business strategies.

Ask a simple question—such as who is my best customer or what is my worst-selling product—and you might get as many answers as you have employees. Databases, data warehouses, and data marts can provide a single source of "trusted" data that can answer questions about customers, products, suppliers, production, finances, fraud, and even employees. They can also alert managers to inconsistencies or help determine the cause and effects of enterprisewide business decisions. All business aspects can benefit from the added insights provided by business intelligence, and you, as a business student, will benefit from understanding how MIS can help you make intelligent decisions.[6]

VISUAL BUSINESS INTELLIGENCE

Informing is accessing large amounts of data from different management information systems. *Infographics (information graphics)* displays information graphically so it can

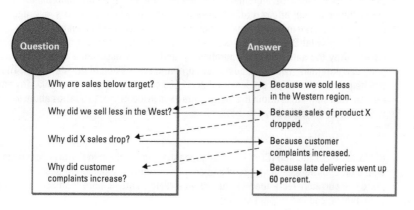

FIGURE 8.7

How BI Can Answer Tough Customer Questions

be easily understood. Infographics can present the results of large data analysis looking for patterns and relationships that monitor changes in variables over time. ***Data visualization*** describes technologies that allow users to "see" or visualize data to transform information into a business perspective. ***Data visualization tools*** move beyond Excel graphs and charts into sophisticated analysis techniques such as pie charts, controls, instruments, maps, time-series graphs, and more. Data visualization tools can help uncover correlations and trends in data that would otherwise go unrecognized. ***Business intelligence dashboards*** track corporate metrics such as critical success factors and key performance indicators and include advanced capabilities such as interactive controls allowing users to manipulate data for analysis. The majority of business intelligence software vendors offer a number of different data visualization tools and business intelligence dashboards.

OPENING CASE STUDY QUESTIONS

1. List the reasons a business would want to display information in a graphic or visual format.

2. Describe how a business could use a business intelligence digital dashboard to gain an understanding of how the business is operating.

3. Explain how a marketing department could use data visualization tools to help with the release of a new product.

4. Assess how Hotels.com is using BI to identify trends and change associated business processes.

Chapter Eight Case: Mining the Data Warehouse

According to a Merrill Lynch survey in 2006, business intelligence software and data-mining tools were at the top of CIOs' technology spending list. Following are a few examples of how companies are using data warehousing and data-mining tools to gain valuable business intelligence.

Ben & Jerry's

These days, when we all scream for ice cream, Ben & Jerry's cuts through the din by using integrated query, reporting, and online analytical processing technology from BI software vendor Business Objects. Through an Oracle database and with BI from Business Objects, Ben & Jerry's tracks the ingredients and life of each pint. If a consumer calls in with a complaint, the consumer affairs staff matches the pint with which supplier's milk, eggs, cherries, or whatever did not meet the organization's near-obsession with quality.

The BI tools let Ben & Jerry's officials access, analyze, and act on customer information collected by the sales, finance, purchasing, and quality-assurance departments. The company can determine what milk customers prefer in the making of the ice cream. The technology helped Ben & Jerry's track more than 12,500 consumer contacts in 2005. The information ranged from comments about the ingredients used in ice cream to queries about social causes supported by the company.

California Pizza Kitchen

California Pizza Kitchen (CPK) is a leading casual dining chain in the premium pizza segment with a recognized consumer brand and an established, loyal customer base. Founded in 1985, there are currently more than 130 full-service restaurants in more than 26 states, the District of Columbia, and five foreign countries.

Before implementing its BI tool, Cognos, CPK used spreadsheets to plan and track its financial statements and line items. The finance team had difficulty managing the volumes of data, complex calculations, and constant changes to the spreadsheets. It took several weeks of two people working full-time to obtain one version of the financial statements and future forecast. In addition, the team was limited by the software's inability to link cells and calculations across multiple spreadsheets, so updating other areas of corporate records became a time-consuming task. With Cognos, quarterly forecasting cycles have been reduced from eight days to two days. The finance team can now spend more time reviewing the results rather than collecting and entering the data.

Noodles & Company

Noodles & Company has more than 70 restaurants throughout Colorado, Illinois, Maryland, Michigan, Minnesota, Texas, Utah, Virginia, and Wisconsin. The company recently purchased Cognos BI tools to help implement reporting standards and communicate real-time operational information to field management throughout the United States.

Before implementing the first phase of the Cognos solution, IT and finance professionals spent days compiling report requests from numerous departments including sales and marketing, human resources, and real estate. Since completing phase one, operational Cognos reports are being accessed on a daily basis through the Noodles & Company website. This provides users with a single, 360-degree view of the business and consistent reporting throughout the enterprise.

Noodles & Company users benefit from the flexible query and reporting capabilities, allowing them to see patterns in the data to leverage new business opportunities. Cognos tools can pull information directly from a broad array of relational, operational, and other systems.[7]

Questions

1. Explain how Ben & Jerry's is using business intelligence tools to remain successful and competitive in a saturated market.

2. Identify why information cleansing is critical to California Pizza Kitchen's business intelligence tool's success.

3. Illustrate why 100 percent accurate and complete information is impossible for Noodles & Company to obtain.

4. Describe how each of the companies above is using BI to gain a competitive advantage.

✳ UNIT SUMMARY

The five common characteristics of quality information are accuracy, completeness, consistency, uniqueness, and timeliness. The costs to an organization of having low quality information can be enormous and could result in revenue losses and ultimately business failure. Databases maintain information about various types of objects, events, people, and places and help to alleviate many of the problems associated with low quality information such as redundancy, integrity, and security.

A data warehouse is a logical collection of information—gathered from many different operational databases—that supports business analysis activities and decision-making tasks. Data marts contain a subset of data warehouse information. Organizations gain tremendous insight into their business by mining the information contained in data warehouses and data marts.

Understanding the value of information is key to business success. Employees must be able to optimally access and analyze organizational information. The more knowledge employees have concerning how the organization stores, maintains, provides access to, and protects information the better prepared they will be when they need to use that information to make critical business decisions.

✳ KEY TERMS

Analytical information, 86
Attribute, 93
Backward integration, 100
Business intelligence
    dashboard, 112
Business-critical integrity
    constraint, 97
Business rule, 97
Content creator, 98
Cube, 106
Content editor, 98
Database, 92
Database management system
    (DBMS), 92
Data dictionary, 93
Data-driven website, 98
Data element (or data field), 92
Data governance, 90
Data model, 92
Data mart, 105
Data mining, 107

Data-mining tools, 107
Data visualization, 112
Data visualization tools, 112
Data warehouse, 105
Dynamic catalog, 98
Dynamic information, 98
Entity, 93
Extraction, transformation, and
    loading (ETL), 105
Foreign key, 94
Forward integration, 100
Informing, 111
Information cleansing or
    scrubbing, 108
Information granularity, 85
Information inconsistency, 87
Information integrity, 97
Information integrity issues, 87
Information redundancy, 97
Infographics (information
    graphics), 111

Integration, 100
Integrity constraint, 97
Logical view of information, 96
Metadata, 93
Physical view of information, 96
Primary key, 94
Query-by-example (QBE)
    tool, 92
Real-time information, 87
Real-time system, 87
Record, 94
Relational database
    management sytem, 93
Relational database model, 93
Relational integrity
    constraints, 97
Transactional information, 85
Static information, 98
Structured query language
    (SQL), 92

UNIT CLOSING CASE ONE

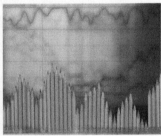
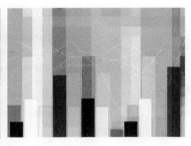

Data Visualization: Stories for the Information Age

At the intersection of art and algorithm, data visualization schematically abstracts information to bring about a deeper understanding of the data, wrapping it in an element of awe. While the practice of visually representing information is arguably the foundation of all design, a newfound fascination with data visualization has been emerging. After *The New York Times* and *The Guardian* recently opened their online archives to the public, artists rushed to dissect nearly two centuries worth of information, elevating this art form to new prominence.

For artists and designers, data visualization is a new frontier of self-expression, powered by the proliferation of information and the evolution of available tools. For enterprise, it is a platform for displaying products and services in the context of the cultural interaction that surrounds them, reflecting consumers' increasing demand for corporate transparency.

"Looking at something ordinary in a new way makes it extraordinary," says Aaron Koblin, one of the more recent pioneers of the discipline. As technology lead of Google's Creative Labs in San Francisco, he spearheaded the search giant's Chrome Experiments series designed to show off the speed and reliability of the Chrome browser.

Forget Pie Charts and Bar Graphs

Data visualization has nothing to do with pie charts and bar graphs. And it's only marginally related to "infographics," information design that tends to be about objectivity and clarification. Such representations simply offer another iteration of the data—restating it visually and making it easier to digest. Data visualization, on the other hand, is an interpretation, a different way to look at and think about data that often exposes complex patterns or correlations.

Data visualization is a way to make sense of the ever-increasing stream of information with which we're bombarded and provides a creative antidote to the analysis paralysis that can result from the burden of processing such a large volume of information. "It's not about clarifying data," says Koblin. "It's about contextualizing it."

Today algorithmically inspired artists are reimagining the art-science continuum through work that frames the left-brain analysis of data in a right-brain creative story. Some use data visualization as a bridge between alienating information and its emotional impact—see Chris Jordan's portraits of global mass culture. Others take a more technological angle and focus on cultural utility—the Zoetrope project offers a temporal and historical visualization of the ephemeral web. Still others are pure artistic indulgence—like Koblin's own Flight Patterns project, a visualization of air traffic over North America.

How Business Can Benefit

There are real implications for business here. Most cell phone providers, for instance, offer a statement of a user's monthly activity. Most often it's an overwhelming table of various numerical measures of how much you talked, when, with whom, and how much it cost. A visual representation of these data might help certain patterns emerge, revealing calling habits and perhaps helping users save money.

Companies can also use data visualization to gain new insight into consumer behavior. By observing and understanding what people do with the data—what they find useful and what they dismiss as worthless—executives can make the valuable distinction between what consumers say versus what they do. Even now, this can be a tricky call to make from behind the two-way mirror of a traditional qualitative research setting.

It's essential to understand the importance of creative vision along with the technical mastery of software. Data visualization isn't about using all the data available, but about deciding which patterns and elements to focus on, building a narrative, and telling the story of the raw data in a different, compelling way.

Ultimately, data visualization is more than complex software or the prettying up of spreadsheets. It's not innovation for the sake of innovation. It's about the most ancient of social rituals: storytelling. It's about telling the story locked in the data differently, more engagingly, in a way that draws us in, makes our eyes open a little wider and our jaw drop ever so slightly. And as we process it, it can sometimes change our perspective altogether.[8]

Questions

1. Identify the effects poor information might have on a data visualization project.
2. How does data visualization use database technologies?
3. How could a business use data visualization to identify new trends?
4. What is the correlation between data mining and data visualization?
5. Is data visualization a form of business intelligence? Why or why not?
6. What security issues are associated with data visualization?
7. What might happen to a data visualization project if it failed to cleanse or scrub its data?

✳ UNIT CLOSING CASE TWO

Zillow

Zillow.com is an online web-based real estate site helping homeowners, buyers, sellers, renters, real estate agents, mortgage professionals, property owners, and property managers find and share information about real estate and mortgages. Zillow allows users to access, anonymously and free of charge, the kinds of tools and information previously reserved for real estate professionals. Zillow's databases cover more than 90 million homes, which represents 95 percent of the homes in the United States. Adding to the sheer size of its databases, Zillow recalculates home valuations for each property every day, so they can provide historical graphs on home valuations over time. In some areas, Zillow is able to display 10 years of valuation history, a value-added benefit for many of its customers. This collection of data represents an operational data warehouse for anyone visiting the website.

As soon as Zillow launched its website, it immediately generated a massive amount of traffic. As the company expanded its services, the founders knew the key to its success would be the site's ability to quickly process and manage massive amounts of data, in real time. The company identified a need for accessible, scalable, reliable, secure databases that would enable it to continue to increase the capacity of its infrastructure indefinitely without sacrificing performance. Zillow's traffic continues to grow despite the weakening real estate market; the company is experiencing annual traffic growth of 30 percent and about a third of all U.S. mortgage professionals visit the site in a given month.

Data Mining and Business Intelligence

Zestimate® values on Zillow use data-mining features for spotting trends across property valuations. Data mining also allows the company to see how accurate Zestimate values are over time. Zillow has also built the industry's first search by monthly payment, allowing users to find homes that are for sale and rent based on a monthly payment they can afford. Along with the monthly payment search, users can also enter search criteria such as the number of bedrooms or bathrooms.

Zillow also launched a new service aimed at changing the way Americans shop for mortgages. Borrowers can use Zillow's new Mortgage Marketplace to get custom loan quotes from lenders without having to give their names, addresses, phone numbers, or Social Security numbers, or field unwanted telephone calls from brokers competing for their business. Borrowers reveal their identities only after contacting the lender of their choice. The company is entering a field of established mortgage sites such as LendingTree.com and Experian Group's Lowermybills.com, which charge mortgage companies for borrower information. Zillow, which has an advertising model, says it does not plan to charge for leads.

For mortgage companies, the anonymous leads come free; they can make a bid based on information provided by the borrower, such as salary, assets, credit score, and the type of loan. Lenders can browse borrower requests and see competing quotes from other brokers before making a bid.[9]

Questions

1. List the reasons Zillow would need to use a database to run its business.
2. Describe how Zillow uses business intelligence to create a unique product for its customers.
3. How could the marketing department at Zillow use a data mart to help with the release of a new product launch?
4. Categorize the five common characteristics of high-quality information and rank them in order of importance to Zillow.
5. Develop a list of some possible entities and attributes of Zillow's mortgage database.
6. Assess how Zillow uses a data-driven website to run its business.

★ MAKING BUSINESS DECISIONS

1. Improving Information Quality

HangUps Corporation designs and distributes closet organization structures. The company operates five different systems: order entry, sales, inventory management, shipping, and billing. The company has severe information quality issues including missing, inaccurate, redundant, and incomplete information. The company wants to implement a data warehouse containing information from the five different systems to help maintain a single customer view, drive business decisions, and perform multidimensional analysis. Identify how the organization can improve its information quality when it begins designing and building its data warehouse.

2. Information Timeliness

Information timeliness is a major consideration for all organizations. Organizations need to decide the frequency of backups and the frequency of updates to a data warehouse. In a team, describe the timeliness requirements for backups and updates to a data warehouse for

- Weather tracking systems.
- Car dealership inventories.
- Vehicle tire sales forecasts.
- Interest rates.
- Restaurant inventories.
- Grocery store inventories.

3. Entities and Attributes

Martex Inc. is a manufacturer of athletic equipment and its primary lines of business include running, tennis, golf, swimming, basketball, and aerobics equipment. Martex currently supplies four primary vendors including Sam's Sports, Total Effort, The Underline, and Maximum Workout. Martex wants to build a database to help it organize its products. In a group, identify the different types of entity classes and the related attributes that Martex will want to consider when designing the database.

4. Integrating Information

You are currently working for the Public Transportation Department of Chatfield. The department controls all forms of public transportation including buses, subways, and trains. Each department has about 300 employees and maintains its own accounting, inventory, purchasing, and human resource systems. Generating reports across departments is a difficult task and usually involves gathering and correlating the information from the many different systems. It typically takes about two weeks to generate the quarterly balance sheets and profit and loss statements. Your team has been asked to compile a report recommending what the Public Transportation Department of Chatfield can do to alleviate its information and system issues. Be sure that your report addresses the various reasons departmental reports are presently difficult to obtain as well as how you plan to solve this problem.

5. Information—Business Intelligence or a Diversion from the Truth?

President Obama used part of his commencement address at Virginia's Hampton University to criticize the flood of incomplete information or downright incorrect information that flows in the 24-hour news cycle. The president said, "You're coming of age in a 24/7 media environment that bombards us with all kinds of content and exposes us to all kinds of arguments, some of which don't always rank all that high on the truth meter. With iPods and iPads and Xboxes and PlayStations—none of which I know how to work—information becomes a distraction, a diversion, a form of entertainment, rather than a tool of empowerment, rather than the means of emancipation."[10]

Do you agree or disagree with President Obama's statement? Who is responsible for verifying the accuracy of online information? What should happen to companies that post inaccurate information? What should happen to individuals who post inaccurate information? What should you remember when reading or citing sources for online information?

6. Illegal Database Access

Goldman Sachs has been hit with a $3 million lawsuit by a company that alleges the brokerage firm stole intellectual property from its database that had market intelligence facts. The U.S. District Court for the Southern District of New York filed the lawsuit in 2010 claiming Goldman Sachs employees used other people's access credentials to log into Ipreo's proprietary database, dubbed Bigdough. Offered on a subscription basis, Bigdough provides detailed information on more than 80,000 contacts within the financial industry. Ipreo complained to the court that Goldman Sachs employees illegally accessed Bigdough at least 264 times in 2008 and 2009.[11]

Do you agree or disagree with the lawsuit? Should Goldman Sachs be held responsible for rogue employees' behavior? What types of policies should Goldman Sachs implement to ensure this does not occur again?

7. Data Storage

Information is one of the most important assets of any business. Businesses must ensure information accuracy, completeness, consistency, timeliness, and uniqueness. In addition, business must have a reliable backup service. In part thanks to cloud computing, there are many data hosting services on the Internet. These sites offer storage of information that can be accessed from anywhere in the world.

These data hosting services include Hosting (www.hosting.com), Mozy (www.mozy.com), My Docs Online (www.mydocsonline.com), and Box (www.box.net). Visit a few of these sites along with a several others you find through research. Which sites are free? Are there limits to how much you can store? If so, what is the limit? What type of information can you store (video, text, photos, etc.)? Can you allow multiple users with different passwords to access your storage area? Are you contractually bound for a certain duration (annual, etc.)? Are different levels of services provided such as personal, enterprise, work group? Does it make good business sense to store business data on the Internet? What about personal data?

8. Gathering Business Intelligence

When considering new business opportunities, you need knowledge about the competition. One of the things many new business owners fail to do is to gather business intelligence on their competitors, such as how many there are and what differentiates each of them. You may find there are too many and that they would be tough competition for you. Or, you may find that there are few competitors and the ones who are out there offer very little value.

Generate a new business idea you could launch on the Internet. Research the Internet to find similar businesses in the area you have chosen. How many sites did you find that are offering the same products or services you are planning to offer? Did you come across any sites from another country that have a unique approach that you did not see on any of the sites in your own country? How would you use this information in pursuing your business idea?

9. **Free Data!**

The U.S. Bureau of Labor Statistics states that its role is as the "principal fact-finding agency for the federal government in the broad field of labor economics and statistics." And the data that the bureau provides via its website are available to anyone, free. This can represent a treasure trove of business intelligence and data mining for those who take advantage of this resource. Visit the website www.bls.gov. What type of information does the site provide? What information do you find most useful? What sort of information concerning employment and wages is available? How is this information categorized? How would this type of information be helpful to a business manager? What type of demographic information is available? How could this benefit a new start-up business?[12]

10. **Explaining Relational Databases**

You have been hired by Vision, a start-up clothing company. Your manager, Holly Henningson, is unfamiliar with databases and their associated business value. Henningson has asked you to create a report detailing the basics of databases. She would also like you to provide a detailed explanation of relational databases along with their associated business advantages.

1. Determining Information Quality Issues

Real People is a magazine geared toward working individuals that provides articles and advice on everything from car maintenance to family planning. *Real People* is currently experiencing problems with its magazine distribution list. More than 30 percent of the magazines mailed are returned because of incorrect address information, and each month it receives numerous calls from angry customers complaining that they have not yet received their magazines. Figure AYK.1 provides a sample of *Real People*'s customer information. Create a report detailing all of the issues with the information, potential causes of the information issues, and solutions the company can follow to correct the situation.

2. Mining the Data Warehouse

Alana Smith is a senior buyer for a large wholesaler that sells different types of arts and crafts to greeting card stores such as Hallmark. Alana's latest marketing strategy is to send all of her customers a new line of hand-made picture frames from Russia. Alana's data support her decision for the new line. Her analysis predicts that the frames should sell an average of 10 to 15 per store, per day. Alana is excited about the new line and is positive it will be a success.

One month later Alana learns that the frames are selling 50 percent below expectations and averaging between five and eight frames sold daily in each store. Alana decides to access the company's data warehouse to determine why sales are below expectations. Identify several different dimensions of data that Alana will want to analyze to help her decide what is causing the problems with the picture frame sales.

3. Cleansing Information

You are working for BI, a start-up business intelligence consulting company. You have a new client that is interested in hiring BI to clean up its information. To determine how good your work is, the client would like your analysis of the spreadsheet in Figure AYK.2.

4. Different Dimensions

The focus of data warehousing is to extend the transformation of data into information. Data warehouses offer strategic level, external, integrated, and historical information so businesses can make projections, identify trends, and make key business decisions. The data warehouse collects and stores integrated sets of historical information from multiple operational systems and feeds them to one or more data marts. It may also provide end-user access to support enterprisewide views of information.

FIGURE AYK.1

Sample Data

ID	First Name	Middle Name	Last Name	Street	City	State	ZIP Code
433	M	J	Jones	13 Denver	Denver	CO	87654
434	Margaret	J	Jones	13 First Ave.	Denver	CO	87654
434	Brian	F	Hoover	Lake Ave.	Columbus	OH	87654
435	Nick	H	Schweitzer	65 Apple Lane	San Francisco	OH	65664
436	Richard	A		567 55th St.	New York	CA	98763
437	Alana	B	Smith	121 Tenny Dr.	Buffalo	NY	142234
438	Trevor	D	Darrian	90 Fresrdestil	Dallas	TX	74532

FIGURE AYK.2

Data Cleansing

CUST ID	First Name	Last Name	Address	City	State	ZIP	Phone	Last Order Date
233620	Christopher	Lee	12421 W Olympic Blvd	Los Angeles	CA	75080-1100	(972)680-7848	4/18/2002
233621	Bruce	Brandwen	268 W 44th St	New York	PA	10036-3906	(212)471-6077	5/3/2002
233622	Glr	Johnson	4100 E Dry Creek Rd	Littleton	CO	80122-3729	(303)712-5461	5/6/2002
233623	Dave	Owens	466 Commerce Rd	Staunton	VA	24401-4432	(540)851-0362	3/19/2002
233624	John	Coulbourn	124 Action St	Maynard	MA	1754	(978)987-0100	4/24/2002
233629	Dan	Gagliardo	2875 Union Rd	Cheektowaga	NY	14227-1461	(716)558-8191	5/4/2002
23362	Damanceee	Allen	1633 Broadway	New York	NY	10019-6708	(212)708-1576	
233630	Michael	Peretz	235 E 45th St	New York	NY	10017-3305	(212)210-1340	4/30/2002
							(608)238-9690	
233631	Jody	Veeder	440 Science Dr	Madison	WI	53711-1064	X227	3/27/2002
233632	Michael	Kehrer	3015 SSE Loop 323	Tyler	TX	75701	(903)579-3229	4/28/
233633	Erin	Yoon	3500 Carillon Pt	Kirkland	WA	98033-7354	(425)897-7221	3/25/2002
233634	Madeline	Shefferly	4100 E Dry Creek Rd	Littleton	CO	80122-3729	(303)486-3949	3/33/2002
233635	Steven	Conduit	1332 Enterprise Dr	West Chester	PA	19380-5970	(610)692-5900	4/27/2002
233636	Joseph	Kovach	1332 Enterprise Dr	West Chester	PA	19380-5970	(610)692-5900	4/28/2002
233637	Richard	Jordan	1700 N	Philadelphia	PA	19131-4728	(215)581-6770	3/19/2002
233638	Scott	Mikolajczyk	1655 Crofton Blvd	Crofton	MD	21114-1387	(410)729-8155	4/28/2002
233639	Susan	Shragg	1875 Century Park E	Los Angeles	CA	90067-2501	(310)785-0511	4/29/2002
233640	Rob	Ponto	29777 Telegraph Rd	Southfield	MI	48034-1303	(810)204-4724	5/5/2002
			1211 Avenue Of The					
233642	Lauren	Butler	Americas	New York	NY	10036-8701	(212)852-7494	4/22/2002
233643	Christopher	Lee	12421 W Olympic Blvd	Los Angeles	CA	90064-1022	(310)689-2577	3/25/2002
233644	Michelle	Decker	6922 Hollywood Blvd	Hollywood	CA	90028-6117	(323)817-4655	5/8/2002
			1211 Avenue Of The					
233647	Natalia	Galeano	Americas	New York	NY	10036-8701	(646)728-6911	4/23/2002
233648	Bobbie	Orchard	4201 Congress St	Charlotte	NC	28209-4617	(704)557-2444	5/11/2002
233650	Ben	Konfino	1111 Stewart Ave	Bethpage	NY	11714-3533	(516)803-1406	3/19/2002
233651	Lenee	Santana	1050 Techwood Dr NW	Atlanta	GA	30318-KKRR	(404)885-2000	3/22/2002
233652	Lauren	Monks	7700 Wisconsin Ave	Bethesda	MD	20814-3578	(301)771-4772	3/19/2005
			10950 Washington					
233653	Mark	Woolley	Blvd	Culver City	CA	90232-4026	(310)202-2900	4/20/2002
233654	Stan	Matthews	1235 W St NE	Washington	DC	20018-1107	(202)608-2000	3/25/2002

Dimension	Value (1–5)	Dimension	Value (1–5)
Product number		Season	
Store location		Promotion	
Customer net worth		Payment method	
Number of sales personnel		Commission policy	
Customer eating habits		Manufacturer	
Store hours		Traffic report	
Salesperson ID		Customer language	
Product style		Weather	
Order date		Customer gender	
Product quantity		Local tax information	
Ship date		Local cultural demographics	
Current interest rate		Stock market closing	
Product cost		Customer religious affiliation	
Customer's political affiliation		Reason for purchase	
Local market analysis		Employee dress code policy	
Order time		Customer age	
Customer spending habits		Employee vacation policy	
Product price		Employee benefits	
Exchange rates		Current tariff information	
Product gross margin			

FIGURE AYK.3

Data Warehouse Data

Project Focus

You are currently working on a marketing team for a large corporation that sells jewelry around the world. Your boss has asked you to look at the following dimensions of data to determine which ones you want in your data mart for performing sales and market analysis (see Figure AYK.3). As a team, categorize the different dimensions ranking them from 1 to 5, with 1 indicating that the dimension offers the highest value and must be in your data mart and 5 indicating that the dimension offers the lowest value and does not need to be in your data mart.

5. Understanding Search

Pretend that you are a search engine. Choose a topic to query. It can be anything such as your favorite book, movie, band, or sports team. Search your topic on Google, pick three or four pages from the results, and print them out. On each printout, find the individual words from your query (such as "Boston Red Sox" or "The Godfather") and use a highlighter to mark each word with color. Do that for each of the documents that you print out. Now tape those documents on a wall, step back a few feet, and review your documents. If you did not know what the rest of a page said and could only judge by the colored words, which document do you think would be most relevant? Is there anything that would make a document look more relevant? Is it better to have the words be in a large heading or to occur several times in a smaller font? Do you prefer it if the words are at the top or the bottom of the page? How often do the words need to appear? Come up with two or three things you would look for to see if a document matched a query well. This exercise mimics search engine processes and should help you understand why a search engine returns certain results over others.

6. Predicting Netflix

Netflix Inc., the largest online movie rental service, provides more than 12 million subscribers access to more than 100,000 unique DVD titles along with a growing on-demand library in excess of 10,000 choices. Data and information are so important to Netflix that it created The Netflix Prize, an open competition for anyone who could improve the data used in prediction ratings for films (an increase of 10 percent), based on previous ratings. The winner would receive a $1 million prize.

Project Focus

The ability to search, analyze, and comprehend information is vital for any organization's success. It certainly was for Netflix, as it was happy to pay anyone $1 million to improve the quality of its information. In a group explain how Netflix might use databases, data warehouses, and data marts to predict customer movie recommendations. Here are a few characteristics you might want to analyze to get you started:

- Customer demographics.
- Movie genre, rating, year, producer, type.
- Actor information.
- Internet access.
- Location for mail pickup.

7. The Crunch Factory

The Crunch Factory is one of the fourth-largest gyms operating in Australia, and each gym operates its own system with its own database. Unfortunately, the company failed to develop any data-capturing standards and now faces the challenges associated with low-quality enterprisewide information. For example, one system has a field to capture email addresses while another system does not. Duplicate customer information among the different systems is another major issue, and the company continually finds itself sending conflicting or competing messages to customers from different gyms. A customer could also have multiple accounts within the company, one representing a membership, another representing additional classes, and yet another for a personal trainer. The Crunch Factory has no way to identify that the different customer accounts are actually for the same customer.

Project Focus

To remain competitive and be able to generate business intelligence The Crunch Factory has to resolve these challenges. The Crunch Factory has just hired you as its data quality expert. Your first task is to determine how the company can turn its low-quality information into high-quality business intelligence. Create a plan that The Crunch Factory can implement that details the following:

- Challenges associated with low-quality information.
- Benefits associated with high-quality information.
- Recommendations on how the company can clean up its data.

8. Too Much of a Good Thing

The Castle, a premium retailer of clothes and accessories, created an enterprisewide data warehouse so all its employees could access information for decision making. The Castle soon discovered that it is possible to have too much of a good thing. The Castle employees found themselves inundated with data and unable to make any decisions, a common occurrence called analysis paralysis. When sales representatives queried the data warehouse to determine if a certain product in the size, color, and category was available, they would get hundreds of results showing everything from production orders to supplier contracts. It became easier for the sales representatives to look in the warehouse themselves than to check the system. Employees found the data warehouse was simply too big, too complicated, and contained too much irrelevant information.

Project Focus

The Castle is committed to making its data warehouse system a success and has come to you for help. Create a plan that details the value of the data warehouse to the business, how it can be easier for all employees to use, along with the potential business benefits the company can derive from its data warehouse.

9. Twitter Buzz

Technology tools that can predict sales for the coming week, decide when to increase inventory, and determine when additional staff is required are extremely valuable. Twitter is not just for tweeting your whereabouts anymore. Twitter and other social-media sites have become great tools for gathering business intelligence on customers, including what they like, dislike, need, and want. Twitter is easy to use, and businesses can track every single time a customer makes a statement about a particular product or service. Good businesses turn this valuable information into intelligence spotting trends and patterns in customer opinion.

Project Focus

Do you agree that a business can use Twitter to gain business intelligence? How many companies do you think are aware of Twitter and exactly how they can use it to gain BI? How do you think Twitter uses a data warehouse? How do you think companies store Twitter information? How would a company use Twitter in a data mart? How would a company use cubes to analyze Twitter data?

AYK APPLICATION PROJECTS

If you are looking for Access projects to incorporate into your class, try any of the following after reading this chapter.

Project Number	Project Name	Project Type	Plug-In	Focus Area	Project Level	Skill Set	Page Number
28	Daily Invoice	Access	T5, T6, T7, T8	Business Analysis	Introductory	Entities, Relationships, and Databases	AYK.17
29	Billing Data	Access	T5, T6, T7, T8	Business Intelligence	Introductory	Entities, Relationships, and Databases	AYK.19
30	Inventory Data	Access	T5, T6, T7, T8	SCM	Intermediate	Entities, Relationships, and Databases	AYK.20
31	Call Center	Access	T5, T6, T7, T8	CRM	Intermediate	Entities, Relationships, and Databases	AYK.21
32	Sales Pipeline	Access	T5, T6, T7, T8	Business Intelligence	Advanced	Entities, Relationships, and Databases	AYK.23
33	Online Classified Ads	Access	T5, T6, T7, T8	Ecommerce	Advanced	Entities, Relationships, and Databases	AYK.23

 ENTREPRENEURIAL CHALLENGE

Build Your Own Business

Project Focus

1. Provide an example of your business data that fits each of the five common characteristics of high-quality information. Explain why each characteristic is important to your business data and what might happen if your business data were of low quality. (Be sure to identify your business and the name of your company.)
2. Identify the different entities and their associated attributes that would be found in your potential relational database model for your sales database.
3. Identify the benefits of having a data warehouse for your business. What types of data marts would you want to extract from you data warehouse to help you run your business and make strategic decisions?

PLUG-IN

B10

Business Intelligence

1. Compare tactical, operational, and strategic BI.
2. Explain the three common forms of data mining.
3. Describe the four categories of BI business benefits.

LO 1. Compare tactical, operational, and strategic BI.

Operational, Tactical, and Strategic BI

Claudia Imhoff, president of Intelligent Solutions, believes it is useful to divide the spectrum of data mining analysis and business intelligence into three categories: operational, tactical, and strategic. Two trends are displayed when viewing the spectrum from operational through tactical to strategic. First, the analysis becomes increasingly complex and ad hoc. That is, it is less repetitive, less predictable, and it requires varying amounts and types of data. Second, both the risks and rewards of the analysis increase. That is, the often time-consuming, more strategic queries produce value less frequently but, when they do, the value can be extraordinary. Figure B10.1 illustrates the differences among operational, tactical, and strategic BI.

These three forms are not performed in isolation from each other. It is important to understand that they must work with each other, feeding results from strategic to tactical to promote better operational decision making. Figure B10.2 demonstrates this synergy. In this example, strategic BI is used in the planning stages of a marketing campaign.

FIGURE B10.1

Operational, Tactical, Strategic BI

	Operational BI	**Tactical BI**	**Strategic BI**
Business focus	Manage daily operations, integrate BI with operational systems	Conduct short-term analysis to achieve strategic goals	Achieve long-term organizational goals
Primary users	Managers, analysts, operational users	Executives, managers	Executives, managers
Time frame	Intraday	Day(s) to weeks to months	Months to years
Data	Real-time metrics	Historical metrics	Historical metrics

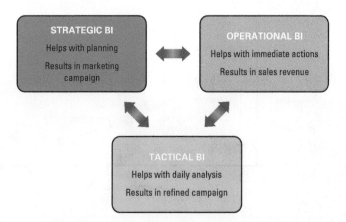

FIGURE B10.2

The Three Forms of BI
Must Work toward a
Common Goal

The results of these analytics form the basis for the beginnings of a new campaign, targeting specific customers or demographics, for example. The daily analyses of the campaign are used by the more tactical form of BI to change the course of the campaign if its results are not tracking where expected.

For example, perhaps a different marketing message is needed, or the inventory levels are not sufficient to maintain the current sales pace so the scope of marketing might be changed. These results are then fed into the operational BI for immediate actions—offering a different product, optimizing the sale price of the product, or changing the daily message sent to selected customer segments.

For this synergy to work, the three forms of BI must be tightly integrated with each other. Minimal time should be lost transporting the results from one technological environment to another. Seamlessness in terms of data and process flow is a must. TruServ, the parent company of True Value Hardware, has used BI software to improve efficiency of its distribution operations and reap a $50 million reduction in inventory costs. The marketing department uses BI to track sales promotion results such as which promotions were most popular by store or by region. Now that TruServ is building promotion histories in its databases, it can ensure all stores are fully stocked with adequate inventory. TruServ was able to achieve a positive return on investment in about five to six months.

BI'S OPERATIONAL VALUE

A leading risk insurance company allows customers to access account information over the Internet. Previously, the company sent paper reports and diskettes to all of its customers. Any errors in the reports would take one to two months to correct because customers would first have to receive the report, catch the mistake, and then notify the company of the error. Now customers spot the errors in real time and notify the insurance company directly through an extranet, usually within a couple of days.

Richard Hackathorn of Bolder Technologies developed an interesting graph to demonstrate the value of operational BI. Figure B10.3 shows the three latencies that impact the speed of decision making. These are data, analysis, and decision latencies.

- **Data latency** is the time duration to make data ready for analysis (i.e., the time for extracting, transforming, and cleansing the data) and loading the data into the database. All this can take time depending on the state of the operational data to begin with.

- **Analysis latency** is the time from which data are made available to the time when analysis is complete. Its length depends on the time it takes a business to do analysis. Usually, we think of this as the time it takes a human to do the analysis, but this can be decreased by the use of automated analytics that have thresholds. When the thresholds are exceeded, alerts or alarms can be issued to appropriate personnel, or they can cause exception processes to be initiated with no human intervention needed.

FIGURE B10.3

The Latency between a
Business Event and an
Action Taken

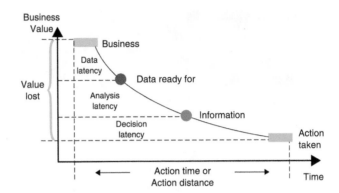

- ***Decision latency*** is the time it takes a human to comprehend the analytic result and determine an appropriate action. This form of latency is very difficult to reduce. The ability to remove the decision-making process from the human and automate it will greatly reduce the overall decision latency. Many forward-thinking companies are doing just that. For example, rather than send a high-value customer a letter informing him of a bounced check (which takes days to get to the customer), an automated system can simply send an immediate email or voice message informing the customer of the problem.

The key is to shorten these latencies so that the time frame for opportunistic influences on customers, suppliers, and others is faster, more interactive, and better positioned. As mentioned above, the best time to influence customers is not after they have left the store or the website. It is while they are still in the store or still wandering around the website.

For example, a customer who is searching a website for travel deals is far more likely to be influenced by appropriate messaging actions then and there. Actions taken immediately, while customers are still in the site, might include:

- Offering customers an appropriate coupon for the trip they showed interest in while searching for cheap airfares.

- Giving customers information about their current purchase such as the suggestion that visas are needed.

- Congratulating them on reaching a certain frequent-buyer level and giving them 10 percent off an item.

A website represents another great opportunity to influence a customer, if the interactions are appropriate and timely. For example:

- A banner could announce the next best product to offer right after the customer puts an item in her basket.

- The customer could receive an offer for a product he just removed from his shopping basket.

- Appropriate instructions for the use of a product could come up on the customer's screen; perhaps warning a parent that the product should not be used by children under three.

LO 2. Explain the three common forms of data mining.

Data Mining

At the center of any strategic, tactical, or operational BI effort is data mining. Ruf Strategic Solutions helps organizations employ statistical approaches within a large data warehouse to identify customer segments that display common traits. Marketers can then target these segments with specially designed products and promotions. ***Data mining*** is the process of analyzing data to extract information not offered by the raw data alone. Data mining can also begin at a summary information level (coarse granularity) and progress through increasing levels of detail (drilling down), or the reverse (drilling up). Data mining is the primary tool used to uncover business intelligence in vast amounts of data.

To perform data mining, users need data-mining tools. ***Data-mining tools*** use a variety of techniques to find patterns and relationships in large volumes of information and infer rules from them that predict future behavior and guide decision making. Data mining uses specialized technologies and functionalities such as query tools, reporting tools, multidimensional analysis tools, statistical tools, and intelligent agents. Data mining approaches decision making with basically a few different activities in mind including:

- ***Classification***—assign records to one of a predefined set of classes.
- ***Estimation***—determine values for an unknown continuous variable behavior or estimated future value.
- ***Affinity grouping***—determine which things go together.
- ***Clustering***—segment a heterogeneous population of records into a number of more homogeneous subgroups.

Sega of America, one of the largest publishers of video games, uses data mining and statistical tools to distribute its advertising budget of more than $50 million a year. Using data mining, product line specialists and marketing strategists "drill" into trends of each retail store chain. Their goal is to find buying trends that help them determine which advertising strategies are working best and how to reallocate advertising resources by media, territory, and time.

Data-mining tools apply algorithms to information sets to uncover inherent trends and patterns in the information, which analysts use to develop new business strategies. Analysts use the output from data-mining tools to build models that, when exposed to new information sets, perform a variety of information analysis functions. The analysts provide business solutions by putting together the analytical techniques and the business problem at hand, which often reveals important new correlations, patterns, and trends. The more common forms of data-mining analysis capabilities include:

- Cluster analysis
- Association detection
- Statistical analysis

CLUSTER ANALYSIS

Cluster analysis is a technique used to divide an information set into mutually exclusive groups such that the members of each group are as close together as possible to one another and the different groups are as far apart as possible. Cluster analysis is frequently used to segment customer information for customer relationship management systems to help organizations identify customers with similar behavioral traits, such as clusters of best customers or onetime customers. Cluster analysis also has the ability to uncover naturally occurring patterns in information (see Figure B10.4).

Data-mining tools that "understand" human language are finding unexpected applications in medicine. IBM and the Mayo Clinic unearthed hidden patterns in medical records, discovering that infant leukemia has three distinct clusters, each of which probably benefits from tailored treatments. Caroline A. Kovac, general manager of IBM Life Sciences, expects that mining the records of cancer patients for clustering patterns will turn up clues pointing the way to "tremendous strides in curing cancer."

A great example of cluster analysis occurs when attempting to segment customers based on zip codes. Understanding the demographics, lifestyle behaviors, and buying patterns of the most profitable segments of the population at the zip code level is key to a

FIGURE B10.4

Cluster Analysis Example

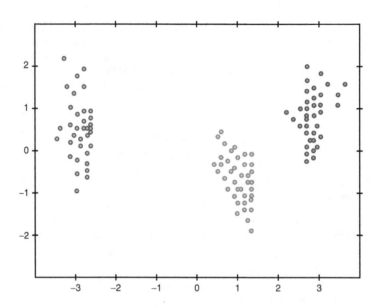

successful target marketing strategy. Targeting only those who have a high propensity to purchase products and services will help a high-end business cut its sales and marketing costs tremendously. Understanding each customer segment by zip code allows a business to determine the importance of each segment.

ASSOCIATION DETECTION

Whirlpool Corporation, a $4.3 billion home and commercial appliance manufacturer, employs hundreds of R&D engineers, data analysts, quality assurance specialists, and customer service personnel who all work together to ensure that each generation of appliances is better than the previous generation. Whirlpool is an example of an organization that is gaining business intelligence with association detection data-mining tools.

Association detection reveals the degree to which variables are related and the nature and frequency of these relationships in the information. Whirlpool's warranty analysis tool, for instance, uses statistical analysis to automatically detect potential issues, provide quick and easy access to reports, and perform multidimensional analysis on all warranty information. This association detection data-mining tool enables Whirlpool's managers to take proactive measures to control product defects even before most of its customers are aware of the defect. The tool also allows Whirlpool personnel to devote more time to value-added tasks such as ensuring high quality on all products rather than waiting for or manually analyzing monthly reports.

Many people refer to association detection algorithms as *association rule generators* because they create rules to determine the likelihood of events occurring together at a particular time or following each other in a logical progression. Percentages usually reflect the patterns of these events; for example, "55 percent of the time, events A and B occurred together," or "80 percent of the time that items A and B occurred together, they were followed by item C within three days."

One of the most common forms of association detection analysis is market basket analysis. *Market basket analysis* analyzes such items as websites and checkout scanner information to detect customers' buying behavior and predict future behavior by identifying affinities among customers' choices of products and services (see Figure B10.5). Market basket analysis is frequently used to develop marketing campaigns for cross-selling products and services (especially in banking, insurance, and finance) and for inventory control, shelf-product placement, and other retail and marketing applications.

FIGURE B10.5
Market Basket Analysis

STATISTICAL ANALYSIS

Statistical analysis performs such functions as information correlations, distributions, calculations, and variance analysis. Data-mining tools offer knowledge workers a wide range of powerful statistical capabilities so they can quickly build a variety of statistical models, examine the models' assumptions and validity, and compare and contrast the various models to determine the best one for a particular business issue.

Kraft is the producer of instantly recognizable food brands such as Oreo, Ritz, DiGiorno, and Kool-Aid. The company implemented two data-mining applications to assure consistent flavor, color, aroma, texture, and appearance for all of its food lines. One application analyzed product consistency and the other analyzed process variation reduction (PVR).

The product consistency tool, SENECA (Sensory and Experimental Collection Application), gathers and analyzes information by assigning precise definitions and numerical scales to such qualities as chewy, sweet, crunchy, and creamy. SENECA then builds models, histories, forecasts, and trends based on consumer testing and evaluates potential product improvements and changes.

The PVR tool ensures consistent flavor, color, aroma, texture, and appearance for every Kraft product since even small changes in the baking process can result in huge disparities in taste. Evaluating every manufacturing procedure, from recipe instructions to cookie dough shapes and sizes, the PVR tool has the potential to generate significant cost savings for each product. Using these types of data-mining techniques for quality control and cluster analysis makes sure that the billions of Kraft products that reach consumers annually will continue to taste great with every bite.

Forecasting is a common form of statistical analysis. Formally defined, ***forecasts*** are predictions made on the basis of time-series information. ***Time-series information*** is time-stamped information collected at a particular frequency. Examples of time-series information include web visits per hour, sales per month, and calls per day. Forecasting data-mining tools allow users to manipulate the time series for forecasting activities.

When discovering trends and seasonal variations in transactional information, use a time-series forecast to change the transactional information by units of time, such as transforming weekly information into monthly or seasonal information or hourly information into daily information. Companies base production, investment, and staffing decisions on a host of economic and market indicators in this manner. Forecasting models allow organizations to consider all sorts of variables when making decisions.

Nestlé Italiana is part of the multinational giant Nestlé Group and currently dominates Italy's food industry. The company improved sales forecasting by 25 percent with its data-mining forecasting solution that enables the company's managers to make objective decisions based on facts instead of subjective decisions based on intuition.

Determining sales forecasts for seasonal confectionery products is a crucial and challenging task. During Easter, Nestlé Italiana has only four weeks to market, deliver, and sell its seasonal products. The Christmas time frame is a little longer, lasting from six to eight weeks, while other holidays such as Valentine's Day and Mother's Day have shorter time frames of about one week.

The company's data-mining solution gathers, organizes, and analyzes massive volumes of information to produce powerful models that identify trends and predict confectionery sales. The business intelligence created is based on five years of historical information and identifies what is important and what is not important. Nestlé Italiana's sophisticated data-mining tool predicted Mother's Day sales forecasts that were 90 percent accurate. The company has benefited from a 40 percent reduction in inventory and a 50 percent reduction in order changes, all due to its forecasting tool. Determining sales forecasts for seasonal confectionery products is now an area in which Nestlé Italiana excels.

Today, vendors such as Business Objects, Cognos, and SAS offer complete data-mining decision-making solutions. Moving forward, these companies plan to add more predictive analytical capabilities to their products. Their goal is to give companies more "what-if" scenario capabilities based on internal and external information.

Business Benefits of BI

LO 3. Describe the four categories of BI business benefits.

Rapid innovations in systems and data-mining tools are putting operational, tactical, and strategic BI at the fingertips of executives, managers, and even customers. With the successful implementation of BI systems an organization can expect to receive the following:

- **Single Point of Access to Information for All Users.** With a BI solution, organizations can unlock information held within their databases by giving authorized users a single point of access to data. Wherever the data reside, whether stored in operational systems, data warehouses, data marts and/or enterprise applications, users can prepare reports and drill deep down into the information to understand what drives their business, without technical knowledge of the underlying data structures. The most successful BI applications allow users to do this with an easy-to-understand, nontechnical, graphical user interface.

- **BI across Organizational Departments.** There are many different uses for BI and one of its greatest benefits is that it can be used at every step in the value chain. All departments across an organization from sales to operations to customer service can benefit from the value of BI.

  Volkswagen AG uses BI to track, understand, and manage data in every department—from finance, production, and development, to research, sales and marketing, and purchasing. Users at all levels of the organization access supplier and customer reports relating to online requests and negotiations, vehicle launches, and vehicle capacity management and tracking.

- **Up-to-the-Minute Information for Everyone.** The key to unlocking information is to give users the tools to quickly and easily find immediate answers to their questions. Some users will be satisfied with standard reports that are updated on a regular basis, such as current inventory reports, sales per channel, or customer status reports. However, the answers these reports yield can lead to new questions. Some users will want dynamic access to information. The information that a user finds in a report will trigger more questions, and these questions will not be answered in a prepackaged report.

  While users may spend 80 percent of their time accessing standard or personalized reports, for 20 percent of their tasks, they need to obtain additional information not available in the original report. To address this need and to avoid frustration (and related report backlog for the IT team), a BI system should let users autonomously make ad hoc requests for information from corporate data sources.

For merchants of MasterCard International, access to BI offers the opportunity to monitor their businesses more closely on a day-to-day basis. Advertising agencies are able to use information from an extranet when developing campaigns for merchants. On the authorization side, a call center can pull up cardholder authorization transactions to cut down on fraud. MasterCard expects that in the long term and as business partners increasingly demand access to system data, the system will support more than 20,000 external users.

CATEGORIES OF BI BENEFITS

Management is no longer prepared to sink large sums of money into IT projects simply because they are the latest and greatest technology. Information technology has come of age, and it is expected to make a significant contribution to the bottom line.

When looking at how BI affects the bottom line, an organization should analyze not only the organizationwide business benefits, but also the various benefits it can expect to receive from a BI deployment. A practical way of breaking down these numerous benefits is to separate them into four main categories:

1. Quantifiable benefits.
2. Indirectly quantifiable benefits.
3. Unpredictable benefits.
4. Intangible benefits.

Quantifiable Benefits

Quantifiable benefits include working time saved in producing reports, selling information to suppliers, and so on. A few examples include:

- Moët et Chandon, the famous champagne producer, reduced its IT costs from approximately 30 cents per bottle to 15 cents per bottle.

- A leading risk insurance company provides customers with self-service access to their information in the insurance company's database and no longer sends paper reports. This one benefit alone saves the organization $400,000 a year in printing and shipping costs. The total three-year ROI for this BI deployment was 249 percent.

- Ingram Micro, a wholesale provider of high-tech goods and technology solutions providers, is working to create a new BI extranet to deliver advanced information to the company's suppliers and business partners. Says Ingram Micro CIO Guy Abramo, "Today it's incumbent on us to provide our partners with sell-through information so they can see what happened once their PCs hit distribution. That's critical for them to do inventory planning and manufacturing planning—helping them to understand what products are selling to what segments of the marketplace."

Indirectly Quantifiable Benefits

Indirectly quantifiable benefits can be evaluated through indirect evidence—improved customer service means new business from the same customer, and differentiated service brings new customers. A few examples include:

- A customer of Owens & Minor cited extranet access to the data warehouse as the primary reason for giving the medical supplies distributor an additional $44 million in business.

- "When salespeople went out to visit TaylorMade's customers at golf pro shops and sporting goods retail chains, they didn't have up-to-date inventory reports. The sales reps would take orders for clubs, accessories, and clothing without confidence that the goods were available for delivery as promised," Tom Collard, information systems director with TaylorMade, said. "The technology has helped TaylorMade not only reduce costs by eliminating the reporting backlog . . . it has eliminated a lot of wasted effort that resulted from booking orders that it couldn't fill."

Unpredictable Benefits

Unpredictable benefits are the result of discoveries made by creative users; a few examples include:

- Volkswagen's finance BI system allowed an interesting discovery that later resulted in significant new revenue. The customers of a particular model of the Audi product line had completely different behaviors than customers of other cars. Based on their socioeconomic profiles, they were thought to want long lease terms and fairly large up-front payments. Instead, the information revealed that Audi customers actually wanted shorter leases and to finance a large part of the purchase through the lease. Based on that insight, the company immediately introduced a new program combining shorter length of lease, larger up-front payments, and aggressive leasing rates, especially for that car model. The interest in the new program was immediate, resulting in over $2 million in new revenue.

- Peter Blundell, former knowledge strategy manager for British Airways, and various company executives had a suspicion that the carrier was suffering from a high degree of ticket fraud. To address this problem, Blundell and his team rolled out business intelligence. "Once we analyzed the data, we found that this ticket fraud was not an issue at all. What we had supposed was fraud was in fact either data quality issues or process problems," Blundell said. "What it did was give us so many unexpected opportunities in terms of understanding our business." Blundell estimated that the BI deployment has resulted in around $100 million in cost savings and new revenues for the airline.

Intangible Benefits

Intangible benefits include improved communication throughout the enterprise, improved job satisfaction of empowered users, and improved knowledge sharing. A few examples include:

- The corporate human resources department at ABN AMRO Bank uses BI to gain insight into its workforce by analyzing information on such items as gender, age, tenure, and compensation. Thanks to this sharing of intellectual capital, the HR department is in a better position to demonstrate its performance and contribution to the business successes of the corporation as a whole.

- Ben & Jerry's uses BI to track, understand, and manage information on the thousands of consumer responses it receives on its products and promotional activities. Through daily customer feedback analysis, Ben & Jerry's is able to identify trends and modify its marketing campaigns and its products to suit consumer demand.

✳ PLUG-IN SUMMARY

Most corporations today are inundated with data—from their own internal operational systems, their vendors, suppliers, and customers and from other external sources such as credit bureaus or industry sales data. The problem with understanding where your company is going is not in the amount of data coming into it. The problem is that this tidal wave of data is not in a form that can easily be digested, comprehended, or even accessed. Ask simple questions like who are your best customers or what are your most profitable products and you will most likely get as many answers as there are employees. Not a comforting position to have in today's era of economic stress.

This is where business intelligence or BI comes in. The goal of BI is to provide the enterprise with a repository of "trusted" data—data that can be used in a multitude of applications to answer the questions about customers, products, supply and demand chains, production inefficiencies, financial trends, fraud, and even employees. It can be used to flag anomalies via alerts, provide visualization and statistical models, and understand the cause and effects of decisions upon the enterprise. Just about every aspect of an enterprise's business can benefit from the insights garnered from BI.

You, as a business student, must understand how technology can help you make intelligent decisions. But at the end of the day, how you interact with a customer face-to-face is the real test of your ability to foster and promote healthy customer relations.

✳ KEY TERMS

Affinity grouping 475	Clustering 475	Estimation 475
Analysis latency 473	Data latency 473	Forecasts 477
Association detection 476	Data mining 475	Market basket analysis 476
Classification 475	Data-mining tools 475	Statistical analysis 477
Cluster analysis 475	Decision latency 474	Time-series information 477

✳ CLOSING CASE ONE

Intelligent Business: Is It an Oxymoron?

In a pilot program by the State of New York, suburban Rockland County announced that it had uncovered $13 million in improper Medicaid claims made over a 21-month period. Because the problems were discovered before the reimbursements were made, Rockland saved itself the headaches it would have faced if it had paid out the money first and asked questions later.

The credit goes not to a crew of hardworking sleuths but to search and analysis software created by IBM that automatically sorted through thousands of forms, plucked out key bits of information, and sized them up against Medicaid rules. Government officials believe that if the program were to be applied statewide, it could deliver $3.8 billion in savings per year. "This may change the Medicaid industry in New York," said Rockland County Supervisor C. Scott Vanderhoef.

This is just one example of a change in the way corporations and governments find and use information. Data are becoming much easier to access and vastly more useful.

Better Understanding

Organizations have huge amounts of data that pass through their computer systems as they place orders, record sales, and otherwise transact business. Much of this information is stored for future use and analysis. But advances in software and hardware make it easier for companies to analyze data in real time—when the data are first whizzing through their computers—and make them available to all kinds of employees.

Technological innovations also make it possible to analyze unstructured data, such as Rockland County's Medicaid claims, that do not easily fit into the tables of a traditional database. The result of all these changes: It is now possible for companies to understand what is happening in their businesses in a detailed way and quickly take actions based on that knowledge.

These improvements have come largely as a result of advances in business intelligence software. This software—a $3 billion segment growing at about 7 percent a year—gathers information in data warehouses where it can easily be reviewed, analyzes the data, and presents reports to decision makers. In the past, the reports had to be painstakingly assembled by tech-savvy business analysts and were typically made available only to top-tier people.

Personal Google

Information easily available to anybody in an organization is a phenomenon industry folks have dubbed "pervasive business intelligence." Companies are moving from a place where only the more technical people had access to information to more of a self-service situation. People can get information themselves, said Christina McKeon, global business intelligence strategist for software maker SAS Institute, based in Cary, North Carolina.

SAS and other BI software makers are reaching out to the masses in a variety of ways. Several of them have hooked up with search leader Google to give businesspeople easier access to those data warehouses via the familiar Google search bar. They have redesigned their business intelligence web portals so people who do Google searches get not only documents that include their keywords, but also others that are thematically related.

For instance, if a business-unit leader searches for first-quarter financial results, he might also get reports on the 10 largest customers in the quarter and the customers who deliver the most profits. "The data warehouse is starting to go mainstream," said analyst Mark Beyer of tech market researcher Gartner.

Directing Traffic

Business intelligence is also being added to other standard run-the-business applications, such as order fulfillment, logistics, inventory management, and the like. Consider a busy warehouse with a limited number of loading docks. Trucking companies do not want their rigs to wait in line for hours, so some of them charge fees for waiting time at the warehouse.

To avoid those costs, companies can build business intelligence into their logistics planning systems that lets them know when trucks are stacking up and directs supervisors in the warehouse to load the trucks that charge waiting fees before those that do not. The supervisors get this information via their PCs or handhelds on the warehouse floor. People are receiving the benefit of business intelligence without knowing it, said Randy Lea, vice president for product and services marketing at Teradata, a division of NCR, a leader in data warehousing software.

This kind of real-time, behind-the-curtains intelligence is even becoming available to end customers. Travelocity, one of the leading travel websites, has long used business intelligence software to help it analyze buying trends and segment customer types so new services can be tailored for them. Now it has rigged its vast data warehouse directly to its consumer website so it can gather and analyze information about what is going on as it is happening.

Computer Intuition

Travelocity links the profile of individual customers who are on the site to a monitor of their current activity and to information about available airplane flights, rental cars, and vacation packages. If a customer begins asking about flights to Orlando over the Fourth of July weekend, Travelocity's system will understand that the customer is probably planning a family vacation and will place advertisements that are relevant to that kind of trip and even pitch special travel promotions. "If we want to, we could give every customer a custom offer," said Mark Hooper, Travelocity's vice president for product development.

What is next in easy-to-use business intelligence? Gartner has a concept it calls "Biggle"— the intersection of BI and Google. The idea is that the data warehousing software will be so sophisticated that it understands when different people use different words to describe the same concepts or products. It creates an index of related information—á là Google—and dishes relevant results out in response to queries.

In computer science, they refer to this capability as non-obvious relationship awareness. "Nobody's doing this yet," said Gartner's Beyer. Judging from the speed of recent advances in business intelligence, though, it may not be long before companies add the term "Biggling" to their tech lexicon.

Questions

1. What is the problem of gathering business intelligence from a traditional company? How can BI solve this problem?
2. Choose one of the three common forms of data-mining analysis and explain how Travelocity could use it to gain BI.
3. How will tactical, operational, and strategic BI be different when applied to personal Google?
4. How is IBM's search and analysis software an example of BI?
5. What does the term *pervasive business intelligence* mean?
6. How could any business benefit from technology such as personal Google?
7. How could a company use BI to improve its supply chain?
8. Highlight any security and ethical issues associated with Biggle.

✳ CLOSING CASE TWO

The Brain behind the Big, Bad Burger and Other Tales of Business Intelligence

Jay Leno, the *New York Times,* and health nutrition advocacy groups have commented on the newest Hardee's fast-food item "The Monster Thickburger," which consists of:

- Two charbroiled 100 percent Angus beef patties, each weighing in at a third of a pound (150 grams)
- Three slices of processed cheese
- Four crispy strips of bacon
- Dollop of mayonnaise
- Toasted butter sesame seed bun

The Monster Thickburger sounds like a hungry person's dream and the dieter's worst nightmare. Yes, this delicious sounding burger nirvana contains 1,420 calories (5945 kilojoules) and an artery-clogging 107 grams of fat. Even though the Monster Thickburger is one of the most fattening burgers on the market—not to mention that most people add a coke and fries to their order—it is selling like crazy, according to Jeff Chasney, CIO and executive vice president of strategic planning at CKE Restaurants, the company that owns and operates Hardee's.

With the national diet obsession and health-related warnings concerning obesity, most fast-food companies probably would never have even put the Monster Thickburger on the menu. CKE confidently introduced the Monster Thickburger nationwide convinced that the product would sell based on intelligence the company obtained from its business intelligence (BI) system. CKE's BI system—known ironically inside the company as CPR (CKE Performance Reporting)—monitored the performance of burger sales in numerous test markets to determine the monster burger's increase to sales and ensure it was not simply cannibalizing other burger sales. CKE monitored several variables including menu mixes, production costs, Thickburger sales, overall burger sales, profit increases, and Thickburger's contribution to the stores' bottom-line. Using its BI system CKE quickly determined that the production costs of the Thickburger were minimal compared to the increase in sales. Armed with burger intelligence CKE confidently paid $7 million in advertising and successfully released the burger nationwide. In its first quarter sales of the burger exceeded CKE's expectations and the company knew the $7 million it paid in advertising was a smart investment.

Hardee's, Wendy's, Ruby Tuesday, T.G.I. Friday's and others are heavy users of BI software. Many of the big chains have been using BI for the past 10 years, according to Chris Hartmann, managing director of technology strategies at HVS International, a restaurant and hospitality consultancy. The restaurants use operational BI to determine everything from which menu items to add and remove to which locations to close. They use tactical BI for renegotiating contracts and identifying opportunities to improve inefficient processes. BI is an essential tool for operational-driven restaurants and if implemented correctly they can highlight operational efficiency and effectiveness such as:

- Carlson Restaurants Worldwide (T.G.I. Friday's, Pick Up Stix) saved $200,000 by renegotiating contracts with food suppliers based on discrepancies between contract prices and the prices suppliers were actually charging restaurants. Carlson's BI system, which at the time was from Cognos, had identified these discrepancies.

- Ruby Tuesday's profits and revenue have grown by at least 20 percent each year as a result of the improvements the chain has made to its menu and operations based on insights provided by its BI infrastructure, which consists of a data warehouse, analytical tools from Cognos and Hyperion, and reporting tools from Microsoft.

- CPR helped CKE, which was on the brink of bankruptcy, increase sales at restaurants open more than a year, narrow its overall losses and even turn a profit in 2003. A home-grown proprietary system, CPR consists of a Microsoft SQL server database and uses Microsoft development tools to parse and display analytical information.

- In June 2003, Wendy's decided to accept credit cards in its restaurants based on information it got from its BI systems. Because of that decision, Wendy's restaurants have boosted sales; customers who use a credit card spend an average of 35 percent more per order than those who use cash, according to Wendy's executive vice president and CIO John Deane.

Other industries could learn a great deal about BI by analyzing such strategic use of BI. "Most BI implementations fall below the midpoint on the scale of success," says Ted Friedman, an analyst with Gartner. It appears that the restaurant industry has avoided the three common barriers to BI success by cleansing voluminous amounts of irrelevant data, ensuring high-data quality, and decreasing user resistance.

Questions

1. What does business intelligence really mean to a business? How did CPR save millions for CKE?
2. What are the negative impacts of CKE's business intelligence?
3. Explain the three forms of data-mining analysis and explain how CKE can use it to gain BI.
4. How can CKE use tactical, operational, and strategic BI?
5. What types of ethical and security issues could CKE face from CPR?

★ MAKING BUSINESS DECISIONS

1. Gaining Business Intelligence from Strategic Initiatives

You are a new employee in the customer service department at Premier One, a large pet food distributor. The company, founded by several veterinarians, has been in business for three years and focuses on providing nutritious pet food at a low cost. The company currently has 90 employees and operates in seven states. Sales over the past three years have tripled, and the manual systems currently in place are no longer sufficient to run the business. Your first task is to meet with your new team and create a presentation for the president and chief executive officer describing tactical, operational, and strategic business intelligence. The presentation should highlight the main benefits Premier One can receive from business intelligence along with any additional added business value that can be gained from the systems.

2. Second Life BI

The virtual world of Second Life could become the first point of contact between companies and customers and could transform the whole customer experience. Since it began hosting the likes of Adidas, Dell, Reuters, and Toyota, Second Life has become technology's equivalent of India or China—everyone needs an office and a strategy involving it to keep their shareholders happy. But beyond opening a shiny new building in the virtual world, what can such companies do with their virtual real estate?

Like many other big brands, PA Consulting has its own offices in Second Life and has learned that simply having an office to answer customer queries is not enough. Real people, albeit behind avatars, must be staffing the offices—in the same way having a website is not enough if there is not a call center to back it up when a would-be customer wants to speak to a human being. The consultants believe call centers could one day ask customers to follow up a phone call with them by moving the query into a virtual world.

Unlike many corporate areas in the virtual world, the National Basketball Association incorporates capabilities designed to keep fans coming back, including real-time 3-D diagrams of games as they are being played.

You are the executive director of BI at StormPeak, an advanced AI company that develops robots. You are in charge of overseeing the first virtual site being built in Second Life. Create a BI strategy for gathering information in a virtual world. Here are a few questions to get you started:

- How will gathering BI for a business be different in a virtual world?
- How can BI help a business become more efficient in a virtual world?
- How will supporting BI in Second Life differ from supporting BI in a traditional company?
- What BI security issues might you encounter in Second Life?
- What BI ethical issues might you encounter in Second Life?

3. Searching for BI

Imagine being able to Google customer phone requests for information, sort through the recorded files of customer complaint calls, or decipher the exact moment when an interaction between a customer and store employee went awry. Being able to query voice records using the same methods as querying textual ones would open up boundless areas of business opportunity. Web surfers can already search audio files and audio/video feeds, but now enterprises can use this technology to help employees search voice mails or recorded calls for keywords and phrases, and, in the end, to decode important customer concerns.

You have recently started your own marketing firm. You have built a BI tool that allows customers to query all of their unique data stores. Now all you need is to prepare your marketing materials to send to potential customers. Create a marketing pitch that you will deliver to customers detailing the business opportunities they could uncover if they purchase your product. Your marketing pitch can be a one-page document, a catchy tune, a video, or a PowerPoint presentation.

4. Mining Physician Data

NPR recently released a story discussing how large pharmaceutical companies are mining physician data. Thousands of pharmaceutical drug company sales representatives visit doctors and try to entice them to prescribe their company's newest drugs. The pharmaceutical companies buy prescription information from pharmacies all over the country describing which drugs are prescribed by which doctors. There is no patient information in the data. The sales representatives receive this BI from their companies and can tailor their sales pitch based on what that particular doctor has been prescribing to patients. Many doctors do not even realize that the sales representatives have this information and know exactly what drugs each individual doctor prescribes. The drug companies love mining data, but critics contend it is an invasion of privacy and drives up the cost of health care. Maine has just become the third state to pass a measure limiting access to the data.

You are working for your state government and your boss has asked you to create an argument for or against pharmaceutical data mining of physician data in your state. A few questions to get you started:

Do you agree that mining physician data should be illegal? Why or why not?

As a patient how do you feel about pharmaceutical companies mining your doctor's data?

As an employee of one of the pharmaceutical companies how do you feel about mining physician data?

5. The Value of Plastic

Accepting credit cards at Wendy's restaurants was a big decision facing corporate executives in early 2003. There was no doubt that customers would appreciate the convenience of plastic, but could this option hurt overall sales? Wendy's executives decided that the best way to determine the value of plastic was to test it at several stores. The BI system was set to monitor how a credit card purchase affects sales, service speed, and cash sales. The intelligence gained from the system told executives that plastic sales were typically 35 percent higher than cash sales. Cash sales typically include a value meal—great for the customer but less profitable for the store. Plastic customers showed a trend of purchasing a la carte items generating a higher bill. Armed with BI, Wendy's introduced credit card readers nationally in June 2003.

You are the vice president of BI for McDonald's restaurants. The board of directors would like you to generate a report discussing the details of how you can use BI to analyze sales trends of menu items for all of its restaurants, including international locations. Identify several different variables you would monitor to determine menu item sales trends.

PLUG-IN T5

Designing Database Applications

1. Describe the purpose of the relational database model in a database management system.
2. List the relational database model's basic components.
3. Describe why entities and attributes are organized into tables.
4. Describe how data redundancy is handled in the relational database model.
5. Explain the need for an entity-relationship diagram in a database management system.
6. Describe the Chen model symbols used in entity-relationship modeling.
7. Explain the purpose of normalization.
8. Describe the first three normal forms typically used in normalization.

Introduction

Businesses rely on their database systems for accurate, up-to-date information. Without those databases of mission critical information, most businesses would be unable to perform their normal daily transactions, much less create summary reports that help management make strategic decisions. To be useful, the information must be accurate, complete, and organized in such a way that it can be retrieved when needed and in the format required.

The core units introduced the *database*, which maintains information about various types of objects (inventory), events (transactions), people (employees), and places (warehouses). A *database management system (DBMS)* is software through which users and application programs interact with a database. The *relational database model* is a type of database that stores its information in the form of logically related two-dimensional tables. This plug-in will build on the core units by providing specific details about how to design a relational database application.

Entities and Data Relationships

There are numerous elements in a business environment that need to store information, and those elements are related to one another in a variety of ways. Thus a database must contain not only the information but also information about the relationships among the information.

The idea behind a database is that the user, either a person working interactively or an application program, has no need to worry about the way in which information is physically stored on disk. A database management system translates between the user's request for information and the physical storage.

A *data model* is a formal way to express data relationships to a database management system (DBMS). The underlying relationships in a database environment are independent of the data model and therefore independent of the DBMS that is being used. Before designing a database for any data model, data relationships need to be defined. An *entity relationship diagram (ERD)* is a technique for documenting the relationships between entities in a database environment.

ENTITIES AND THEIR ATTRIBUTES

An *entity*, sometimes called a table, is a person, place, thing, transaction, or event about which information is stored. A customer is an entity, as is a merchandise item. Entities are not necessarily tangible; for instance, an appointment to see the doctor is an entity. *Attributes,* also called fields or columns, are characteristics or properties of an entity instance. For example, a *CUSTOMER* entity can be described by a *Customer Number, First Name, Last Name, Street, City, State, Zip Code, Phone Number, Credit Card No,* and *Credit Card Exp* (refer to Figure T5.1).

When entities in a database are represented, only the attributes are stored. Each group of attributes models a single entity type in the real world, and values assigned to these attributes represent instances of objects (entity occurrences) corresponding to the entity. For example, in Figure T5.2, there are four instances of a *CUSTOMER* entity stored in a database. If there are 1,000 customers in the database, then there will be 1,000 instances of *CUSTOMER* entities. Instances can sometimes be referred to as records.

Entity Identifiers

An *entity identifier* ensures that each entity instance has a unique attribute value that distinguishes it from every other entity instance (an entity identifier is also referred to as a primary key, which will be discussed later in the plug-in). The primary purpose for entering the information that describes an entity into a database is to retrieve the information at some later date. This means there must be some way of distinguishing one entity instance from another in order to retrieve the correct entity instance. An entity identifier ensures that each entity instance has a unique attribute value that distinguishes it from every other entity instance.

FIGURE T5.1

Entities and Attributes Example

CUSTOMER	ORDER	ITEM	DISTRIBUTOR	ENTITIES
Customer Number First Name Last Name Street City State Zip Code Phone Number Credit Card No Credit Card Exp	Order Number Customer Number Order Date Order Filled	Item Number Title Distributor Number Price Release Date Genre	Distributor Number Name Street City State Zip Code Phone Number Contact Name Contact Phone	Attributes

CUSTOMER #1111
Sam Smith
101 Main Street
Denver Colorado 80208
555-555-5555

CUSTOMER #1212
John Doe
101 Main Street
Vail Colorado 88888
666-666-6666

CUSTOMER #0001
Bill Miller
101 North Main Street
Englewood Colorado 80211
777-777-7777

CUSTOMER #0505
Jane Cook
101 South Main Street
Littleton Colorado 80126
444-444-4444

FIGURE T5.2

Customer Entity Instance

Assume, for example, that a local video store, Mega-Video, has two customers named John Smith. If an employee searches for the items John Smith has ordered, which John Smith will the DBMS retrieve? In this case, both of them. Since there is no way to distinguish between the two customers, the result of the query will be inaccurate. Mega-Video can solve the problem by creating an entity identifier.

Some entities, such as *ORDER*, come with natural identifiers, such as an *Order Number*. Typically, a unique, randomly generated number is assigned to entity identifiers.

A *constraint* is a rule to which some elements in a database must adhere. All entities must have a unique identifier that is a constraint. That is to say, when an instance of an entity in a database is stored, the DBMS needs to ensure that the new instance has a unique identifier. The enforcement of a variety of database constraints helps to maintain data consistency and accuracy.

ATTRIBUTES

There are several types of attributes, including:

- Simple versus composite.
- Single-valued versus multi-valued.
- Stored versus derived.
- Null-valued.

Simple versus Composite

Composite attributes can be divided into smaller subparts, which represent more basic attributes that have their own meanings. A common example of a composite attribute is *Address* (see Figure T5.3). *Address* can be broken down into a number of subparts, such as *Street, City, State, Zip Code. Street* may be further broken down by *Number, Street Name*, and *Apartment/Unit Number*. Attributes that are not divisible into subparts are called *simple attributes*.

Single-Valued versus Multi-Valued

When creating a relational database, the attributes in the data model must be single-valued. *Single-valued* means having only a single value of each attribute at any given time. For example, a *CUSTOMER* entity allows only one *Phone Number*

FIGURE T5.3

Composite Attributes

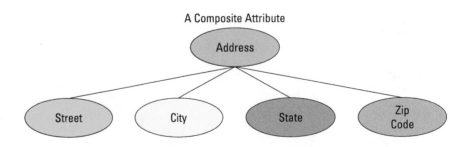

A Composite Attribute

for each *CUSTOMER*. If a *CUSTOMER* has more than one *Phone Number* and wants them all included in the database, then the *CUSTOMER* entity cannot handle them.

The existence of more than one *Phone Number* turns the *Phone Number* attribute into a multi-valued attribute. *Multivalued* means having the potential to contain more than one value for an attribute at any given time. An entity in a relational database cannot have multi-valued attributes. Those attributes must be handled by creating another entity to hold them.

In the case of the multiple *Phone Number*(s), a *PHONE NUMBER* entity needs to be created. Each instance of the entity would include the *Customer Number* of the person to whom the *Phone Number* belonged along with the *Phone Number*. If a customer had two *Phone Number*(s), then there would be two instances of the *PHONE NUMBER* entity for the *CUSTOMER* (see Figure T5.4).

Multi-valued attributes can cause problems with the meaning of data in the database, significantly slow down searching, and place unnecessary restrictions on the amount of data that can be stored. Relational databases do not allow multi-valued attributes for this reason. For example, an *EMPLOYEE* entity with attributes for the *Name(s)* and *Birthdate(s)* of dependents would be considered multi-valued.

When searching a multi-valued attribute, a DBMS must search each value in the attribute, most likely scanning the contents of the attribute sequentially. A sequential search is the slowest type of search available.

Generally, a multi-valued attribute is a major hint that another entity is needed. The only way to handle multiple values of the same attribute is to create an entity for which multiple instances can be stored, one for each value of the attribute. In the case of the *EMPLOYEE* entity, a *DEPENDENT* entity that could be related to the *EMPLOYEE* entity needs to be created. There would be one occurrence of the *DEPENDENT* entity related to an occurrence of the *EMPLOYEE* entity for each of an employee's dependents. In this way, there is no limit to the number of an employee's dependents. In addition, each occurrence of the *DEPENDENT* entity would contain the *Name* and *Birthdate* of only one dependent, eliminating any confusion about which *Name* was associated with which *Birthdate*, as suggested in Figure T5.5. Searching would also be faster because the DBMS could use quicker search techniques on the individual *DEPENDENT* entity occurrences, without resorting to the slow sequential search.

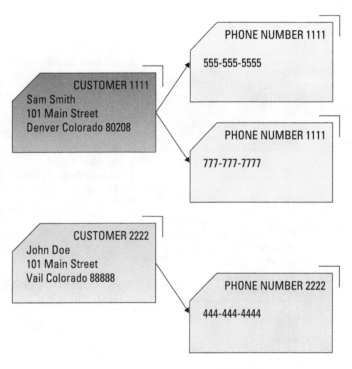

FIGURE T5.4

Customer Entity and Phone Number Entity

Stored versus Derived

If an attribute can be calculated using the value of another attribute, it is called a *derived attribute*. The attribute that is used to derive the attribute is called a *stored attribute*. Derived attributes are not stored in the file, but can be derived when needed from the stored attributes. One example of a derived and stored attribute is a person's age. If the database has a stored attribute such as the person's *Date of Birth*, then you can create a derived attribute called *Age* from taking the *Current Date* (this is pulled from the system the database is running on) and subtracting the *Date of Birth* to get the age.

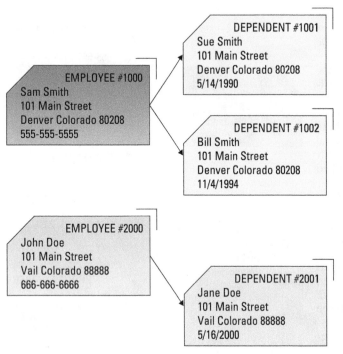

FIGURE T5.5

Employee Entity and
Dependent Entity

Null-Valued

There are cases where an attribute does not have an applicable value for an attribute. For these situations, the *null-valued* attribute is created. A person who does not have a mobile phone would have null stored at the value for the *Mobile Phone Number* attribute. Null can also be used in situations where the attribute value is unknown. There are two cases where this can occur, one where it is known that the attribute is valued, but the value is missing, for example *Hair Color.* Every person has a hair color, but the information may be missing. Another situation is if *Mobile Phone Number* is null, it is not known if the person does not have a mobile phone or if that information is just missing.

Documenting Logical Data Relationships

The two most commonly used styles of ERD notation are Chen, named after the originator of entity-relationship modeling, Dr. Peter Chen, and Information Engineering, which grew out of work by James Martin and Clive Finkelstein. It does not matter which is used, as long as everyone who is using the diagram understands the notation.

The Chen model uses rectangles to represent entities. Each entity's name appears in the rectangle and is expressed in the singular, as in *CUSTOMER.* The original Chen model did not provide a method for showing attributes on the ERD itself. However, many people have extended the model to include the attributes in ovals as illustrated in Figure T5.6.

BASIC DATA RELATIONSHIPS

FIGURE T5.6

Chen Model with
Attributes

The relationships that are stored in a database are between instances of entities. For example, a Mega-Video customer is related to the *ITEM*(s) he or she *ORDER*(s). Each instance of the *CUSTOMER* entity is related to instances of the specific *ITEM* ordered (see Figure T5.7). This is a purely conceptual representation of what is in the database and is completely unrelated to the physical storage of the data.

When data relationships are documented, such as drawing an ERD, types of relationships among entities are shown, displaying the possible relationships that are allowable in the database. Unless a relationship is mandatory, there is no requirement that every instance of an entity be involved in the documented relationships. For example, Mega-Video could store information about a *CUSTOMER* without the customer having any current *ORDER*(s) to which it is related.

Once the basic entities and their attributes in a database environment have been defined, the next task is to identify the relationships among those entities. There are three basic types of relationships: (1) one-to-one, (2) one-to-many, and (3) many-to-many.

One-to-One

A *one-to-one (1:1)* relationship is between two entities in which an instance of entity A can be related to only one instance of entity B and entity B can be related to only one instance of entity A. Consider an airport in a small town and the town in which the airport is located, both of which are described in a database of small town airports (this would not be true for some major metropolitan cities, such as New York City with two major airports). Each of

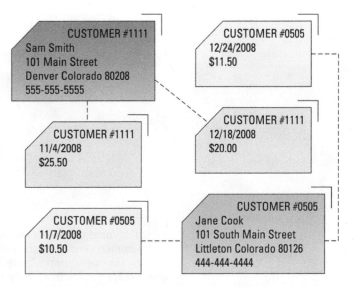

FIGURE T5.7

Entity Relationships

these might be represented as an instance of a different type of entity. As shown in Figure T5.8, the relationships between the two instances can then be expressed as "The airport is located in one and only one town and the town contains one and only one airport." The Chen method, as displayed in Figure T5.8, uses rectangles to document entities, a diamond to represent the relationship, and numbers to show the type of relationship (in this example 1:1).

This is a true one-to-one relationship because at no time can a single *AIRPORT* be related to more than one *TOWN* and no *TOWN* can be related to more than one *AIRPORT*. Although there are municipalities that have more than one *AIRPORT*, the *TOWN(s)* in this database are too small for that to happen.

True one-to-one relationships are rare in business. For example, assume that Mega-Video decides to start dealing with a new distributor of DVDs. At first, the company orders only one specialty title from the new distributor. The instance of the *DISTRIBUTOR* entity in the database is related to just the one merchandise *ITEM* instance. This would then appear to be a one-to-one relationship. Over time, Mega-Video may choose to order more titles from the new distributor, which would violate the rule that the distributor must be related to no more than one merchandise item. Therefore, this is not a true one-to-one relationship (this is an example of a one-to-many relationship, which is discussed next).

What if Mega-Video created a special *CREDIT CARD* entity to hold data about the credit cards that *CUSTOMER(s)* used to secure their rentals? Each *CUSTOMER* has only one credit card on file with the store. There would therefore seem to be a one-to-one relationship between the instance of a *CUSTOMER(s)* entity and the instance of the *CREDIT CARD* entity. In this case, it is a single entity. The *Credit Card Number*, the *Type of Credit Card*, and the *Credit Card Expiration Date* can all become attributes of the *CUSTOMER(s)* entity. Given that only one credit card is stored for each customer, the attributes are not multi-valued; no separate entity is needed.

One-to-Many

A *one-to-many (1:M)* relationship is between two entities, in which an instance of entity A can be related to zero, one, or more instances of entity B and entity B can be related to only one instance of entity A. This is the most common type of relationship. In fact,

FIGURE T5.8

A One-to-One Relationship

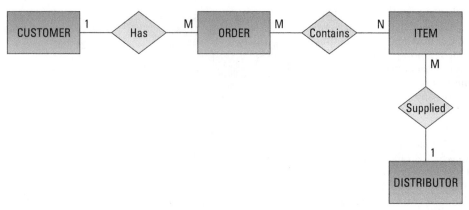

most relational databases are constructed from the rare one-to-one relationship and numerous one-to-many relationships. Mega-Video typically *ORDER(s)* many *ITEM(s)* (in this scenario, an item is a DVD title) from each *DISTRIBUTOR* and a given *ITEM* comes from only one *DISTRIBUTOR* as Figure T5.9 demonstrates. Similarly, a *CUSTOMER* places many *ORDER(s)*, but an *ORDER* comes from only one *CUSTOMER*.

When specifying data relationships, there needs to be an indication of the possible relationships, but an indication is not necessary that all instances of all entities participate in every documented relationship. There is no requirement that a *DISTRIBUTOR* be related to any merchandise *ITEM*, much less one or more merchandise *ITEM(s)*. It might not make much sense to have a *DISTRIBUTOR* in the database from whom the company did not *ORDER*, but there is nothing to prevent data about that *DISTRIBUTOR* from being stored. You will notice that there is an M:N relationship between *ORDER* and *ITEM*, which we will discuss next.

Many-to-Many

A *many-to-many (M:N)* relationship is between two entities in which an instance of entity A can be related to zero, one, or more instances of entity B and entity B can be related to zero, one, or more instances of entity A. There is a many-to-many relationship between a Mega-Video *ORDER* and the merchandise *ITEM* carried by the store (refer to Figure T5.10). A *CUSTOMER* can *ORDER* many *ITEM(s)* and each *ITEM(s)* can be *ORDER(ed)* from many *CUSTOMERs*.

Many-to-many relationships bring two major problems to a database's design. These issues and the way in which they are solved are discussed in the section "Dealing with Many-to-Many Relationships."

RELATIONSHIP CONNECTIVITY AND CARDINALITY

Cardinality expresses the specific number of entity occurrences associated with one occurrence of the related entity. In the Chen model, the cardinality is indicated by placing numbers beside the entities in the format of (x, y). The first number in the cardinality represents the minimum value and the second number stands for the maximum value.

The data relationships discussed thus far have defined those relationships by starting each with "zero," indicating that the cardinality in a given instance of an entity in a relationship is optional. Mega-Video can store data about a *CUSTOMER* in its database before the *CUSTOMER* places an *ORDER*. An instance of the *CUSTOMER* entity does not have to be related to any instances of the *ORDER* entity, meaning there is an *optional* cardinality.

However, the reverse is not true for the Mega-Video database. An *ORDER must* be related to a *CUSTOMER*. Without a *CUSTOMER*, an *ORDER* cannot exist. As a result, an *ORDER* is an example of a *weak entity*, one that cannot exist in the database unless a related instance of another entity is present and related to it. An instance of the *CUSTOMER* entity can be related to zero, one, or more orders. An instance of the *ORDER* entity must be related to one and only one *CUSTOMER*, having a cardinality of (1, 1). The "zero" option is not available to a weak entity. The relationship between an instance of the *ORDER* entity and the *CUSTOMER* is a mandatory relationship, as illustrated in Figure T5.11.

Identifying weak entities and their associated mandatory relationships is important for maintaining the consistency and integrity of the database. Consider the effect of storing an *ORDER* without knowing the *CUSTOMER* to which it belongs. There would be no way to ship the *ITEM* to the *CUSTOMER*, causing a company to lose business.

In contrast, a merchandise *ITEM* can exist in a database without indicating the *DISTRIBUTOR* from which it comes (assuming that there is only one source per item). Data about a new *ITEM* can be stored before a *DISTRIBUTOR* is selected. In this case, the relationship between a *DISTRIBUTOR* and an *ITEM* is actually zero-to-many.

FIGURE T5.11

A Weak Entity and a Mandatory Relationship

Documenting Relationships—The Chen Method

As briefly described earlier, the Chen method uses diamonds for relationships and lines to show the type of relationship between entities. Figure T5.12 displays the relationship between a Mega-Video *CUSTOMER* and an *ORDER*. The number "1" next to the *CUSTOMER* entity indicates that an *ORDER* belongs to at most one *CUSTOMER*. The letter "M" next to the *ORDER* entity indicates that a *CUSTOMER* can place one or more *ORDER(s)*. The word within the relationship diamond gives some indication of the meaning of the relationship.

There is one major limitation to the Chen method of drawing ERDs—there is no obvious way to indicate weak entities and mandatory relationships. An *ORDER* should not exist in the database without a *CUSTOMER*. *ORDER* is a weak entity and its relationship with a *CUSTOMER* is mandatory.

Some database designers have added a new symbol to the Chen method for a weak entity, a double-bordered rectangle, as shown in Figure T5.13. Whenever a weak entity is introduced into an ERD, it indicates that the relationship between that entity and at least one of its parents is mandatory.

FIGURE T5.12

Chen Method Weak Entity Symbol

DEALING WITH MANY-TO-MANY RELATIONSHIPS

There are problems associated with many-to-many relationships. One problem is straightforward—the relational data model cannot handle many-to-many relationships directly; it is limited to one-to-one and one-to-many relationships. This means that the many-to-many relationships need to be replaced with a collection of one-to-many relationships in a relational DBMS.

A second problem is a bit more subtle. To understand it, consider the relationship between an *ORDER* Mega-Video places with a *DISTRIBUTOR* and the merchandise *ITEM* in the *ORDER*. There is a many-to-many relationship between the *ORDER* and the *ITEM* because each *ORDER* can

FIGURE T5.13

Chen Method with Relationship

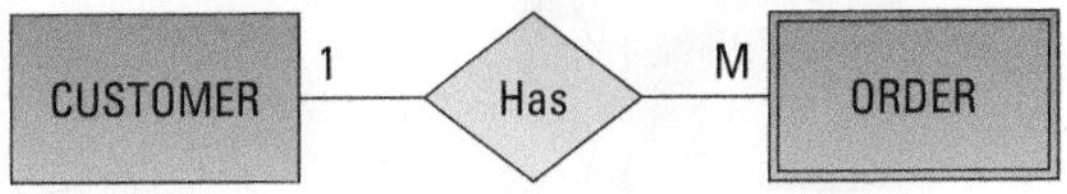

be for many *ITEM(s)* and, over time, each *ITEM* can appear on many *ORDER(s)*. Whenever Mega-Video places an *ORDER* for an *ITEM,* the number of copies of the *ITEM* varies, depending on the perceived demand for the *ITEM* at the time the *ORDER* is placed. Now the question: Where should we store the *Quantity* being ordered? It cannot be part of the *ORDER* entity because the *Quantity* depends on which item is being ordered. Similarly, the *Quantity* cannot be part of the *ITEM* entity because the *Quantity* depends on the specific *ORDER.* To solve this you would need to create a composite entity, which is discussed in the next section.

Composite Entities

Entities that exist to represent the relationship between two other entities are known as *composite entities.* As an example of how composite entities work, consider the relationship between an *ORDER* placed by a *CUSTOMER* and the *ITEM(s)* in the *ORDER.* There is a many-to-many relationship between an *ITEM* and an *ORDER:* An *ORDER* can contain many *ITEM(s)* and over time, the same *ITEM* can appear on many *ORDER(s)* (refer back to Figure T5.9).

What is needed is an entity that displays a specific title that appears on a specific order. In Figure T5.14, there are three *ORDER* instances and three merchandise *ITEM* instances. The first *ORDER* for *Customer Number* 1111 (*Order Number* 1000) contains only one *ITEM* (*Item Number* 9244). The second *ORDER* for *Customer Number* 1111 (*Order Number* 1001) contains a second copy of *Item Number* 9244, but ordered on a different date. *Order Number* 1002, which belongs to *Customer Number* 1211, has two *ITEM(s)* (*Item Number* 9250 and *Item Number* 9255).

Therefore, a composite entity called *ORDER LINE* (think of it as a line item on a packing slip) is created to represent the relationship between an *ORDER* and an *ITEM.* Figure T5.15 demonstrates the Chen notation for ERDs; the symbol for a composite entity is the combination of a rectangle and a diamond.

Each *ITEM* is related to one *ORDER LINE* instance for each *ORDER* on which it appears. Each *ORDER LINE* instance is related to one and only one *ORDER;* it is also related to one and only one *ITEM.* As a result, the relationship between an *ORDER* and its *ORDER LINE* is one-to-many (one order has one or more line items) and the relationship between an *ITEM* and the *ORDER LINE* on which it appears is one-to-many (one item appears in zero, one, or more line items). The presence

FIGURE T5.14

Composite Entity Example

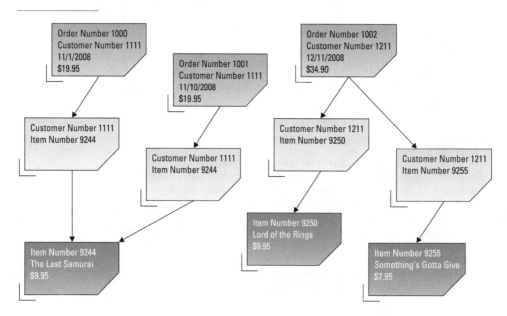

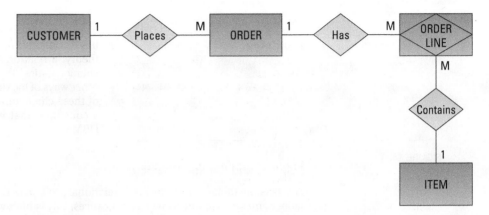

FIGURE T5.15

ERD of Composite Entity

of the composite entity has removed the original many-to-many relationship and turned it into two one-to-many relationships.

SCHEMAS

A *schema* is a completed entity relationship diagram representing the overall, logical plan of a database. This is the way in which the people responsible for maintaining the database will view the design. Users (both interactive users and application programs) may work with only a portion of the logical schema. In addition, both the logical schema and the users' views of the data are at the same time distinct from the physical storage.

The underlying physical storage, which is managed by the DBMS, is known as the *physical schema*. It is for the most part determined by the DBMS (only very large DBMSs give any control over physical storage). The benefit of this arrangement is that both database designers and users do not need to be concerned about physical storage, greatly simplifying access to the database and making it much easier to make modifications.

The Relational Data Model

Once the ERD is completed, it can be translated from a conceptual logical schema into the formal data model required by the DBMS. Most database installations are based on the relational data model.

The relational data model is the result of the work of one person, Edgar (E. E) Codd. During the 1960s, Dr. Codd, trained as a mathematician, began working with existing data models. His experience led him to believe that these were clumsy and unnatural ways of representing data relationships. He therefore went back to mathematical set theory and focused on the construct known as a relation. Dr. Codd extended that concept to produce the relational database model, which he introduced in a historic seminal paper in 1970.

UNDERSTANDING RELATIONS

In mathematical set theory, a relation is the definition of a *table* with columns (e.g., attributes) and rows (e.g., records). The word "table" is used synonymously with "entity." The definition specifies what will be contained in each column of the table, but does not include information. When rows of information are included, an *instance* of a relation is created, such as the *CUSTOMER* relation in Figure T5.16.

Customer			
Customer Number	**First Name**	**Last Name**	**Phone Number**
0001	Bill	Miller	777-777-7777
0505	Jane	Cook	444-444-4444
1111	Sam	Smith	555-555-5555
1212	John	Doe	666-666-6666

FIGURE T5.16

A Sample Customer Relation

At first glance, a relation looks much like a portion of a spreadsheet. Since it has its underpinnings in mathematical set theory, a relation has some very specific characteristics that distinguish it from other ways of looking at information. Each of these characteristics forms the basis of a constraint that will be enforced by the DBMS.

Columns and Column Characteristics

Two or more tables within the same relational schema may have columns with the same names; in fact, in some circumstances, this is highly desirable. But a single table must have unique column names. When the same column name appears in more than one table and tables that contain that column are used in the same operation (e.g., query), the name of the column must be qualified by preceding it with the name of the table and a period, as in:

CUSTOMER.(Customer Number, First Name, Last Name, Phone Number)

Note the proper notation is to capitalize the table name (e.g., *CUSTOMER*) and all columns are in title case (Customer Number) surrounded by parenthesis.

Rows and Row Characteristics

A row in a relation has the following properties:

- Only one value at the intersection of a column and row—a relation does not allow multi-valued attributes.
- Uniqueness—there are no duplicate rows in a relation.
- A primary key—a *primary key* is a field (or group of fields) that uniquely identifies a given entity in a table.

Primary Key

A *primary key* makes it possible to uniquely identify every row in a table. The primary key is important to define in order to retrieve every single piece of information put into a database.

As far as a relational database is concerned, there are only three pieces of information to retrieve for any specific bit of information: (1) the name of the table, (2) the name of the column, and (3) the primary key of the row. If primary keys are unique for every row, then the results will be exactly what was searched for. If they are not unique, then the data being retrieved will be a row with the primary key value, which may not be the row containing the data being searched.

The proper notation to use when documenting the name of the table, the column name, and primary key is as follows:

CUSTOMER(<u>Customer Number</u>, First Name, Last Name, Phone Number)

Again, notice that the table name is capitalized, the primary key is underlined, and it is the first attribute listed containing the column names.

Along with being unique, a primary key must not contain the value null. *Null* is a special database value meaning "unknown." It is not the same as a zero or a blank. If one row has a null primary key, then the data structure is all right. The minute a second one is introduced, the property of uniqueness is lost. The presence of nulls in any primary key column is forbidden. This constraint, known as entity integrity, will be enforced by a DBMS whenever information is entered or modified. *Entity integrity* is a constraint on a relation that states that no part of a primary key can be null.

Selecting a primary key can be a challenge. Some entities have natural primary keys, such as purchase order numbers, as previously mentioned. Primary keys are often arbitrary, unique identifiers, such as those a company attaches to the orders it sends to vendors. Two qualities of all primary keys are:

1. A primary key should contain some value that can never be null.
2. A primary key should never change.

REPRESENTING DATA RELATIONSHIPS

The use of identifiers in more than one relation was mentioned in the preceding section. This is the way in which relational databases represent relationships between entities.

Each table in Figure T5.17 is directly analogous to the entity by the same name in the Mega-Video ERD. The *CUSTOMER* table is identified by a *Customer Number,* a randomly generated unique primary key. The *ORDER* table is identified by an *Order Number,* another arbitrary unique primary key assigned by Mega-Video. The table *ORDER LINE* tells the company which *ITEM(s)* are part of which *ORDER.* This table requires a *concatenated primary key* because multiple *ITEM(s)* can appear on multiple *ORDER(s).* The selection of this primary key, however, has more significance than simply identifying each row; it also represents a relationship between the *ORDER LINES,* the *ORDER* on which they appear, and the *ITEM(s)* being ordered. The *ITEM* table is identified by an *Item Number,* an arbitrary unique primary key.

The *Item Number* column in the *ORDER LINE* table is the same as the primary key of the *ITEM* table. This indicates a one-to-many relationship between the two tables. Similarly, there is also a one-to-many relationship between the *ORDER* and *ORDER LINE* tables because the *Order Number* column in the *ORDER LINE* table is the same as the primary key of the *ORDER* table.

When a table contains a column that is the same as the primary key of another table, the column is called a foreign key. A *foreign key* is a primary key of one table that appears as an attribute in another table and acts to provide a logical relationship between the two tables. The matching of foreign keys to primary keys represents data relationships in a relational database.

FIGURE T5.17

Relations from the Mega-Video Database

CUSTOMER

Customer Number	First Name	Last Name	Phone
1111	Sam	Smith	555-555-5555
0505	Jane	Cook	444-444-4444

Primary key → 1111

ORDER   Foreign key

Order Number	Customer Number	Order Date
1000	1111	11/1/2006
1001	1111	11/10/2006
1002	0505	12/11/2006

ORDER LINE   Foreign key

Order Number	Item Number	Quantity	Shipped?
1000	9244	1	Y
1001	9244	1	Y
1002	9250	1	Y
1002	9255	1	Y

ITEM

Item Number	Title	Distributor Number	Price
9244	The Last Samurai	002	$9.95
9250	Lord of the Rings	002	9.95
9255	Something's Gotta Give	004	7.95

Foreign keys may be a part of a concatenated primary key or they may not be part of their table's primary key at all. Consider a pair of Mega-Video *CUSTOMER* and *ORDER* relations:

CUSTOMER(<u>Customer Number,</u> First Name, Last Name, Phone Number)

ORDER(<u>Order Number,</u> <u>Customer Number,</u> Order Date)

The *Customer Number* column in the *ORDER* table is a foreign key that matches the primary key of the *CUSTOMER* table. It represents the one-to-many relationship between *CUSTOMER(s)* and the *ORDER(s)* they place. However, the *Customer Number* is not part of the primary key of the *ORDER* table; it is a nonkey attribute that is nonetheless a foreign key, which is represented by using the double underline notation.

Technically, foreign keys need not have values unless they are part of a concatenated primary key; they can be null. However, in this particular database, Mega-Video would be in serious trouble if a *Customer Number* was null, since there would be no way to know which *CUSTOMER* placed an *ORDER*.

A relational DBMS uses the relationships indicated by matching data between primary and foreign keys. Assume that a Mega-Video employee wanted to see what *Titles* had been ordered with *Order Number* 1002. First, the DBMS identifies the rows in the *ORDER LINE* table that contain an *Order Number* of 1002. Then, it takes the *Item Number(s)* from the rows and matches them to the *Item Number(s)* in the *ITEM* table. In the rows where there are matches, the DBMS finally retrieves the associated *Title*.

Foreign Keys and Primary Keys in the Same Table

Foreign keys do not necessarily need to reference a primary key in a different table; they need only reference a primary key. As an example, consider the following employee relation:

EMPLOYEE(<u>Employee Number</u>, First Name, Last Name, Department, Manager Number)

A manager is also an employee. Therefore, the *Manager Number*, although named differently from the *Employee Number*, is actually a foreign key that references the primary key of its own table. The DBMS will therefore always ensure that whenever a user enters a *Manager Number*, that manager already exists in the table as an employee. Having a foreign key reference a primary key in the same table is relatively rare.

Referential Integrity

The procedure described in the preceding section works very well unless there is no *Order Number* in the *ORDER* table to match a row in the *ORDER LINE* table. This is undesirable since there is no way to ship the ordered *ITEM* because there is no way to find out which *CUSTOMER* placed the *ORDER*.

The relational data model enforces a constraint called *referential integrity*, which states that every non-null foreign key value must match an existing primary key value. Of all the constraints in a relational database, this is probably the most important because it ensures the consistency of the cross-references among tables.

Referential integrity constraints stored in the database are enforced automatically by the DBMS. As with all other constraints, each time a user enters or modifies data, the DBMS checks the constraints and verifies that they are met. If the constraints are violated, the data modification will not be allowed.

The Data Dictionary

The *data dictionary* is a file that stores definitions of information types, identifies the primary and foreign keys, and maintains the relationships among the tables.

The structure of a relational database is stored in the database's data dictionary, or catalog. The data dictionary is made up of a set of relations, identical in properties to the relations used to hold information. No user can modify the data dictionary tables directly. Data manipulation language commands (e.g., Structured Query Language) that create and remove database structural elements work by modifying rows in data dictionary tables.

The following types of information are typically found in a data dictionary:

- Definitions of the columns that make up each table.
- Integrity constraints placed on relations.
- Security information (which user has the right to perform which operation of which table).

When a user attempts to access information in any way, a relational DBMS first goes to the data dictionary to determine whether the database elements the user has requested are actually part of the schema. In addition, the DBMS verifies that the user has the access rights to whatever he or she is requesting.

When a user attempts to modify information, the DBMS goes to the data dictionary to look for integrity constraints that may have been placed on the relation (see Figure T5.18). If the information has met the constraints, the modification is permitted. Otherwise, the DBMS returns an error message and does not allow the change. All access to a relational database is through the data dictionary.

RELATIONSHIPS AND BUSINESS RULES

In many ways, database design is as much an art as a science. The "correct" design for a specific business depends on the business rules; what is correct for one organization may not be correct for another.

Assume there is more than one store when creating a database for a retail establishment. One of the elements being modeled in the database is an employee's schedule. Before that can be done, the question of the relationship between an employee and a store needs to be answered: Is it one-to-many or many-to-many? Does an employee always work at only one store, in which case the relationship is one-to-many, or can an employee split his or her time between more than one store, producing a many-to-many relationship? This is not a matter of right or wrong database design, but an issue of how the business operates. These types of questions must be answered before you design a database.

Normalization

Normalization is the process of placing attributes into tables that avoids the problems associated with poor database design. Given any group of entities and attributes, there is a large number of ways to group them into relations.

There are at least two ways to approach normalization. The first is to work from an ERD. If the diagram is drawn correctly, then there are some simple rules to use to translate it into relations that will avoid most relational design problems. The drawback to this approach is that it can be difficult to determine whether the design is correct. The second approach is to use the theoretical concepts behind good design to create relations. This is a bit more difficult than working from an ERD, but often results in a better design.

NORMAL FORMS

Normal forms are the theoretical rules that the design of a relation must meet. Each normal form represents an increasingly stringent set of rules. Theoretically, the higher the normal form, the better the design of the relation.

Table Name	Attribute Name	Contents	Type	Length	Format	Range	Req'd	Key	Referenced Table
CUSTOMER	Customer Number	Customer Number	VCHAR	10	X(10)		Y	PK	
	First Name	First Name	VCHAR2	12	X(12)		Y		
	Last Name	Last Name	VCHAR2	15	X(15)		Y		
	Street	Street Address	VCHAR2	20	X(20)		Y		
	City	City	VCHAR2	20	X(20)		Y		
	State	State	VCHAR2	2	X(2)		Y		
	Zip Code	ZIP Code	NUMBER	5	99999		Y		
	Credit Card No	Credit Card Number	NUMBER	15	X(15)		Y		
	Credit Card Exp	Credit Card Expiration Date	DATE	8	MM/DD/YYYY		Y		
ORDER	Order Number	Order Number	NUMBER	5	99999	1-99999	Y	PK	
	Customer Number	Customer Number	VCHAR	10	X(10)		Y	FK	CUSTOMER
	Order Date	Order Date	DATE	8	MM/DD/YYYY		Y		
	Order Filled	Order Filled	DATE	8	MM/DD/YYYY		Y		
ORDER LINE	Order Number	Order Number	NUMBER	5	99999	1-99999	Y	FK	ORDER
	Item Number	Item Number	NUMBER	5	99999	1-99999	Y	FK	ITEM
	Quantity	Quantity	NUMBER	3	999	1-999	Y		
	Price	Selling Price	NUMBER	5	$999.99		Y		
	Shipped	Shipped	VCHAR2	1	X	Y/N	Y		
ITEM	Item Number	Item Number	Number	5	99999	1-99999	Y	PK	
	Title	Title	VCHAR2	25	X(25)		Y		
	Distributor	Distributor	VCHAR2	20	X(20)		Y		
	Price	Price	Number	5	$999.99		Y		

FIGURE T5.18

Data Dictionary Example

As illustrated in Figure T5.19, there are six nested normal forms, indicating that if a relation is in one of the higher, inner normal forms, it is also in all of the normal forms surrounding it. In most cases, if relations are in third normal form (3NF), then most of the problems common to bad relational designs are avoided. Boyce-Codd (BCNF) and fourth normal form (4NF) handle special situations that arise only occasionally. Fifth normal form (5NF) is a complex set of criteria that are extremely difficult to work with. It is very difficult to verify that a relation is in 5NF. Most practitioners do not bother with 5NF, knowing that if their relations are in 3NF (or 4NF if the situation warrants), then their designs are generally problem-free. BCNF, 4NF, and 5NF are beyond the scope of this plug-in; therefore they will not be discussed beyond what is mentioned in this section.

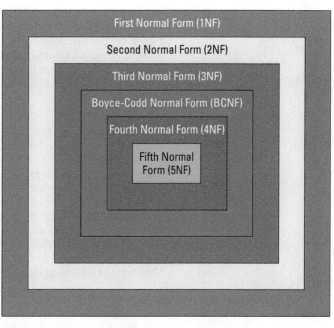

First Normal Form (1NF)
Second Normal Form (2NF)
Third Normal Form (3NF)
Boyce-Codd Normal Form (BCNF)
Fourth Normal Form (4NF)
Fifth Normal Form (5NF)

FIGURE T5.19

Normal Forms

First Normal Form (1NF)

First normal form (1NF) is where each field in a table contains different information. For example, in the column labeled "Customer," only customer names or numbers are permitted. A table is in first normal form (1NF) if the data are stored in a two-dimensional table with no repeating groups.

Although first normal form relations have no repeating groups, they are full of other problems. Expressed in the notation for relations that have been used in this plug-in, the relation notation would look like the following:

ORDER(Customer Number, First Name, Last Name, Street, City, State, ZIP, Phone, Order Number, Order Date, Item Number, Title, Price, Shipped)

The first thing is to determine the primary key for this table. The *Customer Number* alone will not be sufficient because the customer number repeats for every item ordered by the customer. The *Item Number* will also not suffice, because it is repeated for every order on which it appears. The *Order Number* cannot be used because it is repeated for every item on the order. The only solution is a concatenated key, in this example the combination of the *Order Number* and the *Item Number*.

Given that the primary key is made up of the *Order Number* and the *Item Number*, there are two important things that cannot be done with this relation:

- Data about a customer cannot be added until the customer places at least one order because without an order and an item on that order, there is no complete primary key.

- Data about a merchandise item cannot be added without that item being ordered. There must be an *Order Number* to complete the primary key.

First normal form relations can also present problems when deleting data. Consider, for example, what happens if a customer cancels the order of a single item:

- In cases where the deleted item was the only item on the order, all data about the order is lost.

- In cases where the order was the only order on which the item appeared, data about the item is lost.

- In cases where the deleted item was the only item ordered by a customer, all data about the customer is lost.

There is a final type of inconsistency in the *ORDER* relation that is not related to the primary key: a modification, or update, anomaly. The *ORDER* relation has a great deal of unnecessary duplicated data, in particular, information about customers. When a customer moves, then the customer's data must be changed in every row, for every item on every order ever placed by the customer. If every row is not changed correctly, then data that should be the same are no longer the same.

Second Normal Form (2NF)

Second normal form (2NF) is when the relation is in first normal form and all non-key attributes are functionally dependent on the entire primary key. The solution to anomalies in a first normal form relation is to break the relation down so that there is one relation for each entity in the 1NF relation. The *ORDER(s)* relation, for example, will break down into four relations (*CUSTOMER, ORDER, ORDER LINE,* and *ITEM*). Such relations are in at least 2NF.

Although second normal form eliminates problems from many relations, relations that are in second normal form still exhibit anomalies. Assume that each DVD title that Mega-Video carries comes from one *DISTRIBUTOR* and that each *DISTRIBUTOR* has only one warehouse, which has only one *Warehouse Phone Number*. The following relation is therefore in 2NF:

ITEM (<u>Item Number</u>, Title, Distributor, Warehouse Phone Number)

From each *Item Number,* there is only one value for the item's *Title, Distributor,* and *Warehouse Phone Number.* There is one insertion anomaly—data cannot be inserted about a *DISTRIBUTOR* until an item from the *DISTRIBUTOR* is entered. There is a deletion anomaly as well: if the only item from the *DISTRIBUTOR* is deleted, the data about the *DISTRIBUTOR* is lost.

Third Normal Form (3NF)

Third normal form (3NF) is when the relation is in second normal form and there are no transitive dependencies. In terms of entities, the *ITEM* relation does contain two entities: the merchandise *ITEM* and the *DISTRIBUTOR.* The relation needs to be broken down into two smaller relations, both of which are now in 3NF:

ITEM(<u>Item Number</u>, Distributor Number)
DISTRIBUTOR(<u>Distributor Number</u>, Warehouse Phone Number)

NORMALIZED RELATIONS AND DATABASE PERFORMANCE

Normalizing the relations in a database separates entities into their own relations and makes it possible to enter, modify, and delete data without disturbing entities other than the one directly being modified. When relations are split so that relationships are represented by matching primary and foreign keys, DBMS is forced to perform matching operations between relations whenever a query requires data from more than one table. In a normalized database, data is stored about an *ORDER* in one relation, data about a *CUSTOMER* in a second relation, and data about the *ORDER LINE(s)* in yet a third relation. The operation typically used to bring the data into a single table to prepare an output, such as an invoice, is known as a join. A *join* is an operation that combines two relations by matching rows based on values in columns in the two tables. The matching relationship is usually primary key to foreign key.

In theory, a join looks for rows with matching values between two tables and creates a new row in a result table every time it finds a match. In practice, however, performing a join involves manipulating more data than the simple combination of the two tables being joined would suggest. Joins of large tables (those of more than a few hundred rows) can significantly slow down the performance of a DBMS.

✱ PLUG-IN SUMMARY

A database management system, or DBMS, is considered a basic component of data processing. The main advantage of using a DBMS is to enforce a logical and structured organization of the data. Additionally, using a DBMS provides a central store of data that can be accessed by multiple users, from multiple locations. Data can be shared among multiple applications, instead of new iterations of the same data being reproduced and stored in new files for every new application.

The principal type of database used is a relational DBMS. Designing a database requires both a logical and physical design. The organization's data model should reflect its key business processes and decision-making requirements. Entity relationship diagrams and normalization are processes used to design a relational database.

✱ MAKING BUSINESS DECISIONS

1. SportTech Events

SportTech Events puts on athletic events for local high school athletes. The company needs a database designed to keep track of the sponsor for the event and where the event is located. Each event needs a description, date, and cost. Separate costs are negotiated for each event. The company would also like to have a list of potential sponsors that includes each sponsor's contact information such as the name, phone number, and address. Each event will have a single sponsor, but a particular sponsor may sponsor more than one event. Each location will need an ID, contact person, and phone number. A particular event will use only one location, but a location may be used for multiple events. SportTech asks you to create an ERD from the information described above, and then create a normalization structure in 3NF.

2. Course and Student Schedules

Dick Scudder, the chairperson of the information technology department at the University of Denver, needs to create a database to keep track of all the courses offered by the department. In addition, Dick would like the database to include each instructor's basic contact information, such as ID number, name, office location, and phone number. Currently, Dick has nine instructors (seven full-time faculty members and two adjuncts) in the department.

For each course, Dick would like to keep track of the course ID, title, and number of credit hours. When courses are offered, the section of the course receives an ID number, and with that number, the department keeps track of which instructor is teaching the course.

Finally, Dick needs to be able to keep track of the IT students and to know which courses each student has taken. The information he would like to know about each student includes ID number, name, and phone number. He also needs to know what grade the student receives in each course.

Dick has asked you to create an ERD from the information described above, and then create a normalization structure in 3NF.

3. Foothills Athletics

Foothills Athletics is an athletic facility offering services in the greater Highlands Ranch, Colorado, area. All property owners living in Highlands Ranch are members of the Recreation Function of the Highlands Ranch Community Association (HRCA). Foothills Athletics consists of a recreation facility where residents have the opportunity to participate in athletic activities, enroll their children in day camp or preschool, or participate in an HRCA program.

Personnel: Foothills Athletics has a number of employees, primarily fitness course instructors and administrative personnel (e.g., billing clerks, equipment managers, etc.). Records are kept on each employee, past and present, detailing employee name, address, phone number, date of hire, position, and status as either a current or former employee. Employees are assigned a unique four-digit Employee ID number when they are hired.

Members: When joining the Foothills Athletic center, individuals are assigned a unique four-digit Member ID number. This information along with their name, address, phone number, gender, birth date, and date of membership are recorded. At the time of enrollment, each member decides on one of three available membership types along with a fixed membership fee: Platinum ($400), Gold ($300), and Silver ($200). This is a one-time fee that establishes a lifetime membership.

Facilities and Equipment: Foothills Athletics has a variety of facilities and equipment choices. Each facility has a unique room number and a size limitation associated with it. Some of the rooms contain pieces of exercise equipment; all have a serial number (provided by its manufacturer) that is used for inventory purposes. In addition, for each piece of equipment, purchase date and the date of its last maintenance are recorded. Each piece of equipment belongs to a specific equipment type, such as stair master machine, and is assigned a unique three-digit identification number. The description, the manufacturer's model number, and the recommended maintenance interval for that model of equipment are also kept on file. Each equipment type is associated with a single manufacturer that is referenced by a unique two-digit manufacturer ID number. Additional information maintained on each manufacturer is the company name, address, and phone number.

The Task: You have been hired to assist Foothills Athletics with creating a database structure that will incorporate all the features and business rules mentioned above. You should start out developing an ERD and then proceed to create a normalization structure in 3NF.

4. On-the-Vine Vineyard

On-the-Vine Vineyard, Inc., is one of California's largest winemaking facilities in Sonoma Valley, striving to make both a visit to the vineyard and the wine tasting an unforgettable experience. On-the-Vine is a small, family-owned winery, specializing in limited production of premium quality Chardonnay, Sauvignon Blanc, Merlot, Syrah, Zinfandel, Sangiovese, Viognier, and Cabernet.

The Employees: On-the-Vine currently employs over 12 full-time employees, with positions ranging from administrative assistant to winemaker. Among the employees, supervisors have been appointed to manage the work of other employees. Each supervised employee reports to only one supervisor. Each employee is assigned a unique identification number. In addition to the employee's name, position, and identification number, the company also records each employee's Social Security number, address, phone number, and emergency contact.

The Vineyard: The grounds of On-the-Vine Vineyard include the Estate house with an award-winning rose garden, winery, and two vineyard plots of 40 acres each in separate locations. Each vineyard is managed by a single employee and is referred to by its own unique name, Sonoma Cellar and Sonoma Barrel. No employee manages more than one vineyard. Each vineyard is dedicated to the growing of a single grape variety per year.

As mentioned above, On-the-Vine Vineyard currently grows eight different grape varieties:

1. Chardonnay
2. Sauvignon Blanc
3. Merlot

4. Syrah
5. Zinfandel
6. Sangiovese
7. Viognier
8. Cabernet

The Winery: Each wine produced is given a unique identification number in addition to its name. Other information recorded for each wine is its vintage year, category (e.g., dry red, dessert, etc.), and percent alcohol, which is a legal requirement. Also recorded is the employee in charge of making that wine. Winemakers may be responsible for more than one wine at a time.

The composition of a wine may be entirely from a single grape variety or may be a blend of more than one variety. Several of the grape varieties are used in more than one blended wine.

The Customers: On-the-Vine customers are mainly restaurants and wine shops, but the winery also sells to individuals via the Internet. All customers are assigned a unique customer identification number, and this number is recorded along with their address and phone number. Individual customers also have their first name, last name, and date of birth, in order to demonstrate legal age, recorded. Restaurants and wine shops have their company name and tax identification number recorded.

All customers obtain their products by placing orders directly with On-the-Vine. Each order is assigned a unique order number, and the date the order is received, the product or products ordered, and the quantity or quantities desired are all recorded at the same time. A shipment status of "pending" is assigned to an order until it is actually shipped, whereupon the status is then changed to "shipped."

The Task: You have been hired to assist On-the-Vine Vineyard with creating a database structure that will incorporate all the features and business rules mentioned above. You should start out developing an ERD and then proceed to create a normalization structure in 3NF.

PLUG-IN

T6

Basic Skills and Tools Using Access 2010

LEARNING OUTCOMES

1. Describe the primary functions using Microsoft Access.
2. Describe the steps for creating a new database file using Access.
3. Describe the steps for creating and modifying a table and fields using Access.
4. Describe the steps for creating relationships between tables using Access.

Introduction to Access

Microsoft Access 2010 is a powerful database program that allows you to enter and organize large amounts of data. Because Access allows you to relate tables and databases to one another, it is often referred to as a *relational database*. Plug-In T5, "Designing Database Applications," explains relational databases and their structures in detail.

This plug-in introduces the basics of creating a database using Microsoft Access. It is designed to show you the essentials, along with a few added-value features, to get you off to a good start using the program. Additional material, animated tutorials, and simulated practice files that go beyond what we cover in the text can be found at https://misource.simnetonline.com. Figure T6.1 displays many of the tasks and lessons that are provided from this Web site.

In brief, a relational database is a group of tables related to one another by common fields. A *table* (or datasheet) looks similar to a spreadsheet. Each *row* in the table contains all the data for a single *record*. Each *column* in the table represents a specific data value called a *field*. All records in a relational database have the same fields. For example, a table called *EMPLOYEE* might include fields for *Employee ID*, *Last Name*, *First Name*, *Address*, *City*, *State*, and *Zip*. Another table called *TIME SHEET* might have fields for *Time Sheet Number*, *Employee ID*, *Week*, *Hours Worked*, and *Rate of Pay*. The two tables are related by the *Employee ID* field, so the database can generate reports combining information from the two tables. Figure T6.2 displays this relationship.

Access comes with templates for common database categories, including project planning, employee time sheets, expense reporting, and inventory management.

MISource CD **Microsoft Access Lessons**	
Introduction to Access 2010	**Creating and Modifying Queries**
■ Introduction to Access 2010 ■ Opening an Existing Database ■ Creating a New Blank Database ■ Creating a New Database from a Template ■ Creating Relationships ■ Modifying Relationships ■ Entering Data in a Table ■ Navigating Records in a Table ■ Entering Data in a Form ■ Navigating Records in a Form ■ Adding Attachments to Records	■ Using the Simple Query Wizard ■ Creating a Query in Design View ■ Adding Criteria to a Query ■ Adding a Calculated Field to a Query ■ Using Action Queries
Creating and Modifying Tables	**Working with Reports**
■ Designing a Table ■ Creating a New Table ■ Creating a Table from a Template ■ Creating a Table in Design View ■ Setting the Primary Key ■ Defining Table Fields ■ Changing Data Types ■ Adding Fields to Tables ■ Adding a Total Row ■ Using Attachment Fields ■ Modifying Field Properties ■ Modifying Tables ■ Using the Table Analyzer	■ Creating a Simple Report ■ Using the Report Wizard ■ Adding Controls to a Report ■ Grouping Records in a Report ■ Controlling the Page Setup of a Report for Printing
Creating and Modifying Forms	**Organizing Information**
■ Creating a Form Based on a Table or Query ■ Creating a Split Form ■ Creating a Datasheet Form ■ Changing the Look of a Form with AutoFormat ■ Working in Form Design View ■ Adding Controls to Forms ■ Arranging Controls ■ Defining the Tab Order of Controls ■ Creating Subforms	■ Viewing Dependencies ■ Using Text Filters ■ Using Date and Numerical Filters ■ Sorting Records ■ Searching for Information
	Importing and Exporting Data
	■ Importing Data from Excel ■ Exporting Data

FIGURE T6.1

MISource Access Lessons

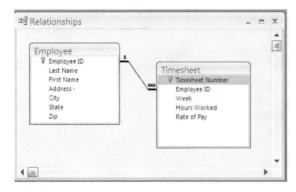

FIGURE T6.2

Database Relationship
Example

An Access database includes more than just data. In addition to tables, an Access database file contains several different types of database objects:

- Saved queries for retrieving and organizing data.
- Forms for entering and displaying data on screen.
- Reports for printing table data or the results of queries.

This plug-in focuses on creating an Access database file, in addition to building tables, fields, attributes, and relationships. Plug-In T7, "Problem Solving Using Access 2010," concentrates on building queries, and Plug-In T8, "Decision Making Using Access 2010," spotlights forms and reports.

CREATING A NEW BLANK DATABASE

When creating a new blank database, the first thing you do is name your database. In Access, the database file cannot be moved to another disk or folder using the *Save As* command, so be sure to save the database to the preferred location when you start. (You can always move the database later using Windows Explorer.)

To create a blank database, follow these steps:

1. Open Access, click the **File** tab, and then click **New.**
2. On the page, under **Available Templates** double click **Blank Database** (illustrated in Figure T6.3).

FIGURE T6.3

Create a New Blank
Database

*Click here to
open a new blank
database.*

*Enter a database
name and click
Create.*

*Double-click
file name to open . . .*

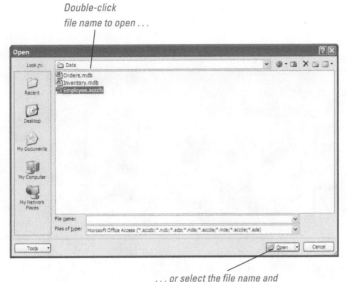

*. . . or select the file name and
click the Open button.*

3. In the Blank Database pane, type **Slopeside Bikes** for the database file name in the **File Name:** box.

4. Click **Create.** Access will save the new blank database in the specified database file (which will have the .accdb extension).

5. Access creates the database with an empty table named **Table1,** and then opens Table1 in **Datasheet** view. The cursor is placed in the first empty cell in the **Add New Field** column.

OPENING AN EXISTING DATABASE

When you start Access, the task pane to the right lists the most recently opened databases. To open a database that is not listed in the task pane, use the Open command. To open a database (refer to Figure T6.4):

1. Click the **File** tab, and then click **Open.**

2. In the **Open** dialog box, browse to the database that you want to open.

3. Double-click the name of the database to open it, or click the name of the database once to highlight it, then click the **Open** button.

USING THE DATABASE TEMPLATES

Access includes a variety of templates to help you get started with some of the most common types of databases.

Templates include databases to manage contacts, expenses, and inventory. Here is an overview on how to create a new database using a template (refer to Figure T6.5):

1. Click the **File** tab, and then click **New.**

2. Several featured templates are displayed under the **Office.com Templates**

3. Click on the template name **Contacts,** then name your file in the **File Name Box,** just below the **Blank Database Preview Box.**

4. Access creates the database and then opens it. A form is displayed in which you can begin entering data.

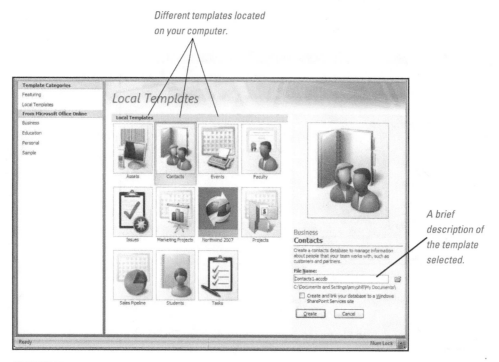

Different templates located on your computer.

A brief description of the template selected.

FIGURE T6.5

Create a New Blank
Database Using
a Template

USING THE DATABASE WINDOW AND OBJECT VIEWS

Whenever a database is open, Access displays the Database window (shown in Figure T6.6), which serves as the central location for working with the database objects (tables, queries, forms, reports, etc.) in the opened database.

The following are among the important ways to work with database objects using the Database window:

■ *To work with a particular type of database object*, click the **Shutter Bar Open/ Close** button (<<) and select the object you want to work with—Tables, Queries, Forms, Reports, Pages, and so on.

■ *To view a database object*, select the object name under the Navigation Pane and double-click the object to open it.

■ *To change the design of a database object*, select the object name under the Navigation Pane, right-click and choose the **Design View** button.

■ *To create a new database object* of the type currently displayed in the Database window, click the **Create** tab and then select the button type to create the new object (Table, Form, Report, Query Wizard, or Data Access Page).

■ *To make a copy of a database object*, right-click the object and choose **Copy** from the shortcut menu. Then right-click a blank spot in the Database window and choose **Paste** from the shortcut menu.

■ *To rename a database object*, right-click the object and choose **Rename** from the shortcut menu.

■ *To delete a database object*, right-click the object and choose **Delete** from the shortcut menu.

■ *To close the current database*, together with the Database window, click the **File** tab, then click the **Close Database** button.

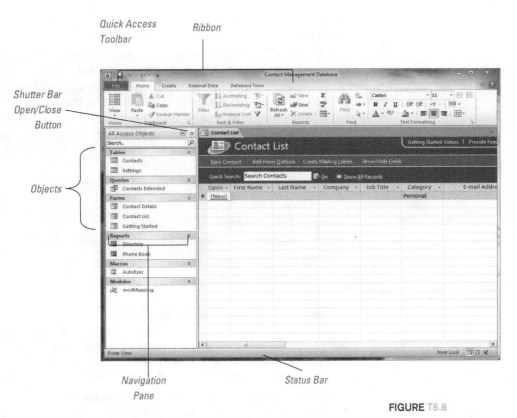

Quick Access Toolbar

Ribbon

Shutter Bar Open/Close Button

Objects

Navigation Pane

Status Bar

FIGURE T6.6

Access Database Window

FIGURE T6.7

Datasheet View

USING TABLE VIEWS

You can open database objects in different views, depending on what you want to do. *Datasheet view* is the view to use when entering data (see Figure T6.7). Use

View button

Datasheet view

Design view when you want to change the structure or properties of the table. To open a table in Datasheet view from the Database window:

1. Under the Navigation Pane, click the **Shutter Bar Open/Close** button and make sure that all of the **All Access Objects** are selected.

2. To automatically open a table in Datasheet View, double-click the name of the table under the **Tables** section of the Navigation Pane. This is the Datasheet view where you can enter data in the table.

3. To change to Design view, click the **View** button in the **Views** group on the toolbar (refer to Figure T6.7). In Design view, you can add or remove fields or change field properties.

4. To switch back to Datasheet view, click the **View** button again.

Creating and Modifying Tables

Access gives you two different ways to create tables:

- Create a table using data entry.
- Create a table in Design view.

CREATING A TABLE USING DATA ENTRY

Sometimes you need to create a very simple table. In this case, the data entry method might be easiest. A new table created with the data entry method appears as a plain datasheet. Fields are named **Field1, Field2, Field3,** etc., until you rename them. To create a table using the data entry method (refer to Figure T6.8):

1. Click the **Create** tab and then click the **Table** button.

2. The new table appears and is ready for data entry.

3. Rename the fields that you are going to use by double-clicking the field name (**Field1, Field2,** etc.) and typing the new field name (First Name, Last Name, etc.).

FIGURE T6.8

Create a Table
by Entering Data

*Field names are labeled Field1,
Field2, etc., until you rename them.*

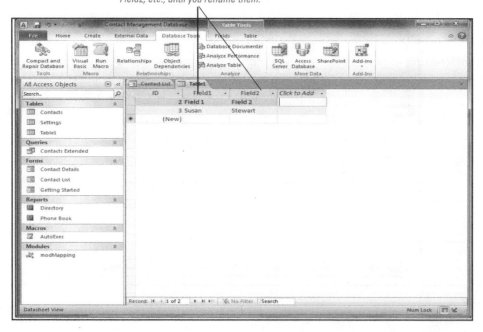

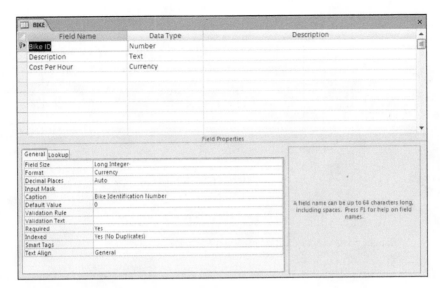

FIGURE T6.9

Bike Table

CREATING A TABLE IN DESIGN VIEW

Most Access objects are displayed in Design view, which allows you to work with the underlying structure of your tables, queries, forms, and reports. In this next step, you will be using the Slopeside Bikes database that you created in the "Creating a New Blank Database" section to use for many of the remaining steps in this plug-in. To create a table using Design view, follow these steps:

1. Click the **Create** tab, and then click the **Table Design** button.

2. Click in the **Field Name** cell and type **Bike ID.**

3. Click in the **Data Type** cell, click the list arrow and select **Number.** To make the Bike ID field a primary key, click on the **Primary Key** button in the **Tools** group on the toolbar. In the **Field Properties** pane (below the table), make sure the **Required** property is set to **Yes** and the **Field Size** is set to **Long Integer.**

4. Using the same steps above, create fields for the following (see Figure T6.9):

   a. Field Name = **Description,** Data Type = **Text,** Field Size = **25,** Required = **Yes**

   b. Field Name = **Cost Per Hour,** Data Type = **Currency,** Required = **Yes**

   Note: Designate a primary key. The *primary key* consists of one or more fields that Access can use to uniquely identify the records contained within the table. A table must have a primary key if it is on the "one" side of a one-to-many relationship, as explained in Plug-In T5.

   When a single field is designated as the primary key, the field's *Indexed* property is automatically set to *Yes (No Duplicates).* This setting cannot be changed. When data in a record are entered or modified, Access will not allow a primary key field to be left blank.

   To designate a field, or a group of fields, as the primary key, select the field or fields in the field list and click the **Primary Key** button. Access will mark the primary key field(s) with a key icon, as shown in Figure T6.10. To remove the primary key designation from a field, select it and click the **Primary Key** button again.

5. Close the table, and click **Yes** to the save changes prompt. Enter **BIKE** as the **Table Name.**

6. Create another new, blank table as before. Enter fields for each entry in Figure T6.11, using field sizes and descriptions as appropriate. Remember to set the **primary key** and ensure that the **Required** property is set to **Yes** as appropriate.

Primary Key button

Select the field that will be the primary key.

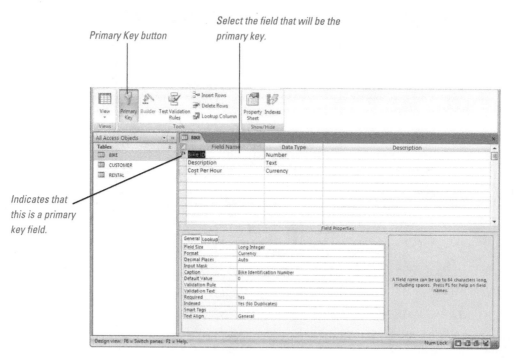

Indicates that this is a primary key field.

7. Close the table, and click **Yes** to the save changes prompt. Enter **CUSTOMER** as the **Table Name.**

8. Create another new, blank table as before. Enter fields for each entry in Figure T6.12, using field sizes and descriptions as appropriate. Since there are three primary keys in this scenario (each acts as a composite key comprised as one primary key), make sure all three (**Drivers License, Date,** and **Bike ID**) are selected by holding down the **CTRL** key when clicking each field, then select the **Primary Key** button.

9. Close the table, and click **Yes** to the save changes prompt. Enter **RENTAL** for the **Table Name.**

FIGURE T6.11

Customer Table

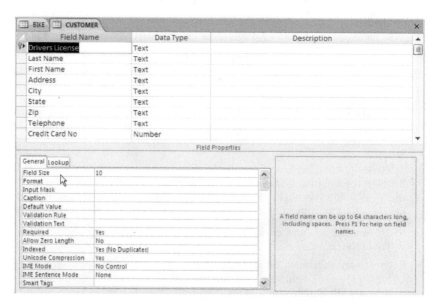

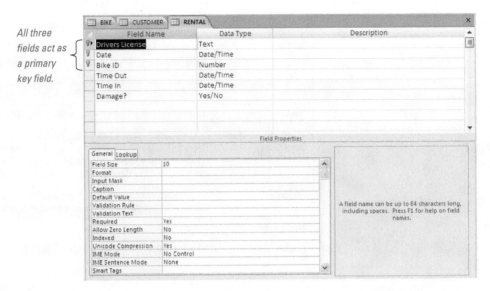

All three fields act as a primary key field.

CHANGING DATA TYPES

By default, the data type for a new field is *Text.* You can change the data type to *Number, AutoNumber, Date/Time, Currency,* or one of the other options available. Specifying the appropriate data type for a field is crucial to designing a useful database. For example, you cannot run calculations on a field with the Text data type, and you cannot sort a date field efficiently unless you use the Date/Time data type.

Carefully consider the type of data you will include in each field before you decide on the data type. To change the data type for a field:

1. In the Navigation Pane, open the table you wish to modify in Design view.

2. Click the existing data type for the field that you want to change.

3. Click the drop-down arrow to see the list of other available data types.

4. Select the appropriate data type for your data (see Figure T6.13).

USING THE INPUT MASK WIZARD

To ensure that users enter data in a particular format, use the *Input Mask* property. Rather than typing the mask format yourself, Access has a wizard that offers samples of the most common data formats. To use the Input Mask Wizard (see Figure T6.14):

1. Open the **CUSTOMER** table in Design view that you created in a previous section.

2. Click the **Telephone** field.

3. Click the **Input Mask** box in the **Field Properties** pane.

4. Click the Build button (the **. . .** ellipsis button) to the right of the box.

5. If you need to save the table, Access will prompt you to do so now.

6. The **Input Mask Wizard** appears. Select **Phone Number** under the **Input Mask:** column.

7. Click the **Next** button to continue.

FIGURE T6.13

Access 2010 Data Types

Access 2010 Data Types	
Text	Any field that does not fit criteria for one of the other data types. This includes not only text, but also formatted numbers like ZIP codes and phone numbers.
Memo	Text descriptions longer than 255 characters.
Number	Quantities; values that will have mathematical calculations performed on them.
Date/Time	Dates and times. There are a variety of date and time formats to choose from. Although you can enter dates and times as Text data types, you must use the Date/Time data type if you want to sort the values.
Currency	Money amounts. Choose from a variety of currency formats. You can perform mathematical calculations on currency values.
AutoNumber	Primary keys or other ID fields.
Yes/No	Fields to which there is only a yes or no response.
OLE Object	Pictures or other graphics. Links to other files such as Word or Excel documents.
Hyperlink	E-mail or Web site addresses.
Lookup Wizard...	Limits the data in the field to values in a list (either from another table or from a list that you create).

8. In this step, you can modify the input mask or change the placeholder character. To change the **Placeholder character:** click the drop-down arrow and select the character you want. You can test the new format by typing values in the **Try It:** box.

FIGURE T6.14

Input Mask Wizard

9. Finally, choose how you want to store the data. Click the **With the symbols in the mask, like this:** radio button.

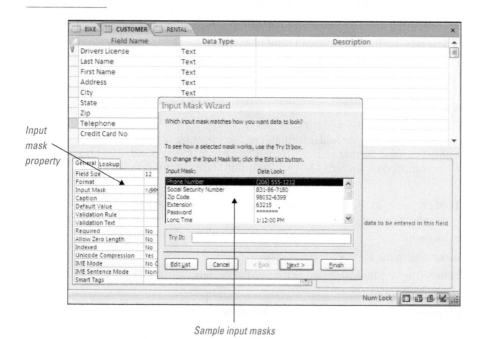

Input mask property

Sample input masks

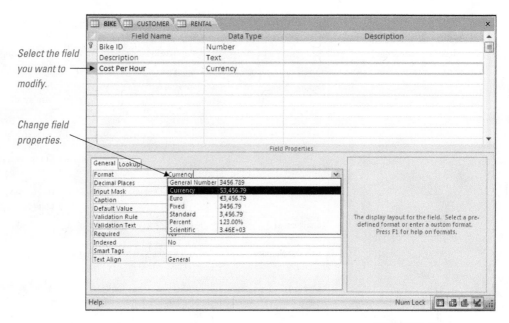

Select the field you want to modify.

Change field properties.

FIGURE T6.15

Format Property

10. Click **Next** to go to the last step.

11. Click **Finish** to complete the input mask.

USING THE FORMAT PROPERTY

Use the format property to ensure that data are entered in a consistent format. You can choose from predefined formats or design your own. To select a predefined format or enter a custom text format (see Figure T6.15):

1. Open the **BIKE** table in **Design** view that you created in a previous section.

2. Click the **Cost Per Hour** field.

3. Click the drop-down arrow under **Format** in the **Field Properties** pane to display the list of predefined formats. Refer back to Figure T6.13 for a list of the data types.

4. Select the **Currency** format.

5. Close the **BIKE** table window and click **Yes** at the save changes prompt.

Note: You can include Autotext in your custom text formats. For example, if you are entering apartment numbers, you could use the format **"Apt. " @-@.** Entering the value **B1** will display **Apt. B-1.** Placing quotation marks around **"Apt. "** tells Access that this is a text string that should be included automatically in each data entry. Notice the space inside the quotation marks to ensure that a space will display between "Apt." and the apartment number. Using this text format will save data entry time. Figure T6.16 displays the different data formats used in Access.

Defining Relationships

Remember that Access is a relational database. Objects in your database are related to one another through relationships defined by common fields between tables. There are three types of relationships: one-to-many, one-to-one, and many-to-many.

FIGURE T6.16

Access 2010 Data Formats

Text Formats		
<	Forces text to lowercase.	Type: Leash, Extra Long Display: leash, extra long
>	Forces text to uppercase.	Type: ca Display: CA
@	Requires character entry or space.	Example: Use for a text field that must always have the same number of characters (like a Social Security Number: @@@-@@-@@@@).
@;none	Controls what value is shown.	Displays value entered; if no value entered, displays "none."
Number/Currency Formats		
General Number	Displays the number as entered. Example: 24000	
Currency	Uses the currency format specified in your Windows Regional Settings, including the comma thousands separator and currency symbol. Example: $24,000.00	
Euro	Uses the standard currency format with the euro symbol. Example: €24,000.00	
Fixed	Uses the number format specified in your Windows Regional Settings. Displays at least one digit. Example: 24000.00	
Standard	Uses the number format specified in your Windows Regional Settings, including the comma thousands separator. Example: 24,000.00	
Percent	Multiplies the value by 100 and adds % symbol. Enter: .03 Displays: 3%	
Scientific	Converts the number to scientific notation. Example: 24E+3	

One-to-many relationships are the most common. In a one-to-many relationship, the primary table contains a primary key field that is included as a field (as a foreign key) in the secondary table. Thus, one record in the first table can relate to many records in the second table.

When these fields have the same names, Access automatically creates the one-to-many relationship for you. However, the fields may have different names. In those cases, you may want to manually create the relationship using the Relationships window.

USING THE RELATIONSHIPS WINDOW

To define relationships between tables follow these steps:

1. Open the **Relationships** window by clicking on the **Database Tools** tab, then clicking the **Relationships** button in the **Show/Hide** group (refer to Figure T6.17).

2. The **Show Table** dialog box appears. Select each table listed (i.e., **BIKE, CUSTOMER,** and **RENTAL**) and click the **Add** button, then click the **Close** button.

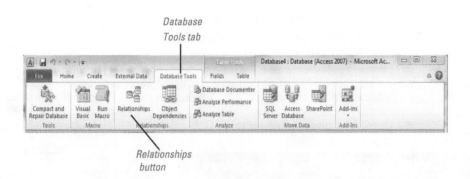

FIGURE T6.17

The Relationships Button

*Database
Tools tab*

*Relationships
button*

FIGURE T6.18

Edit Relationships
Dialog Box

3. The **Relationships** diagram should appear. To define a new relationship, click and drag the **Bike ID** primary key from the **BIKE** table and drop it on the **Bike ID** foreign key in the **RENTAL** table. Make sure the table names and field names being linked are the correct ones. The **Edit Relationships** dialog box should appear (see Figure T6.18). Select **Enforce Referential Integrity.** Then click the **Create** button. Note that related fields do not need to have the same name, only the same data type (although it is best to give the same name to clarify the relationship).

   a. To change the features of a relationship, double-click the relationship's line in the **Relationships** window.

   b. To delete a relationship, click the line to select it and then press the **Delete** key.

4. Complete the diagram with the relationships shown in Figure T6.19.

5. Close the **Relationships** window, and save the layout.

    Notice the symbols on the relationship lines. The **"1"** indicates the "one" table in the one-to-many relationship. The infinity symbol **"∞"** indicates the "many" table. When these symbols appear, you know that the relationship has referential integrity enforced.

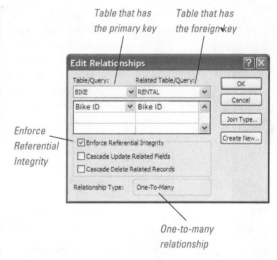

*Table that has
the primary key*

*Table that has
the foreign key*

*Enforce
Referential
Integrity*

*One-to-many
relationship*

FIGURE T6.19

Completed Relationships
Window

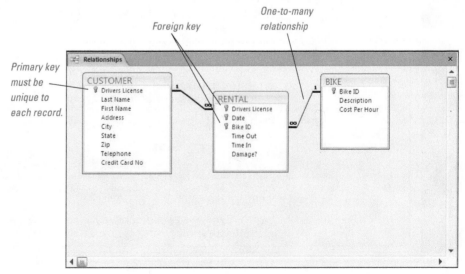

*One-to-many
relationship*

Foreign key

*Primary key
must be
unique to
each record.*

PLUG-IN SUMMARY

Most organizations maintain and manage large amounts of information. One of the most efficient information management computer-based applications is Microsoft Access 2010. Access provides a powerful set of tools for creating and maintaining a relational database. A few of the basic modules that most users utilize when working with Access are building tables and relationships.

MAKING BUSINESS DECISIONS

1. WasteNot Recycling

WasteNot Recycling picks up recyclables from homeowners in Boulder, Colorado. Neighborhoods subscribe to the service so that pickup is cost-effective. WasteNot provides special containers to subscribers for sorting recyclables: a blue container for paper products and a purple container for aluminum, plastic, and glass products.

Subscribers place their recycling containers on the curb for biweekly pickup. Each recycling container is weighed before being emptied. WasteNot drivers carry handheld recording devices used to track each pickup. Subscribers receive quarterly profit-sharing checks based on their contributions. If WasteNot does not make a profit, subscribers are not paid for their recyclables. If WasteNot makes a profit, subscribers share in that profit. WasteNot has asked you to help develop a relational database that will effectively track subscribers, using the data downloaded from the drivers' devices. WasteNot has provided you with a snapshot of two tables you need to create. The Customer table shown here holds static customer information such as name, address, and phone. The Customer Record table holds data about each recyclable pickup.

Specifically, WasteNot needs you to:

Customer Table

Customer ID	Last Name	First Name	Street	City	State	ZIP Code	Phone	First Pickup
1	Wagoner	Sam	5480 Alpine Street	Boulder	CO	80308	(303) 161-5545	05/25/2004
2	Calahan	Eliza	2140 Edgewood Avenue	Boulder	CO	80308	(303) 886-6003	05/25/2004
3	Lake	James	701 Eastman Road	Boulder	CO	80308	(303) 562-4499	08/25/2005
4	Meadows	Sara	Pond Hill Drive	Boulder	CO	80308	(303) 792-3646	02/28/2004
20	Smith	Alto	114 Lexington Street	Boulder	CO	80308	(303) 838-7111	06/02/2004
64	Monarch	Shiela	431 Phillips Lane	Boulder	CO	80308	(303) 352-4847	07/17/2005
65	Guo	Amy	1935 Snow Avenue	Boulder	CO	80308	(303) 555-6731	05/19/2005
80	Rivera	Juan	482 Weston Avenue	Boulder	CO	80308	(303) 815-2456	12/28/2004
85	Williams	Max	230 Southpark Circle	Boulder	CO	80308	(303) 333-0000	07/19/2003

Customer ID	Srvc Date	Weight Paper	Weight Other	Customer Record Table
1	11/22/2007	8	15	
1	10/15/2007	32	85	
1	11/7/2007	12	43	
2	11/7/2007	19	0	
2	11/22/2007	28	174	
3	10/15/2007	5	8	
3	11/22/2007	16	32	
3	12/4/2007	7	12	
20	10/15/2007	18	40	
20	11/22/2007	35	60	
80	10/15/2007	10	10	
80	11/7/2007	9	13	
80	11/22/2007	16	18	
80	12/4/2007	18	21	

1. Create a Microsoft Access database.
2. Create the tables, fields, data types, and primary key(s) for the database.
3. Create the relationship(s) needed between the tables.
4. Populate the database with the data provided above.

2. It's A Grind Coffee Shop

It's A Grind Coffee Shop is an Oakland, California, neighborhood coffee shop. Besides serving gourmet coffee, It's A Grind dishes up sandwiches and desserts. Local bands, Internet connections, and floor-to-ceiling books on every wall provide entertainment. Kate Fitzgerald, the proprietor, has decided that a database would be helpful in the acquisition of new books. Although customers rarely buy books, they do disappear or fall apart from use. Kate needs a way to keep track of which books she has so that she does not pick up duplicates. She has hired you to help design a database to keep track of the books. To assist with the design, Kate has provided you with some data in an Excel spreadsheet, **T6_ItsAGrindCoffee_ Data.xls**. The spreadsheet is not normalized; Kate asks you to assist with that before you start to create the database.

Specifically, Kate wants you to:

1. Create a Microsoft Access database.
2. Create the tables, fields, data types, and primary key(s) for the database using the structure provided in the **T6_ItsAGrindCoffee_Data.xls** file.
3. Create the relationship(s) needed between the tables.
4. Populate the database with the data provided in the **T6_ItsAGrindCoffee_Data.xls** file.

3. Academic Software

Launched in 2005 in Boston, Massachusetts, Academic Software has consistently been the fastest-growing education-focused software retailer in North America. It is committed exclusively to academic customers, offering thousands of full-version software titles at great discounts. Academic Software has partnered with the top technology manufacturers, including

Adobe, Microsoft, Sibelius, Sony Media Software, and Wacom, to offer excellent service and prices, which are available only to students, schools, and teachers.

From the very beginning, Academic Software has relied heavily on technology to ensure a positive shopping experience for its customers. The company's philosophy is simple: Hire amazing people, give them the best tools, and help them deliver an unbeatable customer experience.

One facet of Academic Software's business that needs assistance is its database organization. You have been asked to assist Academic Software with creating a relational database structure for organizing software, vendors, and academic categories. Currently this information is stored in an Excel spreadsheet, **T6_AcademicSoftware_Data.xls,** which Academic Software has provided to you.

Specifically, you are asked to:

1. Create a Microsoft Access database.
2. Create the tables, fields, data types, and primary key(s) for the database using the structure provided in the **T6_AcademicSoftware_Data.xls** file.
3. Create the relationship(s) needed between the tables.
4. Populate the database with the data provided in the **T6_AcademicSoftware_Data.xls** file.

4. On-Campus Health

On-Campus Health is the infirmary located on the campus of the University of Denver. Recordkeeping at the infirmary's pharmacy, although meticulous and professional, is inefficient. Maintaining the recordkeeping using mostly manual systems is becoming more costly as additional people are hired to meet stricter industry regulations regarding the Health Insurance Portability and Accountability Act (HIPAA) and because of state regulations that affect the sale, storage, and dispensing of prescription drugs. Although On-Campus Health succeeded in automating some of the data management for the pharmacy in an Excel spreadsheet, a more substantial change is needed to properly maintain and store data.

Students who use the infirmary can request prescriptions, either by presenting a written order from a doctor or asking for a refill of an existing prescription. The pharmacist adds this request to the system by getting the required information to fill it, including information about the drug, the student's name, the student's health plan, and the prescribing doctor. Use the data that On-Campus Health has provided you in the file **T6_CampusHealth_Data. xls** to complete the following:

1. Create a Microsoft Access database.
2. Create the tables, fields, data types, primary key(s), and the like for the database.
3. Create the relationship(s) needed between the tables.
4. Populate the database with the data provided in the Excel file.

T7

Problem Solving Using Access 2010

1. Describe the process of using the Query Wizard using Access.
2. Describe the process of using the Design view for creating a query using Access.
3. Describe the process of adding a calculated field to a query using Access.
4. Describe the process of using aggregate functions to calculate totals in queries using Access.
5. Describe how to format results displayed in calculated fields using Access.

Introduction

A *query* is a tool for extracting, combining, and displaying data from one or more tables, according to criteria you specify. For example, in a book inventory database, you could create a query to view a list of all hardcover books with more than 500 pages that you purchased in the past five months. In a query, you can sort information, summarize data (display totals, averages, counts, and so on), display the results of calculations on data, and choose exactly which fields are shown. You can view the results of a query in a tabular format, or you can view the query's data through a form or on a report (which is covered in Plug-In T8, "Decision Making Using Access 2010"). In this plug-in, you will learn how to use the Query Wizard and Query-By-Example (QBE) tool to solve problems using Microsoft Access.

Creating Simple Queries

Use the Query Wizard to create a select query. A *select query* displays data from a table or tables, based on the fields that you select, but it does not sort or filter the data. For example, if you owned a bicycle shop and wanted a list of customer names that rented bikes, you could use a simple query that would show fields from a CUSTOMER table.

To create a query using the Simple Query Wizard:

1. Open the file **T7_SlopesideBikes_Data.mdb** from the data file that accompanies this text.
2. You will see a **Security Warning.** Click on the **Options** button and select **Enable this content.** Click **OK.**

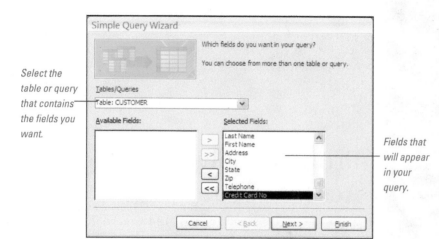

FIGURE T7.1

Create Query by Using Wizard

Select the table or query that contains the fields you want.

Fields that will appear in your query.

3. Click the **Create** tab and then click the **Query Wizard** button.
4. In the **New Query** dialog box, select **Simple Query Wizard** and then click **OK.**
5. Once the wizard opens, click the **Tables/Queries** drop-down arrow. Select **Table: CUSTOMER** (refer to Figure T7.1).
6. Add all the fields by clicking on the **right double arrow** (>>) button.
7. Click **Next.**
8. In the next window, make sure the radio button **Detail** is selected and click **Next.**
9. In the next window, type **Customer Query** as the Query title and select the radio button for **Open the query to view information.**
10. Click **Finish** to view the query in **Datasheet** view (refer to Figure T7.2).
11. Close the query (it will automatically be saved).

By modifying the query in Design view, you can specify that the query display only records that meet certain criteria or that the query display records in a specific order.

Note: Keep in mind that a query database object stores only the query definition—field names, data selection criteria, sorting orders, grouping information, and so on. It does not store the actual data that it displays; that data is stored only in the database tables. Consequently, every time you run a particular query, it shows the current state of the data stored in the database tables.

REORDERING COLUMNS IN THE SELECT QUERY DATASHEET

If you use the Query Wizard, the query datasheet displays fields in the order you added them. You can reorder columns by clicking and dragging.

To reorder columns (refer to Figure T7.3):

1. Open the **CUSTOMER Query** by double-clicking on it in the **Navigation Pane.**
2. Click the **First Name** field selector and then click it again and drag it to the **left** one column (i.e., **First Name** should now be to the left of **Last Name**).

FIGURE T7.2

Query in Datasheet View

FIGURE T7.3

Reorder Column in
Datasheet View Query

*To move a column, click and
drag a field selector.*

Drivers License	First Name	Last Name	Address	City	Sta	Zip	Telephone	Credit Card No
10001ABC10	Sue	Smith	214 Oak Avenue	Philadelphia	PA	19019	(215) 990-0009	111111111
10002DEF20	Mike	Myers	567 5th Street	Minneapolis	MN	55401	(516) 990-8889	222222222
10003GHI30	David	Dunn	3 Ivy Lane	New York	NY	10151	(215) 666-7776	333333333
10004JKL40	Raymond	Elliott	7890 Fishpike Lane	Newark	NJ	07101	(201) 445-8754	444444444
10005MNO50	Lynne	Lapierre	819 River Road	New Orleans	LA	70117	(223) 009-1234	555555555
10006PQR	Randall	Bickford	9 Kiddle Road	Cutbank	MT	59427	(899) 887-8545	666666666
*								0

CUSTOMER Query

Record: 1 of 6   No Filter   Search

3. Notice the dark, thick column border line that appears to the left of the selected column. As you move your mouse across the screen, the column border line will move with it.

4. Close and save the query.

Note: You can select adjacent columns by clicking a field selector and dragging the mouse across other field selectors, then clicking one of them again to drag the whole selection.

CREATING A SELECT QUERY IN DESIGN VIEW

You do not have to use the Query Wizard to create select queries; you can create a new select query in Design view (which can be referred to as a *Query-By-Example*, or *QBE*, tool).

To create a select query in Design view (refer to Figure T7.4):

1. Click the **Create** tab and then click the **Query Design** button in the **Other** group.

FIGURE T7.4

Query in Design View

2. Click the name of the **BIKE** table. Click the **Add** button.

3. Click the **Close** button to continue.

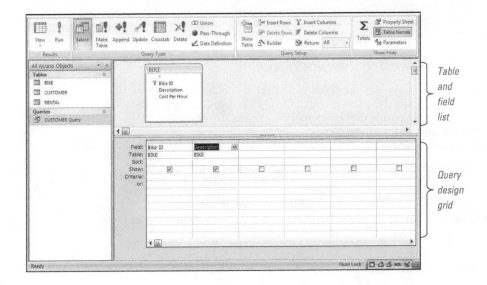

Run button

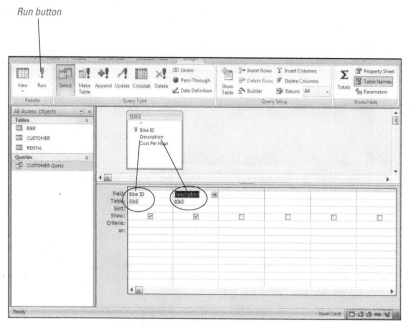

4. Double-click the **Bike ID** field in the field list at the top of the query window. You can also click the name and drag it to the query design grid below.

5. Double-click the **Description** field in the field list.

6. Run the query by clicking the **Run** button in the **Results** group (see Figure T7.5).

7. Close and save the query as **Bike List.**

Note: If you want to include all the fields from a table in your query, click and drag the asterisk (*) to the field row in the query design grid. Notice that rather than listing each field from the table separately, there is only one field called table. The * character represents a wild card. Rather than look for specific field names, the query will look for all the fields in that table. Therefore, if you later add or delete fields, you will not need to change the query design.

You can add tables to the field list by clicking the toolbar button or selecting **Show Table** from the **Query Setup** group of the **Design** tab menu.

ADDING SELECTION CRITERIA TO A SELECT QUERY

Although a select query displays only the fields you select, by default, it will show all of the records. By modifying the select query in Design view, you can refine the query so that it shows only records that meet specific criteria. You can also hide fields so they do not display in Datasheet view.

To specify criteria for a select query:

1. In the **Navigation Pane,** click the **Bike List** query, right-click and click on **Design View.**

2. In Design view, double-click the **Cost Per Hour** field under **BIKE** in the field list.

3. Click in the **Criteria** cell under the **Cost Per Hour** field and type in **<15** (refer to Figure T7.6).

4. Run the query.

5. Close and save the query as **Bikes Under $15.**

FIGURE T7.6

Criteria for a Select Query

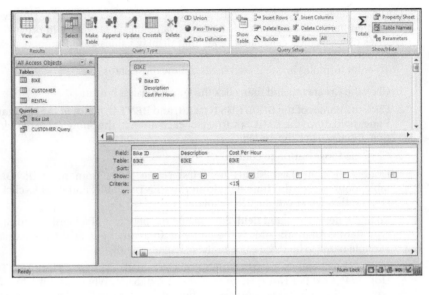

Type the criteria value.

If you need to hide a query field in **Datasheet** view:

1. In **Design** view, click in the **Show** check box, in the query design grid, to remove the checkmark for the field you want to hide.

2. Run the query.

Note: Criteria expressions are not case-sensitive.

SORTING DATA IN A SELECT QUERY

You can control how records in a query appear in Datasheet view by using the *sort feature.*

To modify the select query to sort records:

1. Open the **Bikes Under $15** query that you created in the previous section.

2. In **Design** view, click **Sort** under the **Description** field.

3. Click the drop-down arrow and select the **Ascending** button (**Sort Smallest to Largest).**

4. Run the query.

5. Close and save the query as **Sorted Bikes Under $15.**

If you want to sort the results of a select query while in Datasheet view:

1. Click in the field that you want to sort on.

2. Click the **Sort Ascending** or **Sort Descending** toolbar button in the Sort & Filter group on the ribbon.

Note: If two fields have the sort option selected, Access will sort by the farthest left field first.

Advanced Queries

Database fields generally display the data that are entered into them. However, a calculated field will automatically figure its value based on values in other fields. Queries often include calculated fields that display values based on other values returned by the query.

To enter formulas in calculated fields, follow these steps:

1. Click the **Create** tab and then click the **Query Design** button.

2. Click the names of the **BIKE, CUSTOMER,** and **RENTAL** tables in the **Navigation Pane** (hold down the **CTRL** key to select each one). In the Show Table dialog box that appears, click the **Add** button.

3. Click the **Close** button to continue.

4. Double-click the **Last Name** and **First Name** fields from the **CUSTOMER** table, double-click the **Date** field from the **RENTAL** table, and double-click the **Description** field from the **BIKE** table.

5. To add a **new calculated field,** click inside the field row of a blank column, and type **Rental Amount:**—this is the name of an anonymous field (it is actually a variable name to hold the value of the calculated field).

6. Now you will enter the expression to be calculated. Type in: **([Time In]-[Time Out])*24*[Cost Per Hour]** (refer to Figure T7.7). **Note:** When referring to a field name, enclose the name in brackets. You can use standard mathematical operator symbols like * (multiplication), / (division), + (addition), − (subtraction), and ^ (exponentiation).

7. Click on the **Show** check box under the **Rental Amount** column.

8. Run the query (click **Run** button in toolbar) to see the results of the calculated field.

9. Close and save the query as **Rental Amount.**

FIGURE T7.7

Expression to Be Calculated

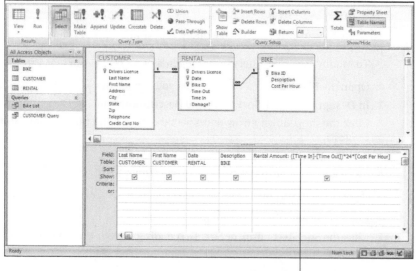

Enter expression to be calculated.

Note: When using a calculated field to combine text fields, you usually want to hide the text fields that are being combined and show only the new calculated field.

USING THE EXPRESSION BUILDER

You do not always have to type your calculated field expressions. The *Expression Builder* lets you construct expressions with just a few clicks of the mouse. It even has a built-in checker, so you will know right away if you have made a mistake.

To create a calculated field with the Expression Builder:

1. Click the **Create** tab and then click the **Query Design** button.
2. Click the names of the **BIKE, CUSTOMER,** and **RENTAL** tables in the **Navigation Pane** (hold down the **CTRL** key to select each one). Click the **Add** button.
3. Click the **Close** button to continue.
4. Double-click the **Last Name** and **First Name** fields from the **CUSTOMER** table, double-click the **Date** field from the **RENTAL** table, and double-click the **Description** field from the **BIKE** table.
5. Position the insertion point in the field row of the next blank column in the query design grid. Click the **Builder** toolbar button, found in the **Query Setup** group.
6. In the Expression Builder dialog box (see Figure T7.8), click the (button, and then double-click the **Tables** folder in the lower left pane.
7. Double-click the **Rental** subfolder. In the middle pane, double-click on **Time In,** click on the – button, double-click on **Time Out,** then double-click the) button.
8. Continue to build the expression in the Expression Builder dialog box.
9. Click **OK** to add the expression to your query.
10. Run the query to see the results of the calculated field.
11. Close and save the query as **Rental Amount 2.**

FIGURE T7.8

Query Expression Builder

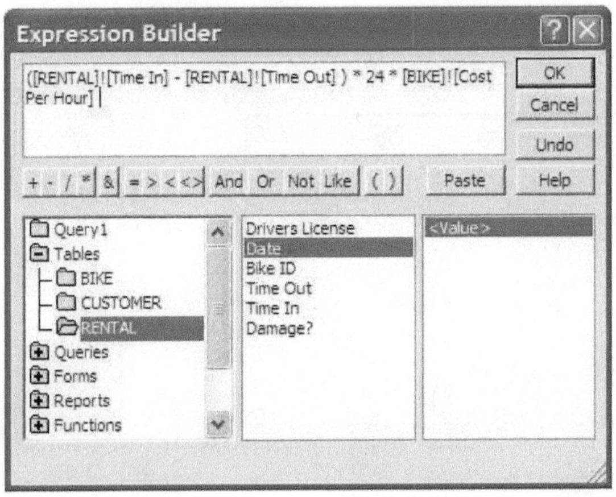

When you create a new calculated field, by default, Access will set the Show option in the query design grid to off. Be sure to check the **Show** check box, or your new field will not show when you run the query.

When you create a calculated field with the Expression Builder, Access will automatically name the field **Expr1.** Rename the field by clicking in the field name box and typing the name you want before the colon that precedes the expression. Be sure not to delete the colon after the name; Access needs it to know that this is a calculated field.

USING AGGREGATE FUNCTIONS TO CALCULATE TOTALS IN QUERIES

Access includes a group of powerful built-in commands known as aggregate (or total) functions. Using *aggregate functions*, you can easily calculate totals for groups of records returned by the query specifications. Aggregate functions can calculate the sum, minimum, maximum, average, count, variance, and standard deviation. In the Query Design window, you should include a field to group by as well as the field that contains the values needed for the calculation. The values of aggregate calculations are not stored in the table; instead, Access recalculates the totals each time the query is run.

To use aggregate functions in queries:

1. Click the **Create** tab and then click the **Query Design** button.
2. Click the name of the **BIKE** table and click the **Add** button.
3. Click the **Close** button to continue.
4. Double-click the **Description** and **Cost Per Hour** fields.
5. Click the **Totals** button (the Sigma icon on the menu bar in the **Show/Hide** group) to add the **Total** row to the query design grid (refer to Figure T7.9).
6. Click in the **Total** row for the **Description** field. Click the drop-down arrow and select the **Group By** function.
7. Click in the **Total** row for the **Cost Per Hour** cell. Click the arrow and select the **Avg** function (refer to Figure T7.9).
8. Click the **Run** button on the toolbar.
9. Notice that the query does not return individual records. Instead, there is one row for each unique value in the **Group By** field. Each row shows the calculated total for that group of records (refer to Figure T7.10).
10. Close and save the query as **Bike Average Cost Per Hour.**

Note: Queries with aggregate calculations are often used to form the basis for strategic analysis or statistical reports.

FORMATTING RESULTS DISPLAYED IN A CALCULATED FIELD

You can specify the format for calculated field results by changing the *format property.*

To use the format property for calculated fields:

1. Open the **Rental Amount** query in **Design** view.
2. Right-click in the **Rental Amount** calculated field.

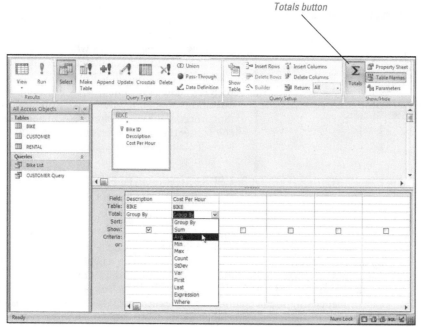

Totals button

FIGURE T7.9

Calculate Totals in a Query

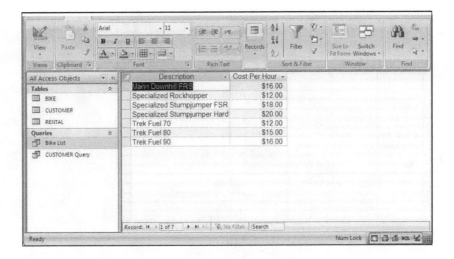

3. Click **Properties . . .** from the shortcut menu.

4. Click in the **Format** box.

5. Click the drop-down arrow.

6. Scroll down and click the **Currency** format.

7. Close the **Field Properties** dialog box by clicking the **close box** in the upper right corner.

8. Click the **Run** button.

9. Close and save the query.

   Note: Be careful that you are viewing the field properties and not the query properties. If the field does not have the Show check box checked, you will open the Query Properties dialog box instead of the Field Properties dialog box.

CREATING AND RUNNING QUERIES TO MODIFY DATA

So far, this plug-in has described one major type of query: the select query. Four additional types of queries, which are known as *action queries,* can actually change your data:

1. A Make Table query.

2. An Append query.

3. A Delete query.

4. An Update query.

   To use action queries:

1. Create a new query in **Design** view as you've done previously.

2. Select the **BIKE** table and click **Add** in the **Show Table** dialog box that appears.

3. Click **Close** to continue.

4. Double-click the **Cost Per Hour** field to add it to the query grid.

5. Convert the query to an action query by choosing the **Update** button in the **Query Type** group on the toolbar (refer to Figure T7.11).

6. Notice that you now have another line—**Update To:**—on the query design grid.

Update button

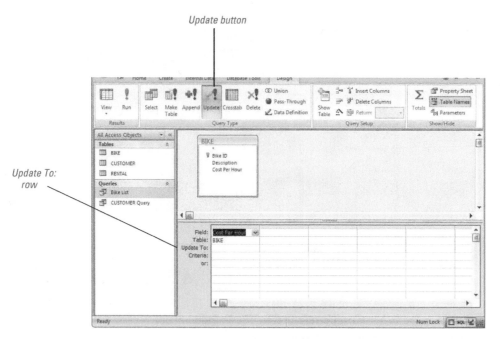

Update To: row

FIGURE T7.11

Query Type Option

7. Click inside the **Update To:** row and type in [**Cost Per Hour**] +**.50** (this will add 50 cents to each cost per hour).

8. Run the query. You will first get a warning message, like that shown in Figure T7.12. Click **Yes.**

9. Close and save the query as **Update Query.**

Note: Make Table, Append, and Delete queries work the same way as the Update Query example above. Before running any of the queries, make a backup copy of your database. These queries can permanently modify your database, possibly removing a large amount of data.

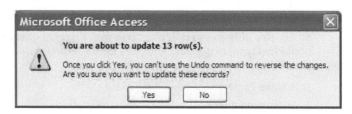

FIGURE T7.12

Query Type Warning

✱ PLUG-IN SUMMARY

A *query* is a tool for extracting, combining, and displaying data from one or more tables, according to criteria you specify. You can use the Query Wizard or Query-By-Example tool to select specific data from a table or tables. You can sort the rows of a query by a particular field, hide a particular field, enter a value to search on, summarize information, and even modify data using a query.

✱ MAKING BUSINESS DECISIONS

1. ProSwing Analysis

Carol Redden had been a part-time tennis instructor for several years. Frustrated with the tennis equipment available in the market, she started her own company. With the aid of her attorneys and investors, she founded ProSwing to design tennis equipment and apparel.

Carol developed a strong product line and was becoming successful in the United States, but she was having trouble with the firm's international marketing strategy. Carol thought that the most effective way to advertise was by getting players to use and wear her products. She wanted to be sure that the players using her line were the players followed by the fans (her target market). She knew that this would bring ProSwing attention from tennis players around the world. She decided to concentrate on the tennis players with the highest current winnings, since they were likely to be very popular and visible to the fans. She would approach the top 25 international men and women players about using ProSwing products. She would then additionally advertise during tennis matches in the four countries most represented by the top players in order to represent both the men and women top players.

Carol prepared a database after finding recent sport statistics on the Web and compiled data on the top players. Included in the database are the player's name, country of residence, most recent winnings, and gender. Carol needs your help to organize the data to plan her international strategy. She has provided you with the database file **T7_Pro-Swing_Data.mdb** in order to complete the following:

1. Create a query that will sort the player data in descending order by winnings. Save the query as **Player Winnings Query.**
2. Create a query that will sort the data in ascending order by Country Name and then in descending order by Winnings within each country. Change the order of the columns so that Country is the first column, followed by Winnings, and then Player. Save the query as **Country Winnings Query.**
3. Create a query that will total the winnings for each country. Use the Country Name for the criteria and sort the Winnings in descending order. Save the query as **Total Winnings for Country Query.**

2. WasteNot Recycling

WasteNot Recycling is an organization that picks up recyclables from homeowners in Boulder, Colorado, as introduced in Plug-In T6. The CUSTOMER table holds static customer information such as name, address, and phone. The CUSTOMER RECORD table holds data about each recyclable pickup. Enough test data has been added to each table to test queries (use the **T7_WasteNotRecycling_Data.mdb** file associated with this text).

The owners of WasteNot Recycling have asked you to assist with creating several queries. Specifically they need you to do the following:

1. Create a query using the CUSTOMER data that will select records for customers who had their first pickup in May 2004. Sort the records by customer's Last Name. Save the query as **May Pickup Query.**

2. Create a query on CUSTOMER RECORD to determine the total weights of paper and other products each customer has had picked up. Use the CUSTOMER Last Name and First Name in the query. Save the query as **Customer Weight Query.**

3. Create a query using the Name, Street, Address, and Weight fields from the CUSTOMER DETAIL table. Enter the criteria that will select customers with less than 10 pounds in either recyclable field. Save the query as **Low Volume Query.**

3. Scale Classic Cars

Johnny Krol runs a body shop that specializes in restoring classic cars. Johnny owns three classics and began collecting scale models when his wife put her foot down and said no to building more garage space for his cars.

Although Johnny frequently used the Internet and e-mail, he had never considered starting an e-business. The Scale Classics Web site began as a technology class project for Johnny's son J.J., who created a basic text and graphics informational site. Johnny liked the site, but wanted a complex site dedicated to the serious collector. He envisioned a storefront, auction house, and collector's forums and had been unable to find such a site in his online searches. Johnny hired a local consultant to build the site, found a processing house to manage orders and payments, and began shipping scale models from the body shop.

The storefront is largely for American classic cars, which come in 1/18, 1/24, 1/43, and 1/64 scale. Popular foreign cars are also available. Johnny has hired you to create some business analysis queries; specifically he wants you to:

1. Use the **T7_ClassicCars_Data.mdb** database.
2. Create a query to select any record with "coupe" in the model name. Include the Make and Model in the query. Save the query as **Coupe Query.**
3. Create a query to select the models that cost less than $35. The query should display the Car ID, Make, Model, and Price fields and sort the result from the highest to the lowest price. Save the query as **Less Than $35 Query.**
4. Create a query listing classic cars grouped by their make. The query should display only the Make, Model, and Price fields. Sort by the model and calculate the average price for each make. Save the query as **Cars By Model Query.**

4. BookFinder.com

BookFinder.com is an open marketplace for books online, a one-stop e-commerce search engine where you can search through more than 100 million new, used, rare, and out-of-print books for sale.

The site is produced by a team of high-tech librarians and programmers, working since 2004 to connect readers with the books they are looking for. They are part of their own audience; members of the BookFinder.com team are heavy readers and buy several dozen books every year using BookFinder.com. They also blog about their work, connecting readers and booksellers from around the world and supporting public access to a strong, diverse bookselling industry.

BookFinder.com was first developed in 2004 by then-19-year-old University of Denver undergraduate Charles Cook (as a personal Web site). Over the years, the site has grown to become one of the best online resources for book-related e-commerce, as evidenced by the great feedback received from users and the press. Whether customers collect rare books or buy cheap paperbacks to read, BookFinder.com is an unbiased marketplace and search engine.

Charles needs help developing some custom queries for his sales and marketing team members. He has provided you with a sample data file, **T7_BookFinder_Data.mdb.** Specifically, what Charles needs is:

1. A query of all authors who have written a book that costs more than $10 and is a novel. The query needs to have the author's First Name, Last Name, Title of Book, Price, and Category displayed. Save the query as **Authors Query.**

2. A query that calculates a 15 percent increase in the purchase price of each book. Format the calculated field with the Currency format. Sort the query on the new calculated field. Save the query as **Book Prices Query.**

3. A query that displays the minimum price of all the books. Save the query as **Min Book Price Query.**

4. A query that updates the price of each book by subtracting 50 cents. Save the query as **Less 50 Cents Query.**

T8

Decision Making Using Access 2010

LEARNING OUTCOMES

1. Describe the steps for creating a form using the Form Wizard in Access.
2. Describe the steps for creating and saving Forms using Access.
3. Describe the steps to modify the properties of a form using Access.
4. Describe the steps for creating a report using the Report Wizard in Access.
5. Describe the steps to modify the properties of a report using Access.

Introduction

This plug-in focuses on the two functions of decision making using Access 2010: creating forms and creating reports. A *form* is nothing more than a graphical representation of a table. You can add, update, and delete records in your table by using a form. Although a form can be named differently from its corresponding table, they both still manipulate the same information and the same data. Hence, if you change a record in a form, it will be changed in the table as well.

A form is useful when you have numerous fields in a table. It allows you to see all the fields in one screen, whereas if you were in the table view (datasheet) you would have to keep scrolling to get to the field you desire.

A *report* is an effective way to present your data in a printed format. Because you have control over the size and appearance of everything on a report, you can display the information the way you want to see it.

Forms

An Access form is a window, similar to a dialog box, that contains a set of controls (such as labels, text boxes, and check boxes) to view, enter, or edit database information, typically one record at a time.

In a form, data are obtained directly from one or more tables or from data that have been extracted using a query. Although it is possible to directly enter and edit the information in tables in Datasheet View, a database usually includes a set of forms that can make entering and editing data considerably easier and can limit the fields that can be viewed or modified.

CREATING A FORM USING THE FORM WIZARD

Forms allow you to enter data one record at a time. Often, it is easier to enter data in a well-designed form rather than in a wide datasheet. You can create a form that has fields from more than one table or query. Like other wizards, the Form Wizard walks you step-by-step through the process of creating a form.

To create a form using the Form Wizard:

1. Open the file **T8_SlopesideBikes_Data.mdb** from the data file that accompanies this text.
2. Click the **Create** tab. Click the **More Forms** button, and then click **Form Wizard.**
3. Click the **Tables/Queries** drop-down arrow and select **Table: BIKE.**
4. Add all BIKE fields by clicking on the double right arrow (**>>**). Click **Next** to go to the next step.
5. Select the **Columnar** form layout. Click **Next.**
6. Select the **Office** style. Click **Next.**
7. Type in **BIKE FORM** for a form title.
8. Click **Finish** to open the form and begin entering data (see Figure T8.1).

Accessing Several Tables or Queries in a Form

When you select the fields for your form in the first Form Wizard dialog box, you can add fields from several tables or queries. To add fields from each table or query, select it in the **Tables/Queries** drop-down list and then use the buttons to move the fields you want to the **Selected Fields** list.

If you add fields from several forms or queries, the wizard will display one or two additional dialog boxes that were not shown in the previous section: one dialog box in which you specify the form or query by which you want to view your data (for example, if you selected fields from the CUSTOMER and the BIKE tables, you would choose to view your data either "by Customer" or "by Bike") and possibly another dialog box in which you select a layout for a subform. The choices you make determine the form's record source.

FIGURE T8.1

Create a Form by Using the Form Wizard

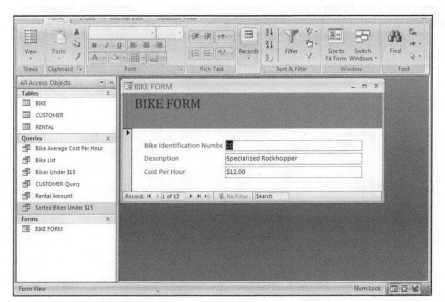

If your form includes fields from two tables that are related in a one-to-many relationship and if you selected to view your data by the primary table, the wizard will let you display the records from the related table in a subform contained within the form. As an alternative, the wizard will let you set up a linked form, which is a separate form that displays the related data and which you open by clicking a button on the main form.

On the other hand, if you chose to view your data by the related table in the one-to-many relationship, when the form displays a record in the related table, it will simply display the unique matching fields from the primary table along with the fields from the current record in the related table.

A form that accesses data from several tables or queries can be complex to design from scratch or to modify. However, if you create the form using the Form Wizard, almost everything is set up for you.

CREATING AND SAVING FORMS

To create a simple form in Access, you can use the form buttons available on the Create tab. You can create a basic form, split form, tabular form using multiple items, blank form, or PivotChart.

To create a form:

1. In the Navigation Pane, select the **CUSTOMER** table.

2. Click on the **Create** tab, and then click on the **Form** button (refer to Figure T8.2).

3. Access automatically creates a Columnar Form based on the CUSTOMER table you selected. Since the CUSTOMER table has a linked relationship to the RENTAL table, Access displays the RENTAL table contents associated with the CUSTOMER information.

4. Close the form by clicking the **Close** box in the upper-right corner.

5. Access will automatically prompt you to save the form. Save it as **CUSTOMER.**

FIGURE T8.2

Create a Form

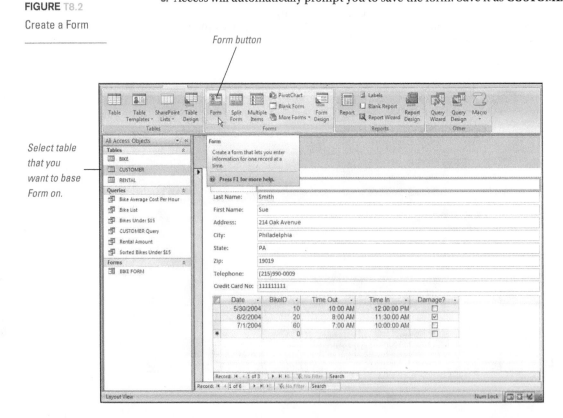

MODIFYING THE PROPERTIES OF A FORM

Once you have created a form, you can still change the way the form looks and functions. The *AutoFormat* button allows you to change the form's graphic style. Opening the Property Sheet dialog box allows you to change other form properties.
Here is a description on how to modify the properties of a form:

1. Select a form in the Navigation Pane, right-click, and click on **Design View.** Click the **Arrange** tab, click the **AutoFormat** group, and then click the AutoFormat design you want to apply (refer to Figure T8.3).

2. To change other form properties, open the **Property Sheet** dialog box by clicking the **Design** tab, and then click the **Property Sheet** button (refer to Figure T8.4).

3. Make sure that you are viewing the properties for the correct form by looking at the box at the top of the dialog.

4. Scroll through the list of properties.

5. Click the box next to the property that you want to change. Some properties have a drop-down list with specific choices. For other properties, you enter a specific value.

6. When you have made the changes you want, close the **Property Sheet** dialog box by clicking the **Close** box in the upper-right corner of the property box.

7. Click on the **View** toolbar button to switch to **Form View** to see the changes you have made.

MODIFYING SPECIFIC CONTROLS ON A FORM

Not all controls on your form may be of equal importance. You may want to modify the look of a specific control to make it stand out, or you may want to modify the control behavior. When designing forms, be careful not to overdesign. Too many different colors, styles, or behaviors can distract from accurate data entry.

FIGURE T8.3

AutoFormat

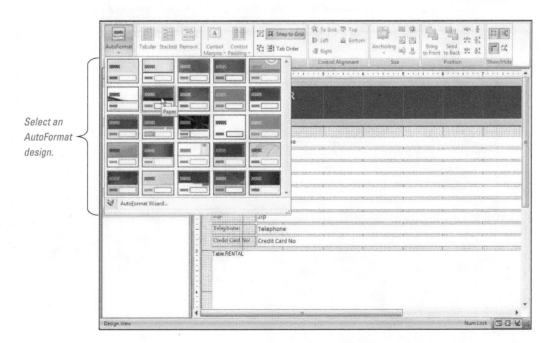

Select an AutoFormat design.

Design tab

Property Sheet button

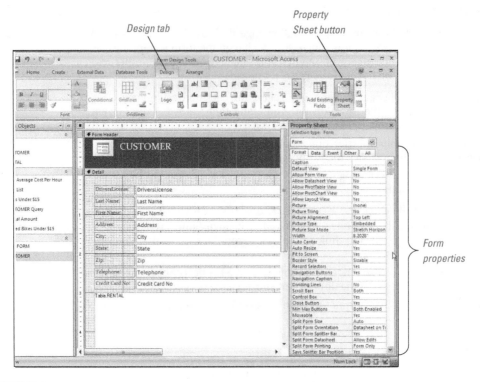

Form properties

FIGURE T8.4

Property Sheet Dialog Box

FIGURE T8.5

Modify Form Properties

To modify the properties of a specific control (refer to Figure T8.5):

1. Open the **BIKE FORM** in **Design View.**
2. Since the BIKE FORM you created using the wizard did not allow you to align the title of the form, you should do that.
3. Click the **Property Sheet** button on the **Design** tab.
4. Under the **Form Header,** select the **BIKE FORM** title object. Notice that there are handles around the object creating a box that is reddish in color.

Select control

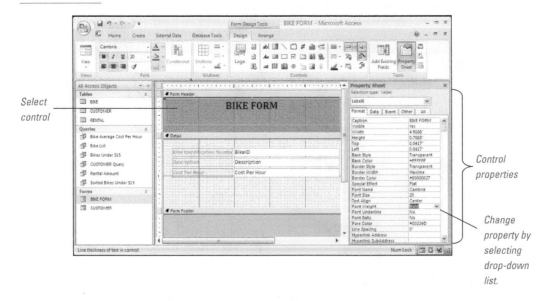

Control properties

Change property by selecting drop-down list.

5. Drag the right-middle handle so that it is as wide as the rest of the form.
6. In the **Property Sheet** dialog box, click the **Format** tab.
7. Click the **Font Weight** property, and select **Bold** in the drop-down list.
8. Click the **Text Align** property, and select **Center** in the drop-down list.
9. Close the **Property Sheet** dialog box.
10. To view your changes, click on the **View** button and select **Form View.**
11. Close and save the form.

Note: Common properties to modify are the use of scroll bars and growing or shrinking the size of the control based on data the user enters. If you turn off scroll bars, users can see only the data that fits within the specific control dimensions. If you turn on *Can Grow* or *Can Shrink,* the control area will grow and/or shrink to fit the data.

Many formatting options are available from the shortcut menu (selecting a control, then right-click). You can change the background color, font color, and which special effect is applied to the control.

Reports

Reports are used primarily for printing selected database information. A report labels, groups, sorts, and summarizes the data it presents. Like a form, a report can display data directly from one or more tables or it can display the results of a query.

Using the Report Wizard

Like other wizards, the Report Wizard walks you step-by-step through the process of creating a report. Unlike forms, which are designed for on-screen data entry, reports are designed for print.

To create a report using the Report Wizard:

1. Click the **Create** tab, and then click the **Report Wizard** button in the **Reports** group.
2. Click the **Tables/Queries** drop-down arrow. Select the **CUSTOMER** table and select all the fields *except* the Drivers License, Telephone, and Credit Card No. Then select the **RENTAL** table and select the **Date** field. Lastly, select the **BIKE** table and select the **Description** field.
3. Click **Next** to go to the next step. **Note:** If you selected fields from more than one table or query in the previous step, the second Report Wizard dialog box asks you to choose one table or query that will be used for grouping the information in the report, if possible.
4. The next step asks how you want to view the report. Double-click **BIKE.** Click **Next.**
5. Make **Date** the first grouping level. (**Note:** Use a grouping level to organize the data into subgroups by the value of a specific field.) Click **Next.**
6. Next, for sort order, specify **State** as the primary data sort. Click **Next.**
7. Select the **Stepped** report layout and **Landscape** orientation. Click **Next.**
8. Select the **Office** style for the report. Click **Next.**
9. Type in **Customer Rental by State Report** for the title and select **Preview the report.**
10. Click **Finish.** Figure T8.6 displays the results.

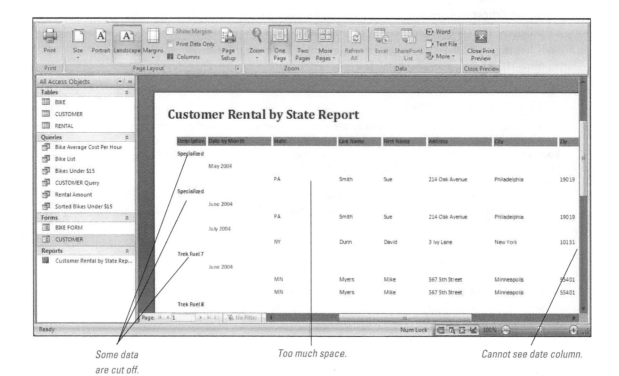

Some data are cut off.   *Too much space.*   *Cannot see date column.*

FIGURE T8.6

View Report

MODIFYING THE REPORT DESIGN

Once you create a report, you can modify the report's design to make it more visually attractive. As with forms, be careful not to overdesign your report. A poorly designed report can distract from the information being presented. To modify the design, you must have the report open in Design View.

To modify the report design:

1. Preview the report first. Double-click the **Customer Rental by State Report** in the Navigation Pane. Notice that the columns and data do not align correctly, some columns are much bigger than they need to be, and we can't even see the date field (refer to Figure T8.6).

2. Switch to **Design View** by clicking the **View** button (under the **Home** tab).

3. Click the **Description** control under the **Bike_Id Header** section, and then **drag** the sizing **right handle** to increase the width of the control box (this will allow more characters to be visible in the report). You can also select **Size** from the **Format** menu. Select **To Fit** to automatically resize the label or control to fit your data.

4. Make sure that you can see the **Date** column control. You may have to adjust the width of that control. Select the **State** column heading and resize that control to have fewer spaces.

5. Switch to **Report View** via the **View** toolbar button to see your changes. You may have to toggle back and forth from the Design View to the Report View several times before you get the results you desire. Figure T8.7 displays the modified report.

Note: Change the graphic style of the report by clicking the **Arrange** tab, then clicking the **AutoFormat** button.

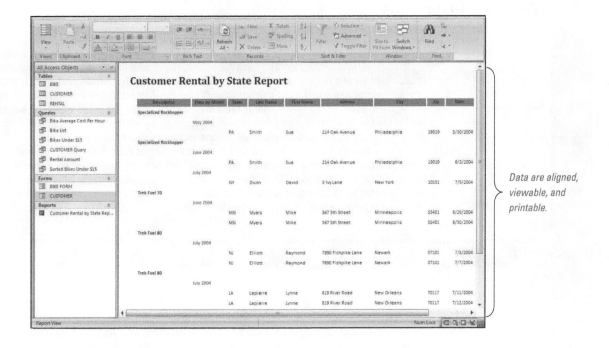

Data are aligned, viewable, and printable.

CHANGING MARGINS AND PAGE ORIENTATION FOR REPORTS

FIGURE T8.7

Modified Report Properties

The default page orientation for a report is *portrait*. This means the height of the page is greater than the width. You may want to change this orientation to *landscape* to accommodate multiple columns of data so they fit on one page. *Margins* are the blank spaces at the top, bottom, left, and right of a report. By adjusting the page margins, you can control the number of records printed on each page. Use the dialog box to adjust margins and page orientation for your reports.

To change the margins for a report:

1. Open the report in **Design View.**
2. Click the **Page Setup** tab, and then click the **Page Setup** button in the **Page Layout** group.
3. Select the **Print Options** tab in the **Page Setup** dialog box.
4. Change the values for the top, bottom, left, or right margin.
5. Click **OK.**

To change the page orientation for a report:

1. Open the report in **Design View.**
2. Click the **Page Setup** tab, and then click the **Page Setup** button.
3. Select the **Page** tab in the **Page Setup** dialog box. Click the radio button for **Portrait** or **Landscape** orientation.
4. Click **OK.**

✴ PLUG-IN SUMMARY

To have Microsoft Access 2010 create a form according to your specifications, select the Form Wizard option. The Form Wizard lets you choose the specific fields to include, and these can belong to one or more tables or queries. To have Access quickly create a form that has a particular configuration (Columnar, Tabular, Datasheet, PivotTable, or PivotChart), based on the record source table or query you select in the drop-down list, select one of the five AutoForm options. Access will immediately create the form, including all fields from the record source and using default options without asking for your specifications.

To have Access help you design a report, select the Report Wizard option. To use default settings to quickly create a report based on a single table or query, with a columnar or tabular layout, select the AutoReport: Columnar or the AutoReport: Tabular option. Either report will include all the fields belonging to the record source table or query that you select in the drop-down list at the bottom of the New Report dialog box.

✴ MAKING BUSINESS DECISIONS

1. **WasteNot Recycling**

   WasteNot Recycling, introduced in Plug-In T6 and reintroduced in T7, picks up recyclables from homeowners in Boulder, Colorado. The owners of WasteNot Recycling have asked you to assist with creating a form and several reports. They have provided you with an updated database file, **T8_WasteNotRecycling_Data.mdb**. Specifically they want you to do the following:

   1. Create a form that will allow the owners to enter data into the CUSTOMER and the CUSTOMER RECORD tables. They have left the design (i.e., aesthetics) up to you. However, they have asked that you locate an appropriate graphic to include on the form. You will want to use the Internet to find such a graphic. Make sure you align all the controls and adjust the size of all the controls to fit the data. Save the form as **Customers**.

   2. Create a report that groups the records by customer. The report should include data on the customer first and last name, service date of pickup, weight of paper, and weight of other. The report should be sorted by customer last name. You will need to create a subtotal for the weights for each customer. Create a report title called **Customer Weights**.

2. **It's A Grind Coffee Shop**

   It's A Grind Coffee Shop, introduced in Plug-In T6, is an Oakland, California, neighborhood coffee shop. Kate Fitzgerald, the proprietor, has decided that she needs a form and a few reports created to help her purchase new books for her coffee shop.

   Kate has provided you with an updated database file, **T8_ItsAGrindCoffee_Data.mdb**. Specifically, Kate wants you to:

   1. Create a form that will allow Kate to add new books to the BOOK table. Kate has asked you to use a Columnar layout and the Sumi Painting style. Kate has given you her logo to add to the form, **ItsAGrindImage.jpg**. Position the logo in the top-left corner. Save the form as **Books**.

   2. Create a report that groups the records by author. Include only the author from the AUTHOR table, and book title, year, and condition from the BOOK table. Sort the report by book title. Create a title labeled **Current Authors**; center the title on the report. Set the label properties to 12 point, bold, italic. Save the report as **Books By Author**.

3. Create a report using the publisher name, book title, year, and author name. Group the report on publisher name and sort on the year the book was published. Create a report title of **Books By Publisher.** Align the columns evenly and use a professional-looking font style and layout. Save the report as **Publishers.**

3. TechIT Seminars

TechIT Seminars is an organization of independent seminar facilitators who provide onsite technical training to large businesses around the world. The facilitators build curriculum that is marketed by TechIT. TechIT books the seminars, arranges facilities, enrolls participants, and collects the money. While the facilitators are not employees of TechIT, they provide the service that is marketed, and their skills and schedules need to be available to all TechIT offices. Deborah Wallbridge has been charged with tracking facilitators and their classification. She has asked you to help develop a form and a few reports to assist in scheduling seminars.

1. Use the **T8_TechITSeminars_Data.mdb** file.
2. Create a data entry form for the FACILITATOR table. Set the form background color to a blue color (hue). Organize and align all controls for effective use and full data display. For the phone data, use the Phone input mask. Save the form as **Facilitators Form.**
3. Use the ENROLLMENT table to create a report listing the students currently enrolled in each seminar. The report field order is Seminar ID, Last Name, First Name, Student Phone, and Student Number. Adjust all controls to display all of their contents. Adjust the color and content of the column headings as shown in Figure T8.8. Align all controls.

FIGURE T8.8

Students by Seminar Report

Students By Seminar Report

Seminar ID	Last Name	First Name	Student Phone	Student Number
TL003				
	Elynuik	Kerry	539-556-3223	115
	Ray	Maria	217-226-4415	135
	Ross	Wilbert	395-444-2247	244
	Timmerman	Henry	123-225-8543	229
	Tsuhara	Gordon	7-1-655-4487	124
	Weinstein	Albert	120-22-547-6684	108
TL010				
	Malone	Sean	894-544-6637	311
	Norgaard	Max	315-554-7787	331
	Rodrigues	Marc	938-224-1135	249
	Tarchuk	Sapphire	217-544-2014	131
	Van Zandt	Willem	439-455-3112	177
TR101				
	Dhaliwal	Frank	452-332-4125	250
	Habib	Akram	315-335-4414	186
	Harrison	Tina	748-441-3352	109
	Kowalski	Byron	976-255-3177	291
	Mahal	Balinder	543-337-8541	308
	McMahon	Lavon	315-225-6634	330
	Nadeau	Pierre	675-441-5511	325
	Oakes	Judy	603-221-4473	255
	Pittman	Dale	43-848-332-6674	455
	Pryor	Deanna	46-438-378-6767	166
	Quinn	Dwayne	315-224-3581	283
	Reyes	Herbert	72-334-6142	208
	Weymouth	Corey	303-335-4712	181

Add a gray line above and below the column headings. Use Sorting and Grouping to sort by Seminar ID, Last Name, and First Name. Place the report date, time, and Page XX of XX in the Page Footer. Format the date and time to long format. Save the report as **Students By Seminar Report.**

4. Scale Classic Cars

Johnny Krol, introduced in Plug-In T7, runs a body shop that specializes in restoring classic cars. Johnny owns three classics and began collecting scale models when his wife put her foot down and said no to building more garage space for his cars. Johnny has decided that he needs a form and a few reports created to help in identifying the buying habits of his customers. Johnny has provided you with an updated database file, **T8_ClassicCars_Data.mdb.** Specifically, Johnny wants you to:

1. Create a form that will allow Johnny to enter new classic cars and update existing records. The form should use a Columnar format and the Sandstone style. Save the form as **Catalog.**

2. Create a report listing classic cars grouped by their make. The report should display all fields from the CATALOG table, sort by model name, and calculate the average price for each make. Use the Formal style. Save the report as **Cars By Model.**